SPAIN UNDER THE HABSBURGS

SPAIN
UNDER THE
HABSBURGS

By

JOHN LYNCH

Reader in Hispanic and Latin American History
University College, London

VOLUME TWO
SPAIN AND AMERICA
1598 – 1700

OXFORD
BASIL BLACKWELL
1969

631 08030 9

Library of Congress Catalog Card No.
64-1472

Printed in Great Britain by
Alden & Mowbray Ltd at the Alden Press, Oxford
and bound by the Kemp Hall Bindery

To
W.K.L.

CONTENTS

		PAGE
I	THE HISPANIC WORLD IN 1600 .	1
II	THE GOVERNMENT OF PHILIP III.	14
	1. King and Favourite .	14
	2. Councils and Councillors .	17
	3. The *Valimiento*	23
	4. The Poverty of Government	30
III	RECESSION AND REACTION	40
	1. Truce in the Low Countries	40
	2. The Expulsion of the Moriscos .	42
	3. Catalonia: the Problem of Intervention	51
	4. Castile and Portugal	55
IV	OLIVARES, CASTILE AND IMPERIAL SPAIN	62
	1. Philip IV and the Rule of Olivares	62
	2. Spain and the Thirty Years War	68
	3. The Cost of War	79
	4. The Cortes of Castile	86
V	THE GREAT CRISIS: 1640 AND AFTER	94
	1. The Union of Arms	94
	2. The Revolt of Catalonia .	101
	3. The Secession of Portugal.	108
	4. After Olivares	115
	5. War and Peace	119
VI	SOCIETY AND ECONOMY	126
	1. Population and Pestilence	126
	2. Aristocracy	130
	3. *La Gente Comun*	137
	4. Agriculture and Industry .	143
	5. Foreign Trade	153
VII	AMERICAN TRADE: CONTRACTION AND CRISIS	160
	1. The Monopoly: Seville and Cadiz	160
	2. Fraud: the Response to Taxation	163

PAGE

3. Foreign Penetration 169
4. Imperial Defence: the Atlantic 173
5. Pacific Defence 178
6. The Collapse of American Trade 184

VIII SPANISH AMERICA: A CHANGING EMPIRE 194
1. The Hispanic World: a New Balance of Power . . 194
2. Mexico: from Mining to Agriculture. . . . 200
3. Peru: Silver Colony, Silver Metropolis . . . 212
4. Inter-American Trade 224

IX GOVERNMENT AND SOCIETY IN THE REIGN OF CHARLES II . 229
1. Privilege and Power: the Rule of Aristocracy . . 229
2. The Last *Validos* 236
3. The Revolt of the Grandees 243
4. Return to Government 247

X THE END OF HABSBURG SPAIN 254
1. Promise and Prejudice in Eastern Spain . . . 254
2. Castile's Tragic Decade 260
3. Bureaucracy and its Reform 267
4. The Precursors 273

APPENDIX I 281

APPENDIX II 282

BIBLIOGRAPHICAL INDEX 285

INDEX 288

ILLUSTRATIONS

FACING PAGE

THE COUNT DUKE OF OLIVARES 70
By Velázquez (*Courtesy of the Hispanic Society of America, New York*)

RECONQUEST OF BAHIA 87
By Juan Bautista Mayno (*Prado Museum, Madrid*)

DEFENCE OF CADIZ AGAINST THE ENGLISH . . . 102
By Zurbarán (*Prado Museum. Madrid*)

ST THOMAS OF VILLANUEVA 119
By Murillo (*Wallace Collection, London*)

LAS HILANDERAS 150
By Velázquez (*Prado Museum, Madrid*)

PROSPECTO DEL CERRO DE POTOSÍ 167
(*Archivo de Indias, Seville*)

MEXICO CITY 214
By Hoefnagle (*Bodleian Library, Oxford*)

CHARLES II 231
By Claudio Coello (*Prado Museum, Madrid*)

MAPS

I   SPAIN IN THE SEVENTEENTH CENTURY 14

II CENTRAL AMERICA AND THE CARIBBEAN IN THE SEVEN-
    TEENTH CENTURY 174

III SOUTH AMERICA IN THE SEVENTEENTH CENTURY . . 212

For Maps II and III grateful acknowledgment is made to Mr. T. Allen of the Cartographic Unit, Department of Geography, University College, London.

CHAPTER I

THE HISPANIC WORLD IN 1600

SPANISH society and economy were built on the twin foundations of land and silver, Castilian agriculture and American mining. The conspicuous luxury of court and aristocracy, the palaces and the mansions, the Baroque splendour of the church, the complex apparatus of bureaucratic government, the fleets and the armies that spanned Europe and the wider world, the entire fabric of this aristocratic society and the power of its empire were supported ultimately on the backs of Castilian peasants and American Indians. The nobles, as well as the crown, drew their wealth from both sources, for in addition to the vast estates and the numerous vassals working for them in Castile, they also primed their fortunes with lucrative viceroyalties and other earnings in the Indies.

These two pillars of Spanish society were interdependent. In the hey-day of empire Castilian agriculture provisioned the Indies fleets and supplied the colonists with grain, oil and wine. And the mineral wealth of America, directly or indirectly, took some of the pressure off the peasants of Castile and lightened their tax burden. In the years around 1600, however, the imperial relationship was profoundly transformed. The changing economies of Mexico and Peru now required not agricultural products but manufactured goods, which Spain was not equipped to supply. Diminishing trade returns, together with recession in silver mining and retention of capital in American hands for local investment, all combined to reduce the yield of empire, and ultimately to shift the burden of responsibility towards the peasants of Castile, as the crown demanded greater sacrifices from its taxpayers, and landlords from their vassals.

Spain was a rural society and land was the source of peninsular wealth. The numerous and growing towns, not being centres of industrial production, were essentially parasitic growths on an agrarian economy. Most people who actually worked lived in the countryside, and their horizons were bounded by the next harvest. But abundant harvests would stimulate other sectors of the national life, and in their wake taxes would be paid, lords and clerics would receive their rents and urban rentiers their interest, artisans would have employment and merchants something to sell. Conversely, if the crops failed, or agriculture became depressed, then the whole nation suffered, from the king downwards. So everyone watched the weather and the work force with acute personal interest, an interest turning to alarm as they noticed the first signs of rural distress. Towards 1575–80 Castile began to experience a reversal of the demographic trend, and by 1600 depopulation was notorious. The primary cause was rural migration, which peasants attributed to 'lack of land'; some of them went to the Indies; others, following the trail of the *hidalgos*, sought their El Dorado in neighbouring towns or in Madrid. 'Lack of land' was a complex phenomenon, but one feature was clear enough —the peasants were losing their commons. The great territorial magnates, the nobles and the church, increasingly encroached on common land as they rounded off their estates, sometimes to increase their grain production in a period of rising prices, sometimes simply for the sake of social prestige.

For one reason or another, many peasants were forced out of agriculture. As the village of Taracena in the province of Guadalajara reported in the late 1570's,

> numbers here have diminished, because many *hidalgos* and *caballeros* have gone to live in the nearby city, although they have their estates in the countryside. The farmers who remain in the village have very little sub-stance; poverty has forced many of them to leave for Guadalajara and Madrid, for the village is so destitute that there is no livelihood in it. The majority of its people are now landless labourers, and some of these are leaving for Guadalajara.[1]

Urban growth, rural depopulation, this was the sombre picture of Castile in the years around 1600.

At a primitive level these agricultural communities were self-sufficient. In New Castile the dominant products were cereals and wine; for a period these crops managed to win the battle for land against the claims of livestock, and they accounted for 70–80 per cent. of agricultural production.[2] Local artisan manufactures, some of them practised by unemployed peasants, supplied the simple needs of farms and villages—coarse textiles, leather, pottery and building materials, soap and candles. There was little surplus capital for more sophisticated consumer goods. Most of the peasants did not own the land they worked: they were tenants or seasonal labourers. And they themselves were 'owned' by great lords, lay and clerical, who possessed *senorío*, conferring rights of service, taxation and jurisdiction over their vassals. The Castilian peasant was closely martialled by seigneurial controls, and these spread their

[1] Quoted by Noël Salomon, *La campagne de Nouvelle Castille à la fin du XVIᵉ siècle d'après les Relaciones topográficas* (Paris, 1964), p. 48.
[2] *Ibid.*, p. 96.

net more widely in the late sixteenth and early seventeenth centuries. Infatuation with noble status, abdication of responsible government, and royal penury, these were the pressures which swept aside the barriers against seigneurial advance erected by Philip II and gradually covered the Castilian countryside with a network of feudalism. Ministers and favourites began a mad scramble for vassals. The duke of Lerma, favourite of Philip III, used his political influence unashamedly to amass *senoríos*. Already before 1600 he owned many townships and villages; at the peak of his power he acquired many more, and in 1611–12 alone he bought a further twelve. Philip IV's financial needs were still more pressing, and he alienated jurisdiction on an even greater scale. In 1625 the crown concluded an *asiento* with a group of bankers, who advanced 1,210,000 ducats to the treasury against the security of 20,000 vassals; these were regarded as property, the sale of which would guarantee the advance. To alienate jurisdiction on this scale the crown needed the formal agreement of the cortes; the size of the transaction disturbed the assembly and it was reluctant to give its sanction. Eventually, to secure agreement, the royal spokesmen had to pull out all the stops of patriotic and religious appeal,

> considering the great and urgent needs of His Majesty caused by the unavoidable expense involved in the capture of Breda, the recovery of Brazil, the provision of the great armed forces maintained by land and sea, and the forces in the Low Countries which are defending the Holy Catholic Faith and the king's patrimony against the assaults of the rebels.[3]

The efforts of the early Habsburgs to curtail and reclaim private jurisdiction were nullified, and the years around 1600 saw a 'feudal reaction', as tens of thousands of Castilian peasants passed from royal to aristocratic control, with harsher taxes, exactions and justice.[4]

Having lost their land and their freedom to the great magnates, the peasants also lost their income, for they were now more vulnerable to service exactions and financial pressure. The Castilian labourer became a beast of burden bearing on his shoulders the whole top-heavy structure of an aristocratic society, church and state, nobles and rentiers, merchants and bankers. The cortes of Castile, by no means a commoner's institution, described in 1573 how one of the basic taxes, the *alcabala* (sales tax), operated in the case of grain:

> The prelates, grandees, lords of vassals and nobles procure all the grain which the peasants produce but do not pay a thing in *alcabala*; the prelates

---

[3] *Actas de las Cortes de Castilla*, 1563–1632 (51 vols., Madrid, 1861–1929), xliii, 125.
[4] See F. Braudel, *La Méditerranée et le monde méditerranéen à l'époque de Philippe II* (Paris, 1949), p. 635, who refers to a 'seigneurial reaction', dating it from an earlier period.

because they are exempt; the grandees and lords of vassals because normally they do not pay this tax but charge it on their wretched vassals; and other nobles because most of them employ similar methods in their villages and estates to divert the tax from themselves. The whole burden therefore falls on the peasants who are unable to escape payment on any grain they sell.[5]

As the cortes of 1593 pointed out, the peculiar tax structure of Castile made the peasants 'the people who sustain this kingdom'.[6] It was their labour which supported Spanish government and society, financed the armies and fleets, and subsidised the allies. In 1600 the distinguished lawyer and *arbitrista* Martín González de Cellorigo argued that the whole social and economic structure of Spain rested on the peasants, 'for the peasant who works in the field has to support himself, his lord, the clergy, the money-lender, and all the others who batten on him'.[7]

What were the various charges which crushed the rural masses? First there was the visible token of their vassalage, payments in money, in kind and in services to their lords. These varied from region to region, and in Castile they were not so oppressive as in Aragon and Valencia, but they were still heavy enough. Even more extortionate was the tithe owed to the church and charged on grain, livestock and other agricultural products. In New Castile the tithe took ten or twenty times more of a peasant's income than did seigneurial payments, and it was impossible to evade or reform, for the church had acknowledged rights to the fruits of the earth, enforced with all the rigour of canon law and spiritual sanctions. The tithe, it is true, financed the pastoral, social and educational work of the church, as well as its more extravagant consumption. But for the peasant it was a nightmare.

In addition to the regular visits of bailiffs and tithe commissioners, the peasant also endured the attentions of the royal tax-collectors, charging *alcabalas*, *servicios* and, from the late sixteenth century, the *millones*, a new tax on basic foodstuffs. Many *arbitristas* considered this the last straw. According to Sancho de Moncada, professor in the University of Toledo, the *millones* took 'the drop of wine from the mouth of the needy farmer, the morsel of meat and oil from the poor widow'.[8] But having paid his taxes, the peasant still had to find the rent he owed his landlord. In New Castile this was even more exacting than the tithe, taking between one-third and one-half of the value of crops produced.[9] Between rent and tithe the peasant was trapped,

[5] *Actas de las Cortes de Castilla*, vi, 369.
[6] *Ibid.*, xii, 505.
[7] *Memorial de la política necesaria y útil restauración de la República de España* (1600), quoted by Salomon, *op. cit.*, p. 214. The *arbitristas* were literally 'projectors' of schemes of financial and economic reform, but they may be regarded as the political economists of the time.
[8] *Fin y extinción del servicio de millones* (Madrid, 1619), fols. 41–41v.
[9] Salomon, *op. cit.*, p. 243.

and the only escape was migration. González de Cellorigo, writing in 1600, regarded rent as the greatest cause of rural distress and the prostration of the Castilian peasants, 'for having paid the tithes owed to God, they pay an even greater amount to the owner of land; and then follow innumerable seigneurial obligations, impositions, payment of debts and dues; and finally the various state taxes to which they are subjected'.[10] Altogether more than half of a peasant's product was consumed in payments which enriched non-peasant classes. On the remainder he had to keep his family, defray his overheads, pay his labourers, and renew his equipment.[11] Is it surprising that he was forced to cut down on production or abandon the land, seeking release from a standard of living which had become intolerable?

The structure of rural society was rigid, a harsh reflection of prevailing values.[12] At the bottom were the *jornaleros*, the landless labourers, who formed more than half the rural population of New Castile and lived more like beasts than human beings, in mud or wooden huts, with no furniture and few belongings, the whole family sleeping on the earth floor. The *jornaleros* were seasonal labourers, moving from place to place in search of work and bread, and in the intervals turning their hands to some rough craft or begging for charity. Above them were the *labradores*, peasant farmers who had actual possession of land by ownership or more commonly on lease. In New Castile they formed 25–30 per cent. of the rural population, and most of them were wretchedly poor, their joyless lives containing few hopes. A farmer was rich if he had 1,000 ducats a year, and perhaps some of them had, but they were a small minority, no more than 5 per cent. of rural inhabitants. These were the only dynamic group among the peasants and they fought to preserve their modest fortunes in the midst of rural crisis, looking down on the *jornaleros* below and resenting the *hidalgos* above. But they were not agents of change, for they themselves aspired to *hidalgo* status and in some cases secured it. So the one vigorous element in the countryside worked not to dissolve the social structure but to reinforce it. As for the *hidalgos* themselves, some were proud and destitute, others were reduced to working for a living, and all of them worked hard at maintaining their tax immunity, if only formally. But the *hidalgos* came well behind the *caballeros* and *titulos* in land, income, and prestige; these were the greatest proprietors, the real landed aristocracy.

The defects of the agrarian structure were becoming more pronounced towards the end of the sixteenth century. Land, jurisdiction, and tax immunity gave the aristocracy a monopoly of power in the countryside, while

[10] Quoted *ibid.*, p. 245.
[11] *Ibid.*, p. 250.
[12] *Ibid.*, pp. 257–302.

the peasant, more vulnerable than ever before, joined a growing exodus to the towns. This was the first cause of rural depopulation. But these over-crowded towns became death-traps of another kind.

In the years around 1600 Spain was struck by devastating disease, the first wave of a repeated assault which decimated the Spanish people and from which no generation of the seventeenth century escaped. The first great bubonic plague entered through Santander in 1596 and spread westwards along the northern coastal provinces, leaving heavy mortality in its wake. About 1598 it penetrated central Spain and began to feed on the two Castiles. In 1599 it reached Andalucía, and in Seville alone claimed 8,000 victims. It is difficult to calculate the total casualties of this prolonged scourge, but they amounted perhaps to 500,000.[13] There was a direct connection between rural depression and the high mortality of these plague-ridden years. Masses of distressed peasantry, already suffering from acute malnutrition, were easy victims of epidemic disease.[14] Once contagion had taken root agriculture further deteriorated, for the labour force was weakened and diminished. As for the densely packed towns, they were particular foci of infection, which shortage of food supplies then prolonged. Coastal districts were open to relief, for emergency supplies could be rushed in by sea. But the heartland of Castile, at the mercy of a slow and inefficient transport system, was isolated from the outer world. Its enclosed rural communities depended on their own agricultural resources, and to them the coincidence of famine and plague brought disaster—and panic. As towns were placed under quarantine, move-ment of the meagre food supplies available became even more difficult. And it was the urban poor, living in unsanitary slums and shanty towns, who suf-fered most; while the wealthy could escape to their country houses and isolate themselves behind armed guards, the poor had no refuge and if they fled from the towns they were driven off from country villages at gunpoint.

The great plague of 1596–1602, a precursor of other lethal epidemics, in-augurated a century of demographic recession. A decade later, inspired with a kind of death wish, Spanish society purged itself of impurity and expelled the moriscos, the last remnants of Islam in the peninsula. These two amputa-tions deprived Castile of some 600,000 to 700,000 people, about one-tenth of its population, within the short period of 1596–1614. Spain bore the scars for many decades to come. According to González de Cellorigo, 'the loss of the strength, valour and greatness of Spain' was due to the 'lack of people which

[13] Antonio Domínguez Ortiz, *La sociedad española en el siglo XVII* (Madrid, 1963), pp. 68–70. The prolific writings of this distinguished historian, full of research and understanding as they are, have made him one of the greatest authorities on the Spanish seventeenth century; this book is particularly indebted to his works.

[14] J. Nadal and E. Giralt, *La population catalane de 1553 à 1717* (Paris, 1960), discusses the relation between famine and pestilence.

has become apparent in recent years'. This lack was particularly noticeable in the Castilian plain watered by the River Duero, a region which included Valladolid, Burgos and Medina del Campo; but the provinces of Toledo and Seville were not far behind. And there was no respite. The years 1630–32 were particularly harsh, with a crushing combination of crop failure, famine and plague. In 1632 the cortes lamented:

> Many people have died, and many have abandoned their houses and farms, with great loss to agriculture. Livestock is scarce, savings are consumed, and many villages are so destitute that they ought to be relieved of their burdens rather than be asked for more to contribute to the needs of other kingdoms.[15]

But plague and depopulation had secondary consequences, for they disrupted trade and business, and labour shortage inflated wages to an unprecedented level.

Demoralised by death and destruction, the people of Castile were further castigated in these years by a rampant rise in the cost of living. After a century of relentless inflation prices suddenly spiralled beyond all control. In Andalucía the price of grain rose from 430 maravedis a fanega in 1595 to 1,041 in 1598, in Castile from 408 in 1595 to 908 in 1599.[16] The price revolution culminated in 1601 when prices reached their peak. Thereafter, inflation did not cease, in spite of demographic recession and the precipitous fall of silver receipts from America; now it was caused by the progressive depreciation of base money, especially from the early 1620's. In Andalucía and the two Castiles the average price level showed a downward tendency in 1601–10, and trade, particularly to America, began to recede.[17] Prices then remained stable in 1611–20, with a slight trend upwards. This stability was upset by the enormous coinage of vellon (debased copper coinage) in 1621–25, as the government sought to create quick money for itself. On average the indices rose about 20 per cent. in 1621–30; in 1626–27 Castile experienced one of the most violent price upheavals in its history, its average indices rising 20·21 points in two years.[18] This was caused not by economic activity nor by the American trade—imports of precious metals fell sharply in 1630—but almost exclusively by monetary inflation. There was a further price rise in 1636–38, with an advance of 21·8 points in Old Castile. After a brief fall, prices surged upwards again in 1641–42, owing to the heavy increase in vellon during the wars and revolutions of the early 1640's, but they were brought

[15] *Actas de las Cortes de Castilla*, li, 97.
[16] Earl J. Hamilton, *American Treasure and the Price Revolution in Spain*, 1501–1650 (Cambridge, Mass., 1934), pp. 215–16.
[17] *Ibid.*, pp. 217–21.
[18] Base 1571–80.

B

down in 1642 by official deflation. This did not last long, and further depreciation of vellon caused another great upswing in Castile in 1646–50, while
the rise was aggravated in Andalucía by the great plague of 1648. The
average price level in Andalucía, the two Castiles and Valencia was approximately 38·7 per cent. higher in 1650 than in 1625. 'Hence the net advance
under the stimulus of vellon inflation in Castile and silver inflation in
Valencia in the second quarter of the seventeenth century was not far behind
the most violent upheaval of silver prices in any quarter century of the Price
Revolution'.[19]

Grains, particularly wheat, were the most important item of consumption
of the vast majority of the population and consumed a high percentage of the
income of the common people. Until about 1570 there was little divergence
between grain prices and those of other commodities. Up to 1650 this still
held good for Old Castile and Valencia. But in Andalucía and New Castile
grain prices rose much more than those of general commodities in the period
1575–1650. The rise of the New Castilian indices in the first half of the seventeenth century, in spite of demographic recession, was probably due to
exports to other parts of Spain and to over-planting of vineyards on wheat
land after the steep rise of wine prices in the previous century. And the lag of
grain prices in Old Castile behind those of other regions is probably accounted
for by depopulation and price control.[20]

The wage rise of the sixteenth century continued into the seventeenth.[21]
The demographic reversal caused by the great plague of 1596–1602 led to an
abrupt increase of wages; a labourer in Castile who was paid 3,470 maravedis
in 1599 received 9,000 in 1603. Under the stimulus of vellon inflation money
wages continued to rise from 1626, and the wage index for 1650 exceeded
that of 1600 by 47·77 per cent. But a labourer had to buy food and clothing
and house his family, and his real earnings were eroded by inflation. In the
course of the sixteenth century the purchasing power of labourers suffered
by almost 30 per cent. It also suffered in the first half of the seventeenth
century. Prices responded much more rapidly than wages to the great
depreciation of vellon money in 1622–27, and this disparity caused real wages
to drop more than 20 per cent. From then onwards wages never caught up
with the steep rise in the cost of living. The index for real wages in 1650 was
about 10 per cent. less than in 1645 and considerably under that for 1627. For
the labouring masses of Castile, therefore, the inflation induced by vellon
debasement was a calamity; it defrauded them of their wages and depressed
their already low living standards to the margin of subsistence.

Historians have been tempted to argue that Spain forged its own economic
ruin by tolerating the sharp increase of wages in the early seventeenth century,

[19] Hamilton, *op. cit.*, p. 220.   [20] *Ibid.*, pp. 241–42.   [21] *Ibid.*, pp. 273–82.

especially in the period 1611–20 when real earnings briefly attained a summit. In these years, it is suggested, wages did not lag sufficiently behind prices to allow the accumulation of capital for investment in production.[22] The argument is not convincing. It is unrealistic to suppose that Spain needed a policy of compulsory saving at the expense of depressed labouring groups. Surplus capital already lay in other hands, innocent of useful employment. And there is no evidence to suggest that better industrial profits would have been invested productively. Spanish entrepreneurial and manufacturing groups, few in numbers and low in spirits, thwarted by state policy, war, social values and economic adversity, were already in difficulties by the end of the sixteenth century. And there could be no improvement until the agrarian structure had been remodelled, for the depressed rural sector did not provide a market for consumer goods. The towns themselves, swarming with unemployed or underemployed migrants from the countryside, were simply an extension of rural depression, so they in turn provided little outlet for agricultural expansion.

Towards the end of Philip III's reign the sense of crisis rose to a new pitch. Amidst a chorus of lamentations from officials and economists, from towns and countryside, the crown commissioned the Council of Castile to report on measures needed to revive the ailing economy. In its celebrated *consulta* of 1 February 1619 the Council examined the causes of depopulation and depression, and concluded, among other things, that the 'excessive burdens and contributions' imposed on the people had led to the 'greatest depopulation', for in order not to die of hunger people were forced to emigrate to other regions or overseas.[23] In a gloss on this report, the *arbitrista* Pedro Fernández Navarrete argued that the income from agriculture, the country's basic economic activity, was not sufficient to cover various costs such as taxes, rent to the landowner, and interest payments to money-lenders; in his view, output was falling because the costs of production were too high.[24] A somewhat different opinion was expressed by Sancho de Moncada. Writing in 1619, he dated rapid deterioration as beginning during 'the last four or five years'; this would coincide with the expulsion of the moriscos and the first stage of recession in the American trade. But Moncada did not regard poor harvests as the root cause of depression; following the crop shortages of 1606–7, he argued, production had improved.

[22] See Earl J. Hamilton, 'American Treasure and the Rise of Capitalism, 1500–1700', *Economica*, ix (1929), 338–57.

[23] Angel González Palencia, *La Junta de Reformación, 1618–1625 (Archivo Histórico Español*, v, Valladolid, 1932), doc. 4.

[24] *Conservación de Monarquías* (1626) (*Biblioteca de autores españoles*, xxv, Madrid, 1947), pp. 445–47.

Many parts of Castile and elsewhere are depopulated by the very abundance of crops, and we see grain and grapes remaining to be harvested. The
reason is the lack of demand, which arises from the dearth of people and
money for buying essentials; for those who remain have no means of
earning money to spend on food.[25]

He saw the depression as the inevitable consequence of a diminishing population, excessive import of foreign goods, and a social mentality which inhibited
industrial production. Yet a further viewpoint was given by the count of
Gondomar, Spanish ambassador to England, who referred to the 'depopulation, poverty and deprivation in contemporary Spain; foreigners proclaim
that to travel through our country is more painful than to traverse any other
waste land of Europe, for there are no beds, lodgings or meals, on account of
the great and oppressive taxes the natives pay'.[26]

Government revenue was heavily compromised by Philip III. He did not
create new taxes, but he anticipated revenue by several years and he inaugurated one of the great evils of the century, monetary inflation. From 1618 in
particular, to finance Spain's entry into the Thirty Years War, his government debased the currency on a large scale, a practice continued with even
less responsibility by Philip IV. Unwilling to reduce expenditure, which was
regarded as essential for national defence, or to increase taxation, which would
be unpopular, the government persisted in reckless borrowing, until it
reached the point of inevitable bankruptcy in 1627. This year was a further
stage in the crisis. Castile now staggered under the impact of vellon inflation,
diminution of American trade, and a year of poor harvests. In 1628 the
Dutch captured the Mexican silver fleet, and hostilities with France pushed
up defence expenditure still higher. Adverse weather conditions in the
following years caused further crop failures. Emergency grain supplies were
desperately sought in the Mediterranean, North Africa and the Baltic; and
the few existing stocks were bought up by the powerful and wealthy, while
the mass of the people lived next to starvation.[27]

The syndrome of rural poverty, depopulation, financial chaos, and recession of American trade produced Spain's first great crisis in the modern
period.[28] The crisis can be dated between 1598 and 1620, and it was a crisis of
change, denoting a reversal of the economic trends of the sixteenth century.
The worst was still to come. From 1640 political disintegration and military

[25] *Restauración política de España y deseos públicos* (1619), quoted by Domínguez Ortiz, *La sociedad
española en el siglo XVII*, pp. 26–27.
[26] Gondomar to Philip III, 1619, *Documentos inéditos para la historia de España* (New series, 4
vols., Madrid, 1936–45), ii, 131–46.
[27] Domínguez Ortiz, *La sociedad española en el siglo XVII*, pp. 33–34.
[28] See P. Vilar, 'Le temps du "Quichotte" ', *Europe*, xxxiv (1956), 3–16, for an interpretation.

collapse compounded the economic disorder and reduced Spain to absolute depression. And by this time there was no hope of relief from America.

In the sixteenth century the economy of the Hispanic world was an integrated economy. Spain expended men, money and prolonged effort in the colonisation of America and the development of its resources. The annual shiploads of American treasure, therefore, were the returns on an investment —the greatest investment by any country in the sixteenth century—and not the rewards of a parasite. The injection of expanding amounts of silver into the peninsula compensated to some degree for the failings of the domestic economy. These receipts stimulated some sectors such as shipbuilding and, at first, agriculture; they bridged the gap in the balance of payments; they alleviated the tax burden; and they joined the contributions of the Castilian peasantry to maintain the nation's armies and fleets, and to support its war effort in northern Europe. In the years around 1600 the continuing yield of colonial wealth redeemed the poor performance of domestic agriculture and still more of industry by providing capital to buy abroad. But this closely-knit economy was bound to contract when its most fruitful branch began to wither. Between 1606–10 and 1646–50 gross tonnage in the American trade dropped by 60 per cent., from 273,560 tons to 121,308. This long period of recession can be dated from 1609, and the trend was never reversed.[29] No doubt the crisis of the transatlantic trade was aggravated by the attack of foreign enemies and the penetration of foreign interlopers. But its basic cause was the transformation of the colonial economies and the shift of economic power within the Hispanic world.

The American colonies were no longer exclusively orientated towards mining production. The trends of silver output, of course, differed between Mexico and Peru. From 1545 to the mid-1560's Peru disgorged a vast amount of treasure, especially from Potosí. There followed a recession in the late 1560's and early 1570's until the adoption of the *patio*, or amalgamation, process unlocked the lower grade ores and released an immense and rising output. While this was not sustained throughout the seventeenth century, Peru remained a mining economy, more 'colonial' and less developed than Mexico. But Peru, too, had other sources of wealth and these now absorbed more of the colony's capital, leaving a reduced surplus for Spain. Mexico's mining output was more erratic in the sixteenth century until the introduction of mercury amalgamation in 1553. Thereafter silver production rose steadily, though at its peak, in the 1580's and 1590's, it probably amounted to no more than a third or quarter of that of Peru. And from the beginning of the seventeenth century it receded to the point of collapse. The fall in silver

---

[29] See the references to H. and P. Chaunu, *Séville et l'Atlantique* (1504–1650) (8 vols., Paris, 1955–59), in Chapter VII below.

returns from America, therefore, reflected in some degree the great depression in the mining industry, which was itself a consequence of demographic catastrophe among the Amerindians, labour shortage, technical deficiencies and rising costs. But it was also evidence of the development of the colonial economies, the decrease of their primitive dependence on mining, their exploitation of other sources of wealth, and their retention of capital for local use in administration, defence contracts, public works and private investment. In Mexico the demographic factor alone was sufficient to stimulate a new investment pattern. The simultaneous growth of the white population and decimation of the Indians caused the colonists to overcome shortage of labour and therefore of food supplies by renewed investment in agriculture, to concentrate more on land and less on mining.

Spain was powerless to prevent these developments. Indeed she had necessarily assisted them. In the process of colonisation Spaniards introduced from the peninsula and the Canary Islands the domestic animals, cereals, vegetables and fruits which flourished in the temperate and highland regions of the New World; they also transferred tropical and sub-tropical plants, such as the orange, sugar cane, and later coffee and rice, which took root in the humid and warmer lowlands. Furthermore, a number of plants cultivated by the Amerindians—cacao, cotton and maize—were taken over by the colonists and produced in quantities to become, with sugar, hides and woods, important articles of trade. Towards colonial industry and commerce Spanish policy was at best liberal and at worst too inconsistent to be a serious obstacle. Some American products such as wine—the vine too was transplanted from Spain—expanded into direct competition with Spanish exports, but by the time this was identified as a danger, towards the 1590's, the development could not be reversed. The textile industry was specifically authorised. Mexico produced raw and manufactured silk, and being well endowed with wool had a sizeable cloth industry. Peru also had a textile industry; this became a target of restrictive policy, but too many Peruvian interests were involved to permit its curtailment. While colonial textiles were inferior in quality and could not command the luxury market, they could certainly satisfy the mass market and remove it from Spanish control. Many of the new products were sold outside the colony which produced them; inter-colonial trade developed a buoyancy of its own, independent of the Spanish liaison, and carried by a merchant marine constructed in American shipyards.

Economic shift was accompanied by social change. By 1600 the first generation of American-born Spaniards had taken root and occupied dominant positions as landowners, manufacturers, merchants and capitalists. Mexican-born whites and meztizos now called themselves *criollos* and were conscious of a difference between themselves and peninsula-born Spaniards, whom they called *gachupines*. They were subjects of the crown, of course, and not basically hostile to Spain, but nor were they closely attached and they would brook no interference with their private interests. The depression of imperial trade and navigation provided favourable conditions for the growth of an independent society, and in the course of the seventeenth century an American aristocracy came into being, an aristocracy of land and large-scale commerce, the guardians of creole interests, whom imperial administrators could not ignore.

The crisis in the transatlantic trade in the years after 1600, therefore, was rooted in economic forces over which Spain had no control. The development of the empire, the new variety of its economic activities, and its growing self-absorption, were all signs that America was detaching itself from peninsular requirements and was no longer content to be a mere provider of precious metals for the metropolis. By the 1640's certain sectors of the American economy—shipbuilding, agriculture, and investment in overseas trade—were far more buoyant than their counterparts in Spain. The economic independence of America, and its superior capital resources, denoted a fundamental shift of balance within the Hispanic world. Economically at least the dominant partner was now America, and America did not share the peninsular and European interests of Spain, nor did it now contribute in any significant degree to Spain's defence needs and foreign policy. If this interpretation is correct, Spain lost her colonial wealth not so much to foreign rivals and interlopers—the familiar heroes or scapegoats according to point of view—as to her own American subjects who now appropriated their own resources for themselves.

The reorientation of the Hispanic world in the years around 1600 has gone largely unnoticed in European historiography.[30] Observers have been so impressed by the waning of Spanish power in Europe that they have tended to see this exclusively in terms of the depression and depopulation within the peninsula, the suicidal foreign policy of Spain's rulers between 1621 and 1658, and the relative improvement in the power of other states. In these terms, however, how can we explain the enduring facts of the case—that an enfeebled metropolis retained its American empire unimpaired for another two centuries, and that the unity of the Hispanic world survived all assaults until 1810? The reason, of course, is that this was still a great complex of wealth and power, though the centre of gravity had moved across the Atlantic. America in effect preserved its own territory, and in addition defended imperial communications. America was now the guardian of empire. This is the story of the seventeenth century—not the waning of the Hispanic world, but the recession of Spain within that world.

[30] Except of course by Chaunu; see below, pp. 194–200.

CHAPTER II
THE GOVERNMENT OF PHILIP III

1. KING AND FAVOURITE

PHILIP II died on 13 September 1598, leaving to his son, then aged twenty-one, the government of the largest, the most powerful and the most complex empire in the world. He delivered his charge with some misgivings: 'God, who has given me so many kingdoms, has denied me a son capable of ruling them'. And, referring to the aristocratic friends hovering about the heir to the throne, he confided to his secretary a few days before his death, 'I fear they are going to rule him'.[1]

Ill-endowed in mind and character for his vast responsibilities, regarded by his officials and his subjects with a mixture of indulgence and exasperation, and condemned by later opinion as totally unfit to rule, Philip III put personal monarchy to the severest test it had yet endured.[2] Physically he seemed to have shed the ill-health of his childhood. Short in stature and inclined to stoutness, he was agreeable enough in appearance, with the red hair typical of his dynasty but without the degenerate physiognomy of the later Habsburgs. His education and upbringing had followed conventional lines for an heir to the throne, and he had lived a courtly life in the company of clerical tutors, spiritual advisers, and aristocratic friends. His father had arranged his betrothal, predictably, to a Habsburg cousin, Margaret of Austria, whom he married in Valencia on 18 April 1599; she bore him eight children, five of whom survived infancy, and she died in childbirth in 1611. Benign and pious, he impressed contemporaries for his moral virtues at least. If his court was frivolous and extravagant, it was probably an inevitable reaction to the austerity of Philip II's household. The king himself had no strong interests, except perhaps eating and hunting. He travelled extensively and seemed to prefer country houses, above all the Escorial, to Madrid. But his mind was empty, his will supine. His political ideas were based on a belief in the divine

---

[1] Modesto Lafuente, *Historia general de España* (30 vols., Madrid, 1850–67), xi, 77–78.

[2] There is no adequate modern study of the reign of Philip III. Ciriaco Pérez Bustamente, *Felipe III. Semblanza de una monarca y perfiles de una privanza* (Madrid, 1950) is a useful source of information though not of analysis. The distinguished works of the nineteenth-century statesman and historian, Antonio Cánovas del Castillo, *Historia de la decadencia española* (Madrid, 1854, 2nd ed. 1911) and *Bosquejo histórico de la Casa de Austria* (Madrid, 1869, 2nd ed. 1911) are still valuable for their scholarship and judgment.

SPAIN IN THE
SEVENTEENTH CENTURY

OA

BÉARN

RRE

ROUSSILLON

Urgel

Gerona

CATALONIA

Zaragoza

Lérida

pila

ARAGON

Barcelona

Tarragona

VALENCIA

BALEARIC I.s.

Valencia

Alicante

urcia

Cartagena

Marseilles

Toulon

100 miles

mission of Spanish kingship, and he identified the interests of religion with those of Spain, interpreting the vicissitudes of Spanish policy in terms of divine pleasure or displeasure. Otherwise he seemed to view his office primarily as a source of patronage for the Spanish aristocracy. His irresponsible generosity drove his treasury officials to despair, though it was never directed, as far as is known, to cases of real destitution. Even more damaging to the interests of good government, however, was his incurable apathy. Philip III was the laziest king in Spanish history.

The new monarch could not hope to emulate his father. Philip II, as well as being a great king, had been a great civil servant. But his system of government, in which the king was at once his own counsellor, policy-maker and executive, placed an intolerable burden on the incumbent. Philip III at least recognised his own limitations. He took one look at the situation and promptly withdrew. Before doing so he made, for a Spanish monarch, an unprecedented decision: he delegated power to a chief minister. Even in this rare moment of resolution, however, he could not escape his own mediocrity. His choice fell upon Francisco de Sandoval y Rojas, marquis of Denia and soon promoted duke of Lerma, his closest friend and confidant, and a man no more fit to exercise power than he himself was.

Though not a Castilian—he came from Valencia—Lerma was impeccably aristocratic. Indeed his social status and his friendship with the king were his only qualifications for office. Intelligence and judgment he possessed to only a moderate degree. He was also deficient in political experience; he had occupied, without distinction, only one major office, that of viceroy of Valencia, and he had been given this by Philip II not on his merits but in order to remove him from proximity to the impressionable prince. Ranke believed that Lerma possessed qualities verging on statesmanship.[3] And it is true that he consistently advocated a policy of peace and sought to disengage Spain from imperial commitments in northern and central Europe. But these qualities would have been more convincing had Lerma shown any disposition to use peace as a means of reassessing Spanish priorities, of relieving the tax-payer, and of pursuing a policy of retrenchment and reform. As it was he seemed to have little interest in the details of government. In this respect at least he was far from being a precursor of Olivares, the great favourite of Philip IV. Lerma wanted power not in order to make policy but in order to acquire prestige and, above all, wealth. In pursuit of wealth he was active and uninhibited. Beginning his public career in financial difficulties he gradually amassed a vast personal fortune and used his political power shamelessly to

---

[3] Leopold von Ranke, *L'Espagne sous Charles-Quint, Philippe II et Philippe III* (Paris, 1845), 219–23.

sustain and extend it.[4] If Philip III was the laziest ruler Spain has had, Lerma was incomparably the greediest. And his care for his own interests was closely followed by that for his family and friends. He dismissed García de Loaysa, archbishop of Toledo, and Pedro de Portocarrero, inquisitor general, and gave both posts to his uncle Bernardo de Sandoval. He distributed titles and offices to select favourites until he had an entire faction beholden to him. Lerma's venality can hardly be questioned. Whether he had a corrupting influence on Spanish public life is more difficult to determine. The distribution of favours to political clients is one thing; perverting an entire administration is another. It is hardly likely that the hard core of the bureaucracy was affected by Lerma's influence. The Spanish civil service was not so sensitive to change.

The novelty of a weak king and a powerful favourite so impressed contemporary Spaniards that they regarded the year 1598 as the end of an age. Political theorists, too, reacted quickly to the change. In Spain the age of the great political philosophers, like the age of the great kings, had passed. The successors of Vitoria, Soto and Suárez were mediocrities, writers who compiled precepts of moral philosophy for the instruction and edification of the ruler and his ministers.[5] They took for granted that the perfect form of government was personal monarchy; they did not question that sovereignty should be absolute; and it never occurred to them to consider the role of representative institutions. They were looking, indeed, not for the origins and nature of power but for the ideal Christian prince. Their search was appropriate but in vain; Spanish kingship was never so weak as when it was exposed to most exhortation. As though despairing of the monarchs, some political theorists turned to the monarchs' favourites and began to preach on the education, qualities and tactics of the *perfecto privado*. This type of literature reached the depths of bathos in the conclusions drawn by Padre Joseph Laynez: 'If the favourite is as good as he ought to be then he is the noblest and richest gem in the crown of the king'. And as kings rule by divine right so do favourites: 'God chooses the favourite as he does the king'.[6] However preposterous Spanish political theory became in its didactic period, it reflected the view that Spanish kings needed encouragement and their favourites recognition. This in itself was a radical change from the theory and

---

[4] 'The circumstances of the marquis of Denia are extremely reduced', Mateo Vázquez to Philip II, 12 January 1585, *Correspondencia privada de Felipe II con su secretario Mateo Vázquez, 1567–1591*, ed. C. Riba García, vol. i (Madrid, 1959), p. 351; according to the Venetian ambassador, Lerma was bankrupt in 1598, Simon Contarini, *Relazione* of 1605, in Luis Cabrera de Córdoba, *Relaciones de las cosas sucedidas en la corte de España desde 1599 hasta 1614* (Madrid, 1857), p. 579. On Lerma see also Cánovas, *Decadencia*, p. 60.

[5] J. A. Maravall, *Teoría española del Estado en el siglo XVII* (Madrid, 1944).

[6] *Ibid.*, pp. 303–17.

practice of kingship in the reign of Philip II. Later historians, too, have seen the year 1598 as a turning point in the history of Spain, the time when personal rule by the monarch gave way to the rule of favourites.[7]

Yet these developments masked a basic continuity in Spanish history, a continuity of institutions, personnel and policy. This was appreciated by an older tradition of Spanish historiography: 'the truth is that, with less power and less fortune, neither Philip III nor Philip IV professed any other principles of government than Philip II established and practised'; and it has even been claimed that it was not in the *valimiento*, the office of favourite, but in the councils 'in which resided in effect all the political power at that time'.[8] No doubt this is an exaggeration. The formulation of policy is not the same as the exercise of sovereignty. Nor was it the councils in general which formulated basic policy but one council in particular, the Council of State.[9] Nevertheless, in underlining the continuity provided by the administrative machine, these views have a certain validity.

2. COUNCILS AND COUNCILLORS

Spain continued to be governed by the conciliar apparatus developed by the earlier Habsburgs. In this system power was distributed among a number of agencies which specialised in different aspects of government. But it was not distributed evenly. At the top was the Council of State which considered major policy and had exclusive jurisdiction over foreign policy. This council had no president, as the king was regarded as its convenor. And all the other councils were subordinate, either formally or in practice, to its jurisdiction. It was the parent body of the Council of War, which had begun its career as little more than a specialised sub-committee of the senior council. In the last decades of Philip II's reign, in response to Spain's growing military commitments, the Council of War had acquired its own secretariat and a distinct identity, but it was still basically a subordinate of the Council of State both in function and membership; all the councillors of state were *ex-officio* members of the Council of War, though they did not all necessarily attend it, and its role was simply to administer the military consequences of policy decided in the Council of State.

There was a group of superior or supreme councils, so called because they were theoretically independent of any other. In order of rank these were the Council of Castile, the Council of the Indies, the Council of Aragon, the Council of the Inquisition, the Council of Italy, the Council of Flanders, and

[7] Pérez Bustamente, *op. cit.*, p. 7.
[8] Antonio Cánovas del Castillo, *Estudios del reinado de Felipe IV* (2 vols., Madrid, 1888), i, 258.
[9] Charles Howard Carter, *The Secret Diplomacy of the Habsburgs, 1598–1625* (New York, 1964), pp. 71–72.

the Council of Portugal. Constitutionally 'supreme', in fact they were, to a greater or lesser degree, essentially administrative agencies, applying policy not making it; matters of importance, particularly those affecting defence and security, had to be referred to the Council of State. The Council of Aragon considered the affairs of the three realms of the Crown of Aragon, that is Aragon proper, Catalonia and Valencia. It acted as a liaison between the king in Madrid and his viceroys in Zaragoza, Barcelona and Valencia. Like the other councils in this group it had its own president and secretariat, and a membership which was a mixture of minor nobility and *letrados*; but it also possessed a unique 'constitutional' feature in that all its councillors, with the exception of the treasurer-general, had to be natives of the Crown of Aragon.[10] The Council of Castile had administrative and judicial jurisdiction in the territories of the Crown of Castile alone, and was the nearest Spain approached to a council for home affairs. But even within this specialised field major policy-decisions—the expulsion of the moriscos, for example— had to be referred to the Council of State. The councils specialising in regional affairs outside Castile and Aragon—the Council of Italy, the Council of Flanders, and the Council of Portugal—had an even more humble role. They handled the day-to-day trivia of administration, much of it concerned with applications for pensions and preferment, and any business of importance within their areas went to the Council of State. The Council of the Indies, on the other hand, occupied a more distinguished position in the administrative hierarchy, corresponding to the importance of the overseas empire which it administered. It had competence in every sphere of colonial government, legislative, financial, judicial, military, ecclesiastical and commercial.[11] And so specialised was its function that it was necessarily the major influence in the formation of colonial policy. Nevertheless, in matters concerning imperial defence and security it might have to defer to the Council of State; and its control over Indies revenue and expenditure was severely limited by the general fiscal jurisdiction of the Council of Finance.[12] The latter administered the crown's revenue and expenditure; and although in the field of taxation its jurisdiction was confined to Castile in effect it had international responsibilities, for it was Castile which financed the general policy of the Monarchy. But as this policy was formulated in the Council of State, the Council of Finance was little more than a service department for its superior.

Conciliar government, which was essentially government by committees, was weak in two respects: it provided neither an efficient executive nor

[10] See *Spain under the Habsburgs*, i, 3, 11, 48, 182–84, 337–38.

[11] Ernesto Schäfer, *El Consejo real y supremo y de las Indias* (2 vols., Seville, 1935–47) provides an authoritative and detailed study of the Council of the Indies, a task which has not been performed for any other council.

[12] *Ibid.*, i, 102–10.

sufficient centralisation. It was subject, of course, to relentless pressure. Over the vast expanse of the Hispanic world, from the Low Countries to the Philippines, hundreds of officials spent much of their working lives writing reports to the central government, posing problems, requesting advice, demanding action. As wave after wave of paper reached Madrid it was processed according to a procedure which was now fairly standardised. Each conciliar secretary selected and prepared his particular material for the attention of the king; the latter, working with the secretary, decided what the appropriate council should see and requested its opinion; the council discussed the matter and presented its conclusions in a *consulta*, which was a document drawn up by the secretary summarising the various arguments and recording the vote of each councillor; this then went to the king for his decision, a decision which would be returned to the secretary and/or council for action. Before they were subverted by declining standards of appointments in the course of the seventeenth century, the councils themselves and their secretaries worked with reasonable efficiency and despatch. And the *consulta* was a useful instrument for the formulation of policy. The weakness of the system lay in the excessive reliance it placed upon the executive, the king. Too much depended on his personal action. Under Philip II, who worked prodigiously, the machinery was already beginning to creak; under his successors it almost ground to a halt. Delay occurred at two key points: having received the incoming material the king took too long to send it to council for an opinion; and having received the opinion he took too long to act upon it. The efficiency of the subordinate councils in particular was blunted by the evasive tactics of the king in sending their *consultas* to the Council of State for a further *consulta* and even then delaying his decision. The precious decision, once obtained, had to reach a distant agency, or a number of agencies, for actual enforcement. This was the final flaw in the system.

Conciliar government, radiating from the centre though it did, was not really a centralised system of administration. Reflecting to some degree the constitutional structure of the Monarchy, with its semi-autonomous regional components, it could hardly aspire to centralisation. But regional barriers were not the only ones. Madrid was not linked with its outlying provinces by a bureaucracy. Few of the councils—the Inquisition and the Council of the Indies were exceptions—employed their own officials in the localities; liaison between the centre and the periphery hardly penetrated beyond viceregal level. Thus the councils could only govern indirectly. The Council of Finance, for example, which had most need of its own local officials, had to rely for the collection of taxes on tax-farmers who were not responsible to the central government.[13] The regional councils had virtually no full-time

[13] Antonio Domínguez Ortiz, *Política y hacienda de Felipe IV* (Madrid, 1960), 171–80.

administrative officials in the areas under their jurisdiction. Even Castile, within its own boundaries, lacked bureaucratic centralisation.

Philip III inherited these structural defects in Spanish administration and aggravated them by his own habits of work. But his very indolence allowed the councils to assume greater direction of their affairs and to this extent promoted institutional development. This was particularly noticeable in the Council of State. Under Philip II, who did his own work, its powers were limited and its meetings irregular. From about 1600, however, it began to meet regularly—about once a week—and to assume a more active and comprehensive role in the formulation of policy. This can be seen in the greater number of *consultas* coming from the Council of State, indicating that Philip III was sending it more material and relying more on its advice than his father had ever done. This advice he normally accepted. The only drawback was the intolerable length of time he took to do so.

In the first three years of his reign Philip III grossly neglected his responsibilities. He was unbelievably slow in sending incoming material to the councils, and he sometimes took as long as six months and frequently two or three months to reply to a *consulta*. From about 1602 he seemed to bestir himself, but his performance was still erratic. His addiction to public ceremonial and his excessive travelling habits further isolated him from officials, who were left to administer affairs of state as best they could, waiting with increasing frustration for the king's perfunctory agreement to their *consultas*. Liaison with the councils he left in the hands of Lerma, who pushed material around from one to another and kept an eye on their activities. But it is difficult to determine the extent to which Lerma influenced conciliar decisions. He rarely attended the Council of State and he seems to have been content to let the administration get on with its own job. Councillors, of course, had other means of knowing the favourite's opinions than listening to them at the council table; and he was known to be a dangerous man to cross. But in many respects Lerma was the image and likeness of the king; he was remote, itinerant, and just as ready to accept conciliar advice as his master. There were two subjects, however, in which he took a close interest—finance, especially expenditure, and patronage. On these matters at least he made it clear who was in command.

The remoteness of the executive threw greater responsibility on the councils and forced them to review their own procedure. They reacted to the growing burden of work by producing from within themselves a number of juntas, or sub-committees, whose function was to consider urgent and special problems of the moment. They were usually composed of a few members of the parent body reinforced by specialists from other councils or from outside the councils. The Council of the Indies, whose problems encompassed many areas of government, sought relief in the junta system. In 1600 it produced a *Junta de guerra de Indias*, specialising in the military and naval affairs of the empire, and composed of four councillors of the Indies and four members of the Council of War. In the same year it also formally constituted a special finance committee, the *Junta de hacienda*, to which were added two members of the Council of Finance; this was an *ad hoc* body which had first appeared in 1595 and operated until 1605.[14] Finally, appointments and patronage in the Indies were put in the hands of a small standing committee, the *Consejo de cámara de las Indias*; constituted in 1600, this committee soon acquired a reputation for the venality associated with the duke of Lerma and it was abolished in 1609, an indication perhaps of conciliar resistance to blatant corruption. The junta system was particularly useful to the Council of State and enabled it to cope with the increasing business coming its way. It set up a number of sub-committees to specialise in the various areas of foreign policy, such as the *Junta de Italia*, the *Junta de Inglaterra*, and the *Junta de Alemania*. In this way the Council could have a number of urgent matters considered simultaneously without tying down the whole Council to one problem. The proliferation of juntas in the reign of Philip III has usually been regarded as a disorderly process and a symptom of decline in standards of government. In fact it was a realistic development, sponsored by the administration itself, in response to the growing burden of work.[15] And it had perfectly respectable precedents in the reign of Philip II.

Continuity between the old regime and the new can also be seen in the personnel of Philip III's administration. The new king did not take over the conciliar team of his father in its entirety. Some officials were demoted and new ones were brought in. Among the latter Lerma himself was the out-standing example, and he is often supposed to have had a pernicious influence on the new administration by filling it with his own creatures. The Venetian ambassador reported: 'In Spain the Council is everything, but it is not free, or only nominally so, for no one dares to give his opinion freely, especially if it is against the will of the duke of Lerma. For having done so García de Loaysa, archbishop of Toledo, fell in disgrace, and Rodrigo Vázquez, president of the Council of Castile, was deprived of his office and expelled from court. The same happened to Pedro Portocarrero, inquisitor general, and to don Pedro de Guzmán, royal chamberlain, who spoke ill of the duke to the king'.[16] The Venetian ambassadors were not infallible guides to the Spanish political system. It can be queried whether there was anything sinister in these dismissals and whether they were due exclusively to the

[14] Schäfer, *op. cit.*, i, 170–74, 203–6.
[15] See Carter, *op. cit.*, pp. 73–74, for a vigorous reappraisal of the junta system.
[16] Contarini, *op. cit.*, p. 579.

favourite's malice. García de Loaysa and Vázquez de Arce had both been members of the junta appointed by Philip II for the education of the heir to the throne, and it may be that the latter had seen enough of them not to require their services further. A new regime, moreover, might be expected to react against members of the old who take their power and influence too much for granted. This seems to have been the case with Cristóbal de Moura, former secretary of Philip II; while not dismissed by the new king, he was posted away from Madrid, returning subsequently to the Council of State a strangely muted figure.[17] Baltasar de Zúñiga, was also posted abroad, but this was because his great diplomatic talents were especially needed in the key embassies at Brussels, Paris and Vienna; and he too returned to conciliar office for a brief, though influential, term.[18] Lerma's patronage can certainly be seen in appointments to a certain number of offices, including some at secretarial level; but there is no evidence that he attempted the impossible task of subverting the entire administration.

The Council of State provides a good example of the new dispensation. Most of the men who were now brought in—the duke of Alba, the duke of Infantado, and the constable of Castile—were obvious candidates for preferment by reason of their noble rank, their experience, and their past service to the crown. The inclusion of the royal confessor, Fray Gaspar de Córdoba, was acceptable by the standards of the time and he too had experience of administration under Philip II. Even the count of Miranda, regarded by many historians as an obvious creature of Lerma, had viceregal and conciliar experience in the previous reign and qualified for further office on his own merits.[19] The clearest line of continuity, however, was provided by two men who had been among the principal officials of Philip II, Juan de Idiáquez, comendador of León, and the count of Chinchón. The latter was a seasoned and forceful administrator, whom Philip II had employed on various councils and had marked with his approval. Idiáquez had been brought into the royal secretariat after the fall of Antonio Pérez and was one of those men around whom Philip II had built a new and hard-line administration in the 1580's. As a member of the junta which had supervised his education he was well known to the new king, who now appointed him to the Council of State; there he became one of the most influential members. A tough, faceless, and realistic administrator, Idiáquez was a witness to the survival of professionalism in government.[20] Fashioned round men like this, the new Council of State was no irresponsible creation. The criterion of appointment

[17] Matías de Novoa, *Memorias* (*Colección de documentos inéditos para la historia de España*, lx–lxi, lxix, lxxvii, lxxx, lxxxvi, Madrid, 1875–78), lx, 58.

[18] Carter, *op. cit.*, pp. 70, 208, 281.

[19] Schäfer, *op. cit.*, i, 178; Cánovas, *Decadencia*, p. 61.

[20] See *Spain under the Habsburgs*, i, 306.

seems to have been experience and talent, not favouritism. By the end of the first decade of the reign, with the departure of Chinchón and Miranda, its composition was modified; the marquis of Spinola and the marquis of Villafranca were brought in, while Cristóbal de Moura returned in 1612. But its character remained unchanged. It was a conservative body and a fairly unanimous one, applying the received doctrines of Spanish policy on which virtually the whole ruling class was agreed. It was not a body which could be bullied or corrupted by the duke of Lerma, even if he had tried.

The members of the Council of State were drawn almost exclusively from the higher aristocracy, as they had been under Philip II. In the other councils Philip III, like his father, employed a greater proportion of middle and lesser nobility and a hard core of *letrados*, whose university qualifications were usually enhanced by gentry status. Like his father, he rarely, if ever, employed commoners. Granted the bias towards aristocracy, Philip III's choice of servants seems to have been guided by a concern for expertise and efficiency. The count of Miranda, for example, president of the Council of Castile and a specialist in home affairs, had numerous *ad hoc* duties assigned to him in the field of internal administration, all of which he performed with great competence. Another experienced official inherited from the previous regime, the secretary Esteban de Ibarra, was used as an executive in military and defence matters and as a man who could keep the Council of War on its toes and implement its decisions. These and others like them, such as the secretaries Andrés de Prada, Antonio de Aróstegui and Juan de Ciriza, were professional bureaucrats who formed a reserve of talent on which the king could draw to reinforce the various juntas and commissions which were busy examining Spanish policy and problems. And their presence in the administration enabled it to absorb amateurs like the royal confessor and Lerma's *criados* without too much damage to standards of government.

3. THE 'VALIMIENTO'

After 1598 Spanish government began to move beyond the system of personal rule practised by Philip II and to break through the restraints imposed on its development. Much of the impetus towards change came from the administration itself. But Philip III, out of his own inadequacy, was responsible for the greatest change of all, the creation of an office closely resembling that of chief minister. The fact that the office was unnamed, that the minister of his choice was his closest friend the duke of Lerma, and that Lerma's appointment initiated a permanent line of *validos*, or favourites, whose chief qualification was their personal friendship with the king, has tarnished the development in the eyes of later historians and obscured those

c

elements in it which represented real institutional growth.[21] It is true that the appointment of *validos* was in part a device by which the later Habsburgs, lacking the talent and the will for personal rule, sought to shield themselves from the problems of government. But it was more than this. It was, in the first place, an adjustment to circumstances. The burden of governing Spain and its vast empire had grown beyond the point where one man could carry it alone. As a mere administrative problem, with paper mounting inexorably day by day, it was more than a one-man executive could be expected to resolve. The time had come for the king to share his burden and delegate power.

In the past the crown had shared administrative work, though not policy making, with its secretaries. Less than a minister, the secretary had become more than a clerk. He had access to all state papers, his advice was sought by the king, and he was the main link between king and council. The secretaries of the Council of State in particular were key figures in the administration, especially under Philip II who had worked his secretaries hard and his Council little. Indeed the secretaries' permanent access to the king, contrasting with the irregular meetings of the Council, must have been galling to aristocratic councillors, who regarded themselves as the king's rightful advisers. For it was clear to them that the secretaries were no longer merely the Council's clerks: the *secretario de estado* had become the *secretario del rey*. Yet the development of the secretaryship did not alter the character of the secretary. He remained a professional bureaucrat without political ambition; he usually had a university qualification and some previous administrative experience; and socially he came from the lesser nobility, a matter of preference to Philip II and of resentment to the grandees.

The rise of the *valido* meant the decline of the secretary. Writing in the 1620's, Francisco Bermúdez de Pedraza, an authority on the office, lamented the passing of the golden days of the secretaryship in the sixteenth century and its depreciation at the hands of the *validos*:

> Philip III did not have a private secretary, because the grandees of Spain in his administration made sure they discussed verbally with the king the *consultas* and files of the secretary. It is the exercise of the office which counts, not the title. And it was the grandees who were now exercising the real function of the office; the secretaries were left with the title but they were merely clerks, deprived of the most important part which is to discuss and resolve personally with the king the highest affairs of state.[22]

[21] Francisco Tomás Valiente, *Los validos en la monarquía española del siglo XVII* (Madrid, 1963) provides an illuminating institutional study of the *valido*, to which the following pages are indebted; see also Carter, *op. cit.*, pp. 66–71, for a notable revision of the subject.

[22] Quoted in Valiente, *op. cit.*, 50.

The grandees had won their point. The secretaries of state were now literally secretaries of the Council of State. They were no longer private counsellors of the king. They were no more than civil servants, important ones no doubt, but completely over-shadowed by the *valido*. It was the *valido* who now supervised the councils, managed the written instruments of government, and advised the king. His office had greater political content than the secretary-ship had ever had; it was unique, undivided, and carried more power. The *valido*, moreover, was closer to the king, whose friendship was at once his badge of authority and his chief qualification for office. Finally, the *valido* had greater social assets than the secretary: he almost invariably came from the higher aristocracy.[23]

The rise of the *valido* reflected not only the inadequacy of the king and the growth of administration but also the ambitions of the aristocracy. In the role of Lerma and his successors one can observe perhaps a certain reaction of the higher nobility against the type of secretary who had stood between them and the king in the reign of Philip II. In this sense the emergence of the *valido* represented an aristocratic bid, if not to control, at least to monopolise the crown, and the outcome was a political victory of the grandees over the *hidalgos* and the lesser nobility. For although the grandees, like other elements in Spanish society, overtly criticised the *validos*, their criticism was directed at individual incumbents, not at the office, and it was motivated by resentment of a rival's success or in expectation of similar preferment. This was only to be expected, for the *valido* was simply the apex of a system which permeated the whole of Spanish society, as it did other European societies in the early modern period, the system of patronage and clientage.[24]

The Spanish crown was regarded not only as a law-giver but also as a benefactor. From all parts of Spain and its dependencies a constant stream of suitors pressed on Madrid in search of appointments, honours, privileges, pensions, and grants of all kinds. They could hardly expect to reach the fount of patronage itself, the crown, so they would try to get someone highly placed to intercede for them, a councillor or an important official who had the king's ear, and naturally they would be expected to pay for this service in one way or another. Clients, then, sought to attach themselves to a powerful patron who disposed of influence and wealth, and the most influential of all was the king's favourite, and after him the favourite's favourite. For their part patrons, anxious to build up a large following as a measure of their own power and status, were willing to oblige. This accounts for the manoeuvring

[23] *Ibid.*, pp. 51–53, 109–10.
[24] The penetrating study of patronage and faction in England by Sir John E. Neale, 'The Elizabethan Political Scene', *Proceedings of the British Academy*, xxxiv (1948), provides an interpretation which can usefully be applied to Spain.

for strategic positions around the king and for the constant agitation at court. Fray Antonio de Guevara, one of the many observers of the scene, recorded: 'I see the majority of courtiers swearing, blaspheming, muttering and snarling about the evils and evil-doers there are at court. But I am confident that their discontent does not stem from the vices they see practised there but from the simple fact that their rivals are prospering in the king's favour while they are not.'[25]

The patronage system had political implications. There were, of course, no political parties: these could not develop in a situation where the crown controlled policy, where the obligation of councillors to the crown was a personal and not a corporate one, and where the ruling class was agreed about basic objectives. This did not mean that there were no political differences among statesmen. But the form these differences took was faction. The rivalry of factions was concentrated on what mattered most, namely influence over the king and thereby control of patronage and all that this meant. It meant not only wealth but power. If a politician disposed of patronage and influence he could attract a large following and so create a faction of men who expected their patron to sponsor their interests at court. It was inevitable, therefore, that just as Lerma and his successors sought the king's patronage, so they in turn should distribute patronage to their clients and thus acquire their own *validos*. It was at this point that the patronage system engendered corruption. Don Pedro Franqueza, for example, younger son of impoverished Catalan gentry, became a *valido* of Lerma and through him acquired a title, count of Villalonga, and the offices of secretary and councillor of Finance; but success went to his head and after a brief if spectacular career he was purged from the administration for blatant venality. The most notorious example of the private *valido* was Rodrigo Calderón whose rapid rise from obscurity to fame and fortune at once fascinated and scandalised contemporaries.[26] Beginning as a retainer in Lerma's household he soon became his principal liaison officer, in much the same way as Lerma was the king's. His patron procured him numerous offices and grants, including the titles of count of Oliva and marquis of Siete Iglesias, and put him in the way of a large income. Calderón in turn had his creatures, rather lower down the ladder, and predictably a large number of enemies. His disreputable behaviour made him particularly vulnerable once his patron fell. Indeed his fate was worse than Lerma's. He was arrested on various charges ranging from murder to peculation, and after lengthy imprisonment he was tortured, convicted and executed at the hands of a rival faction in the following reign. The downfall of Lerma and Calderón attested to the ruthlessness of the patronage system and the

[25] Quoted in Valiente, *op. cit.*, p. 54.
[26] Cánovas, *Decadencia*, pp. 61–62.

vindictiveness of the 'outs' when they became the 'ins'. There was too much at stake to expect clemency.

The crown itself was a passive spectator of these events, trapped in a system it had helped to create. Instead of distributing their favour among a number of ministers, who could be played off one against the other, the later Habsburgs allowed one man to monopolise patronage and power. They thereby lost their independence, for they were subject to the pressure of a single interest. They became victims of powerful *validos* and aristocratic factions. What had begun as delegation of power ended as abdication of control.

Yet their original objective was valid enough. They may not have been able to formulate the problem precisely, but they were searching in effect for a chief minister. The term is actually used in contemporary texts and state papers, and although its meaning is not precise its use is sufficient to identify the official and public status of the *valido* as head of the central administration. Some political commentators viewed the development with the deepest misgivings; that a king should share his sovereignty was thought to be incompatible with absolute monarchy. And, paradoxically, in order to control the *valimiento* they sought to institutionalise it. Diego Saavedra Fajardo, the distinguished diplomat, was affronted in all his instincts by the emergence of the *valido*, and his writings show a deep concern to reduce the position to acceptable limits. The *valimiento*, he argued, 'is not only a grant, it is an office; it is not a favour but a delegation of work'.[27] For Saavedra the *valimiento* was an office without a name; far better that it be regarded as a public institution than allowed to drift into crude personal power.

As an institution the *valimiento* was not static but evolved throughout the course of the seventeenth century. The first important stage of its growth was the long tenure of the duke of Lerma, who occupied the position for twenty years. The decision of the young king to share his responsibilities with his friend and mentor must have been taken before his accession to the throne. At any rate within a few days of his father's death, and in spite of the disapproval of Moura and Idiáquez, he dissolved the small junta which Philip II had created to ease the transition, and he thus left the way open for Lerma to acquire a unique position. Simultaneously he seems to have given Lerma verbal authority to sign state papers in the king's name, in order to legitimise that position. The delegation of power can be inferred from a remarkable decree issued some years later, in 1612, in which the king declared his complete satisfaction with the service rendered by Lerma and confirmed the power given to him at the beginning of the reign. The decree ordered each council and its president 'to comply with whatever the duke instructs or

---

[27] *Idea de un Príncipe político-cristiano* (1640) (*Biblioteca de autores españoles*, 25, Madrid, 1947), p. 126.

orders . . . and also to furnish him with any information he requires'.[28] This was the formal instrument of delegation, with retrospective validity to the beginning of the reign. It stated in effect that orders signed by Lerma had the force of royal orders, and thus placed the entire conciliar system at the disposition of the *valido*. This was how Lerma himself interpreted his powers. He received incoming material from the secretary, distributed it to the councils, and made executive decisions on the councils' *consultas*. No doubt he discussed these matters with the king privately, and he was always careful to couch his instructions in the form of a written or verbal order from the king himself. But he was acting in fact as the executive. This was so in his relations with the Council of State, the chief policy-making body; and as he exercised his own discretion in deciding what matters should be remitted from the other councils to the Council of State he became the controlling link in the whole system, though not a particularly efficient one.[29] Towards the other councils, such as the Council of Aragon and the Council of the Indies, he also assumed the attitude of the executive, though preserving the form of merely transmitting 'the king's orders'.[30] The Council of Finance, it is true, was an object of more particular interest to the king, and he usually looked more closely at its *consultas*, though he also usually agreed with them. But Lerma himself sent frequent and peremptory orders, overtly in the king's name, to the president of the Council of Finance, ordering payments of various kinds, including military expenditure. Finally, Lerma was careful to keep control of patronage in his own hands. In July 1605 he instructed the secretary of the Council of State that matters concerning appointments and grants must be submitted directly to the king, and that the Council could only consider them if they were expressly remitted to it by the king. In practice all decisions on patronage matters were sent by Lerma, again acting in the name of the king, to the secretary for communication to the applicant.[31]

For twenty years, until 1618, Lerma was chief minister in all but name. In the course of this time he grew in wealth and in unpopularity; inevitably he became the target of criticism of Spain's economic condition and international policies. His unbridled greed, his unscrupulous use of patronage, and the scandalous behaviour of some of his clients, notably Calderón, outraged public opinion; his enemies began to sharpen their knives and his subordinates to edge away. In the course of twenty years the king too grew, if not in wisdom at least in maturity. The tutelage of his childhood mentor, to which

---

[28] Valiente, *op. cit.*, pp. 9, 161.

[29] *Ibid.*, pp. 63–64.

[30] For examples of Lerma's relations with the Council of Aragon see J. Reglà, 'La expulsión de los moriscos y sus consecuencias', *Hispania*, xiii (1953), 215-67; for the Council of the Indies see Schäfer, *op. cit.*, i, 188–89.

[31] Valiente, *op. cit.*, p. 68.

he had clung with relief as a young king of twenty-one, was becoming increasingly ridiculous as he approached middle age. After about 1615, moreover, a sense of disillusionment possessed him, as he became aware of the
shortcomings of Lerma and his clients, of growing dissatisfaction in the
country, and above all of the real state of government finances. Meanwhile,
as the king emancipated himself from Lerma, new voices were making
themselves heard in council, especially those of Baltasar de Zúñiga, now
returned from his embassies abroad, and of Fray Luis de Aliaga, the new
confessor. On the international front Spain was facing new problems. The
situation in Germany was deteriorating; Spain's commitment to the Habsburg cause and her position in the Low Countries had to be reappraised.
Lerma stood for a policy of peace and non-intervention in the affairs of
northern Europe, a policy which in itself had much to recommend it but
which coming from Lerma lacked moral conviction.

Court and administration lived in expectation, trying to detect the next
candidate for royal favour; and clients awaited the decision of the supreme
patron. Opposition to the ageing favourite was mobilised by Aliaga, whose
opinions on foreign policy coincided with those of Lerma but who otherwise
abhorred the latter's influence on public affairs. An anti-Lerma faction began
to form, grouped around a new contender for the *valimiento*, none other than
Lerma's own son, Cristóbal de Sandoval y Rojas, duke of Uceda. And in the
Council of State the views of Zúñiga, the principal advocate of a hard-line
policy in northern Europe, began to win support. Faction and policy alike
were moving against Lerma. In a desperate attempt to strengthen his position
he procured a cardinalate from Rome, a typical move by a man who viewed
politics almost exclusively in terms of personal prestige. Even Philip III was
unimpressed. From about April 1618 he began to withdraw his confidence
from Lerma, restricting his access to state papers and warning him to prepare
for retirement. When during July and August the Council of State was
uncharacteristically divided over a major policy issue, whether or not to
intervene in Germany, Lerma found himself in a distinct minority, powerless
to keep Spain out of a war that was going to ensnare her for forty years. On 2
October he was summoned to the king's presence in the Escorial, and after an
interview lasting two hours he emerged shaken, incredulous, and discarded.
He retired to his estates in Valencia where he died in 1623 at the age of
seventy-one, having been forced by those who came to power under Philip
III's successor to disgorge a large part of his fortune.

Philip III acted with unwonted resolution in dismissing Lerma. According
to an anonymous chronicler, 'even the lamb has to roar once; for it was important that His Majesty should overcome his meekness and show his favourites that he was determined enough to perceive and punish misdeeds and

dismiss their authors'.[32] Lerma's clients, moreover, inevitably felt the cold wind blowing through the Escorial, and his particular favourites like Calderón were mercilessly pursued by their enemies in the new regime. Yet his fall was not the occasion of a general upheaval of government, and the hard core of the administration continued unchanged. As for government by *valido*, that was too valuable to the king to be relinquished and he still clutched at the support which it offered him.

Uceda succeeded Lerma in the *valimiento*, and the transfer of power was instantaneous.[33] It was also incomplete. On 15 November 1618 Philip III issued a decree which had the effect of revoking that of 1612; from now onwards all policy statements, orders and matters of patronage emanating from the royal will were to be signed by the king and by no one else.[34] This ended, formally at least, the almost total delegation of power by king to *valido*, and it meant that the councils were not so dependent on Uceda as they had been on Lerma. It is a sign perhaps that Philip III had learnt some lessons and was determined this time not to abandon all his responsibilities. If this is so, he did not keep his resolution. Before long Uceda was handling a good deal of conciliar business on behalf of the king, and the administration seemed to regard him as chief minister. Nevertheless, his position was never as well-defined as that of Lerma. He did not monopolise liaison between king and councils; and to some extent traditional avenues of communication reasserted themselves. Uceda himself had no political gifts and there was a certain hollowness about his regime. Was this featureless man a figure-head behind whom other advisers operated, Aliaga, the keeper of the king's conscience, and, in foreign affairs, Baltasar de Zúñiga? If the suspicion is correct it would signify a sharing of delegated power, in itself a healthier political development. But the evidence is too vague to yield firm answers. If the chroniclers are to be believed, Philip III died repentant of having abandoned power into the hands of *validos*. And on the day of his death, at the express wish of the new king, Uceda was obliged to hand over state papers and the management of government to Baltasar de Zúñiga.

4. THE POVERTY OF GOVERNMENT

The empire which Philip III inherited was based on Castile, but it was not governed by the laws of Castile or assessed by the taxes of Castile. Even Philip II, absolutist though he was, had not attempted to challenge the autonomy of his various kingdoms or to incorporate them into a centralised

---

[32] Quoted *ibid.*, p. 9.
[33] On the fall of Lerma and the succession of Uceda see Novoa, *Memorias*, lxi, 145–59.
[34] Valiente, *op. cit.*, pp. 10–11, 162.

state. Although Philip III described himself as king of Spain, he was first and foremost king of Castile and his power was absolute only in Castile. Even within the kingdom of Castile the provinces of Vizcaya (Biscay), Guipúzcoa and Alava enjoyed a degree of fiscal and administrative autonomy. Outside Castile separatism was even more pronounced. The Crown of Aragon, which included the realms of Aragon, Catalonia and Valencia, had its identity enshrined in highly developed *fueros*, or constitutional rights. Each of these realms was governed independently, each had its own laws and tax system, and in each the king was represented by a viceroy. Castilian sovereignty was even more attenuated in Italy, where the kingdoms of Sicily and Naples and the duchy of Milan were governed for the king of Spain by viceroys or governors and administered by their own institutions. In the Low Countries Spanish sovereignty, where it was effective, was exercised by the archdukes, who were something less than independent rulers and something more than mere governors, and who ruled through local institutions with the assistance of local personnel.[35] This constitutional structure cannot be described as a federal one, for there was no federal agency at the centre, other than the crown itself. It was a personal union, which fully respected the independence of each of the parts. In practice Castilian power made itself felt to some degree. The permanent residence of the king in Castile, the preponderance of Castilians in public office, and the situation of the councils in Madrid made unity rather more effective in practice than it was in theory. But there was one area of government where the constituent kingdoms were particularly sensitive to attacks on their prerogatives—in matters of finance. One of the greatest problems of the Castilian government was to persuade them to contribute to common expenditure in proportion to their resources.

The Spanish Low Countries contributed only modest amounts to the general expenses of the Monarchy and these were swallowed up in local administration; defence expenditure was subsidised from Castile. From the time of the dissolution of the States General in 1600 a subsidy (*subsidio ordinario*) of 3,600,000 florins was collected annually; this was voted by the various provincial estates, but it was understood that they could not refuse it without compromising the king's sovereignty; and in order to allow them to discuss it without danger the administration usually asked them for a higher amount than it was likely to get.[36] In addition, and more reluctantly, they also voted an extraordinary subsidy of varying amounts. The Italian dependencies contributed much more to imperial expenditure than did the Low Countries.[37]

[35] Charles Howard Carter, 'Belgian "autonomy" under the Archdukes, 1598–1621', *Journal of Modern History*, xxxvi (1964), 249–59.
[36] H. Pirenne, *Histoire de Belgique* (3rd ed., 7 vols., Brussels, 1909–32), iv, 402.
[37] Domínguez Ortiz, *Política y hacienda de Felipe IV*, pp. 161–64.

For Spanish policy imposed upon them an important and costly role in Europe and the Mediterranean, a role which they sustained to a great extent out of their own resources; these resources were severely strained by tax demands which, at the end of the sixteenth century, were being met to the tune of 5½ million ducats a year by Sicily, Naples and Milan combined.

Within the peninsula Portugal was completely autonomous in fiscal matters and contributed nothing to the general expenses of the Monarchy. The Basque provinces, though part of Castile, were also immune from Castile's demands.[38] They did not pay the *alcabala*, the *millones*, or the other standard taxes of Castile, and they even complained that merchandise imported from Castile was already charged with these taxes. The only revenue which the king received from the Basque provinces was the yield from his feudal and seigneurial rights, and this was hardly enough to cover the cost of his administration in the area. In Vizcaya, for example, his patrimonial revenue—some 30,000 to 40,000 ducats a year—was normally expended on the grants and pensions of various kinds with which he was expected to regale his subjects in the province. The latter resisted all attempts of the central government to introduce ordinary taxation, no matter how temporary, for that would have compromised their *hidalguía* and consequently their permanent immunity from taxation. The attitude of the Basques, however, was not unreasonable, for theirs were small provinces, sparsely populated and economically undeveloped. Whenever Spain was at war with France they defended the frontier at their own cost, and to this extent contributed to imperial finances.

The Crown of Aragon was equally stubborn in its resistance to the tax demands of the central government, and actually contributed less than the Italian dependencies to general expenses. Royal income from Valencia was effectively confined to the revenue from crown property and seigneurial jurisdiction. This yielded the modest sum of about 100,000 libros a year which was consumed in the maintenance of royal administration in the area. In the reign of Philip III the cortes of Valencia voted only one subsidy, in 1604, amounting to 400,000 ducats. From the cortes of Catalonia he received in 1599 a subsidy of 1,100,000 ducats. And from the cortes of Aragon he received nothing. In Aragon and Catalonia most of the taxes on merchandise were in the hands of the towns or of individual proprietors; the crown had the right to one-fifth (*quinto*) of these revenues annually, but in many cases had allowed it to fall into disuse. Philip III's local administration began to reclaim the *quinto* for the crown, and those towns which could not produce proof of legal immunity from the claim were gradually, and against much opposition, forced to pay. The campaign for the *quinto* was particularly intense in Catalonia, and when it reached Barcelona the latter flatly refused

[38] *Ibid.*, pp. 159–60.

to contribute. The refusal was accompanied by the usual appeal to Catalan liberties, an appeal which would have been more convincing had the not inconsiderable revenues of Barcelona been administered with integrity by the municipal oligarchy. In any case nothing was further from the intention of Philip III's government than to initiate constitutional change.

Castile continued to be the treasury of the Monarchy. And general expenditure continued to outstrip Castile's resources. In the first decade of the reign defence expenditure, especially in the Low Countries, was still the major charge on revenue. In addition Philip III inherited the considerable debts incurred by his father. He made matters worse by his own extravagance. He spent far too much money on himself and almost as much on his favourites. Among the numerous gifts to the duke of Lerma was one of 50,000 ducats made in the euphoria engendered by the arrival of the Indies fleet. On the occasion of the king's marriage in 1599 his lavish gifts to various favoured subjects passed all reason; the whole extravaganza cost 950,000 ducats, 300,000 of which were disposed of by Lerma. Philip III, in fact, behaved as though the public treasury was his private property. Traditionally this may have been a valid assumption, though the political economists of the time, the *arbitristas*, were beginning to challenge it.[39] Indeed Juan de Mariana, the Jesuit political philosopher, was quite clear on the subject: 'The king is not allowed to spend at liberty the money granted to him by his subjects as if it were income from his private possession'.[40] It was obvious, even to Philip III, that the grants of the cortes had a public character which placed them out of his reach; in any case they were usually appropriated to specific items of expenditure. But there were numerous other revenues on which he could lay his hands. In addition to his private patrimony, moreover, the king, as the highest official, possessed a kind of civil list—some 600,000 ducats a year—charged on public revenues. This, however, by no means covered all his expenses—royal household, secret service payments, gifts to clients, to mention only a few. The maintenance of the royal family alone cost Castile about 1,300,000 ducats a year under Philip III—over 10 per cent. of the budget—compared to 1,000,000 a year under his two predecessors and his immediate successor.

The scale of expenditure called for greater revenue than the government possessed. Yet there was a real reluctance to impose new taxes. These were known to provoke resistance and criticism of government policies. And as its own conduct was particularly vulnerable to criticism, the government of

[39] José Luis Sureda Carrión, *La Hacienda castellana y los economistas del siglo XVII* (Madrid, 1949), pp. 77–79.
[40] *De mutatione monetae*, in John Laures, *The Political Economy of Juan de Mariana* (New York, 1928), p. 299.

Philip III and Lerma preferred not to stir up hostile interests or alienate public opinion; its policy was to let sleeping dogs lie. There were, in fact, two alternatives to heavier taxation. One was to reduce defence expenditure, an expedient which appealed to Philip III not out of conviction but on the assumption that peace was easier than reform. As other nations too had an interest in ending the long and costly conflict inherited from the previous century, the Spanish government was able to continue the process of peace-making begun by the Franco-Spanish treaty of 1598. Peace was made with England in 1604, and in April 1607 a cease-fire was arranged with the Dutch, followed by the Truce of Antwerp in 1609. Disengagement in northern Europe, of course, did not mean disarmament elsewhere, and Spain continued to have heavy defence commitments in Italy, the Mediterranean and the Atlantic. But recourse had already been had to a second expedient, one which branded the government as bankrupt of ideas as well as of money—debasement of the coinage.

In 1599 Philip III departed from a long Spanish tradition of sound money and issued in Castile a vellon coinage of pure copper in order to save the silver with which it had previously been alloyed. The 100 per cent. profit accruing to the government from this operation encouraged it to decree even heavier issues of copper vellon in 1602 and 1603, in spite of the bitter protests of the cortes. In 1608, in return for a subsidy, Philip III promised the cortes not to coin further vellon for twenty years, but the enormous budget deficit in 1617 caused him to seek release from his promise, and the cortes agreed to a further issue sufficient to yield a profit of one million ducats. This was followed in 1621 by yet another issue, designed to yield a profit of 800,000 ducats. Altogether Philip III issued copper vellon to the amount of 27 million ducats.[41] The consequences were predictable, at least to many outside the government. Monetary instability drove gold and silver out of circulation. Vellon receded from parity with the precious metals; the average annual premium on the exchange of vellon for silver rose from 1 per cent. in 1603 to 3 per cent. in 1619. As taxes were paid in vellon and defence expenditure abroad had to be made in silver, the crown itself was one of the biggest losers. Currency debasement, moreover, prolonged into the seventeenth century the great price inflation generated by American silver in the sixteenth century, but with an important difference; whereas the price revolution of the sixteenth century had been a steady and continuous process, the new inflation moved by fits and starts and was periodically interrupted by sudden deflation, thus causing great harm to business activities and to all those who lived on annuities, pensions and fixed incomes. And inflation hit the

---

[41] Earl J. Hamilton, *American Treasure and the Price Revolution in Spain*, 1501–1650 (Cambridge, Mass., 1934), pp. 73–79, 88–93, 102–3.

greatest consumer of all, the government itself. Many of these disadvantages were identified by contemporaries, by the cortes and the *arbitristas*. Mariana wrote a treatise on the subject which he published in Germany in 1609. He denounced Philip III's monetary policy as hidden taxation and warned that it would drive out gold and silver and lead to inflation. But on this subject the government was hypersensitive. Mariana was arrested by the Inquisition and charged with lèse-majesté for criticising the monetary policy of the king before a foreign audience; and although he was released after a year his treatise was put on the Spanish Index.[42]

What were the main sources of revenue from Castile? First, there was the ordinary income from the *alcabala* and the customs. The latter covered a wide range of charges on internal and foreign trade and constituted a basic item of revenue, though one highly vulnerable to fraud. The *alcabala* was a 10 per cent. tax on sales, which the larger towns had previously compounded for an agreed yearly payment. By 1612 it was raising 2,754,766 ducats a year, more than twice the amount yielded in the 1570's.[43] This was still well below its potential yield, for many places and people, including all ecclesiastics, had acquired exemption from the tax or paid at a reduced rate. In many parts of Castile, moreover, the *alcabala* had fallen into the hands of private proprietors, either through grants to powerful nobles in the middle ages or by purchase in the course of the sixteenth century; and the improvident government of Philip III continued the process of alienation in exchange for a quick though short-term income. These traditional revenues of the crown were supplemented by grants of the cortes.[44] The *servicio ordinario y extraordinario* was granted by the cortes every three years and since 1591 had been fixed at 405,000 ducats a year. The most important grant, however, was the *millones*, a tax on basic foodstuffs, which was supposed to yield 2 million ducats a year but in fact grew to 3 million in the early years of the reign, reverting to 2 million by the end of the reign. In an age of inflation the value of these fixed grants effectively declined, though the *millones* occasionally responded to rising prices. In addition to this ordinary and extraordinary income, the crown had revenues from ecclesiastical sources, and these extended beyond Castile into all the king's dominions.[45] The most important was the *cruzada*, the revenue from the sale of bulls of indulgence, whose average annual yield in Spain alone was 800,000 ducats paid in silver by the banker who administered the revenue; the *subsidio*—some 420,000 ducats a year—was a proportion of church revenues paid to the crown for the upkeep of the naval establishment

[42] Laures, *op. cit.*, p. 282; see also G. Lewy, *Constitutionalism and Statecraft during the Golden Age of Spain: A Study of the Political Philosophy of Juan de Mariana, S.J.* (Geneva, 1960), pp. 30–32.

[43] Domínguez Ortiz, *Política y hacienda de Felipe IV*, pp. 194–203.

[44] *Ibid.*, pp. 232–38.

[45] *Ibid.*, pp. 241–49.

in the Mediterranean; and the *excusado* was an income of 250,000 ducats a year derived from ecclesiastical property. Finally, the crown possessed its celebrated revenue from the Indies.[46] The decade 1610–20, however, saw the beginning of a precipitous decline in silver remittances from America, reflecting the profound crisis in the Indies trade which hit both public and private returns.[47] For the five-year period 1611–15 the crown received 7,212,921 pesos, compared with 10,974,318 pesos in the peak period 1596–1600. In the years 1616–20 there was an even sharper drop, to 4,347,788 pesos, a level from which the American revenue never substantially rose during the rest of the seventeenth century.

In 1598 the crown's estimated revenue amounted to 9,731,405 ducats.[48] Of this, 4,634,293 ducats—drawn principally from major taxes such as the *alcabala*, customs, and the *subsidio*—were either already assigned in advance to permanent items of expenditure, principally *juros* (state bonds) and certain defence commitments, or had been recently alienated to tax proprietors. The rest of the revenue, just over 5 million ducats—derived from the *millones* and *servicio* granted by the cortes, the *cruzada* and the income from the Indies—was theoretically free of charges but in fact much of it was committed in advance to bankers in payment of previous *asientos*, or defence contracts. Most of the defence expenditure was incurred in the Low Countries, which in the first twelve years of the reign consumed over 40 million ducats.[49] As commitments increased the time came when the whole of the 'free' revenue for several years in advance was assigned to bankers and there was nothing left to cover further *asientos*. This point was reached in 1607; the government had now anticipated revenue up to 1611 and the total debt stood at 22,748,971 ducats.[50] For this situation there was a classical remedy, known at the time as the *medio general*: contracted revenues were released from their commitments and the bankers were indemnified with *juros*.[51] Operations of this kind, though frequently called bankruptcies, were in effect forced conversions of debts; Philip II had recourse to them on three occasions, roughly every twenty years. In using the device once, Philip III could claim not to have exceeded his quota, but once was enough to worsen the crown's credit, and the government was forced to re-think its defence policy. Suspension of payments in 1607, therefore, was followed by suspension of war in the Low Countries in 1609. Yet although Spain was no longer involved in

---

[46] Hamilton, *American Treasure*, pp. 34–38.

[47] See below, pp. 168, 186.

[48] Domínguez Ortiz, *Política y hacienda de Felipe IV*, pp. 3–18.

[49] 'Relación del dinero remitido a Flandes', 13 September 1598–20 June 1609, *Colección de documentos inéditos para la historia de España*, xxxvi, 509.

[50] *Actas de las Cortes de Castilla, 1563–1632* (51 vols., Madrid, 1861–1929), xxiii, 543–59.

[51] See *Spain under the Habsburgs*, i, 134.

a major war, her financial troubles were not at an end. A number of localised conflicts in Italy, defence spending in Germany, the Mediterranean and the overseas empire, and the expenses of court and government actually raised expenditure beyond previous wartime levels. In 1615 the year's expenditure was expected to exceed 9 million ducats.[52]

On the eve of the Thirty Years War, therefore, Spanish finances were badly overstrained. Much of the appropriated revenue in 1617 failed to meet its commitments. The remaining 'free' revenue amounted to 5,357,000 ducats, compared with an expenditure which had risen to some 12 million ducats. This comprised 5 million in defence costs (principally in the Low Countries, where Spain was now re-priming the military establishment, and Milan), 3 million owed in unpaid *juros*, and the remainder for the royal household, officials' salaries, delayed debts and sundry other expenses.[53] The budget for 1618 looked even worse: 'free' revenue had now dropped to 1,601,000 ducats and was utterly inadequate for existing commitments. It was at this point that Spain intervened in Germany, on a modest scale at first but sufficient to aggravate expenditure. Long before its arrival the public income from the Indies for 1619 was assigned to bankers on account.

What could the government do? Advice there was in plenty. The Council of Castile took a long look at the economic situation before producing its notable *consulta* of 1619 on the state of the nation.[54] It drew attention to the damaging effects of excessive taxation on Castile, and underlined two particular causes of rising expenditure—the extravagant doling out of grants and pensions, and the exaggerated growth of the bureaucracy, much of which was becoming at once venal and superfluous. The results, it concluded, could be seen in the financial situation: the whole of the crown's income was committed in advance, except for the 'free' revenue, and this had been anticipated in *asientos*. But Philip III's mind was closed to argument of this kind. In the same year, in spite of the Council's advice to cut conspicuous expenditure, he decided to take a long-planned trip to Portugal to have his son recognised as heir apparent, an excursion which proved to be inordinately expensive. Yet he still shrank from taking the extreme step of imposing new taxes. He preferred more devious methods, such as issuing further quantities of vellon, sequestering a portion of private treasure on the Indies fleet in return for *juros*, and, of course, anticipating income. The last *asiento* contracted by Philip III shortly before his death in March 1621 was for $4\frac{1}{2}$ million ducats, most of it for defence expenditure in the Low Countries, the

[52] J. H. Elliott, *The Revolt of the Catalans. A Study in the Decline of Spain* (1598–1640) (Cambridge, 1963), pp. 187–88.
[53] 'Relación de la Real Hacienda', 1617, *Actas de las Cortes de Castilla*, xxx, 15–32.
[54] Angel González Palencia, *La Junta de Reformación, 1618–1625 (Archivo Histórico Español, 5,* Valladolid, 1932), doc. no. 4.

Atlantic and the Mediterranean. This consumed all his current 'free' revenue and that of the future up to 1624.

The crushing weight of defence expenditure fell almost exclusively on Castile. Inevitably Castilians began to demand that the tax burden should be shared by other parts of the Monarchy. The argument was developed by a number of *arbitristas*. In a paper presented to Philip III on his accession Baltasar Alamos de Barrientos pointed out that 'in other states all the parts contribute to the maintenance and greatness of the head, as is only fair. . . . But in ours, it is the head which does the work and provides the other members with their sustenance'.[55] Pedro Fernández Navarrete echoed these sentiments at the beginning of the following reign:

> It is only fair that the burdens should be properly apportioned; that Castile should continue to provide for the royal household and for the defence of its own coasts and the route to the Indies; that Portugal should pay for its own military defences and for the East Indies fleets, as it did before incorporation with Castile; and that Aragon and Italy should defend their own coasts and provide the necessary military and naval forces for this. It is quite wrong that the head should be impoverished and weakened while the other members, wealthy and populous as they are, remain spectators of its burdens.[56]

In the eyes of Castilians, therefore, Aragon's constitutional barriers preserved a fiscal immunity which was at once outmoded and unjust. The *fueros* of the eastern kingdoms, of course, were not designed with the welfare of the underprivileged in mind; peasants and urban workers in those lands did not live in a tax-free paradise. But the taxes they paid went to the local governing bodies, dominated, as in the rest of Spain, by the aristocracy and the urban patriciate. They certainly did not go to the crown. There was, therefore, truth in the charge that the periphery paid much less revenue to the crown than did the centre.[57] In 1610, for example, income from Aragon, Catalonia and Valencia together yielded no more than 600,000 ducats, whereas in Castile the *alcabala* and *millones* alone (taxes which the east did not pay) produced 5,100,000.[58] There is evidence, indeed, that Castile was actually subsidising the administration and particularly the defence establishments of the eastern kingdoms.[59] It is not surprising that Philip III's treasury officials should have joined the *arbitristas* in demanding a fairer distribution of fiscal obligations among the component parts of the Monarchy. Their demands

[55] Quoted in Elliott, *The Revolt of the Catalans*, p. 184.
[56] *Conservación de Monarquías* (1626) (*Biblioteca de autores españoles*, 25, Madrid, 1947), p. 496.
[57] For a quantitative comparison see Elliott, *The Revolt of the Catalans*, p. 185.
[58] Sureda Carrión, *op. cit.*, p. 114.
[59] Elliott, *The Revolt of the Catalans*, p. 190.

were reinforced by the Council of Castile in its *consulta* of 1619, when it advocated, among other things, that the various partners should make greater revenue contributions in order to relieve Castile; for it was only just that 'they should provide, and should be requested to provide, some assistance, so that the whole burden should not fall on one weak and exhausted victim'.[60] To implement proposals like this, however, would mean attacking the laws and provoking the susceptibilities of the eastern kingdoms. And this was not the stuff that Philip III's government was made of.

[60] González Palencia, *op. cit.*, p. 16.

D

CHAPTER III
RECESSION AND REACTION
1. Truce in the Low Countries

THE government of Philip III was a conservative government. The national objectives developed in the course of the sixteenth century—defence of Spanish interests in northern Europe and, within the peninsula, maintenance of an equilibrium between the power of Castile and the rights of the regions—these it accepted in their essentials. But it was no longer possible to apply the classical precepts of Spanish policy undiluted. The environment was different. Economic circumstances were beginning to move against Spain; a basic sector of the economy, the Indies trade, after a century of almost constant growth, entered a period first of stagnation, then of depression. In a time of acute economic disorder political strategy developed its own neuroses. Financial stringency induced uncertainty and vacillation: in foreign policy aggression alternated with inertia, and at home Castile began to readjust its relations with the periphery.

The financial crisis in the last years of Philip II's reign was enough in itself to check Spanish action in northern Europe. Peace with France in 1598 was a recognition that Spain could not fight a war on three fronts simultaneously. In the Low Countries the transfer of sovereignty to the archdukes was a belated attempt to end the struggle with the northern provinces by peaceful means and to close one of the gaping holes of Spanish expenditure. The Archduke Albert was a realist and he used his sovereignty to reduce commitments still further. On his own initiative he sent an ambassador to London to open negotiations with the new king of England, James I, and he urged Madrid to take the dispute to the conference table; the policy bore fruit in the Treaty of London (1604) which ended the long Anglo-Spanish war. With the exception of Lerma, the government of Philip III was not enthusiastic over military withdrawal in northern Europe. But even Madrid had to bow to financial arguments. It was now clear that the economy was suffering severe dislocation. In the Atlantic sector, although the long period of growth had not yet finished its course, a series of fluctuations from 1597 brought the first signs of contraction in the Indies trade and the first indication that Spain could no longer rely on constant returns from America.[1]

[1] P. Chaunu, *Séville et l'Atlantique* (1504–1650) (8 vols., Paris, 1955–59), viii, 2, 1, pp. 767–68.

It was the Low Countries, always the severest test of Spanish resources, which reacted most sharply to Spain's difficulties.[2] Events in 1600 were ominous. The war against the United Provinces was now being fought on yet another front—the Indian Ocean—and in the Low Countries itself a mutiny of unpaid troops worsened Spanish prospects. Yet Philip III's determination to continue the struggle was suddenly rewarded.[3] In 1602-3 a cyclical expansion in the Indies trade brought returns comparable to those of the peak years of 1584-87 and enabled the government to send larger remittances to the Low Countries. These provided the means for renewing military operations and led to the successful siege of Ostend, conducted by a brilliant new military commander, Ambrosio Spinola. The victory at Ostend in 1604 was the prelude to a large-scale offensive in which Spinola penetrated into Frisia with the object of driving a wedge into the United Provinces and cutting their communications with Germany. But the Yssel campaign came to an abrupt conclusion in 1606. The difficult terrain and the skilful tactics of the Dutch brought a halt to the Spanish offensive. But they were not the only obstacles. Yet another large-scale mutiny of Spanish troops, in 1606, crippled the war effort from within; and mutiny was caused by lack of pay under the financial stringency imposed by the fall in returns from the Indies in the years 1604-5.[4]

The revolt of the *tercios* in 1606 shook Spain's belief in the possibility of reconquering the United Provinces; combined with the suspension of payments in 1607 and the losses suffered in the Indies trade in the same year, it persuaded the Spanish government that the time had come to negotiate. Again, however, it was the administration in Brussels which first faced up to realities. The Archduke Albert appreciated that the United Provinces would never agree to unconditional surrender. They were now a state, recognised as such by many European powers; they possessed an effective administration, a buoyant overseas trade, and natural protection against an invading army. The recent campaign, for all its initial success, simply showed the impossibility of reducing the Dutch by force. On his own initiative the archduke concluded a cease-fire with the Dutch in March 1607; containing as it did a recognition of Dutch sovereignty for the duration of the cease-fire, this was an enormous concession of principle.[5] Subsequent negotiations for a formal truce conceded even more. For it was clear that Spain would have to recognise Dutch sovereignty in such terms that there would be no saving clause in favour of Catholics. These were serious blows to Castilian pride, so much so

[2] P. Chaunu, 'Séville et la "Belgique" (1555–1648)', *Revue du Nord*, xlii, 2 (1960), 259–92.
[3] Joseph Lefèvre, *Spinola et la Belgique, 1601–1627* (Brussels, 1947), 29–31.
[4] Chaunu, *Séville et l'Atlantique*, viii, 2, 2, pp. 1143–57, 1189–1252.
[5] Lefèvre, *op. cit.*, 36–44.

that Madrid was loath to follow the pacificatory advice of the archduke, supported though it was by the military expert, Spinola. Philip III sought to evade the ultimate decision. The year 1608 was a record year in the transatlantic trade; and in August a sense of euphoria induced by massive returns from the Indies caused the Spanish government to toy with the idea of breaking off the peace negotiations and subsidising a new offensive.[6] But the income of one exceptional year could not solve Spain's financial problems. This was recognised even in Madrid, and the government was forced to accept the inevitable and to conclude a twelve years' truce with the United Provinces in 1609.

The decision of 1609 marked a stage in Spanish policy. In the Low Countries it gave Spain a breathing space. Overseas, it is true, the Dutch onslaught on Iberian positions continued, though directed perhaps more at Portugal than at Spain. But by any standards Spain had suffered a political, military, and ideological defeat; and the affront to its prestige was immense. A defeat for Spain was essentially a defeat for Castile, for it was Castile which provided the policy and the sustenance for Spain's role as a world power. Thwarted abroad, wounded in its self-esteem, Castile developed a new and a heightened sensitivity in its political relations; it began to seek compensation nearer home and to look more closely at its position within the peninsula.

2. THE EXPULSION OF THE MORISCOS

The Truce of Antwerp was signed on 9 April 1609. On the same day Philip III took another decision—to expel the moriscos from Spain.[7] The two events were not a coincidence. Spanish statesmen of the time measured out their policy by calculation, not by accident, and Spanish policy was never more calculating than it was in 1609. The international situation was at last propitious for a measure which was regarded as one of national security. The detente achieved by peace with England in 1604 and with the United Provinces in 1609 enabled Spain to concentrate her land and sea forces in the Mediterranean in order to ensure the security of the operation against the moriscos.[8] But there was a further and more complex connection between the events of 1609. Behind them loomed the worsening economic situation, of which the fluctuations in the Indies trade were at once a symptom and a

---

[6] Chaunu, *Séville et l'Atlantique*, viii, 2, 2, pp. 1276–95.

[7] On the expulsion of the moriscos see particularly two modern works, J. Reglà, 'La expulsión de los moriscos y sus consecuencias. Contribución a su estudio', *Hispania*, xiii (1953), 215–68, 402–79, and H. Lapeyre, *Géographie de l'Espagne Morisque* (Paris, 1959). On the sixteenth-century background see *Spain under the Habsburgs*, i.

[8] F. Braudel, *La Méditerranée et le monde méditerranéen à l'époque de Philippe II* (Paris, 1949), pp. 592–93.

cause. On Spain's position in the Low Countries the impact of economic restriction was direct. Its effect on the position of the moriscos was more insidious. In a period of declining living standards—the years 1604-5 saw a pronounced cyclical recession in the Indies trade after a long period of expansion—the resentment of the masses towards a successful minority might be expected to become more acute. Not that the Spanish government responded directly to public opinion; but its decision reflected the general malaise. It also reflected the state of mind of Castile's leaders. The time had passed when they could impose their will in northern Europe; they had been forced to recognise the sovereignty of people they regarded as rebel subjects and to abandon the religious interests of their Catholic brethren. But in Spain at least they were still masters and here they could find moral compensation for their retreat abroad.[9] To expel the moriscos was to rid Spain of a group long identified as national enemies and simultaneously to strike a blow for religious orthodoxy, vindicating at once Castilian power and prestige. In a government which wanted victories on the cheap the psychological factor was not insignificant.

Ironically the war with Islam had lost much of its urgency and by 1609 it was no longer a major preoccupation.[10] Of course the depredations of the Barbary corsairs and their Ottoman allies continued to pose a security problem in the western Mediterranean; Spanish shipping was still subject to constant attack, and Spanish prisoners were still held for ransom money by the enemy in North Africa. To this relentless pressure the Spanish naval authorities reacted with vigour and some success, and in the period 1601–16 they took the war into the enemy's own camp. But no one seriously believed in waging a war of religion, and there was no real danger of an invasion of Spain or of military collusion between Algiers and the moriscos. The strategic argument, therefore, had lost much of its point. But it was still used. Lerma himself used it. In 1596, as viceroy of Valencia, he had reported his fears of an attack by sea combined with an insurrection of the moriscos. But the Council of Aragon thought he exaggerated the danger and argued that, even were the Turkish fleet to approach, the moriscos were in no position to act, 'for they possess neither arms, nor supplies, nor fortified positions, nor a base for the Turkish fleet'.[11]

The basic problem of the moriscos was a problem of integration. The moriscos remained a class apart, with their own language and religion and a

[9] P. Chaunu, 'Minorités et conjoncture. L'expulsion des Morisques en 1609', Revue Historique, ccxxv (1961), 81–98.

[10] See Spain under the Habsburgs, i, 233–35.

[11] Tulio Halperin Donghi, 'Recouvrements de civilisation: les Morisques au Royaume de Valence au XVI siècle', Annales. Economies. Sociétés. Civilisations, xi (1956), 154–82; for the quotation see p. 178.

way of life directed by Islamic law. In Aragon and Valencia, descendants of those who had submitted to forced conversion, they were a genuine enclave of Islam within Spain, resistant to christianisation and hispanisation, with their own leaders and upper class, their rich and their poor, all equally immune to integration. And as their spiritual home was outside Spain so, it was suspected, was their political allegiance. In Castilian eyes it was an abnormal and monstrous situation, an admission of the failure of past policies. On the whole the country was unanimous in its opposition to the moriscos and in favour of expulsion. There was no question of toleration: everyone agreed that Islam was an inveterate enemy of the Catholic faith and of Spain. But there was a division of opinion over one issue: could not some moriscos be genuinely assimilated into Christian belief and society? A number of ecclesiastics such as Fray Luis de Aliaga, the royal confessor, and the bishops of Tortosa and Orihuela, came to the defence of 'well-disposed' moriscos and of genuine converts. But their advocacy was outweighed by the fanatical voices of Jaime Bleda, Dominican friar and member of the Inquisition of Valencia, who sometimes spoke as though he favoured the extermination of the moriscos as a final solution, and of Juan de Rivera, archbishop of Valencia, whose religious intolerance was accompanied by the argument that the king could profit from confiscating morisco property and from enslaving moriscos for work in the galleys and mines or from their sale abroad 'without any scruples of conscience'. Among secular opinion, too, there was a certain division of opinion, reflected in the Council of State, between the majority who followed the advocacy of Idiáquez for total eviction and those who favoured the pleas of the duke of Infantado for the exercise of discrimination. The most committed defenders of the moriscos, of course, were self-interested ones, the aristocracy of Aragon and Valencia, on whose estates they provided the labour force as tenants or vassals. But the nobles were not the only owners of morisco property: there was another group of proprietors, urban rentiers, clergy and religious houses, who were paid extremely low quit-rents—further devalued by contemporary inflation—and who had an incentive to get rid of their tenants in order to dispose of the land more profitably.[12] As for the mass of Christian peasants, they viewed their morisco rivals with envy and resentment and regarded them as satellites of the landowning aristocracy.

At the root of the morisco problem lay a matter of demography. On the eve of the expulsion the morisco population of Spain stood at 300,000 out of a total of some $8\frac{1}{2}$ million inhabitants.[13] But this 300,000 was not distributed

[12] *Ibid.*, p. 178.

[13] Lapeyre, *op. cit.*, pp. 203–4. For a somewhat higher estimate of morisco demography see Domínguez Ortiz, *La sociedad española en el siglo XVII*, pp. 83–85.

evenly throughout the peninsula. More than 60 per cent. of the moriscos were concentrated in the south-east quarter of the country. In Valencia, where the concentration was greatest, they amounted to 135,000, or about 33 per cent. of the population, one morisco for every two Christians. In the eyes of the government, whose officials kept it extremely well informed on these matters, the problem was aggravated by the fact that the morisco population was growing more rapidly than the Christian. In Valencia, between 1565 and 1609, population growth among the moriscos was in the order of 69·7 per cent., compared with 44·7 per cent. in the non-morisco sector.[14] In Aragon a similar situation prevailed, though on a smaller scale. There the moriscos numbered some 61,000, or about 20 per cent. of the population, and again their growth rate was outstripping that of the Christians. In the area between Zaragoza and Alicante, therefore, there was a vast *morería* of some 200,000 aliens, facing a Christian population of 600,000 and growing faster than it. This was the real morisco problem, and it appeared insuperable. For the two communities lived in different worlds. The towns were Christians, the suburbs morisco; the rich lands of the plains were Christian, the hill scrub and the highlands were morisco. And the two worlds did not meet.

In Castile the situation was less tense. The ancient communities of *mudejares*, a tiny minority, had never posed a problem. The dispersion of the moriscos of Granada throughout Castile after the suppression of their revolt in 1570 hardly altered the demographic picture. Together, *mudejares* and Granadine moriscos numbered no more than 80,000 or 90,000 people, unpopular people no doubt, but hardly a threat to Castile's 6½ million Christians. The two morisco communities were not even integrated among themselves; and they had little in common with their co-religionists in Aragon and Valencia. So it was not against this poor minority of small traders and artisans that the measure of 1609 was taken. Muslim Spain was south-eastern Spain. It was here that the real danger was seen to lie. The rapid population growth of the moriscos of Valencia and Aragon threatened soon to restore the balance of power between the two communities and eventually perhaps to tip it in favour of Islam. The expulsion of 1609, therefore, can be regarded as the second act of the Reconquest.

This was one matter on which the duke of Lerma was an active policy maker and executive. Under his direction the Council of State debated the issue, and on 4 April 1609 it advised expulsion. The king accepted the advice: on 9 April it was decided to expel the moriscos from the whole of Spain, beginning with Valencia. It was here, as has been seen, that the problem of the moriscos was considered most acute, because of their numbers, their

---

[14] Lapeyre, *op. cit.*, p. 30.

concentration in mountain fastnesses, their situation near a coast-line easily accessible from North Africa. It was logical to expel them first, before they organised their defence or called in outside aid.[15] Preparations were begun in the utmost secrecy. The Mediterranean galleys were assembled; the Atlantic fleet was brought in; troops were mobilised. By September naval squadrons were stationed at three ports, Alfaques, Denia and Alicante; and three *tercios* withdrawn from Italy occupied strategic positions in the north and south of Valencia. On 22 September the viceroy of Valencia, the marquis of Carazena, ordered the publication of the decree of expulsion. This included a provision excepting children under four years—subsequently raised to fourteen years—if their parents agreed to their remaining; and Archbishop Rivera protested in vain that all morisco children should be reduced to slavery for the good of their souls. The decree also authorised six families out of every hundred in each village to stay behind in order to main-tain 'houses, sugar-mills, rice crops and irrigation works, and to initiate the new settlers'.[16] In fact very few took advantage of this permit and it was subsequently abolished.

The landed aristocracy of Valencia, task-masters and protectors of the moriscos, had already held various meetings and organised a protest to Mad-rid, arguing that expulsion would mean destruction of their estates and loss of their revenue.[17] Their protest was fruitless, though Lerma had in mind some form of compensation. The moriscos were allowed to take with them their moveable property, but their houses, seeds, crops, trees and other assets were to go as compensation to their lords, with the death penalty for any act of destruction or burning. But these orders were variously interpreted, and many moriscos quickly unloaded their products and property on to the market.[18] Otherwise they caused no trouble. They quietly left their villages, and under the direction of special commissioners they made their way in long columns to the ports of embarkation.

There, from 30 September, they were herded aboard the waiting vessels, most of them foreign merchantmen attracted by the good freightage oppor-tunities; for, as a final affront, the moriscos were forced to pay their own passage. They left in successive convoys under naval escort to North Africa. In the first twenty days of October some 32,000 moriscos were transported across the Mediterranean. Incidents were few, but those which occurred had repercussions. There were some isolated cases of robbery and violence by ships' captains; and a few groups of moriscos were attacked and robbed by

[15] Pascual Boronat, *Los moriscos españoles y su expulsión* (2 vols., Valencia, 1901), ii, 150–51.

[16] Boronat, *op. cit.*, ii, 190–93; Julio Caro Baroja, *Los moriscos del reino de Granada* (Madrid, 1957), pp. 232–33.

[17] Boronat, *op. cit.*, ii, 183–84.

[18] Reglà, *op. cit.*, p. 231.

Arabs in North Africa. When news of these incidents reached Valencia it heightened the fears of those who had not yet embarked. Rebellion broke out on 20 October in the remote valley of Ayora in the south of the kingdom; about 6,000 insurgents defied the authorities and entrenched themselves in the wilderness of the Muela de Cortes. Five days later a more serious uprising of 15,000 moriscos occurred in an area near the coast of southern Valencia, and the rebels took up positions in the valley of Laguar.[19] The government sent in the *tercios* and the local militia, and meanwhile continued the embarkations in order to stop the revolt spreading. By the end of November the rebels were overwhelmed; those who survived the slaughter were either sent to the galleys or summarily expelled. By now even the most recalcitrant were resigned to their fate, and few escaped the efficient machinery which operated the expulsion. In the first three months of the operation 116,022 moriscos were transported to North Africa. And when, by 1612, the stragglers and escapees had been rounded up, a total of 117,464 had been expelled from Valencia.

The operation was equally efficient in Aragon, where it was conducted in the course of 1610, once the security of Valencia was assured. Here too the aristocracy protested, and here too their protests were in vain.[20] By mid-September some 41,952 moriscos, including a few from Catalonia, had been expelled to North Africa via the port of Alfaques. The rest of the Aragonese moriscos, some 13,470, were sent over the Pyrenees into France, to be shepherded by exasperated French authorities to the port of Agde for shipment across the Mediterranean, and forced to pay transit dues as well as sea fares.[21] From Andalucía, where the moriscos were more difficult to identify because of their relative affluence, 36,000 were expelled by mid-1610. In the rest of Castile the operation was not a problem in point of numbers but was complicated by the existence of two groups of moriscos, the ancient *mudejares* and the more recent emigrés from Granada. First, by decree of 28 December 1609, they were given the opportunity of emigrating voluntarily via France to Tunis. Many took advantage of this, and the remainder were expelled by decree of 10 June 1610, departing via the ports of southern Spain. By mid-1600 about 32,000 had left.

Although Spain had now expelled most of its moriscos, the operation was not absolutely complete. It took from 1611 to 1614 to round up the stragglers, who were particularly elusive in Castile. Those who regarded themselves as true Spaniards made desperate efforts to avoid expulsion, either by litigation

[19] Florencio Janer, *Condición social de los moriscos de España: causas de su expulsión y consecuencias que esta produjo en el orden económico político* (Madrid, 1857), pp. 321–26; Boronat, *op. cit.*, ii, 225–27, 234–37, 557–60.

[20] Boronat, *op. cit.*, ii, 296–98; Reglà, *op. cit.*, pp. 252–55.

[21] Lapeyre, *op. cit.*, pp. 100–5; Reglà, *op. cit.*, pp. 258–62.

or by sheltering under ecclesiastical authority. Some of these were successful; others managed to remain illegally, and yet others returned clandestinely.[22] Gradually the mopping-up operations were completed, and by 1614 from the whole of the country some 275,000 moriscos had been expelled.[23] Most of them had gone to North Africa, to Morocco, Oran, Algiers and Tunis, where they got a mixed reception but eventually contributed their industry and skills to their new homelands. A few made their way to Salonica and Constantinople.[24] Perhaps about 10,000 managed to remain in Spain.

Spain had finally settled her account with Islam. But how was she herself affected by this vast diaspora? Most of the *arbitristas* considered the event to be of slight consequence for the economy of the country as a whole: the government itself professed indifference to the economic implications of the measure; and when the Council of Castile reported on the state of the nation in 1619 it did not even refer to the expulsion. This complacency was probably justified in the case of Castile, where the demographic and economic consequences of the expulsion could only have been slight. While the diligence and efficiency of the moriscos are not in doubt, it is a myth that they were the only productive classes in Spain; most of the trades and occupations in which they specialised, including irrigation, were also practised by Spaniards. And even in Valencia they had not been the only efficient farmers. The expulsion, of course, represented a loss of capital as well as of labour, for in spite of regulations to the contrary the moriscos sold as much of their property as they could and took the cash with them; but it is impossible to quantify this flight of capital. If we are to judge by wage and price levels in those sectors of the economy where the moriscos had been most productive, the expulsion had little material consequence, even in Valencia, and economic activity continued undisturbed.[25]

When all this has been said, however, the fact remains that the expulsion of the moriscos was a major event in Spanish history which cannot be explained away by reference to wage and price levels. The loss of 20 per cent. of the population of Aragon–Valencia could not leave the area unaffected. The towns suffered less than the countryside; industry and commerce less than agriculture. But where the moriscos left a vacuum, disaster was complete.

[22] Reglà, *op. cit.*, pp. 407–15.
[23] Lapeyre, *op. cit.*, 204–5.
[24] Caro Baroja, *op. cit.*, 249–57.
[25] Earl J. Hamilton, 'The Decline of Spain', *Economic History Review*, viii (1937–38), 168–79, who indicates that wages in morisco-type occupations and prices of commodities, such as sugar and rice, which moriscos had produced underwent little significant change in the years after the expulsion. Hamilton's article, which is somewhat exaggerated in its interpretation and unreliable in its morisco population figures, was a reaction against previous historiography; a more balanced note has been struck in the works of Reglà and Lapeyre.

Forty years later, in 1646, Valencia remained depopulated.[26] Not only had the old morisco villages disappeared, but most Christian ones were depleted too; not only were the highland regions still empty but even the fertile *huertas* around Játiva and Gandia were underpopulated compared with their situation in 1609. With the exceptions of the province of Castellón and the *huerta* of Valencia, every region of the kingdom of Valencia suffered a loss of vital manpower. Many of these areas were too poor to attract new settlers; and much morisco land was too heavily charged with ground rents and other dues to make it a good investment.

Almost all the seigneurial lords in Valencia, and to a lesser extent in Aragon, had mortgaged their morisco property up to the hilt; the mortgagees were usually private investors and ecclesiastical communities who were thereby assured of a regular income charged on seigneurial revenue. Now the seigneurial proprietors were driven to demand from new tenants extremely heavy rents or else to default on their payments to creditors. The government attempted to compensate the landlords by assigning them ownership of morisco property and reducing the interest rate on mortgages, but neither of these expedients was adequate. So the landowners fell back on charging the few incoming tenants excessive rents, which only deterred other settlers; and they still failed to meet their mortgage payments. Another group of creditors hit by the expulsion were those who had invested directly in agriculture by providing credit to morisco farmers. For many creditors the revenue from morisco agriculture was their only income. As most of them were ecclesiastical communities and middle-income groups in the towns it is clear that the effects of the expulsion extended far beyond the countryside.[27] It was a further blow at the middle sectors in Spanish society and a further disincentive to investment in an already under-capitalised agriculture.[28]

As an administrative exercise the expulsion of the moriscos could hardly be faulted. Few government machines in Europe could have collected the statistical information on which it was based, or have organised the assembly and transport of so many people.[29] This was one test which the Spanish bureaucracy passed with vigour and efficiency; to conduct an operation of this magnitude and complexity was a sign of strength not of stagnation. Even the much-maligned Lerma emerged with credit—as an administrator if not as a policy-maker. It was an example, moreover, of central policy and direction reaching effectively into the provinces, on this occasion at least belying

---

[26] Boronat, *op. cit.*, ii, 324–54; Reglà, *op. cit.*, pp. 419–22; Lapeyre, *op. cit.*, 71–73; Domínguez Ortiz, *La sociedad española en el siglo XVII*, pp. 85–86.

[27] On the mortgage implications of the expulsion see particularly Reglà, *op. cit.*, 417–43.

[28] J. Reglà, 'La expulsión de los moriscos y sus consecuencias en la economía valenciana', *Hispania*, xxiii (1963), 200–18.

[29] Lapeyre, *op. cit.*, pp. 212–13.

the usual criticism of Spanish government. This aspect of the operation had implications beyond the problem of the moriscos.

The expulsion of the moriscos was a policy decided in Castile and executed by Castile. To this extent it further altered the balance of forces within the peninsula. From the beginning of Philip II's reign the power of Castile had over-shadowed the eastern kingdoms: to finance the policy of Spain was to control the policy of Spain. But the government of Philip II had been careful not to encroach on the rights and resources of the non-Castilian parts of the nation. Now, by expelling the moriscos from Aragon and Valencia, Madrid was attacking the immunity of these kingdoms and increasing the dis-equilibrium between the centre and the periphery. This meant in effect an attack on the non-Castilian aristocracy. In its origin the aristocracy of Aragon was a military aristocracy, with pronounced feudal and seigneurial characteristics, owing its initial existence to its control over a large morisco population.[30] During the second half of the sixteenth century the feudal power of the higher nobility had already been eroded by royal jurisdiction, which had also begun to curb the severity of private seigneurial authority.[31] The expulsion of the moriscos was a further blow at the power and wealth of the Aragonese aristocracy. The same was true of Valencia, where the higher nobility was severely hit by the fall in income from seigneurial property after 1609.[32] The *fueros* of the eastern kingdoms were essentially the possession of the upper classes of the towns and countryside; to strike at the landed aristo-cracy, therefore, was to strike at the constitutional immunity of these regions. In the process Castile broke whatever power Aragon and Valencia possessed within the Monarchy, for it was there that the economic consequences of the expulsion were most severe. It was for this reason that the government of Castile remained indifferent to the economic arguments against expulsion. From the point of view of Castile, smarting under its defeat in the Low Countries where it alone sustained Spain's position without help from Aragon and Valencia, the policy of 1609 was not unreasonable. But this policy added two more dead weights to the empire, and made of Aragon and Valencia, as Castile had already made of the Low Countries, a liability rather than an asset to Spain.

There remained in eastern Spain one region virtually unaffected by the policy of 1609. Catalonia possessed few moriscos and on this issue at least did not enter the calculations of the central government. Catalonia's problems went deeper than the possession of a dissident minority. Indeed they were

---

[30] On the Aragonese aristocracy see Domínguez Ortiz, *La sociedad española en el siglo XVII*, pp. 300–3.

[31] See *Spain under the Habsburgs*, i, 337–45.

[32] Domínguez Ortiz, *La sociedad española en el siglo XVII*, pp. 303–5.

such as to justify a reappraisal of its relations with Madrid: Castile had much more reason to intervene in Catalonia than in Aragon and Valencia. Whether it was prepared to do so remained to be seen.

3. CATALONIA: THE PROBLEM OF INTERVENTION

The crippling blows dealt at Aragon and Valencia in 1609 left Catalonia pre-eminent among the eastern kingdoms. Her advantage was a relative one, of course, for the Catalan economy was by no means buoyant. In the period 1599–1615 Catalan trade in the Mediterranean was receding, incapable of competing with that of France and Italy.[33] The French were actually making inroads into the Catalan domestic market. One of the reasons for this was the poor industrial performance of Catalonia; with textile production slumping, Catalonia was becoming an exporter of raw materials alone.[34] Urban society reflected these conditions. Municipal government was controlled by urban oligarchies composed largely of businessmen; and this aristocracy of the towns, with a resentment born of frustration, was only too ready to attribute its difficulties to outsiders, especially the central government. The rural sector was faring no better. Agriculture in the principality suffered from poor technique and, in certain areas, from lack of irrigation. There was, it is true, some agricultural prosperity in the first half of the seventeenth century, at least in eastern Catalonia.[35] But elsewhere production was hit by the farmers' policy of keeping output down in order to keep prices up, and by the policy of Barcelona merchants whose commercial relations with Sicily involved the import of Sicilian corn.[36] The pressure of a growing population on limited food supplies and the inability to earn a sufficiency by foreign trade led to a price rise and severe unemployment. These conditions bred banditry, as in many other Mediterranean regions. And banditry was, in part at least, an aristocratic phenomenon.

The higher aristocracy of Catalonia was almost indistinguishable from that of Castile. Few in numbers and including only one grandee, the duke of Cardona, it co-operated with the crown and in general played its part in the public life of the Monarchy.[37] But it was not typical of Catalonia. The typical Catalan noble was poor, ignorant, far removed from the life of the court with its offices and opportunities; in seventeenth-century Spain he was an anachronism. Whereas the poor *hidalgos* of northern Spain either resigned themselves to a plebeian standard of living or sallied forth in search of careers

[33] Pierre Vilar, *La Catalogne dans l'Espagne Moderne* (3 vols., Paris, 1962), i, 588–92.
[34] *Ibid.*, i, 593–99. [35] *Ibid.*, i, 599–602.
[36] Elliott, *The Revolt of the Catalans*, pp. 56–59.
[37] On the Catalan aristocracy see Domínguez Ortiz, *La sociedad española en el siglo XVII*, pp. 305–9.

in Castile or the Indies, in trade, office or military service, the Catalan nobles showed little inclination to leave their homeland; they were rarely to be found in the Indies, the army, the central bureaucracy, or the commercial houses of Seville and Cadiz. Their alienation from the life of the nation was not due entirely to the exclusivism of Castile. It was also due to the parochialism of Catalonia. To reject the burden was to forfeit the fruits of empire. In any case the mass of the Catalan aristocracy was virtually unemployable, being more addicted to guns than to books. This petty nobility and gentry, harsh with its inferiors, narrow in its political vision, ill-qualified for office even within Catalonia, either remained unemployed or released its energies in crime and extortion. Banditry, contraband, counterfeiting money, these were the principal occupations of many of the Catalan nobility. For these men the Catalan *fueros* were a vital defence mechanism against the interference of royal officials.

The king's power in Catalonia was constitutional and contractual; the exercise of sovereignty depended on his observing the *fueros*. Philip III visited Catalonia in 1599 and held a session of the cortes.[38] In return for various concessions—he confirmed aristocratic privileges, distributed many new honours, and cancelled the arrears of taxes owed to the crown—he was given a subsidy of 1,100,000 ducats, more than twice the amount of the largest subsidy granted to his predecessor. Philip III and Lerma were content to leave things at that. For the moment they had little option; their preoccupations first in northern Europe then in Moorish Spain left them little room for manoeuvre in Catalonia until some years after 1609. A series of innocuous viceroys maintained a holding operation against considerable odds. The Catalan aristocracy may have been impecunious but it was not powerless. Its extensive seigneurial jurisdiction—71 per cent. of all jurisdiction in Catalonia was in private hands—was a major obstacle to royal sovereignty.[39] Its poverty was matched by that of the crown, which did not have the revenue in Catalonia, nor reserves from outside, to implement a policy. And when all else failed, the aristocracy could fall back on the so-called Catalan liberties, which it virtually monopolised in its own sectional interests. In these years a campaign against the carrying of arms, which was thought to have the benefit of cheapness, did little to restrict banditry for it was frustrated by the aristocracy with the usual invoking of the *fueros*. As Viceroy Monteleón reported in August 1603, 'the majority of these people live in a state of mutual conflict, belonging to bands and factions, which give rise to infinite excesses'. But if the crown took action then it was probably breaking some Catalan

---

[38] On the policy of Philip III's government in Catalonia see Elliott, *op. cit.*, pp. 49–51, 65–66, 104–47, and J. Reglà, *Els segles XVI i XVII: els virreis de Catalunya* (Barcelona, 1956), 123–28.
[39] Elliott, *op. cit.*, p. 98.

law, for as the viceroy explained, 'justice here is shackled by the laws and constitutions'.[40] The Catalans were a difficult people to govern; they resented intervention and they criticised indifference. The crown could hardly win.

During the viceregency of the marquis of Almazán (1611–15) the crisis in Catalonia reached a peak. Banditry was now feeding voraciously on the country. Bandits had their protectors, chiefly among the rural nobility, who took a commission for their services; they had their enemies, in rival bands; and neutrals were bribed or terrorised into silence. A mafia-type regime prevailed in parts of Catalonia, sustained by violence and extortion.[41] By 1615, such was the anarchy in the country, even local interests looked to the crown to rescue them. The bishop of Vic reported in 1615 that 'the people of this principality are blaming the bishops for not getting together to consider these evils [banditry] and request a remedy for them; and they say that if the king sends troops to occupy the country they will all support him in order to establish justice as in Castile and remove the perverse laws and customs which impede it'.[42] An exaggeration, no doubt, but a reflection of prevailing desperation.

At last the government of Philip III decided to act. In the post-1609 phase of policy reappraisal the moment was right from Castile's point of view: having secured peace in the Low Countries and expelled the moriscos, it had liquidated for the moment its major policy problems and was ready to turn its attention to Catalonia. The government appointed a tough viceroy, the duke of Alburquerque, a Castilian aristocrat uninhibited by constitutional ideas. Alburquerque was realist enough to appreciate that strong government could only be applied at the expense of the Catalan *fueros*; believing that what masqueraded as liberty was really licence, he announced in advance that he would 'put the entire principality in the galleys'.[43] When he took office in March 1616, in fact, he discovered that he had some allies, at least among those who valued law and order—businessmen, property owners in town and country, peasant proprietors. But he also had some enemies, and the bitterest of these was the *Diputació*, the standing commission of the cortes, supposedly the guardian of the *fueros* and the representative of the whole Catalan people; in fact it was a corrupt oligarchy serving the interests of the aristocratic sector alone. The *Diputació* was the centre of an anti-government movement on the part of discontented nobles. It was also a financial power to be reckoned with; it had an income over four times as large as that of the royal

[40] Quoted by Reglà, *Els virreis de Catalunya*, pp. 124–25.
[41] J. Carrera Pujal, *Historia política y económica de Cataluña (siglos XVI–XVIII)* (Barcelona, 1947), i, 165–75.
[42] Quoted by Reglà, *Els virreis de Catalunya*, pp. 127–28.
[43] F. Soldevila, *Història de Catalunya* (3 vols., Barcelona, 1935), ii, 262.

administration in Catalonia, and it was hardly a secret that its members were lining their own pockets from the tax revenue they were supposed to administer.[44]

The new viceroy set about detaining and executing delinquents on a large scale; and he reached out to frighten off their aristocratic allies by destroying the latters' castles and strongholds. Predictably there was an outcry that the constitutions were being violated; and a nervous central government, once Alburquerque was seen to have the situation under control, ordered him to observe the *fueros*. By the time he left office in 1619, however, he had restored some order out of chaos and his policy could hardly be reversed. It was continued by his successor, the duke of Alcalá, who provoked even more opposition than Alburquerque. His personal qualities were less attractive than those of his predecessor, but it was basically to his policy that interested parties in Catalonia objected. To strengthen the royal administration Alcalá decided to intensify the fiscal policy of Alburquerque and to reclaim for the crown the royal 'fifth' from those towns which were not already paying it and could not prove exemption.[45] In view of the revenue enjoyed by the *Diputació* the object was not unreasonable. Amidst growing protest Alcalá stubbornly extended the list of towns to be assessed, and in 1620 he decided to tackle Barcelona itself, including its arrears since 1599. But Barcelona refused to pay, and it was still refusing when the reign of Philip III ended in March 1621. The stand taken by Barcelona strengthened the Catalan resistance to further intervention from Castile. In the process of restoring law and order to the principality the crown and its representatives had alienated two groups, the rural aristocracy, who made an issue of the attack on firearms and the destruction of castles, and the urban oligarchies, who took their stand on resistance to the 'fifth'. Yet they themselves had no policy for the salvation of Catalonia. Who could take seriously the Catalans' plea for more royal government, given their record of impeding it? These were men who could obstruct government but were incapable of promoting it. The initiative would have to come from the central government. Philip III's administration recognised the problem, and in its general readjustment of the balance of power within the peninsula it made a tentative approach to re-ordering Castile's relations with Catalonia. But it did not have the nerve to risk a political confrontation with the principality, and the problem was left unresolved.

The attitude of Catalonia towards Castile and the central government seems to have been conditioned by an assumption—subsequently underwritten by Catalan historians—that as the Catalans did not receive the benefits of

[44] Elliott, *op. cit.*, pp. 92, 101, 120–21.   [45] See above, p. 32.

empire they could hardly be expected to share its obligations.[46] In particular
Castile's monopoly of the Spanish Indies has been cited as an example of her
exclusiveness, which reaped its logical reward in the alienation of Catalonia.
Historically, however, the situation had not developed in this way. The
Catalans asserted and practised their liberties long before Spain assumed an
imperial role in Europe and America. Their opposition to Castilian laws and
taxes was not the result of their exclusion from the Indies trade but preceded
it.[47] Indeed the Castilians might have justly inverted the argument: the
Catalans could not expect to be admitted to Castilian privileges if they
rejected Castilian responsibilities. But these were, and remain, debating points.
The Catalan liberties had a long history, so long in fact that they were now
out of joint with the time and the place; the world in which they had been
forged had little relevance to the problems of seventeenth-century Spain.

4. CASTILE AND PORTUGAL

The year 1609 was a critical one for Castile, and it inaugurated a new stage
in the political equilibrium within the peninsula. Peace in the Low Countries
gave Castile the opportunity and the incentive to eliminate the last vestige
of Islam in Spain. This involved breaking the constitutional barriers surrounding Aragon and Valencia and reducing them to Castile's will. And
this in turn left Catalonia exposed in a Spain which was becoming increasingly
unfavourable to the possession of special status and fiscal immunity. But
1609 was also significant for Castile's relations with Portugal. The policy of
peace with the United Provinces was decided by Castile and for Castile.
Portugal, whose overseas interests were particularly sensitive to international
change, had no say in the conduct of her international affairs. Consequently
she had no say in Spanish policy towards the United Provinces, though the
latter were the greatest threat to her empire.

The population of Portugal, hit by emigration overseas and by the
virulent epidemics of 1580 and 1598–99, underwent no real growth in this
period, moving from about 1,100,000 in 1580 to 1,200,000 in 1640.[48] The
effects of emigration were seen in periodic crises of food supplies, for there
were not enough peasants to feed the growing urban centres with a sufficient
margin for safety. The non-productive sectors of society—clerics, university
graduates, the military and bureaucrats—were increasing in numbers. The
nobility, in search of pensions and preferment, joined the service of the king

[46] See, for example, J. Vicens Vives, *Aproximación a la historia de España* (Barcelona, 1952).
[47] On the position of the subjects of the Crown of Aragon in relation to the Indies see below,
pp. 160–62.
[48] On Portuguese society and institutions under Habsburg rule see Damião Peres, ed., *História
de Portugal* (8 vols., Barcelos, 1929–35), v, vi.

E

at court, in the administration, or in the empire. Commerce was largely in the hands of the New Christians, nominally converts or the descendants of converts from the Jewish religion. Regarded by the Portuguese, probably justifiably, as crypto-Jews, they were persecuted by crown and Inquisition alike. They had two main avenues of escape—the purchase of immunity or emigration to Amsterdam. Those who remained performed an essential entrepreneurial function and constituted in effect a middle sector of society, though with second class status.

Although Portugal was annexed to the crown of Castile in 1580, she retained her separate identity. Philip II observed the conditions of autonomy to which he had agreed at the cortes of Thomar. Portuguese offices were reserved to Portuguese. The Portuguese empire was administered by Portugal alone and its trade monopolised by Portuguese subjects; it remained, indeed, more firmly closed to Spaniards than the Spanish empire did to Portuguese. And Portugal retained its own institutions. Sovereignty, of course, resided in the king, and he was the head of the government structure. He was represented in Lisbon by a viceroy or by a board of three governors. But their jurisdiction was limited and matters of importance had to be remitted to Madrid; there they were considered by the Council of Portugal, which produced *consultas* for the king's decision. In Lisbon there was a Council of State to advise the royal representatives on major items of government, but it was a purely government council without precise administrative competence. Already, before 1580, it had employed two secretaries of state, one for home affairs and one for the colonies, whose functions were to transmit the king's decisions to the appropriate agencies. Philip II retained these officials. He also retained the *Mesa da Consciencia e Ordens* (Board of Conscience and Military Orders), which was at once a tribunal and council of religious affairs and the military orders, with jurisdiction in the metropolis and the colonies. And he preserved the *Desembargo do Paço*, the supreme tribunal of the kingdom which supervised the administration of justice. He did make, however, one significant institutional change: in 1591 he replaced the *Vedores da Fazenda* by a *Conselho da Fazenda*, which now became the supreme financial tribunal. Composed of a president, four councillors and four secretaries, this council conducted day-to-day financial administration on its own initiative, though it remitted important matters to the king. As Portugal's most important financial and economic interests lay in her overseas colonies, the *Conselho da Fazenda* constituted in fact a tribunal for colonial affairs. All normal and routine decisions regarding the Portuguese empire were made in Lisbon by the *Conselho da Fazenda*, which worked in close contact with, and often included in its membership, the viceroy of Portugal; major policy decisions they would remit, with their recommendations, to the king or the Council of Portugal in Spain. Co-ordination in policy matters between these two bodies was achieved by routine correspondence between the Council of Portugal on behalf of the king and the *Conselho da Fazenda* in Lisbon.

Philip II's conservative approach to Portugal and her institutions was not continued by his successor. In 1601 the duke of Lerma created a *Junta da Fazenda*, composed of three Spaniards, with power to intervene in the *Conselho da Fazenda*. This was correctly interpreted in Portugal as an attempt to centralise financial administration in the interests of Spain and of Lerma's policy; the *Junta* was viewed with extreme mistrust, and it was abolished in 1605.[49] A further attempt to modify the structure of government was made with the creation of the *Conselho da India* (25 July 1604). The new council had a president and four councillors, and was given jurisdiction over colonial affairs, though the financial and economic business of the empire remained in the hands of the *Conselho da Fazenda*. This, too, was viewed with reservation in Portuguese government circles; the new agency clashed with the jurisdiction of the *Mesa da Consciencia e Ordens*, and it did not survive beyond 1614.[50] But there were other avenues into the Portuguese administration. Philip III began to appoint Spaniards to the Council of Portugal in Madrid and to the *Conselho da Fazenda* in Lisbon. In 1615 he attempted to appoint a Spaniard, the count of Salinas, as his representative in Portugal, but he bowed to the inevitable protest and appointed the archbishop of Lisbon instead. In 1617, however, he did in fact appoint the count of Salinas, bestowing on him the Portuguese title of marquis of Alenquer.

Behind this attempt to infiltrate the Portuguese administration lay another object. The crown's economic difficulties were causing it to look more closely at Portugal as a possible source of revenue. By the terms of the union Portugal enjoyed fiscal autonomy. But this was not impenetrable. Lerma proposed to raise a revenue by selling privileges to New Christians. They were first granted permission to leave Portugal in return for 170,000 cruzados. They were then offered the right to remain, together with a general pardon and admission to all offices in Portugal, but for a larger fee—ten times larger. Portuguese opinion was outraged: in a single deal the Spanish crown would simultaneously raise a revenue and soften up the administration. The three archbishops were sent to Spain to object. They offered the crown an alternative, 800,000 cruzados from the Portuguese towns; but there was one drawback to this—the designated taxpayers refused to pay. So Madrid reopened negotiations with the New Christians. In the new bargain the right to office was dropped and they were offered only toleration for the full sum of 1,700,000

[49] Fortunato de Almeida, *História de Portugal* (6 vols., Coimbra, 1922–31), v, 19–22.
[50] See F. P. Mendes da Luz, *O Conselho da India* (Lisbon, 1952), pp. 81–93, 97–195.

cruzados, which was in fact converted into an exaction. There was worse to come: in 1610 all the concessions granted to the New Christians were withdrawn and the Inquisition resumed its operations. One of the few escape routes left to the New Christians was to marry into distressed Christian families, which gave them some guarantee, producing what the Inquisition called 'half-Jews' or 'quarter-Jews'.

The attempt to tap the resources of Portugal was not, for the moment, carried further. As in the case of Catalonia, the government of Philip III did not really have the courage of its own convictions. But if in the union of the crowns Portugal did not lose its administrative and fiscal independence, it did lose its control over foreign policy. And while it acquired a powerful sovereign, it also acquired a powerful enemy. Whether the Dutch would have stayed their hand against an independent Portugal indefinitely, of course, is a matter of speculation. Philip II's policy in the 1590's, when he put an embargo on Dutch shipping in the Tagus and prohibited further trade between the Portuguese and the Dutch, was possibly provocative, but it was hardly more effective than the ban on Spanish trade with the Dutch, and it may be queried whether it was the policy of embargo which drove the Dutch to go direct to the Far East for goods which they had previously procured in Lisbon and thus initiated the Dutch attack on the Portuguese Asian empire. It can hardly be doubted that the Dutch would have made their way to the Far East even without provocation by Philip II. And if Spain brought enemies she also brought bullion to Portugal; for its trade with Asia Portugal needed a constant supply of silver, which the Spanish Indies alone could provide.[51] There was, therefore, an economic case for closer integration between the two countries. At the same time Dutch pressure in the Far East helped to precipitate a shift in Portuguese colonial interests. Although Portugal's Asian empire gradually succumbed to enemy penetration in the early seventeenth century, a second empire began to take shape in America. Brazil became the focus of increasing attention and by the 1620's had developed into a prosperous plantation colony; it possessed an expanding sugar industry, attracted growing emigration, and yielded more money to the metropolis than it cost in administration and defence.[52] Simultaneously Portuguese merchants made use of their advantageous position under the union of the crowns to ease their way into the American trade of Seville and to infiltrate into Castile's colonial possessions.[53] Although the Portuguese received no special privileges to enter Spanish

---

[51] Chaunu, *Séville et l'Atlantique*, viii, 1, 261.

[52] See C. R. Boxer, *Salvador de Sá and the Struggle for Brazil and Angola* (London, 1952), pp. 1–39.

[53] On the Portuguese in Spanish America see Alice P. Canabrava, *O comércio português no Rio da Prata*, 1580–1640 (São Paulo, 1944); Boxer, *Salvador de Sá*, p. 31; Lewis Hanke, 'The Portuguese in Spanish America, with special reference to the Villa Imperial de Potosí', *Revista de Historia de América*, no. 51 (1961), 1–48; Chaunu, *Séville et l'Atlantique*, iv, 570.

America and were legally regarded as foreigners there, even in the period 1580–1640, in fact their status was much superior to that of other foreigners— unlike the English and the Dutch they were allies of Spain—and they were allowed to travel and settle in the Spanish empire with relative immunity. In the years after 1580 they were particularly active and were to be found in all parts of Spanish America, as seamen and settlers, merchants and artisans; and by the second generation they had made their way into offices in church and state. Their preference was for the Río de la Plata and Peru; and Potosí was one of their principal targets. Brazil afforded a convenient base for their operations. Portuguese exports to Brazil far exceeded the colony's needs; many of them were designed as re-exports to the Río de la Plata and, beyond the pampas and Tucumán, to Upper Peru, where they competed with legitimate Spanish trade routed via Panama and Peru; and Portuguese traffic in slaves and merchandise siphoned off quantities of silver from Potosí.

As the Portuguese shifted the focus of their imperial interests from the Far East to America, so the Dutch followed them remorselessly. The Dutch had already penetrated Spanish imperial defences at certain points.[54] From the 1580's they were active in the Caribbean; and at the beginning of the seventeenth century they began the occupation and exploitation of the salt-pans of Punta de Araya on the coast of Tierra Firme, which became a base of an extensive contraband trade until the Spaniards hit back in 1605.[55] Conditions of war or peace made little difference to the Dutch. And although the Portuguese had no say in the Spanish decision to conclude a truce with the Dutch in 1609, it may be doubted whether any other decision would have altered the balance of power overseas. The chief obstacle to the truce negotiations was Dutch insistence on a right to trade in the East and West Indies, and Spain's refusal, following her usual practice, to admit in an international treaty any statement reflecting on her colonial monopoly. But one of the reasons which forced Spain to come to terms was the success achieved by the Dutch East India Company from 1602, which had effectively breached one sector of the Iberian monopoly. Spain, unable to defend both Asia and America simultaneously, was concerned to assert its determination to preserve the latter, in which Portugal too had a stake. The fourth clause of the treaty, therefore, was worded in such a way that it could be interpreted as allowing the Dutch a relatively free hand in the East Indies but not in America.[56] This merely recognised the existing situation, for treaties could not alter facts. It

[54] Frédéric Mauro, *Le Portugal et l'Atlantique au XVII siècle* (1570–1670). *Étude économique* (Paris, 1960), p. 463.
[55] Engel Sluiter, 'Dutch Maritime Power and the Colonial Status Quo, 1585–1641', *Pacific Historical Review*, xi (1942), 29–41.
[56] C. R. Boxer, *The Dutch in Brazil, 1624–54* (Oxford, 1957), p. 2.

also reflected the policy of the 'peace party' of the burgher oligarchs in the United Provinces, who preferred to trade in the East Indies than to fight their way into America. Consequently, during the period of the truce (1609–21), the Dutch continued their progress in Asia, consolidating the dominant position in the Indian Ocean and the Far East which they had begun to acquire in the period 1600–9.

America, however, was another matter. The treaty of 1609 implied that, whatever happened in the Far East, America was to be regarded more strictly as an Iberian preserve. This too reflected the balance of power overseas. Spain sustained her position in the New World by virtue of occupation, military defence and naval power. The Dutch might make minor inroads into the Spanish monopoly; but they could not overthrow it. There was, it is true, a 'war party' in the United Provinces which advocated an attack on South America comparable to that in South-East Asia. This party argued that the truce of 1609 should be limited to Europe, with war continuing 'beyond the line'. Through the ambiguous wording of the fourth clause of the treaty the truce was in fact virtually limited to Europe. But there was also a limit to what the Dutch could accomplish in Spanish America. The latter remained immune from penetration on a large scale. In any case, as the Dutch could trade with relative freedom to the Iberian peninsula in the years of peace, it was easier to conduct a re-export trade to Spanish America from Seville than to breach the monopoly by direct assault. Portugal, however, was more vulnerable than Spain. So Dutch activity in America tended to focus on Brazil. During the years of truce Dutch trade with Brazil made a notable spurt.[57] The Spanish crown issued constant and explicit prohibitions of foreign trade with the colony, but its policy was subverted from within Portugal itself. The Dutch traded with Brazil through the connivance of Portuguese officials and of Portuguese merchants—New Christians in most cases—in Vianna and Oporto; it was they who provided the necessary facilities of cover agents and a flag of convenience.[58] Dutch merchants estimated that by the 1620's they had secured between one-half and two-thirds of the carrying trade between Brazil and Europe. By the end of the truce fifteen ships were being built yearly in the United Provinces for the Brazil trade alone, while some 50,000 bales of sugar, apart from Brazil-wood, cotton and hides, were being imported in Dutch vessels by way of Portugal. Most of this Brazilian produce was shipped via Oporto and Vianna, where duties on imports and re-exports were substantially lower than at the monopoly port of Lisbon. There was also an outward flow of traffic, for Brazil was a market for Dutch linens and textiles. A sector of opinion in the United Provinces wanted more than a contraband trade with Brazil: it sought the

[57] Mauro, op. cit., p. 261.   [58] Boxer, Dutch in Brazil, p. 20.

colony's annexation. This was viewed with alarm by the 'peace party', which believed that a profitable trade would only be damaged by war with the Iberian powers. According to one Dutch writer, the king of Spain regarded Portuguese Asia 'as his concubine, who can shift for herself if need be, but he does not count the cost of maintaining America, which he regards as his lawful wife, of whom he is exceedingly jealous and firmly resolved to maintain inviolate'.[59] And Dutch critics of an expedition to Brazil in the 1620's were convinced that the Spanish government would react more vigorously towards an attack on America than it had done in the Far East.

Portuguese opinion, too, disillusioned with the union of the crowns, subsequently tended to attribute Portuguese losses in the Far East to Spanish neglect. The charge was less than just to Spain. By the terms of the union the empires of the two powers remained independent, their burdens and their fruits in separate possession. This was what Portugal wanted. It was easy for the Dutch to identify the weaker member of the partnership and to focus their attack accordingly. In any case, Portugal's Asian empire, being essentially a trading complex with the minimum of political dominion, was not an easy object to defend by conventional methods of imperial defence, such as could be applied in America. There was little to prevent other trading powers moving in, if they had sufficient maritime resources. Spain could hardly be held responsible for failing to defend two empires at once. This was recognised at the time. There was no sign of resentment against Spain among the Portuguese officials administering and defending their Asian empire, and it seems to have been taken for granted that there was a division of labour over the defence of their respective possessions. The test of relations between Spain and Portugal would come if the Dutch attacked Brazil; then it would be seen if Spain had the will and the ability to come to the assistance of a Portuguese dominion situated within the heart of the Iberian monopoly. Meanwhile, however, Spaniards were taking note that while they possessed no legal status, much less privilege, in the Portuguese empire, the Portuguese were swarming over the empire of Spain. Again this raised the question, in Castilian minds at least, should not those who received benefits assume obligations? The government of Philip III was aware of the question but left it unanswered.

[59] Quoted *ibid.*, p. 16.

CHAPTER IV
OLIVARES, CASTILE AND IMPERIAL SPAIN

1. Philip IV and the Rule of Olivares

Philip III died prematurely (31 March 1621), leaving the government of Spain and its empire to his son, a youth of sixteen, who had yet to be introduced to affairs of state and was already dominated by his childhood mentor, Gaspar de Guzmán, count of Olivares. The accession of Philip IV, therefore, was accompanied by his virtual abdication. His precipitate induction into kingship was enough in itself to cause him to reach desperately for the guiding hand of a powerful minister; and the habit of relying on the judgment of Olivares acquired in the early years of the reign proved difficult to outgrow. When, by about 1630, he had gained some maturity and experience and was in a position to question the decisions taken in his name, it was too late to assert his independence, had he so wished; for, under pressure of foreign wars and domestic crises, Spanish policy had become committed to certain objectives which were difficult to reverse and which the king could only leave to the government machine and the man who ruled it.

Modern historiography has attempted to rescue Philip IV from the obloquy heaped on the later Habsburgs.[1] Contemporaries certainly recognised him as an improvement on his father, if not in appearance—he had the pendulous lower lip and exaggerated jaw characteristic of the Habsburgs—at least in intellectual and political virtues. After the inertia and corruption of the previous reign the new king was hailed as a leader and a reformer. Popular enthusiasm was reflected even by the satirist Quevedo: 'His actions promise another Charles V; his words and decrees recall his grandfather; his religion reflects his father'.[2] He himself claimed that, having served no apprenticeship in kingship, he was forced to learn it as he went along, by secretly attending council meetings, by reading history, and by examining 'all the reports

---

[1] There are few general studies of the reign. One of the first modern historians to attempt a reappraisal was A. Cánovas del Castillo, *Estudios del reinado de Felipe IV* (Madrid, 1888, 2nd ed. 2 vols., Madrid, 1927), a valuable work still. Martin Hume, *The Court of Philip IV. Spain in Decadence* (London, 1907) is based on original documentation and has considerable utility, in spite of its defects of analysis. For a character description of Philip IV see José Deleito y Pinuela, *El declinar de la monarquía española* (4th ed., Madrid, 1966), pp. 46–63.

[2] Quoted J. Juderías, *Don Francisco de Quevedo y Villegas. La época, el hombre, las doctrinas* (Madrid, 1923), p. 110.

which come from the councils, juntas and individual ministers on every matter concerning my kingdoms'.[3] And it is true that he did a considerable amount of paper work, annotating the conciliar material with his comments and decrees, sometimes extensive and in his own hand.[4] But these efforts were sporadic and inconclusive, little more than signs of periodic remorse, a substitute for policy-making not a means towards it. Philip IV was essentially a courtier, with a courtier's tastes and interests. His notorious patronage of literature, the theatre and the fine arts was that of a dilettante with too much leisure and too little judgment. He was even more interested in outdoor sports, particularly equestrian sports and bull-fighting. But his passion for horses yielded second place to his passion for women, which turned him into a jaded voluptuary well before middle age. His relentless self-indulgence marred his family life both with his first wife, Isabel of Bourbon, and his second, Mariana of Austria; and while he had great difficulty in providing an heir to the throne, his progeny of bastards numbered between twenty and thirty.

It has been argued that Philip IV delegated power to Olivares not out of feebleness of mind and will but because he believed that Olivares was the best man for the job.[5] But this is not the whole story. Philip IV was basically frivolous and irresponsible, a king who preferred private pleasure to public duty. He sought in the able and determined Olivares the counterpoise for his own irresolution and lack of judgment. It is true that his decision to delegate power corresponded to the conditions of seventeenth-century government, and was a necessary admission that the king of Spain could no longer administer the affairs of his vast empire unaided.[6] His freedom of choice, moreover, was limited, for the higher aristocracy of Castile would not tolerate supreme power going to anyone outside their own ranks. Olivares was the only member of the ruling class whom Philip IV knew well enough to trust. These were the grounds on which he subsequently justified his abject reliance on a favourite minister, contrasting the man of his choice with the many 'pernicious ministers' who surrounded him, 'those people who to my way of thinking are more concerned with their own interests than with the service of God and the king'.[7] Self-justification of this kind, however, could not disguise the fact that Philip IV did more than delegate

---

[3] Quoted in Cánovas, *Estudios*, i, 231.

[4] For attempts to rehabilitate Philip IV based on this kind of evidence see Cánovas, *Estudios*, i, 157–59, 259, 297, and Antonio Domínguez Ortiz, *Política y hacienda de Felipe IV* (Madrid, 1960), *passim*. Cánovas describes Philip IV as a *rey papelista*.

[5] Domínguez Ortiz, *Política y hacienda de Felipe IV*, p. 9.

[6] See above, pp. 23–25.

[7] Philip IV to Sor María de Agreda, 30 January 1647, in Appendix VIII, Valiente, *Los validos en la monarquía española del siglo XVII*, pp. 181–84.

power: he abdicated control. This is implied in the barbed advice given by the same Quevedo who had once welcomed the young king. To give political power to a *valido*, argued Quevedo, was to alienate sovereignty: 'Whoever relieves the king of the work and the fatigue of his office is a thief, for he takes away the honour, pride and fruits of that office'; and again, 'the minister who lets the king sleep does not serve him, he buries him'. Quevedo addressed himself directly to Philip IV: 'Most powerful, mighty and excellent Lord: kings are workers, and you are worth no more than you labour; to be idle is to forfeit your wages'.[8] Philip IV's neglect of public duty became an obsession with Quevedo and he returned to the theme in one of his most mordant verses:

> Filipo, que el mundo aclama
> Rey del infiel tan temido,
> Despierta, que por dormido
> Nadie te teme, ni te ama.[9]

The man who relieved Philip IV of these burdens was Gaspar de Guzmán, son of Enrique de Guzmán, ambassador and viceroy under Philip II.[10] The family was ambitious, and its pretension probably outstripped its resources. These, however, were substantial enough. The Guzmán were a junior branch of a famous noble dynasty headed by the duke of Medina Sidonia; they came from Andalucía where they had estates in the region of Seville, allegedly yielding the incumbent an income of some 60,000 ducats a year. But they aspired to higher things, and for years Gaspar de Guzmán, as his father before him, sought to convert his peerage of Castile into a grandeeship of Spain. After a socially, if not academically, productive career at the University of Salamanca—as contemporaries remarked, he became Rector before he even graduated—he succeeded to his father's title and estates in 1607 and thenceforth devoted his energy and patrimony to penetrating the source of power, the court of Philip III. In 1615 he received the first return on his investment: he was appointed to the household of Prince Philip, the heir to the throne, who first apparently regarded his dominating senior with some aversion but soon came to rely on him in every detail of his life. Olivares secured complete control of the young prince's household, packing it with his own

---

[8] *Política de Dios y Gobierno de Cristo*, in *Obras* (*Biblioteca de autores españoles*, 23, Madrid, 1946), pp. 23, 69, 72.

[9] 'Philip, whom the world acclaims, king who keeps the infidel in fear, wake up! For while you sleep no one fears you and no one loves you!' Quoted in Hume, *op. cit.*, p. 355, n. 1.

[10] Olivares is studied in the distinguished 'psychological' biography by Gregorio Marañón, *El conde-duque de Olivares (la pasión de mandar)* (Madrid, 1936, 4th ed., 1959), a valuable source of personal detail but lacking in political content. This, and much more, is supplied by Elliott, *The Revolt of the Catalans*, pp. 193 ff.

creatures. And as he monopolised the heir to the throne, so he indoctrinated him against Lerma and then against the remains of the Lerma faction. These were scattered in 1621 when Philip succeeded his father and Olivares succeeded Uceda. With his pupil on the throne Olivares received all the offices and honours he desired; in 1625 he was made duke of Sanlucar la Mayor, and came to be known universally as the count duke. But what he desired above all was political power.

On the political front Olivares moved at first with caution, overtly deferring to the greater experience of his uncle, Baltasar de Zúñiga, and careful not to offend the susceptibilities of the new king, who seems to have had a brief period of aversion to rule by *valido*. But, as the king's closest friend, his tactical position was assured. Gradually and discreetly he began to intervene in matters of government, gaining confidence as he went along. By August 1622 he was a member of a junta consisting of all the presidents of councils whose function was to advise the king on major items of policy. There was now talk of disagreement between Olivares and Zúñiga, who was regarded by courtiers and officials as merely the uncle of the new favourite.[11] Zúñiga's death (7 October 1622) clarified the situation. The king now handed power officially and exclusively to Olivares, making it clear that he alone enjoyed his absolute confidence.

Now in his early thirties, Olivares was dark and heavy in appearance, with hard eyes and an imperious bearing. His shortcomings were there for all to see —ruthless ambition, obstinacy, impatience with fools and opponents, and dangerous illusions induced by the power he wielded. But his qualities, too, were on a large scale. He possessed great political vision and he was capable of great magnanimity. In the king's service he worked himself to a standstill. He lived in the royal palace and attended to his master's slightest whim as well as to every aspect of government. He worked non-stop from early morning to late at night, interviewing, attending councils and juntas, reading dispatches, writing memoranda, and seeing the king.[12] He brought to his office not only dedication but also a marked instinct for absolute rule and the ability to go with it. If there was a field of government which he did not understand, such as finance, he mastered it quickly. If there was an urgent problem which officials could not resolve he stayed up all night to resolve it. In a sense his vigour and impatience were his undoing, for he tried to take short-cuts to objectives which required a more elaborate approach. His vision of a greater Spain was too ambitious for the period of recession in which he lived, and he himself had no talent for political manoeuvre and compromise.

Unlike many seventeenth-century *validos* and ministers, Olivares was more

---

[11] Marañón, *op. cit.*, pp. 43–52.
[12] *Ibid.*, pp. 167–72.

interested in government than in patronage. Philip IV gave him almost exclusive power in matters of patronage, and he used it, to reward friends and
punish enemies. But he did not like it and he tried to relinquish it, believing
that it was a matter for the king, while he concentrated on policy and
government. He was quite explicit about this, and one of his reasons was
that control of patronage was the mark of a *valido*, while he preferred to be a
minister. In a paper which he wrote for the king (4 September 1626) he
argued that if the king assumed control of patronage 'there would be no need
for the name and office of *privado*, for this is its essential feature. . . . At the
same time your Majesty's ministers would be relieved of the lengthy negotiations which patronage involves and would be able to concentrate on your
royal service'.[13] Olivares seems to have sought a working partnership and a
division of labour between himself and the king. But this, he recognised,
depended on the king doing much more work than he had hitherto done:
'the problems of government are such that your Majesty cannot evade
assuming your share of the burden, under pain of grave and mortal sin'.
Olivares never sought to reduce the king to a cipher; nor did he aspire to a
valimiento, which, like many of his contemporaries, he seems to have regarded with distaste. He preferred power to prestige, politics to patronage.
He saw himself in effect as a prime minister, an office which Spanish government needed but did not possess. In default of a single great office of state,
therefore, Olivares had to acquire a number of offices in order to buttress his
position and give it legal form. He was not entirely devoid of acquisitive
motives, but he was not as greedy as Lerma and he was primarily interested
in the institutional content of his offices.

One title to which he was particularly attached was that of *Canciller Mayor
y Registrador de las Indias*, granted by the king on 27 July 1623.[14] This was an
office which had long since lapsed and was now revived in order to give
Olivares a base in an important institution, the Council of the Indies, and to
enable him to share its jurisdiction over Spain's overseas empire.[15] At the
other end of the scale he formalised his influence over the local government
of Castile through the offices of *procurador* in the cortes and *regidor* in the
towns represented there; these offices enabled him to intervene not only in
the cortes but also in the internal affairs of the constituent towns. His most
important office, of course, was that of Councillor of State, which gave him
legal entry to the highest policy matters. He became a member of the
Council in 1622 and soon came to dominate it. The extent of his dominance
is seen in the fact that he did not normally attend, though when he did his

[13] Olivares to Philip IV, 4 September 1626, in Valiente, *op. cit.*, Appendix V, pp. 171–74.
[14] *Ibid.*, Appendix IV, pp. 162–70.
[15] See Schäfer, *El Consejo real y supremo de las Indias*, i, 217–27.

interventions were extensive and decisive. They were equally decisive when he operated, as a king would do, from outside the Council. He controlled its assembly, its agenda and, by making known his opinions in advance, its decisions. If, in spite of all this, its *consultas* still did not meet with his approval, he sent them back for revision without even showing them to the king. What the king finally received, therefore, if he received it at all, was a *consulta* censored by Olivares, and what he gave in return was a decision advised by Olivares. The secretaries of state, whose status had already been eroded in the previous reign, were further demoted by the role of the count duke.[16] They were now merely officials who handled his communications for him and furthered the details of his policy. It was he who controlled relations between the various councils and co-ordinated their activities. He was particularly interested in the Council of Finance, which had to find the resources for his policy, and those brusk and admonitory decrees descending so frequently on the Council, though signed by Philip IV, bear all the marks of Olivares-inspired documents.

The junta system, which had taken firm root in the previous reign, proliferated even more under Philip IV.[17] It is usually regarded as a device by which Olivares side-stepped the councils and placed administration in the hands of his creatures. Whether he needed to do this is debatable. In any case he did not invent the system nor was it necessarily a sinister development. It probably represented no more than the perennial habit of administrators who have to work through committees to create sub-committees for specialised tasks. Most of the new juntas had administrative, not political, implications. The *junta de armadas* specialised in naval affairs, the *junta de presidios* in frontier garrisons. Inevitably most of the juntas were concerned with raising or administering money. Some, such as the *junta de media anata*, the *junta del papel sellado*, the *junta de donativos*, were created for the administration of extraordinary revenues which the Council of Finance's machinery did not cover. Others were designated *juntas de medios* and ordered to find the 'means' to resolve the ever-present financial problems. These were usually composed of councillors of Castile and Finance, with a few ecclesiastics and Olivares; their object was to circumvent the ponderous and frequently unimaginative councils and to find answers to urgent questions of the day. They were smaller in composition than the councils and drawn from a fairly restricted number of public figures.[18] The *junta de estado* was in a different category, and it is not easy to discern the difference of jurisdiction

[16] See above, pp. 24–25.
[17] See above, pp. 20–21.
[18] Domínguez Ortiz, *Política y hacienda de Felipe IV*, pp. 185–86. There was even a curious *junta de conciencia*, created in 1643, to consider the justification of new taxes, particularly as they affected the church.

between it and the Council of State. Both dealt with the same matters, mainly foreign policy, and some members of the Council also belonged to the junta. The junta, like the Council, depended for its agenda on items submitted to it by the king or Olivares, and, like the Council, it directed its *consultas* to the king for action in fact by Olivares. Perhaps it was intended that the junta should provide a second opinion on *consultas* which Olivares considered had not been sufficiently aired in Council. Or perhaps it was an attempt to endow the *valido* with a type of council of his own, meeting in his private apartment, more flexible than the Council of State, and directly subordinate to his will.[19]

Possessed of the main instruments of power and secure in the backing of the king, Olivares set the direction and controlled the momentum of Spanish policy for the next twenty years. In domestic affairs he was essentially a reformer. But domestic affairs were of secondary interest to him, a means to an end. His prime concern was the preservation of Spain as a world power, and this he conceived as a problem not of internal resources but of foreign and military policy.

2. SPAIN AND THE THIRTY YEARS WAR

Olivares viewed the international role of Spain with the eyes of a traditionalist. He did not question the inherited ideas of Spanish foreign policy nor did he create new ones. He simply sought to apply received doctrine with greater vigour and more powerful resources. In a paper dated 28 November 1621, for the advice of the new king, 'the greatest monarch in the world in kingdoms and possessions', he reminded him of his essential duty: 'Almost all the kings and princes of Europe are jealous of your greatness. You are the main support and defence of the Catholic religion; for this reason you have renewed the war with the Dutch and with the other enemies of the Church who are their allies; and your principal obligation is to defend yourself and to attack them'.[20] Although this policy is frequently described as Spanish 'imperialism', in fact it was empty of aggressive content and of expansionist aims.[21] Spain had neither the desire nor the means to acquire new dominions in southern, central or northern Europe, and encroachment on French sovereignty and territory was now unthinkable. Why then, Spaniards were never tired of asking, did their policy provoke such suspicion and hostility throughout Europe?

[19] Valiente, *op. cit.*, pp. 81–83.

[20] 'Documento de gobierno del Conde-Duque de Olivares al Rey, en 1621', in Marañón, *op. cit.*, pp. 438–40.

[21] For a sensible discussion of Spanish foreign policy on the eve of the Thirty Years War see Carter, *The Secret Diplomacy of the Habsburgs, 1598–1625*, pp. 23–49.

The answer lay in two facts. First, Spain was an 'imperial' power in Europe in the sense that she possessed dominions outside her metropolis, in Italy and in the Low Countries. Secondly, to preserve communications between herself and these possessions she had to cut across spheres of interest and influence jealously guarded by other powers. The situation was aggravated by the conviction abroad that Spain was motivated by an aggressive Catholicism as well as imperialism. The conviction was largely misplaced: while Spanish statesmen might piously invoke religious arguments, they were under no illusions about the possibility of extending Catholicism by force. Here too, as with political dominion, they spoke only of defending existing positions. There was some justification for their attitude. Seventeenth-century Spain had inherited certain possessions in Europe which would have been difficult to relinquish even had she so wished. Most of these possessions were not ready for national independence, and it was arguable that no power had a better title to them than Spain. The one flaw in the argument was the United Provinces, which Spain regarded as rebel provinces but which by any realistic standards were a sovereign state. But even here Spain could invoke arguments of legitimate defence. For the Dutch were ready to subvert the Spanish position in the southern Netherlands and they waged outright war on the overseas possessions of the Iberian partners. At stake in the Low Countries, therefore, was imperial defence. And from the basic premise of defence in the Low Countries the rest of Spanish foreign policy flowed with a remorseless logic. To prevent the isolation of the Low Countries Spain was led to intervention in Germany, a break with England, conflict in northern Italy and eventually war with France.

Spain's response to the outbreak of the Thirty Years War in 1618 was carefully defined. To the emperor she sent financial subsidies and a token force of Spanish troops; these were present at the battle of the White Mountain in November 1620 when the imperial army defeated the Protestant forces, put the Elector Palatine to flight, and crushed the Bohemian revolt. Meanwhile Spain had directed her principal military effort to targets closer to her immediate interests. In July 1620 Spanish troops under the duke of Feria, governor of Milan, occupied the Alpine valley of the Valtelline, an essential pass linking the Spanish and Austrian Habsburgs, and an equally important passage for Spanish troops on their way from Milan to the Low Countries.[22] In September the powerful Spanish army of the Low Countries, under its distinguished commander, Ambrosio Spinola, struck quickly into western Germany, crossed the Rhine and occupied the Lower Palatinate. The object of this operation was not primarily to deprive the Elector Palatine

---

[22] On the Valtelline and Spanish lines of communication see P. Marrades, *El camino del Imperio. Notas para el estudio de la cuestión de la Valtelina* (Madrid, 1943).

of his patrimony while he was absent fighting the forlorn battles of the Bohemians. It was to safeguard the communications of the Low Countries with allied positions in Germany and with Spanish positions in northern Italy by securing control of the passage of the Rhine.

Spain's presence in the Lower Palatinate was resented by the German princes, including the Catholic electors and the duke of Bavaria, who had himself acquired the Upper Palatinate and wanted the rest. But it was regarded by Spain as a place of great strategic importance, not least because the Dutch truce was due to expire in April 1621, and she was determined to stay until she had achieved the security of the Low Countries. In the early stages of the German war the Spanish Council of State had many reservations over giving continued assistance to the emperor. The money was badly needed in the Low Countries, and there seemed little point in promoting the ambitions of the emperor's ally, Maximilian of Bavaria. But in the ultimate analysis it was appreciated that Spain had too few allies in Europe to allow the destruction of the Austrian Habsburgs, and that she had a particular interest as well as a dynastic obligation in sustaining the imperial cause. From 1618 to 1640, therefore, in a period of appalling financial difficulties, Spain assigned substantial funds to the war in Germany.[23]

The basic reason for Spain's commitment in Germany was to be found in the Low Countries. If the imperial cause, and Catholicism, receded in Germany, the Spanish Netherlands would be correspondingly more isolated and vulnerable. Spain wanted the political frontier of the Habsburgs and the religious frontier of Catholicism maintained beyond the Low Countries. Here the moment of decision was approaching, one of the first big decisions Olivares had to make. The advice from Brussels was virtually unanimous: the Truce of Antwerp should be renewed, for with existing resources there was no possibility of winning a war. This was the policy of the Archduke Albert and after his death in July 1621 it was continued by his widow Isabella and her military expert, Spinola. They were overruled by Olivares and his advisers in Madrid, and their decision is usually regarded as a mistake. The renewal of the Dutch war, it is true, was a crippling blow to the Spanish economy. But the decision to renew it was not Spain's alone. The United Provinces too had a war party, led by Prince Maurice and including Calvinist extremists and Amsterdam merchants. The latter looked for profits in maritime war against the Iberian colonies. They had not wasted their time during the years of truce. The Dutch offensive against Portuguese positions in the tropics continued unabated, and if they were less successful against the

---

[23] There is no full-scale study of Spain and the Thirty Years War, but Spanish relations with the Austrian Habsburgs and Germany are well discussed in Bohdan Chudoba, *Spain and the Empire* 1519–1643 (Chicago, 1952), pp. 229–61.

The Count Duke of Olivares

Facing p. 70

Spanish empire this was due not to Dutch inhibitions but to Spanish defences. Now, with the prospect of official war, there would be even greater scope for action in the East and West Indies.[24] The Dutch colonial offensive justifiably bore great weight in Spain's decision to renew the war. In 1588 Philip II had dispatched his Armada against England in order to strike at the source of the greatest attack on his overseas empire. Similarly, in 1621, Spain resumed the struggle with the Dutch in order, in part, to remove the most serious contemporary threat to the Iberian empires. The motives in each case are intelligible, the means adopted less so. Experience had shown that land warfare against the Dutch was expensive and unproductive. The millions of ducats poured into the Low Countries might have been more profitably invested in maritime and imperial defence where, in the case of the Spanish empire at least, the Dutch had shown that they were not invincible. The Portuguese empire was the more vulnerable of the two. With the expiration of the truce of Antwerp plans for the establishment of the Dutch West India Company were immediately implemented, and in the course of 1623 an expeditionary force was mobilised for an attack on Brazil. Spanish intelligence kept Portugal fully informed of Dutch preparations and destination, but it was difficult to defend the vast Brazilian coastline—one of the deterrents to heavy investment in imperial defence—and in May 1624 the Dutch force captured Bahia and took a large booty in sugar and other products.[25] With a foothold in Brazil the Dutch were now a greater menace to Spanish America.

While America entered into Spain's calculations in Europe, America also contributed to Spain's war effort there. Spain entered the Thirty Years War and renewed the conflict with the Dutch under favourable conditions in at least one sector of her economy, the Atlantic sector. The years 1616–20 were a kind of Indian summer in the Indies trade, with private treasure receipts shooting up from 17·8 million pesos in the previous five-year period to 25·7 million.[26] The crown's receipts dropped, it is true, from 7·2 to 4·3 million pesos, but the crown benefited indirectly from the boost given to the private sector and directly from its sequestrations of private treasure. In the period 1621–25 the crown's receipts were maintained at the previous level, while private returns dropped by about 3·5 million, but in general the favourable trading cycle was sustained, with marked results for the Spanish war effort. In December 1621 the Tierra Firme fleet was shipwrecked with much loss of treasure, and in the following year the New Spain fleet also suffered

[24] On the Dutch colonial offensive see C. R. Boxer, *The Dutch Seaborne Empire* 1600–1800 (London, 1965), pp. 25–27.
[25] C. R. Boxer, *Salvador de Sá and the Struggle for Brazil and Angola*, pp. 41–52.
[26] Hamilton, *American Treasure and the Price Revolution in Spain*, pp. 34–35; Chaunu, 'Séville et la "Belgique" (1555–1648)', *op. cit.*, pp. 277, 291.

F

losses. Income from America, therefore, was poor in the years 1622–23, and military operations in the Low Countries were unspectacular. But in October 1624 both fleets reached Spain safely with one of the largest bullion deliveries in the history of the Indies trade.[27] There was nothing wrong with the Spanish army in the Low Countries that money could not repair. Now, with money available, Spinola led it to a spectacular success in May 1625 when he captured Breda after a ten-month siege. Perhaps even more interesting evidence of Spanish revival was the construction and equipment of a naval squadron based on Ostend and Dunkirk to wage maritime war on Dutch trade and shipping, though in the event it had to be employed primarily in a defensive role in protecting Spanish convoys through the Atlantic and the English Channel.[28]

In the Americas the Spanish war effort was equally robust. Madrid reacted promptly to the capture of Bahia, if only because it was believed, as the Council of Portugal informed Philip IV, that the ultimate objective of the Dutch was 'not so much to make themselves masters of the sugar of Brazil as of the silver of Peru'.[29] This coincidence of interests produced a remarkable example of Luso-Spanish co-operation. A joint expeditionary force consisting of 52 vessels, carrying 12,566 men and 1,185 guns, was assembled under the command of Don Fadrique de Toledo; it quickly struck at Bahia and after a month's siege forced the Dutch garrison to surrender on 1 May 1625. The Spanish contingent followed up this success by pursuing the enemy in the Caribbean, and there too the Dutch were repulsed, notably at Puerto Rico. The Dutch, of course, had not yet shot their bolt. During the years 1626–27 the squadron under Piet Heyn wrought considerable damage on Portuguese shipping in the South Atlantic. But for the moment Spanish naval defences were equal to the threat and the silver fleets continued to get through. And this in spite of the fact that Spain was now at war with two naval powers.

Since 1604, and more particularly since 1618, peace with England had been one of the key objectives of Spanish foreign policy. On it was thought to depend the security of the Low Countries and Spain's freedom to intervene in Germany. During the crucial early years of the Thirty Years War Spain had neutralised England by means of the Anglo-Spanish marriage negotiations, under cover of which Spinola had struck into Germany and taken the patrimony of the Elector Palatine, son-in-law of James I of England.[30] In

[27] A. Domínguez Ortiz, 'Los caudales de Indias y la política exterior de Felipe IV', *Anuario de Estudios Americanos*, xiii (1956), 311–83, particularly pp. 338–39.

[28] Lefèvre, *Spinola et la Belgique, 1601–1627*, pp. 82–83.

[29] Quoted in Boxer, *Salvador de Sá*, p. 55; see *ibid.*, pp. 56–66 for the recapture of Bahia, and the same author's *The Dutch in Brazil, 1624–1654*, p. 28.

[30] Garrett Mattingly, *Renaissance Diplomacy* (London, 1955), pp. 255–68; Carter, *The Secret Diplomacy of the Habsburgs, 1598–1625*, pp. 120–33.

1624, when the marriage negotiations had collapsed in ruins and the English were convinced of Spanish bad faith, English neutrality was even more important to Spain because of the latter's expanding commitments in the Low Countries, Germany and northern Italy. Olivares shied away from the impending war; indeed it was not until an English fleet appeared at Cadiz in the autumn of 1625 that the Spanish government reconciled itself to war with England. Once war was joined, however, Olivares and his collaborators indulged in an orgy of planning and for several months they seriously discussed a project for an invasion of England on a scale even greater than that contemplated by Philip II. But while the Spaniards discussed incongruities the English practised them. At Cadiz, with a force of 90 vessels and 9,000 men, they committed every conceivable mistake. The Spanish Indies fleet was allowed to take evasive action; the attack on the town was badly conducted and was repulsed by local levies; and the whole operation ended in calamity, with loss of 1,000 men and 30 vessels. This war was not entirely of Spain's seeking. Charles I began it in 1625 because negotiations with Spain had failed to secure the restoration of the Elector Palatine's patrimony. While Philip IV had promised to use his influence with the emperor to further the cause of the elector, he had understandably refused to accept the English demand that he should undertake the restoration of the entire Palatinate by force of arms if necessary.

With France, too, Spain sought peace but was disposed for war. And here, too, the problem was one of preserving communications with the Low Countries, particularly through the Valtelline pass, a route which France and Spain's enemies in northern Italy were equally anxious to compromise. In January 1625 the French occupied the Valtelline and made an alliance with Venice and Savoy against Genoa, Spain's traditional ally. At the same time French naval forces blockaded Genoa and threatened to cut the vital supply lines between Barcelona, Milan and the Low Countries. Without a formal declaration of war, France and Spain confronted each other. In Spain French property was sequestered, while France prohibited trade with Spain. The Spanish government intrigued with the Huguenots while the French helped the Swiss Protestants. More to the point, a squadron under the marquis of Santa Cruz raised the blockade of Genoa, and troops led by the duke of Feria forced the French to retire across the Alps. These successes, combined with political instability within France, gave Spain the edge and enabled her to emerge unscathed. By the Treaty of Monzón (March 1626) peace was restored to Italy and the status quo to the Valtelline. Spain could continue to use the pass for military purposes.

The years 1624–26 were triumphant years for Philip IV and Olivares. Overseas Spain's naval and imperial defences had withstood and repulsed

Dutch probings. In Europe Spain's military prowess had again been vindicated, moving Velázquez to celebrate it in his famous *Las Lanzas* depicting the capture of Breda. In a message to the Council of Castile on the state of the nation Philip IV alluded to the harsh economic consequences for Castile of this massive war effort, but he could not restrain his jubilation at the renewal of Spanish military power:

> Our prestige has been immensely improved. We have had all Europe against us, but we have not been defeated, nor have our allies lost, whilst our enemies have sued me for peace. Last year, 1625, we had nearly 300,000 infantry and cavalry in our pay, and over 500,000 men of the militia under arms, whilst the fortresses of Spain are being put into a thorough state of defence. The fleet, which consisted of only seven vessels on my accession, rose at one time in 1625 to 108 ships of war at sea, without counting the vessels at Flanders, and the crews are the most skilful mariners this realm ever possessed. . . . This very year of 1626 we have had two royal armies in Flanders and one in the Palatinate, and yet all the power of France, England, Sweden, Venice, Savoy, Denmark, Holland, Brandenberg, Saxony, and Weimer could not save Breda from our victorious arms.[31]

Yet the following years were an anti-climax and the big push forward in the Low Countries did not materialise. The reason was shortage of money, particularly from the Indies, that bonus on which Spanish foreign policy was so dependent. There was a close correlation in the period 1626–28 between mediocre returns from the Indies—total treasure receipts in the quinquennium 1626–30 showed a drop of more than 2 million pesos on the previous period—and the pause in the Spanish war effort.[32] In 1626 the Tierra Firme fleet brought 1·5 million ducats, which were immediately swallowed up in debts and current expenditure. In 1627, the year in which the crown was forced into a declaration of bankruptcy, American revenue yielded only 1 million ducats. But the greatest catastrophe was still to come. In 1628 Piet Heyn's Atlantic squadron captured the entire New Spain silver fleet in the Cuban harbour of Matanzas, and the Spaniards offered virtually no resistance. This was the biggest blow to Spain's pride and purse since the discovery of America, and for the Dutch a windfall from which they financed another invasion of Brazil two years later. Piet Heyn owed his triumph to a combination of good luck and good seamanship. But the incident was out of character with current Spanish naval performance on the Indies run, and this accounts in some degree for the exasperation it caused in Spain. The com-

[31] Quoted in Hume, *op. cit.*, pp. 156–57.
[32] Hamilton, *American Treasure and the Price Revolution in Spain*, pp. 34–35; Domínguez Ortiz, 'Los caudales de Indias y la política exterior de Felipe IV', *op. cit.*, pp. 340–41.

mander of the fleet, Admiral Juan de Benavides, was brought to trial for gross dereliction of duty; and after five years' litigation he was publicly beheaded in Cadiz.[33] Philip IV subsequently remarked: 'Whenever I speak of the disaster the blood runs cold in my veins, not for the loss of treasure but because we lost our reputation in that infamous defeat, caused as it was by fear and cowardice'.[34] But the loss to his treasury was grievous enough—1 million ducats, and three times that amount if the galleons and artillery are included; and for private individuals the losses totalled about 6 million ducats. It happened, moreover, at a very inopportune moment.

Thwarted by the need to fight the Dutch and the English simultaneously, on resources inadequate to the task, Spain turned to her allies in Germany. From as early as 1624 Olivares had been thinking in terms of a Habsburg league, whereby Spain would unite with the emperor and the Catholic princes for the destruction of their respective enemies in Germany and the Low Countries.[35] As Spain had not hesitated to assist the emperor in his moment of need, it was thought reasonable that the Germans should reciprocate by lending their assistance against the Dutch. The idea was revived in 1626 but it made little headway in Germany.[36] While the emperor and Maximilian of Bavaria were anxious for Spanish aid in Germany, especially since Danish intervention there in 1626, they were not prepared to dissipate their resources on the Spanish war in the Low Countries. A concomitant of Olivares's proposed league was a plan for a Habsburg naval and merchant base in the Baltic. In the course of 1626–28 he pushed the idea of a Habsburg–Hanseatic trading company to be based on ports in East Friesland. While this would challenge Dutch control of the Baltic trade, a Habsburg–Hanseatic fleet would strike at Dutch shipping and attack the enemies of the Iberian overseas empires near their homeland.[37] An indispensable preliminary of this commercial and maritime league was Habsburg possession of a Baltic port. For this Olivares depended on the emperor, and the emperor's refusal to pledge himself not to lay down his arms until such a port was obtained virtually killed the scheme; the death blows were added by Hanse and Bavarian hostility. The only consequence of Olivares's project was that it alarmed

[33] A. Domínguez Ortiz, 'El suplicio del almirante Benavides', *Archivo Hispalense*, xxiv (1956) 159–71.

[34] Quoted in Domínguez Ortiz, 'Los caudales de Indias y la política exterior de Felipe IV', *op. cit.*, p. 341.

[35] Michael Roberts, *Gustavus Adolphus. A History of Sweden, 1611–1632* (2 vols., London, 1953–58), ii, 315–16.

[36] Philip IV to Archduchess Isabella, 9 September 1626, 4 July 1628, in Henri Lonchay, Joseph Cuvelier, and Joseph Lefèvre, eds., *Correspondance de la Cour d'Espagne sur les affaires des Pays-Bas au XVIIe siècle* (6 vols., Brussels, 1923–37), ii, 899, 1242.

[37] Rafael Ródenas Vilar, 'Un gran proyecto anti-holandés en tiempo de Felipe IV. La destrucción del comercio rebelde en Europa', *Hispania*, xxii (1962), 542–58.

Gustavus Adolphus and reinforced his motives for taking Sweden into the Thirty Years War.[38]

The frustrations he encountered in northern Europe caused Olivares to seek more fruitful terrain for the Spanish war effort. His eyes fell on northern Italy, where in December 1627 the duke of Mantua died leaving a succession problem. The most convincing claimant to the duchy was the French duke of Nevers, but Olivares feared that the succession of a French client would endanger Spain's interests in northern Italy and threaten her strategic communications. In March 1628, therefore, he ordered the governor of Milan, Gonzalo Fernández de Córdoba, to occupy Montferrat, a key position in the Mantuan estates situated on Milan's western frontier.[39] But what Olivares had conceived as a quick and decisive operation degenerated into a costly and bloody war. A French army predictably crossed the Alps and soon Spain was fighting to save Milan. The great Spinola was sent to command the Spanish and imperial forces, but when he died (25 September 1630) victory was no nearer and the Spaniards were thankful to accept an armistice, a prelude to the peace of Cherasco (April 1631) which ended the sterile conflict. Spain gained nothing from the War of Mantua, and her responsibility for it was a departure from the doctrine of defence on which her foreign policy was professedly based. On both counts her prestige suffered. So did her resources: by this miscalculation Olivares sabotaged any hopes his administration may have entertained of financial recovery. The Italian front swallowed up all the crown's returns from the Indies and a good portion of private returns. Of the 3 million ducats of private revenue brought on the Tierre Firme fleet in 1629 the crown laid its hands on 1 million and added it to its own 800,000 for immediate dispatch to Italy. In 1630 the crown received about 1·8 million ducats from the two fleets, a healthy sum for the time, which together with a 'loan' of half a million from Seville merchants also disappeared in defence costs.[40] In 1631 about 5 million ducats of American treasure went to the bottom of the sea through shipwreck. The Italian war had been no less wasteful.

The War of Mantua was a distraction from, not a contribution towards, the central issue of Spanish policy, the war against the Dutch. Coinciding as it did with the financial stringency caused by the loss of the New Spain fleet in 1628, it brought the campaign in the Low Countries virtually to a halt. This intractable problem was extensively debated in the Council of State in the course of 1628, as the Spanish government doggedly sought the way to success. Spinola—temporarily recalled to Madrid—outlined two possible

[38] Roberts, op. cit., ii, 317-18.

[39] See Manuel Fernández Alvarez, Don Gonzalo Fernández de Córdoba y la Guerra de Sucesión de Mantua y del Monferrato (1627–1629) (Madrid, 1955).

[40] Domínguez Ortiz, 'Los caudales de Indias y la política exterior de Felipe IV', op. cit., pp. 342–49.

policies, either a firm renewal of a lengthy truce with the Dutch, or the dispatch of sufficient funds to permit a determined offensive. He himself favoured a truce, on the ground that the past sixty years had shown the impossibility of reducing the Dutch by force. The reply of Olivares was astonishingly unrealistic even for him. He demanded an energetic renewal of hostilities, without the slightest indication of how they were to be paid for; the object should be not a truce but a definitive peace treaty which would make the United Provinces a vassal state of Spain, forcing them to recognise explicitly the sovereignty of the king of Spain and to undertake to break off all alliances with Spain's enemies; they must accept a Spanish delegate in all their councils, promulgate their laws in the name of Philip IV, and perform a yearly act of deference to him.[41] Yet Olivares's policy, with all its delusions, was in substance the policy which Spain continued to follow. Not surprisingly Spinola declined to implement it and refused to return to his post. In 1629 the Spaniards lost Bois-le-Duc in Brabant, and in the following year the Dutch, switching their attack back to Brazil, began the conquest of Pernambuco.

What options were left to Spain? American revenue provided few windfalls in these years. Throughout the 1630's the crown's treasure receipts did not rise above the current yearly average of 1 million pesos; and returns to the private sector, on which the Spanish economy depended, dropped from 20·3 million pesos in 1626–30, to 12·3 million in 1631–35, to 11·6 million in 1636–40.[42] Peace was made with England in 1630 and with France in 1631. But Sweden's powerful descent upon Germany worsened the prospects of the Habsburgs, and Spain had no confidence in the peace with France. Hitherto France had confined herself to giving subsidies to the enemies of the Habsburgs, but in the early 1630's she seemed to be making more warlike preparations. From 1632 to 1635 Spanish policy was indecisive, fearful of sudden attack but uncertain whether to strike first. The Councils of War and of State constantly returned to the problem, and they began to make plans for an *exército real*, an army led by the king himself with all the nobility and their retainers. It was never clarified whether the role of this army would be defensive or whether it would strike beyond the Pyrenees; and the whole idea made little sense except in so far as it was a pretext for getting money in lieu of service out of the Spanish nobility. Meanwhile the Rhine fortresses fell into the hands of the Protestants, Spain had to send reinforcements to Germany and the Low Countries, and the latter were now threatened in the rear by France. As one front after another deteriorated, Olivares turned once more to Germany.

---

[41] Lefèvre, *Spinola et la Belgique*, pp. 92–100; on Spinola, see also A. Rodríguez Villa, *Ambrosio Spinola, primer marqués de los Balbases* (Madrid, 1905).
[42] Hamilton, *American Treasure and the Price Revolution in Spain*, pp. 34–35.

Spain still possessed one card in Germany, the Lower Palatinate, which was now regarded as an essential part of her strategic communications. As Philip IV remarked in 1638, 'the Palatinate is the best guarantee of our continued possession of the Low Countries and Italy'.[43] And in spite of German pressure Spain was determined to keep it until her possessions in northern Europe were secure. It was the only compensation she had ever received from the Empire for her military and financial aid, and it was a useful bargaining counter in her periodic attempts to interest her German allies in the problems of the Low Countries. From 1630 to 1648 Spain had strong diplomatic representation in Germany, including the count of Oñate, the architect of Habsburg collaboration in 1618, and Diego Saavedra y Fajardo, a theoretician of government as well as a distinguished diplomat.[44] Their object was to persuade the emperor and the Catholic princes that the survival of Habsburg rule in the Low Countries was as important to Germany as to Spain. Their arguments were reinforced by subsidies to the Catholic electors, who were expected to counter the influence of the duke of Bavaria. The latter's opposition to German intervention in the Low Countries and his neutralism with regard to France made him a great security risk in Spanish eyes, and it was Saavedra's task to watch him, to contain his influence, and to get him positively committed to the Habsburg cause, especially in the Low Countries. It was recognised by Spanish planners that subsidies and diplomacy were not sufficient in themselves to procure active German co-operation in the war against the Dutch or in any war against France. Spain would have to convince by her example, to contribute a powerful military contingent to a joint Habsburg force which would serve at once imperial interests in Germany and Spanish interests in the Low Countries. The need was all the more pressing because of two recent developments: at the end of 1631 the armies of Gustavus Adolphus and his German allies occupied the Lower Palatinate, and a few months later Richelieu acquired some strategic positions in Lorraine. Communications between Italy and the Low Countries were threatened anew.

Attacked by Sweden and threatened by France, the Habsburg cause required renewed collaboration between Vienna and Madrid. In February 1632 they signed a treaty of mutual help, and Olivares stirred himself to implement it.[45] Overwhelming problems of war and finance had momentarily reduced Olivares to a state of acute melancholia, and he seemed to despair of the future of Spain.[46] But his planning on this occasion was sound enough. In the course of 1633–34 a powerful army was assembled under the

[43] Philip IV to the Cardinal Infante, 5 November 1638, Lonchay, *Correspondance*, iii, 807.
[44] See Manuel Fraga Iribarne, *Don Diego de Saavedra y Fajardo y la diplomacia de su época* (Madrid, 1956).
[45] On plans for Habsburg military collaboration see Chudoba, *op. cit.*, p. 259.
[46] Marañón, *op. cit.*, pp. 80–82.

command of the Cardinal Infante Ferdinand, younger brother of Philip IV, a man who wore his sword more frequently than his cardinal's hat.[47] Moving north across the Alps from Milan he was joined by imperial forces under general Gallas and inflicted a crushing defeat on the Swedes at Nördlingen in September 1634. This campaign, one of the most spectacular of the war, brought a halt to Swedish successes, cleared southern Germany for the Habsburgs, and gave renewed confidence to the emperor and his allies. But it brought imperial armies no closer to the Low Countries. Count Oñate finally got the emperor's signature to an offensive and defensive treaty against the Dutch in October 1634. His active participation in the war was more difficult to procure. When France intervened in 1635 and thus opened a new front in the Low Countries, Spanish appeals for imperial and German assistance became more insistent.[48] But apart from a token and temporary imperial contingent Spain received no German aid in the Low Countries.

Far from inaugurating an anti-Dutch Habsburg league, the victory of Nördlingen only worsened Spanish prospects. For it increased France's aversion to Habsburg power and reinforced her determination to enter the war, which she did in May 1635. This not only opened up new fronts for Spain but placed in jeopardy all the lines of communications with northern and central Europe which she had so laboriously built up over the years. And while France entered the war relatively fresh, Spain had been fighting for over fifteen years. The search for untapped resources now seemed hopeless. The Spanish economy was in a state of depression, its last prop, the Indies trade, suffering progressive contraction.[49] Between 1629 and 1631 occurred a decisive fall in the volume of the transatlantic trade and from then onwards it never permanently recovered. This was reflected in the mediocre silver returns of the 1630's which never came near to covering the deficits from defence expenditure.[50] The government was only too aware of this, and so was the Castilian taxpayer.

3. The Cost of War

In financial matters Philip IV was served by the most professional of all his councils, the Council of Finance. Established in 1523, reorganised in 1593, and reformed in 1621, it now consisted of a president, six councillors, a fiscal and

[47] See A. Van der Essen, *Le Cardinal-Infant et la politique européenne de l'Espagne* (1609–1634). Vol. I (Brussels, 1944), and 'Le rôle du Cardinal-Infant dans la politique espagnole du XVIIᵉ siècle', *Revista de la Universidad de Madrid*, iii (1954), 357–83.

[48] Cardinal Infante to Castañeda, 24 August 1637, Lonchay, *Correspondance*, vi, 399.

[49] Chaunu, *Séville et l'Atlantique*, viii, 2, 2, pp. 1643–83.

[50] Domínguez Ortiz, 'Los caudales de Indias y la política exterior de Felipe IV', *op. cit.*, pp. 350–52.

a secretary.[51] The president tended to be a professional administrator rather than a member of the higher nobility, and the councillors were a mixture of bureaucrats, minor nobility and bankers. Its basic function was to administer the royal revenue, either farming it out on lease or keeping it under government administration. From the product it paid the *juristas* (owners of state bonds), and provided guarantees to the bankers for their *asientos* (contracts for the actual defraying of expenditure at home and abroad). The Council of Finance employed very few of its own officials in the collection of revenue.[52] *Sisas* (excise) and subsidies granted by the cortes were collected by local authorities; the *alcabala* was a composition tax paid by the localities; customs duties and taxes on wool, tobacco and such-like were usually on lease, with the lessees employing their own personnel and paying the product direct to the owners of *juros* charged on the revenue in question. Although administrative costs were apparently slight, in fact the system was expensive to the treasury and oppressive to the taxpayer. The lessees, often Portuguese Jews, pressed hard on the taxpayers in order to make a profit, and they not infrequently siphoned off the funds and declared themselves bankrupt. Municipal administration of taxes was often fraudulent, to the profit of those with places or creatures in the municipalities, powerful people who did not themselves pay but used the money of those who did for their own financial advantage. Fraud and evasion became more common as the state's demands became more pressing and its administration less efficient, as it did towards the end of Philip IV's reign. Excesses of this kind made Spanish taxation, which was not in itself immoderate, a highly discriminatory instrument and one regarded by those who suffered from it as an intolerable abuse.[53] But this was not the only trouble.

In the course of Philip IV's reign many new taxes were introduced. According to a report made to the cortes in 1623, Castile contributed more than 9 million ducats annually, of which 5½ million were assigned to the payment of *juros*; this did not include revenue from America which, as has been seen, was now falling steeply. At the beginning of the following reign the Council of Finance reported (1667) an income of 12·7 million ducats, of which 9·1 million were already alienated; but this statement did not include revenues administered by other bodies, the profits from debasement of coinage, or income from benevolences and sale of office; counting these, annual income probably then reached an average of 20 million ducats. These figures reflect the new taxes created during the reign of Philip IV. Some of them were more

[51] See Ramón Carande, *Carlos V y sus banqueros. La Hacienda Real de Castilla* (Madrid, 1949), chapter 2; Cristóbal Espejo, *El Consejo de Hacienda durante la Presidencia del marqués de Poza* (Madrid, 1924); Domínguez Ortiz, *Política y hacienda de Felipe IV*, pp. 171–76.

[52] Domínguez Ortiz, *Política y hacienda de Felipe IV*, pp. 176–80.

[53] For an attempt to estimate the level of taxation see *ibid.*, pp. 180–85.

harmful in their consequential effects than the amount they yielded justified; devices such as coinage debasement, sale of office, and sale of common lands were extremely damaging to different sectors of public and private life. But the greatest cause for complaint was that this taxation was only part of the burden which the taxpayer had to carry. For it covered only part of the expenditure of the public sector—the royal household, diplomacy, administration, and above all defence, which together with the public debt represented by the *juros* absorbed the greater part of taxation. There still remained many services—public works, social welfare, education, medical facilities— which today the state assumes but which in seventeenth-century Spain were a charge on private or local enterprise and financed from various sources, such as tithes, municipal taxes, pious foundations. The tithes alone represented taxation comparable in volume to all the regular revenues of the Castilian treasury put together, and it weighed exclusively on farmers and peasants, most of whom were already subject to payment of rents and seigneurial dues. Public taxation, therefore, while not in itself excessive, fell on a sector of the population already burdened with other payments. Little wonder that it produced depopulation of entire villages.

Financial reform was a favourite theme in the early years of the new regime. It was canvassed principally by Olivares and coincided conveniently, some thought, with his desire to punish his opponents of the previous reign. The duke of Osuna, former viceroy of Sicily and Naples, was put on trial for peculation; the aged Lerma and his son Uceda were also brought to account and forced to disgorge some of their takings. But Olivares's attack on corruption went beyond vindictiveness: his reforms represented a determined attempt to impose financial restraint on the administration and the public alike. He had to begin with the king, who regarded the treasury as his privy purse and, to the exasperation of his officials, gave from it lavishly to an endless line of impecunious nobles, orphans, widows, ex-officers and other suitors who thronged the court, some deserving, many less so. Olivares insisted on restraint in the granting of *mercedes*, and as long as he held influence they were in fact severely rationed and many previously granted were pruned; it was only in the last decades of the reign that the weak and irresponsible monarch shed the restrictions imposed by his former minister and lavished grants on begging suitors from a treasury which could not afford them. The royal household was another problem. In the reigns of Charles V and Philip II its maintenance had cost the taxpayers of Castile about 1 million ducats a year, about 10 per cent. of the budget; under Philip III this had grown to 1,300,000 ducats, and the cortes were agitating for its reduction.[54] Under the prompting of Olivares, Philip IV began to reduce his household

[54] *Ibid.,* pp. 168–71.

expenses, reducing the numbers of courtiers and officials, cutting their salaries, stopping the extravagant perquisites to which they had been entitled, and generally saving money. The 'reduced' household was still enormous, but a start had been made and an example set. Two years after these measures, in 1626, the king wrote: 'I have twice reformed my household, and although my servants may be more numerous than before, I have had no other money to pay them with than honours, and they have received no pecuniary pay. As for my personal expenses, the moderation of my dress and my rare feasts prove how modest it is, and I spend no money voluntarily on myself, for I try to give my vassals an example to avoid vain ostentation'.[55] There was a measure of self-delusion in these claims, but if the financial records are to be believed Philip IV did manage to restore the level of royal household expenditure to that of the sixteenth century.[56]

Olivares also attempted to reform the administration, partly by reducing the conciliar and municipal bureaucracy, partly by imposing new standards of integrity. In 1622 he set up a *junta de la reformación de costumbres* to prevent peculation among office-holders. The junta was to register the property of all senior officials appointed since 1592 and to compare it with the total of their possessions before their term of office began. It was further decreed (16 January 1622) that in future all senior appointees before taking office should make a sworn inventory of their private property and repeat the process at each promotion. These measures were extremely unpopular and in view of the resistance they met it is unlikely that they were permanently enforced. Olivares finally tried to impose restraint on private spending. In the 1620's he caused to be enacted a series of sumptuary laws so extensive in their application—they embraced an incongruous range of items from clothes to coaches and from bullion to brothels—as to be quite unenforceable.[57] And like all sumptuary laws they attacked only symptoms. In any case, all Philip IV's protestations of good faith and all Olivares's reforms suffered from a basic weakness: they regarded financial reform not as a function of the internal needs of Spain but as a means to practise foreign policy, a policy which was far more costly than that of any other reign and brought very few returns.

In July 1621, soon after the revival of hostilities in the Low Countries, the Council of Finance informed the king that he was beginning his reign with an empty treasury; much of his revenue was anticipated up to 1625, and 'resources are so exhausted that we do not know where to turn'.[58] The bankers, too, were aware of the facts and they advanced not the 1½ million

[55] Quoted in Hume, *op. cit.*, p. 35.
[56] Domínguez Ortiz, *Política y hacienda de Felipe IV*, p. 179.
[57] Hume, *op. cit.*, pp. 131–32, 137–40.
[58] Domínguez Ortiz, *Política y hacienda de Felipe IV*, pp. 12–13.

ducats requested but a mere 600,000, secured on various extraordinary revenues. The Low Countries, however, were soon absorbing annually not 1½ million ducats as in the last years of the truce but 3½ million, while naval defence in the Atlantic, a prerequisite in any war with the Dutch, more than doubled its cost to 1 million ducats. In spite of a reduction in court expenditure, therefore, the first budget of the reign produced an expenditure of 8·2 million ducats, almost double that of the last budget of Philip III. As available revenue up to 1625 only reached 5·8 million ducats, there remained an enormous deficit. Philip IV and Olivares were not impressed by these difficulties: they regarded them as a legacy for which they were not responsible; and nothing could shake their conviction that political problems took precedence over pecuniary ones, which were never insuperable. In the early years of the reign, to 1626, they simply adopted expedients which had been well tried in the past. First, they anticipated revenue. When this proved insufficient they continued the coinage of vellon initiated by Philip III, but on an even more massive scale. On 24 June 1621 the king decreed the coining of 4 million ducats, arguing that 'my chief obligation is to preserve and defend the kingdom against my enemies, and this does not admit delay'.[59] The decision was taken without reference to the cortes and it broke one of the conditions attached to previous subsidies. As a financial device it was extremely clumsy: copper was expensive to import and to coin; profits were slow and inadequate; and the consequent monetary disorder damaged the economy. But what was the alternative? The government was still reluctant to create new taxes, and it was still thought, as in Lerma's time, that there must be some way of procuring great sums without anyone having to pay them. This was the classical period of the *arbitristas*, those contrivers of schemes, or *arbitrios*, who searched for a 'universal means' to improve the situation; many of them favoured the invention of a single tax, though there was much disagreement as to the commodity on which it should fall.

Meanwhile the government was frantically searching for money to rush to the Flanders front, remittances for which it wished to increase to 300,000 ducats a month in 1623. When the Council of Finance complained that it could not lay its hands on the money for these and other defence costs, it was rebuked by Philip IV: 'There is no need to warn me about the state of my treasury, for I am not responsible for its present situation. . . . It behoves the Council of Finance not to spend all its time pointing out difficulties but to attempt to resolve them'.[60] But the Council of Finance was not alone in its reservations about current financial policy. The bankers too were becoming restless, weary of being fobbed off with *juros* instead of hard cash, and steadily pushing up their rates of interest. For the contracts which backed the successful

[59] Quoted *ibid.*, p. 14.   [60] Quoted *ibid.*, p. 21.

war effort of 1624–26 they insisted on extremely rigorous conditions, and at the beginning of 1626 Olivares had to stay up a whole night arguing with them before they agreed to the contracts for that year. The Genoese bankers, hitherto the mainstay of royal finances, were now anxious to cut their losses and retire from the *asiento* business. But this year, for the first time, a consortium of Portuguese Jewish financiers offered Olivares a loan of 400,000 escudos for payment in the Low Countries. Their capital resources were small compared to those of the Genoese, but Olivares encouraged their initiative as a means of keeping down the interest rates and as an alternative for the future.[61]

The Genoese had foreseen a crash. It came at the end of January 1627 when the crown, unable to anticipate revenue further, declared its bankruptcy, suspended its servicing of debts, and compensated its creditors with *juros*. Philip IV and Olivares were more complacent about this operation than were the bankers, regarding it simply as a conversion of short-term into long-term debts, as in a sense it was; it had become a regular device, adopted roughly every twenty years, and it was sometimes the prelude to financial restraint and reform. But it was useless to look to Philip IV and Olivares for financial reform: they regarded the treasury as an instrument for defraying defence costs. The late 1620's were bad years for Castile, with renewed inflation depressing living standards still further for its long-suffering people. Inflation was aggravated by bad harvests and by the scarcity of imported goods caused by a partial closing of the frontiers during wartime. But it had already been induced by the massive coinage of vellon from the very beginning of the reign. Between 1621 and 1626 the crown minted 19·7 million ducats of vellon, from which it made a profit of 13 million ducats. The premium on silver soared from 4 per cent. in 1620 to 50 per cent. in 1626.[62] The treasury itself was a victim of this monetary disorder. At one point in the war it had to guarantee the Fuggers 180,000 ducats in vellon to make a payment of 80,000 ducats in silver in Germany. 'How am I going to rescue my stricken kingdoms from the oppression of vellon?', cried Philip IV to the Council of Finance.[63] One answer was to stop further issues. By a decree of 8 May 1626 minting was suspended. And on 7 August 1628 the crown reduced the tariff of vellon by 50 per cent.[64] This savage deflationary measure—which the crown promised was its last word on vellon—reduced the premium on silver, though at the cost of great hardship to individual holders of vellon, who were not compensated and suffered losses totalling some 14 million ducats. But it

[61] *Ibid.*, p. 31.
[62] Hamilton, *American Treasure and the Price Revolution in Spain*, pp. 80–81, 96; Domínguez Ortiz, *Política y hacienda de Felipe IV*, pp. 256, 276, n. 16.
[63] Quoted *ibid.*, p. 38.
[64] Hamilton, *American Treasure and the Price Revolution in Spain*, p. 83.

brought relief to the treasury by the reduction in the premium it had to pay the bankers for silver. And, in conjunction with the suspension of payments of the previous year, it could have been the point of departure for a new financial policy. In 1627 the Indies fleets returned with substantial remittances of precious metals. And on all fronts—England, the Low Countries and Germany—the war was dormant.

It was at this point that Olivares chose to go on the offensive and launched the aggressive and, in the event, fruitless war of Mantua, the only war which ever troubled the conscience of Philip IV. The heavy costs of the Italian war coincided (1628) with the loss of the treasure-laden New Spain fleet in the bay of Matanzas. The Tierra Firme fleet brought only 800,000 ducats for the crown, which took a forced loan of 1 million ducats from the silver which had arrived for private investors. Olivares could only complete the *asientos* for 1629 by bringing in the Portuguese financiers and persuading them to accept 15 per cent. interest in place of the current 24–30 per cent. This was accompanied by minor palliatives such as selling *hidalguías*, seigneurial jurisdiction and municipal offices, in an attempt to meet the defence costs of 1629–30. The years 1627–34, therefore, saw no financial reform, only greater financial irresponsibility as the crown searched frantically for new sources of income.[65]

As the war in northern Europe gathered momentum in 1632 Olivares turned his frightening gaze once more on the taxpayers of Spain, and they rested as usual on those of Castile.[66] The cortes, which had already been held to a particularly long session in 1623–29, were convoked again in February 1632. They were asked to vote a three-year subsidy of 9 million ducats and given ten days to decide. They were understandably reluctant, pointing to the parlous state of the country, the multitude of taxes, the pernicious effects of debasement, the forced sale of offices and *hidalguías* to towns that had to pay for them out of municipal funds for want of takers, to all of which they added their customary warnings about rural deprivation and depopulation, concluding that 'the people ought to be relieved of impositions rather than given new ones for the benefit of other kingdoms'.[67] Then the browbeating began. The king warned them that he had been advised by the Council of Finance to send home those members who did not obey. Olivares tried to impress them with a statement of expenditure totalling, with some exaggeration, more than 18 million escudos. And the usual trading in pensions and honours was not neglected. Eventually the cortes voted $2\frac{1}{2}$ million ducats over six years, 416,666 ducats a year, to be raised from new taxes on sugar,

---

[65] Domínguez Ortiz, *Política y hacienda de Felipe IV*, pp. 40–49, 359–64, 388–89.
[66] He was also, of course, unsuccessfully attempting to tax Catalonia; see below, pp. 98–101.
[67] On the proceedings of this cortes see *Actas de las Cortes de Castilla*, xlix.

paper, chocolate, fish and tobacco; they also doubled the regular *millones* subsidy to 4 million ducats a year by raising the taxes on basic foodstuffs, thus further depressing the living standards of the poor.

The expedition of the Cardinal Infante Ferdinand to Germany and the Low Countries in 1634 was a major financial undertaking, and on this occasion ecclesiastical revenue came to the rescue. The costs of the campaign were met in part by the numerous ecclesiastical benefices held by Ferdinand, particularly the wealthy see of Toledo and the Portuguese abbacies of Thomar and Crato; by the sale of seigneurial jurisdiction and municipal offices; and by the sale of a portion of the future *millones* revenue to financiers. But the victory of Nördlingen, presaging as it did French intervention in the war, only produced another financial nightmare. During 1634 Olivares worked feverishly with the Council of Finance and the *junta de medios* (committee of ways and means) to find supplies for the following year. A decree of 23 September fixed the expenditure for 1635 at 7,256,000 escudos: 5,656,000 for the Low Countries, 600,000 for Germany, 500,000 for northern Italy, and the rest for Spain. This was one of the largest Habsburg defence budgets ever. Olivares and his advisers appreciated the impossibility of the bankers providing such a sum, and they decided to negotiate for 5 million escudos, trying other expedients for the balance. The king rejected the advice indignantly: 'I do not know how you have the nerve to make such a proposal, which is offensive to my Council of State and, what is worse, to me. . . . I order you to set to and complete the negotiation with the bankers by dint of work, interest and prerogative'.[68] He ordered all senior ministers to buy *juros*, and local officials were instructed to promote a similar sales campaign in their districts. Foreigners were forced to pay to the treasury half of a year's returns on the *juros* they held. And, disregarding his promise of 1628, the king ordered further debasement of the coinage in March 1636.[69] This inaugurated a new period of financial disorder. From 1635 Castile entered a period of total war and its economy was subject to unprecedented pressure by the demands of defence expenditure. The financial planners ceased to plan and simply reacted despairingly to one circumstance after another, improvising from day to day and returning ever more frequently to the defenceless taxpayers of Castile. The people looked in vain for relief to their king. And they could expect no protection from their own representatives.

4. The Cortes of Castile

One of the sternest critics of the crown's financial practices was the cortes of Castile. In 1617 the town of Zamora instructed its representatives to

---

[68] Quoted in Domínguez Ortiz, *Política y hacienda de Felipe IV*, p. 48.
[69] Hamilton, *American Treasure and the Price Revolution in Spain*, p. 84.

Reconquest of Bahía, with Olivares and Philip IV in allegory of victory

Facing p. 87

resist further demands for subsidies and to seek a reduction of its tax assessment which had been set at 29,000 ducats fifteen years previously. 'The misery and poverty of this region and the great tax burden it bears are causing a daily flight of capital and labour. The countryside is exhausted, its farming and stock consumed. Trade, cattle and crops are down to a third of their previous volume'.[70] Denunciations like these were part of the stock-in-trade of the seventeenth-century cortes. But while they spoke like lions they acted like lambs.

The crown negotiated with the higher nobility and the clergy outside of the cortes, and these estates had long since ceased to attend. So the cortes in fact comprised the representatives of eighteen cities and towns of Castile— Burgos, León, Seville, Córdoba, Murcia, Jaén, Toledo, Zamora, Toro, Soria, Valladolid, Salamanca, Segovia, Madrid, Avila, Guadalajara, Cuenca and Granada. Throughout the sixteenth century representation in the cortes was confined to these towns, each of which sent two *procuradores*, or deputies. Unrepresented towns resented their exclusion, not because they wished to bring themselves to the attention of the crown, but because in the actual voting and administration of taxes those who were represented were able to favour themselves at the expense of those who were not. In the reign of Philip IV, when most things were up for sale, seats in the cortes too could be bought. In 1625 Galicia bought representation; so too, at the end of the reign, did Palencia. In 1639 Jerez sought to buy its way in, for a sum of 85,000 ducats, in order to free itself from the dominance of Seville. The cynical arguments used by the Council of Finance against the application were an interesting commentary on the role of the cortes. To admit Jerez, observed the Council, would simply give the government more trouble and expense, with one more town to manage in procuring majority votes, and two more deputies to satisfy with grants and honours; to raise 85,000 ducats the town councillors of Jerez, who alone would benefit from representation, would have to impose taxes on the mass of the citizens, who would get no benefit at all; in any case Jerez was already in arrears in its normal taxes and highly unlikely to be capable of raising the offered sum.[71] In the event the king granted the application on condition that the money came from the pockets of the twenty-four town councillors and not from taxes on the citizens. At that point the application was withdrawn.

The cortes of Castile existed not to make laws, which was an exclusive

---

[70] Manuel Danvila y Collado, *El poder civil en España* (6 vols., Madrid, 1885–87), vi, 67, 76–77.
[71] Consulta del Consejo de Hacienda, 21 July 1639, in Domínguez Ortiz, *Política y hacienda de Felipe IV*, appendix XII, p. 372. See also the same author's 'Concesiones de votos en Cortes a ciudades castellanas en el siglo XVII', *Anuario de Historia del Derecho Español*, xxx (1961), 175–86.

G

prerogative of the crown, but to vote taxes.[72] In taxation the crown's sovereignty was limited by the basic principle, established since the beginning of the fourteenth century, that new taxes could not be imposed without the consent of the cortes. During most of the sixteenth century ordinary sources of income—existing taxes, ecclesiastical revenue, and returns from the Indies—enabled the crown to pay its way without going frequently to the cortes for extraordinary supplies. But the rising defence expenditure of Philip III and Philip IV forced these monarchs to have frequent and lengthy recourse to the cortes in search of new taxes. Philip III convoked the cortes on six occasions, Philip IV on eight occasions, one of which was a session lasting six years (1623–29). The cortes depended for their assembly on royal summons. There was no general rule regulating the election of deputies, and practices varied from town to town, some proceeding by elections, others by rotation or lot. The Spanish monarch did not normally go in person to his cortes but was represented by a minister, who opened the session with a speech from the throne, the *Proposición*, outlining the reasons for summoning the cortes, particularly the state of the treasury and its new needs, and exhorting them to do their duty. Having studied this message, and if proceedings went smoothly, the deputies then agreed on a sum to be granted, indicating the taxes by which it was to be raised, and imposing as a condition of the grant that it be applied to the expenditure for which it was requested. And in order to ensure the conditions of appropriation the cortes administered the grant through a commission of deputies which gradually became a permanent bureaucratic body subordinate to the royal treasury.

These specific, if limited, powers, combined with the needs of the crown, gave the cortes a certain bargaining capacity which they sometimes used to effect. They were particularly critical of the monetary policy of the crown and made more than one attempt to stop debasement of the coinage. In 1608, for example, as a condition of the *millones* grant of 2½ million ducats a year for seven years, they procured a promise from the king not to coin additional vellon under any circumstances for the next twenty years.[73] But in 1617 in view of the enormous budget deficit, they released him from his promise and subsequently agreed to a vellon issue yielding 1 million ducats profit.[74] After this Philip III continued his inflationary measures without much reference to the cortes, and Philip IV issued vellon without reference to

[72] On the cortes of Castile see Manuel Colmeiro, *Introducción a las Cortes de los antiguos reinos de León y de Castilla* (2 vols., Madrid, 1888); Danvila, *El poder civil en España*, vi; and Danvila's series of articles, primarily documentation, on the cortes of Castile in the reign of Philip IV in *Boletín de la Real Academia de la Historia*, xv (1889), 385–433, 497–542, xvi (1890), 69–164, 228–90, xvii (1890), 273–321.

[73] *Actas*, xxiv, 637–39.

[74] *Actas*, xxx, 109–19, xxxi, 191–93, 196–201.

them at all, though he occasionally consulted them on some of its consequences. In April 1628 the deputies voted to have five hundred masses
celebrated for the 'enlightenment of their intelligence' in studying the reform
of vellon.[75] The cortes were in a stronger position when some particular
financial proposal required the positive co-operation of the public. In 1623,
for example, searching frantically for additional sources of income, the
government advanced the idea of forming public banks, capitalised by forced
loans from the public graded according to income; these banks would bor-
row at 3 per cent. and lend at 5 per cent. This proposal met with the utter
opposition of the cortes and the towns they represented, on the grounds that
the contributions would be obligatory and unequal in incidence; and the
matter had to be dropped.[76]

The government of Philip IV was particularly contemptuous of the cortes,
and it was possibly in reaction to this, as well as to the rising demands for
supplies, that the towns of Castile attempted to put some teeth into the cortes
by modifying their procedure. Traditionally, in attaching conditions to grants,
the cortes had presented petitions to the crown for redress of grievances.
These were notoriously ignored. In 1623, therefore, many towns gave
their deputies only the power of a *voto consultivo*, or provisional vote, reserving
to themselves the *voto decisivo*, that is ratification of the grant offered;
and the deputies were instructed that ratification would be withheld until the
crown agreed to the conditions or gave good reasons why it should not.

The new procedure was soon put to the test. In 1623, under government
prodding, a commission of the cortes produced proposals for a number of
new taxes; these included a 12 per cent. tax on public offices, a 'fifth' on all
grants from the crown yielding the recipient an income, including *encomiendas*
in the Indies, a 5 per cent. tax on luxury textiles and on *juros* and *censos*.
These proposals were a rare and promising development in tax policy, for
they were aimed at the haves rather than the have-nots and would have
spared the labouring masses in town and country. It was precisely for this
reason that the cortes chose to dig in their heels. The deputies for Seville,
Juan Ramírez de Guzmán and Francisco Ruidiaz de Pineda, opposed most of
the new proposals on the grounds that they would impose further burdens
on an already overtaxed city, whose returns from the Indies were under
constant threat of sequestration. And they declared their incapacity to vote
on the proposals as their municipality had reserved to itself the *voto decisivo*.[77]
The opposition of Seville, however, was not as firm as it looked for its
municipality was divided into two factions, the partisans of Olivares, who

[75] Hamilton, *American Treasure and the Price Revolution in Spain*, p. 83, n. 3.
[76] *Actas*, xxxviii, xxxix, *passim*.
[77] *Actas*, xl, *passim*.

were backed by the Asistente, the crown's official in the area, and an independent faction including most of the twenty-four proprietary office-holders in the municipality; the latter were inspired by the local aristocracy led by the wealthy family of Ortiz de Malgarejo, personal opponents of Olivares. One of the objects of Philip IV's visit to Seville in March 1624 was to break this opposition. While the king was being regaled in a series of fiestas, Olivares presided over a session of the *cabildo* and handled it with such effect that it not only ratified agreement to the proposals before the cortes but also granted the king a benevolence of 30,000 ducats.

Meanwhile, however, other towns had decided to withhold ratification, and the cortes continued discussing the issue throughout 1624.[78] They maintained their opposition to virtually all the new taxes, particularly to those on offices, grants, *juros* and *censos*, for these affected the vital interests of the minor nobility, whom the cortes in effect represented. The result was that these particular taxes, advantageous in their social as well as their financial implications as they would fall on the privileged and the unproductive, were eventually dropped, and the cortes confined themselves to approving a continuation of the *millones*, at the rate of 2 million ducats a year for six years, the money to be raised by taxes on basic consumer goods. Among the conditions attached to this grant was one that the crown should impose no extraordinary taxation outside the cortes; although the king agreed his ministers soon found ways of evading it. As for the attempt of the towns to retain in their own hands ratification of votes on subsidies, this hardly survived the cortes of 1623–29. The crown disliked the device: it insisted on deputies having full voting powers, and it met with little resistance. The incident, in fact, simply underlined two characteristics of the cortes of Castile, their class interest and their limited function.

How can the subservience of the cortes be explained? The basic reason was their lack of legislative power, which deprived them of a bargaining device and prevented them from insisting on redress of grievances before grant of supplies. They were, moreover, subject to government pressure of various kinds, ranging from holding the cortes to inconveniently lengthy sessions to outright corruption. The deputies were not paid a salary by their constituencies but received emoluments of one kind and another from the government. Their expenses were defrayed from a percentage of the subsidies they voted; in addition they spent much of their time in Madrid negotiating for offices, pensions and honours for themselves and their relatives, most of which were forthcoming if they co-operated with the crown. Methods of blatant bribery and corruption were first introduced by Lerma; Olivares and his successor, Luis de Haro, employed a mixture of cajolery and intimidation.

[78] *Actas*, xlii, *passim.*

As though this were not enough they were forced to admit to full member-ship of their sessions senior ministers of the crown, such as the president of the Council of Finance and the favourites Lerma and Olivares.[79]

Yet these factors do not in themselves completely account for the co-operation of the cortes of Castile with the crown. Their subservience was more apparent than real and it masked a measure of self-interest. They were generous, no doubt, but their generosity tended to be at the expense of sectors of society other than the ones they represented. The cities and towns of Castile were dominated by aristocratic oligarchies; more particularly their government and economy were in the hands of the middle and lower nobility, who secured in the localities power to which they could not aspire at the centre. They were strategically placed to defend their property and their interests, for many taxes, and all those granted by the cortes, were administered by the municipalities. And, through the deputies whom they sent to the cortes, they were in a position to influence the actual incidence of taxation. In the sixteenth century the oligarchies of the larger towns had insisted on compounding the *alcabala*, one of the major taxes of Castile, for an agreed yearly payment. The reasoning behind this move was that in an age of inflation, with expanding trade and profits, it was advantageous to stabilise a sales-tax at a fixed level, particularly as this was one of the few taxes from which the nobility were not exempt. Subsequently, to compensate the crown for its losses on the *alcabala*, the cortes authorised a series of subsi-dies known as the *servicios ordinarios y extraordinarios*, payment of which was confined to commoners.[80] Thus the nobility arbitrarily passed on the tax burden to others. As there were relatively few commoners in northern Spain, a region notoriously populous in *hidalgos*, the north was effectively over-assessed compared to the centre and the south, with consequent economic hardship. The difficulties experienced by some regions in meeting their quota caused this tax, too, to be stabilised, and from 1591 its yield was fixed at 405,000 ducats a year. Consequently, like the *alcabala*, its yield to the crown failed to keep up with inflation. So it in turn was supplemented by a further series of subsidies known as the *servicios de millones*, which were first voted by the cortes towards the end of Philip II's reign. These were designed to raise 2 million ducats a year, by means of taxes on the *cuatro especies*, that is on wine, meat, oil and vinegar. These subsidies were generously renewed throughout the reigns of Philip III and Philip IV, and under pressure of the crown they showed a tendency to rise and to be extended to further

[79] Cánovas, *Estudios*, i, 125–33; Marañón, *op. cit.*, p. 333.
[80] On the grants of the cortes see Domínguez Ortiz, *Política y hacienda de Felipe IV*, pp. 232–80, and the same author's 'La desigualdad contributiva en Castilla durante el siglo XVII', *Anuario de Historia del Derecho Español*, xxi–xxii (1951–52), 1222–68.

commodities. In 1626 the cortes raised the *millones* subsidy from 2 million to 4 million ducats a year, by means of new taxes on paper, salt, and ship anchorage. In 1632 they granted an extra subsidy of 2½ million ducats every six years. And temporary subsidies were voted from time to time for specific items of expenditure and charged on various consumer goods.

From the *millones* the nobility were not exempt: in the grant of 1611 it was explicitly stated that there were to be no exemptions. Did this imply a change of fiscal policy on the part of the cortes? The change was more apparent than real. In the first place the affluent sectors whom they represented were less sensitive to taxes on basic foodstuffs than were the masses of labouring poor; in conjunction with the *alcabala* and local excise duties the *millones* were an intolerable burden on agriculture and on the farmers and peasants who practised it. Secondly, in a period when the financial officers of the crown were looking with disfavour on fiscal privilege, it obviously made sense for the nobility to choose the lesser of two evils, a purchase tax rather than a property tax. This is precisely what the cortes did when, as has been seen, they sabotaged the crown's proposals for taxes on public offices, pensions, *juros* and *censos*—all of which were vital property interests to the middle and lower nobility—and preferred instead to renew the *millones*. Finally, through their control of local government, the nobility were able so to administer the *millones* that they themselves paid as little as possible and even in some cases made a profit out of them, as did those officials who actually handled the tax and those nobles who sold untaxed goods from their own estates in their own houses in a respectable form of contraband.

Once the cortes had defined, and the crown had accepted, the type of taxation they preferred, there was little reason for their further convocation. They continued to meet in the 1630's and 1640's, and they were summoned again in 1655 and 1660, but their renewal of the *millones* was now fairly automatic. The last cortes of Castile to be held in the seventeenth century were those of 1662. From 1668 the *millones* were renewed by the *junta de asistentes a cortes*, the administrative commission of the cortes, which maintained the legal fiction of representation by sending circular letters to the towns indicating the need to renew the grant for a further six years.

Castile had been taxed too long and too heavily for anyone to mourn the demise of its cortes. Yet in one sense at least the cortes spoke for Castile. In the late sixteenth and early seventeenth centuries they often tried to insist that the money voted be spent exclusively on Castile, particularly on naval armament and defence of the Indies trade, and they had tried to appropriate supplies to this effect.[81] Their priorities were sound enough, and they

[81] José Martínez Cardos, 'Las Indias y las Cortes de Castilla durante los siglos XVI y XVII' *Revista de Indias*, xvi (1956), 207–65, 357–412.

were based on the conviction that Castile was bleeding itself in order to send supplies to other provinces which did not contribute fairly to their own defence, much less to the common cause of the Monarchy. As taxation of Castile reached saturation point and brought diminishing returns, this conviction began to be shared by royal officials and advisers, and the non-Castilian provinces came under closer scrutiny. The call to action was given by Olivares.

CHAPTER V

THE GREAT CRISIS: 1640 AND AFTER

1. THE UNION OF ARMS

THE defence of Spanish interests in Europe and overseas was more than Castile could bear alone. The Thirty Years War laid an extra burden on a land already depopulated and impoverished by previous calls on its resources. Increasing demands on Castile coincided with rapid diminution of Castile's remaining assets. The transatlantic trade now entered a period of severe crisis; it experienced a major contraction in the years 1629–31, which anticipated the great collapse of 1639–41.[1] The crown was thus starved of its revenue and the economy of its life-blood. It was not Castilian prejudice, therefore, but fiscal and military emergency which caused the central government to look more closely at the non-Castilian provinces and to seek to tap their resources.

Economists and ministers alike were calling for a more equitable distribution of taxation within the empire and demanding that the various provinces should pay at least for their own defence. In the reforming environment of the early 1620's the demands became more pressing. Fernández Navarrete spoke for many *arbitristas* when he argued that Castile was paying more than its fair share of defence costs: 'as far as possible there should be a just and proportionate adjustment of taxation in the Provinces, so that the whole weight does not fall on the centre'.[2] In April 1622 the Council of Finance was even more explicit:

> The greatest benefit from these frontier garrisons accrues to the provinces themselves, and so they should reasonably be expected to maintain them, and Castile should not have to bear the entire burden, especially when the royal revenues are in such an impossible state, and the Castilians so exhausted and oppressed with tributes.[3]

Similar arguments had long been used by the cortes of Castile. A royal decree of 28 October 1622 to the towns represented in the cortes discussed the possibility of replacing the *millones* by a subsidy guaranteed to maintain 30,000 troops and of extending this to other provinces:

[1] Chaunu, *Séville et l'Atlantique*, viii, 2, 2, pp. 1797–1848.
[2] *Conservación de monarquías*, p. 496.   [3] Quoted in Elliott, *Revolt of the Catalans*, p. 192

The greatest reform would be an arrangement whereby the other provinces, Aragon, Portugal, Navarre, Vizcaya and Guipúzcoa, made an equivalent contribution towards troops, for although they benefit equally from the defence and conservation of the Monarchy they have hitherto escaped the costs. They have no justification for their exemption. Natural justice insists that all those who enjoy common benefits should make appropriate contributions. Moreover, they do not possess *fueros* or laws granting exemption; and, even if they did, they would not be justified in invoking them.[4]

These were likely to remain pious aspirations unless the central government was prepared to force the issue. The Italian states, it is true, contributed towards imperial defence in Italy, and they probably bore the greatest burden after Castile. The Low Countries contributed less, granted their resources, but they were in the front line of almost permanent warfare. Navarre, Aragon and Valencia gave only small and occasional amounts. Portugal and Catalonia utterly refused to contribute to general defence costs, as though what happened beyond their frontiers was no concern of theirs.[5] But the constitutional structure of the Spanish empire, and the diversity of laws within it, prevented the central government from taxing the periphery by executive means, and raised the issue of royal prerogative *versus* regional privilege. This was the problem which Olivares inherited in 1621 and to which he brought his feverish and dynamic talents. He took up ideas of fiscal uniformity which had been in the air for some time and incorporated them into a theory of empire. He then spent the rest of his political life attempting to apply the theory.

It was the object of Olivares to rationalise the imperial machinery in order to make it an efficient instrument of defence; this could be done by drawing into a common pool all the Monarchy's resources of manpower and revenue for deployment where and when they were needed. To do this the empire had to be unified, and the obstacles were the different constitutions of the component parts. A precondition of uniform recruitment and taxation was a uniform law, and this inevitably meant Castilian law. But responsibilities would bring rewards. In return for their constitutional sacrifices, the provinces would receive the fruits of empire—offices and opportunities—as well as its burdens. To this extent Olivares was a champion not of Castile but of Spain, of a new and unified Spain where rights and duties were equally shared.[6]

---

[4] Quoted in González Palencia, *La Junta de Reformación*, p. 406.
[5] See Domínguez Ortiz, *Política y hacienda de Felipe IV*, pp. 157–59.
[6] Elliott, *op. cit.*, pp. 198–208.

These ideas were developed by Olivares in a secret memorandum which he presented to Philip IV early in 1625.[7] At the heart of his argument was the idea of unification:

> The most important thing in Your Majesty's Monarchy is for you to become king of Spain: by this I mean, Sir, that Your Majesty should not be content with being king of Portugal, of Aragon, of Valencia and count of Barcelona, but should secretly plan and work to reduce these kingdoms of which Spain is composed to the style and laws of Castile, with no difference whatsoever. And if Your Majesty achieves this, you will be the most powerful prince in the world.

But how was this object to be achieved? One method, according to Olivares, was to follow a policy of attraction, offering non-Castilians favours, offices, titles and brides in Castile; this was the best method, but the slowest. Alternatively the king could negotiate with the various provinces, but he should do this from a position of strength while his armed forces were not occupied on foreign fronts. There remained a 'third way'. The king could go in person to the province in question and provoke a rebellion there; this would give him a pretext for using an army to restore law and order, and thereby provide an opportunity to reorganise the province in conformity with Castile on the basis of conquest. This method, though not so justified as the others, would be more effective.

Olivares seems to have included the 'third way' in order to give the king a complete picture of the various options open to him, not because he favoured its adoption. There is no evidence that he ever sought to implement the proposal, while there is ample evidence that he preferred the ways of attraction and negotiation. For he recognised the aspirations of the non-Castilians and their resentment at exclusion from honours, offices and privileges, and he always argued that they should have equality of opportunity with Castile. These are not the sentiments of a crude Castilian nationalist: they imply a concept of empire transcending particularism, either of Castile or of the other parts. In the years following this memorandum, it is true, Olivares did little to widen the distribution of offices, apart from appointing an Aragonese, Miguel Santos de San Pedro, to the presidency of the Council of Castile. But the reason for his diffidence may have been the difficulty of synchronising this reform with evidence of co-operation from the periphery. Such a plan would certainly provoke opposition in Castile and would have to be accompanied by a clear demonstration that the periphery was assuming its obligations.

[7] Printed in part in Marañón, *op. cit.*, appendix xviii, pp. 440–47; see also Elliott, *op. cit.*, pp. 199–203; Eulogio Zudaire Huarte, 'Ideario político de D. Gaspar de Guzmán, privado de Felipe IV', *Hispania*, xxv (1965), 413–25; Hume, *op. cit.*, pp. 142–43.

And this, as will be seen, was something which Olivares could not guarantee. Yet he remained remarkably free of the prejudices shared by most Castilian aristocrats, who regarded their regional neighbours with some contempt and treated them as second-class citizens. Olivares had no time for this attitude, and in the Council of State in 1632 he rebuked those who made discriminatory remarks against Catalans: 'In saying "Spaniards" it must be understood that there is no difference between one nation and another of those included within the limits of Spain, and the same is to be understood of the Portuguese as of the Catalans'.[8]

As assimilation was a lengthy process and force not seriously contemplated, the memorandum of 1625 remained a long-term plan, to be achieved by evolutionary rather than revolutionary means. For the immediate defence of the empire and relief of Castile he had a second plan, more pragmatic in its approach, the co-called Union of Arms. This was designed to secure an army of reservists, 140,000 strong, recruited and paid in appropriate proportions by the various provinces, for deployment wherever and whenever an emergency occurred. From each according to its resources, to each according to its needs. The idea was sound enough in principle and promising in prospects, for military and financial co-operation could be a step towards political unification. But it still came up against the autonomous rights of the regions. A decree from Madrid was not likely to overcome constitutional objections to raising money and troops in Aragon, Valencia and Catalonia for use outside these provinces. These may have been archaic privileges, inappropriate in a seventeenth-century state, but they could not be circumvented. There was no short cut to unification, only a long and tortuous road, with many pitfalls and obstacles. And at the end of it what had Olivares to offer the provinces? An interminable war and a devastated Castile, objects not of attraction but revulsion.

The eastern regions prepared for battle, mobilising their legal reserves and polishing their constitutional weapons. Their first line of defence was their cortes. In January 1626 Philip IV opened the cortes of Aragon at Barbastro; despite the efforts of Olivares—a mixture of bullying and bribery—they proved decidedly refractory, and they had offered nothing to the Union of Arms when in March the king moved on to Monzón, where he had summoned the cortes of Valencia. The Valencians, too, were stubborn; they pleaded great poverty as a result of the expulsion of the moriscos and, like the Aragonese, they refused to supply troops for service outside the province. Olivares thereupon lowered his demands, making the military service voluntary but still insisting on the money to pay the men. After long and acrimonious debates the cortes of Valencia were finally persuaded to vote a

[8] Quoted in Elliott, op. cit., p. 204.

subsidy of 1,080,000 ducats on these terms; this the king accepted as sufficient to maintain 1,000 infantrymen for fifteen years, at the rate of 72,000 ducats a year. Eventually the Aragonese accepted similar terms, offering either 2,000 paid volunteers for fifteen years or 144,000 ducats a year to maintain this number of men.[9]

The Catalans were more difficult. They had already had one brush with Philip IV over their refusal to accept a viceroy nominated by Madrid before the king had visited them and taken the traditional oath to observe their laws; to resolve this conflict the central government had had to back down on two important items it had fought for in the previous reign, the carrying of arms and the Barcelona 'fifths'.[10] When, on 28 March 1626, the king opened in Barcelona the first cortes for twenty-seven years the Catalans were no more ready to co-operate.[11] The Catalan cortes, unlike those of Castile, had legislative powers, and they regarded law-making as their first function; their second function was to secure redress of grievances. Only after securing satisfaction on these two matters would they pass to the third stage of their proceedings, the granting of supplies; these depended on unanimity throughout the three estates of the cortes and were accompanied by receipt of *mercedes*, or royal favours. The cortes possessed a formidable instrument of resistance—the act of dissent, which any member could make in matters of grace and justice and which, if accepted, then stopped all proceedings. The crown could only overcome this tactic if it were prepared to buy agreement with huge concessions.

Olivares merely wanted a quick vote of subsidy, but he restrained himself and accepted the order of proceedings with good grace. By 18 April, however, the royal patience was wearing thin, and the cortes were presented with an urgent message from Philip IV:

> My children, one and a thousand times I say and repeat that I have no wish to remove your *fueros* and immunities, but only to give you many new ones. To serve with paid men, as is proposed to you, is not to infringe your constitutions nor to do anything contrary to custom, but to revive the glory of your nation, and the name that for so long has been forgotten, but was once feared throughout Europe. And by this means I wish your countrymen to obtain the leading places in my kingdoms—places to which their valour and heroism will surely take them.[12]

---

[9] Danvila, *El poder civil en España*, iii, 59–76, for extracts of debates at Monzón and Barbastro. The sums voted, small in themselves, were further eroded by resistance to actual collection.

[10] Elliott, *op. cit.*, pp. 148–81; Eulogio Zudaire Huarte, *El Conde-Duque y Cataluña* (Madrid, 1964), pp. 1–33; see above, pp. 51–55.

[11] Elliott, *op. cit.*, pp. 215–47; Zudaire Huarte, *op. cit.*, pp. 35–59.

[12] Quoted in Elliott, *op. cit.*, pp. 230–31.

The cortes were not impressed by this call to greatness, but looked instead at its cost, 16,000 men. This, they argued, was beyond the capacity of Catalonia and a violation of its laws. So they returned to their practice of dissent; one town after another laid claim to fiscal and administrative concessions, and Barcelona led the way. No monarch could possibly submit to such demands if he wished to remain sovereign and solvent. The most that Olivares was prepared to concede was to cancel the request for paid infantrymen and to take instead a subsidy of 250,000 ducats a year for fifteen years. 'The money is to be spent solely in this province, for the defence of its frontiers and the upkeep of galleys, not galleons. It is to be entirely collected by natives of the province, and is not to pass through the hands of royal officials.'[13] But the cortes found the new version no more acceptable than the old.

Olivares's estimate suffered to some degree from defective statistics. He assumed—as many Catalans did—that the population of the principality amounted to about 1 million. In fact it was probably no more than 400,000.[14] This population paid some 160,000 *lliures* a year in local taxes to the *Diputació*, the standing committee of the cortes. In addition Olivares was asking for 260,000 *lliures* a year for the central government. He was probably asking too much. Did the Catalans protest too much? The principality, if not as wealthy as Olivares imagined, was certainly wealthier than Aragon and Valencia, and these provinces decided, reluctantly, to co-operate with the crown. Could not the funds of the *Diputació* serve to defray a portion of the Catalan contribution? Unfortunately, in spite of the *Diputació's* regular income over the last twenty years, its funds had been exhausted by a combination of peculation and maladministration. Catalan institutions were better equipped to resist than to govern. Olivares tried to ease the task of the local administration by offering to cancel the arrears of 'fifths' of all towns which voted the required subsidy and to make no further claims on them until the next cortes. But weeks of argument, negotiation and bribery were of no avail. On 3 May, in conditions of near riot, the cortes refused to vote the subsidy.[15] The next day the king left Barcelona in disgust.

On his return to Castile Olivares published the Union of Arms as though it were an accomplished fact and Castile were now going to be relieved of its burdens. But this was propaganda and no one was deceived. Castile and its dependencies continued to bear the brunt of defence expenditure. Peru was assigned a quota of 350,000 ducats, Mexico 250,000, to be applied to naval defence on the transatlantic route. So the colonies, already heavily taxed,

---

[13] Quoted *ibid.*, p. 237.

[14] J. Nadal and E. Giralt, *La population catalane de 1553 à 1717* (Paris, 1960), pp. 40-41, 341-44; Vilar, *La Catalogne dans l'Espagne moderne*, i, 617-20, 630.

[15] Carrera Pujal, *Historia política y económica de Cataluña*, i, 196.

made their contribution to the Union of Arms and in a form which became in fact a new permanent tax.[16] But Catalonia continued to resist, becoming, in its very isolation, a political as well as a fiscal problem, and one which Olivares had committed himself to solving. To the accompaniment of mounting resentment in Catalonia and of growing anti-Catalan sentiment among the Castilian ruling class, Olivares began to turn the screw more tightly on the principality, at a time, 1629–32, when commercial depression and plague were further reducing its fiscal capacity.[17] His methods were various. First he subverted the independence of the Council of Aragon, which he regarded as too closely tied to regional interests. In February 1628 the king replaced the office of vice-chancellor, hitherto a preserve of natives of the eastern provinces, by that of president, after the fashion of the other councils; and to the new office was appointed the marquis of Montesclaros, a close friend of Olivares. The duke of Medina de las Torres, Olivares's son-in-law, became treasurer-general. But the key man in Olivares's system was Jerónimo de Villanueva, an Aragonese from a long-established bureaucratic dynasty. Nominally Villanueva was simply *protonotario* of the Council of Aragon, an official in the chancery section of the Council. In fact he was to Olivares what Olivares was to the king, a *valido*. From 1626 he began to dominate the Council of Aragon and to control its business with the eastern provinces. He became, in addition, secretary of the Council of State, a member of the Council of War, and a member of all the important juntas. A powerful, intolerant, and ruthless man, with a hint of religious heterodoxy about him, Villanueva was eager to relieve Olivares of the day-to-day burden of eastern affairs, much as Olivares relieved the king of the burden of empire.

Catalonia, meanwhile, with Barcelona in the lead, stubbornly refused to co-operate. Olivares therefore decided to appeal once more to the Catalan cortes. It is difficult to see what he hoped to achieve. In matters of *fueros* there were probably only two courses of action, either to leave well alone or to act with speed and force. Lengthy discussion was likely to produce neither peace nor profit. Yet in this his second appeal to Catalonia Olivares was prepared to give the cortes even more time to make up its mind. The king's place in Barcelona was taken by his brother, the Cardinal Infante Ferdinand, who acted simultaneously as president of the cortes and viceroy of Catalonia, while the count of Oñate was appointed his political adviser. The results were not encouraging. The business of the cortes was brought to a halt while the city of Barcelona wrangled interminably over its rights, privileges and demands, and resisted any concession to the crown. There is some evidence that members of the corrupt *Diputació* were working to sabotage relations

[16] Domínguez Ortiz, 'Los caudales de Indias y la política exterior de Felipe IV', *op. cit.*, pp. 317–19.
[17] Elliott, *op. cit.*, pp. 248–72.

between the cortes and the crown in order to prevent investigation of the *Diputació* itself. But subversion, if it took place, was hardly necessary. By now the crown did not even know how to withdraw from the conflict without loss of prestige. In August 1632 its exasperated officials in Barcelona were instructed to display the utmost 'tolerance and gentleness, and be prepared to consider any measure that would conclude the Cortes to the general satisfaction, even if it brings little benefit to the royal treasury'.[18] For the crown there was little satisfaction and even less benefit. At the end of October the cortes were prorogued. Catalonia still remained outside the Union of Arms and still constituted the major obstacle to Olivares's plans for fiscal uniformity.

2. THE REVOLT OF CATALONIA

For the government of Philip IV Catalonia was first a fiscal problem. Since 1626 it had also been a political problem. In May 1635, with the outbreak of the Franco-Spanish war, it became part of Spain's international problems. France's entry into the Thirty Years War had been foreseen for some time, but, harassed as it was on many fronts, the Spanish government was ill-prepared for the emergency. Now it had to improvise the raising of troops and money from a depopulated and impoverished community. Its methods were arbitrary taxation reinforced by appeals to patriotism.[19] *Juros* were heavily taxed, millions of ducats of vellon were coined, offices were sold on an unprecedented scale, and the cortes of Castile were browbeaten into voting new subsidies. Ministers were sent into the provinces to raise troops and loans. The higher nobility were ordered to raise companies at their own cost, *hidalgos* to hold themselves ready for military service. In Castile there was some response to these promptings, but it seemed like a drop in the ocean of Spain's commitments. Defence expenditure for 1636 exceeded 9 million escudos, most of it for the Low Countries. In 1637 defence and government costs rose to over 13 million escudos, while income was no more than 7¼ million; and *asientos* were becoming more difficult to obtain. The government now lived from hand to mouth, in the midst of financial chaos which lasted until the end of the reign.

The military returns from this expenditure were not impressive. In 1635 the Cardinal Infante took the offensive against France, striking hopefully from the Low Countries towards Paris; by August 1636 his army had reached Corbie. But his superiors in Madrid could not help him by opening a second front in southern France, and the Spanish war effort gradually lost its momentum. In October 1637 the Dutch recaptured Breda. In December 1638 Bernard of Weimar took Breisach, thus cutting the route from Milan

[18] Quoted *ibid.*, p. 282.   [19] Domínguez Ortiz, *Política y hacienda de Felipe IV*, pp. 51–60.

to the Low Countries. Attempts to supply and reinforce the northern army by sea were extremely hazardous and culminated in a major naval disaster; on 21 October 1639 Admiral Tromp destroyed the fleet of Antonio de Oquendo at the battle of the Downs. These reverses were due not so much to Spain's weakness as to her inability to concentrate her not inconsiderable military power on any one sector at any one time. She was now seriously overcommitted, with too many enemies and no major allies. Olivares appreciated the situation and in the late 1630's he seriously sought peace. 'God wants us to make peace', he remarked, 'for he is visibly depriving us of all the means of making war'.[20] By 1640 he had drastically reduced his terms in an effort to liquidate the war with France. But there was a limit to what he could concede. He could not countenance Dutch conquests in Brazil and expect to retain Portuguese allegiance.[21] And Richelieu refused to break his alliance with the Dutch and to press them into relinquishing their position in Brazil. So Olivares had to continue to plan for war. But where could he get additional supplies? American revenue in 1639 was not enough to cover the *asientos*; in 1640 nothing arrived from the Indies, and the whole budget was thrown out of gear. In these circumstances contributions from outside Castile were more urgently needed than ever. So attention was again focused on Catalonia.

By now, however, the Catalan problem had acquired a new dimension. From the standpoint of Madrid Catalonia was no longer simply a source to be exploited but a strategic problem to be solved, for Catalonia was France's immediate neighbour and Spain's outer defence against French invasion. Was Catalonia a security risk? The suspicion haunted some minds in Castile, but not that of Olivares. With typical ebullience he saw war on the Pyrenees front as a challenge which, if firmly grasped, might transform Catalonia from a liability into an asset. It became his policy in fact to force Catalonia into contributing to imperial defence by making the province a theatre of operations in the war with France.[22] This was not the sinister project so frequently attributed to Olivares. It was not his intention to put an army into Catalonia in order deliberately to provoke a rebellion, the crushing of which would then be a pretext to abolish Catalan liberties; even Olivares at his most extreme did not plan the total destruction of the Catalan constitutions. He simply wanted to involve Catalonia in the problems, and therefore the finances, of the Monarchy, and so to end its political and fiscal immunity.

Olivares worked on this principle from late 1635. But it was not easy to implement. Catalan resistance to taxation continued. Between 1626 and

---

[20] Report of Olivares to king, March 1640, in Cánovas, *Estudios*, i, 414.
[21] See below, pp. 110–12.
[22] Elliott, *op. cit.*, pp. 356–61, 375–90; Zudaire Huarte, *op. cit.*, pp. 119–26.

Defence of Cadiz against the English

1637, it is true, Barcelona provided 308,500 *lliures* in loans or gifts to the crown; but this was only half the value of arrears of 'fifths' owed by the city since 1599.[23] And it was not taxation. Recruitment of troops was equally difficult. The Catalans refused to supply a contingent for the hard-pressed Italian front. In the course of 1637 they also refused to supply troops for a diversionary blow into Languedoc to relieve the pressure on Italy and the Low Countries. In 1638, when French forces penetrated into Guipúzcoa and laid siege to Fuenterrabía, contingents from virtually the whole of Spain, including Aragon and Valencia, came to the rescue of the beleaguered town. Again Catalonia was absent. The Catalans, of course, invoked their constitutions, which prevented their recruitment for duties outside their own frontiers. But no power could possibly conduct a war on these principles, with one hand tied behind its back, never able to anticipate an attack or to take the offensive. Yet the Catalans were adamant. And now the resistance of Barcelona was reinforced by that of a resurgent *Diputació*, posing once again as the defender of the laws and liberties of the fatherland and taking advantage of the crown's financial difficulties to bargain more toughly.

If the laws of Catalonia frustrated legitimate defence interests there was an arguable case for changing the laws. This, at any rate, seems to have been the assumption of Olivares and his advisers. When they planned military operations for 1639 they deliberately chose Catalonia as the front on which to fight France, in order, among other things, to force Catalonia to contribute to the war effort, 'finding itself directly involved, as up to now it seems not to have been involved, with the common welfare of the Monarchy and of these kingdoms'.[24] In the event the campaign brought little credit to Madrid or Barcelona. Operations were seriously handicapped by constant bickering over the raising and payment of troops in the principality, and by mutual recriminations over Castillian charges that Catalan troops were deserting on a large scale. Military ineptitude compounded the confusion; and Salces, having been foolishly lost, was extravagantly recovered, at heavy cost in Catalan lives. Nevertheless, as a result of this campaign, Catalonia had been hounded into raising troops, these had been harried to the front, and a royal army about 9,000 strong now wintered in Catalonia in preparation for the spring campaign in 1640. Inevitably the army infringed the constitutions, for these defined Catalan obligations of billeting in such a way that they were insufficient for basic maintenance. This in turn affected the behaviour of the troops, whose excesses Viceroy Santa Coloma was too weak to prevent and the Catalans too exasperated to stomach.

By the end of February 1640 the patience of Olivares was exhausted. 'We always have to look and see if a constitution says this or that', he wrote to

---

[23] Elliott, *op. cit.*, p. 333.　　　　　　　　　　[24] Quoted *ibid.*, p. 361.

Santa Coloma. 'We have to discover what the customary usage is, even when it is a question of the supreme law, of the actual preservation and defence of the province. . . . The Catalans ought to see more of the world than Catalonia'.[25] He ordered firmer measures for billeting and payment of troops in Catalonia, and for further recruitment there. A member of the *Diputació* and two members of Barcelona city council were gaoled. And preparations were made to involve Catalonia irremediably in the campaign of 1640. Malice played no part in the count duke's policy: far from trying to provoke the Catalans into revolt, he was complacent enough to believe they were basically loyal.

The Catalans, too, had had enough. Suddenly, in the first weeks of May 1640, the pent-up resentments of the last four decades and the more immediate anger at the presence of the royal army exploded into rebellion. Peasants in the western areas of Gerona and La Selva attacked the *tercios* which were billeted on them. Violence was ruthless, organised, and inflamed by agitators. By the end of May peasant forces had infiltrated Barcelona. In June they were joined by the *segadors*, casual labourers, who soon had the city at their mercy. Royal judges were hunted like animals at bay, and the viceroy was killed on a beach of Barcelona as he sought to embark for safety.

The reaction of Madrid to these events was predictable. Ministers urged that the time had come to crush Catalonia once and for all. Olivares did not share this view. He still clung to his belief that reasonable accommodation was possible and that the Catalans would respond to a genuine offer of equal status and opportunity within the Monarchy.[26] He therefore advocated leniency and the granting of a general pardon. The murder of the viceroy, however, shattered even Olivares; in a mood of hatred and despair he now lost his faith in the Catalans and appreciated that he had a major rebellion on his hands which no government could condone. But for the moment the government was impotent. Its armies and resources were already committed on several fronts and could not be focused on Catalonia.

If the rebellion was beyond the control of the government, it was soon out of the hands of the Catalan leaders. For alongside the political opposition which they represented there was a social revolution over which they had no control. From the beginning the rebels had attacked the property and the persons of wealthy citizens. Rural agitators infiltrated into the towns and collaborated with lawless elements among the urban poor. The leadership of Barcelona and its oligarchy was brushed aside as the forces of agrarian discontent swept into action. This was a rebellion of impoverished and landless peasants against wealthy farmers and noble landowners; of the underprivileged

[25] Olivares to Santa Coloma, 29 February 1640, *ibid.*, pp. 400–1.
[26] *Ibid.*, pp. 433–42.

in the towns against the urban oligarchies; of repressed bandit elements against the forces of law and order.[27] The Catalan leaders had unleashed a tiger, and soon their country was rent by civil war as well as by revolution. Caught between the authority of the king and the radicalism of the mob, the leaders of the political revolution turned to France. The inconsistency of their position was now fully exposed. For all their opposition to the king they were incapable of ruling Catalonia independently, and so they sought the protection of the king's enemies. The *Diputació*, or people acting on its behalf, seem to have established contact with France as early as April 1640, before the revolution began.[28] The initiative was taken by Pau Claris, canon of Urgell, member of the *Diputació* and a leader of resistance to Madrid, and Francesco de Tamarit, another member of the *Diputació*, whose political activities had recently landed him in jail. And for his part Richelieu had his agents in Catalonia.

As the news from Catalonia became worse, Olivares too was caught in a dilemma. To offer reconciliation might be interpreted as weakness and set a bad example to other equally hard-pressed provinces. To crush Catalonia by military action, on the other hand, he really needed peace with France, as Richelieu knew to his advantage. Yet military action was now called for. Since the loss of Barcelona the government had used the port of Tortosa for the movement of troops to Italy and for supplying the remnants of its forces on the Catalan front. But in July Tortosa too revolted and deprived Spain of a vital link in its imperial communications. So preparations were made to send an army against Catalonia. Even now the intention of Olivares was not to destroy Catalonia's constitutions but only 'those laws which specifically obstruct good government and the administration of justice, and which stand in the way of uniformity with the other kingdoms of the Crown'.[29] As Castile laboriously mobilised, Catalonia too began to look to its defences. The *Diputació* could not rely on patriotism alone, for the Catalans were no more disposed to accept military service for defence against Castile than they had been for defence against France. So on 24 September the *Diputació* submitted a formal request to Paris for French protection and military assistance. And in October it entered into an agreement with France whereby it allowed French ships to use Catalan ports and undertook to pay for the upkeep of 3,000 troops which France would send to Catalonia.[30]

As Olivares remarked, Spain had another Holland on its hands. He was now dispirited and pessimistic, believing that this was a war which no one

[27] *Ibid.*, pp. 431–32, 459–65; Zudaire Huarte, *op. cit.*, pp. 249–82.
[28] José Sanabre, *La acción de Francia en Cataluña en la pugna por la hegemonía de Europa* (1640–1659) (Barcelona, 1956), pp. 91–94; Zudaire Huarte, *op. cit.*, pp. 283–86, 299–300.
[29] Paper by Olivares, 11 August 1640, in Elliott, *op. cit.*, pp. 497–98.
[30] Sanabre, *op. cit.*, pp. 103–6.

could win, 'for one cannot talk of success in an action against one's own vassals, in which all gain must be loss'.[31] He had great difficulty in mobilising
an army in Castile and he had to rely on methods which had hardly changed
since the middle ages. City militias were ordered to stand to, nobles to arm
their vassals, *hidalgos* and *caballeros* of the military orders to follow the king
to war.[32] The result was disappointing. Barely 1,000 nobility and gentry
answered the call, and troops were equally difficult to find. When an army of
20,000 was finally assembled, it seemed the height of folly to entrust this
precious commodity to the command of the marquis of los Vélez, viceroy
elect of Catalonia, who had no military experience and few qualities of leadership. Tortosa was taken without much opposition at the end of November,
but in the advance on Barcelona the army's behaviour, particularly the mas-
sacre of prisoners, reinforced the Catalans' determination to resist. On 23
January 1641 the principality placed itself under the government of the king
of France in return for French military protection. The joint Catalan–French
forces successfully defended Barcelona against the army of Castile, and the
incompetent los Vélez promptly ordered a retreat. There would be no prompt
return.

While Spain suffered temporary dismemberment by the revolt of Catalonia, the Catalans suffered much more. Now, with cruel irony, they had
achieved a kind of parity with Castile: in the years following 1640 they too
became the victims of war, and they too were forced to endure heavy defence
expenditure, monetary inflation, economic stagnation, plague, famine, and
finally loss of fertile territory.[33] They acquired the burden of power without
any of the fruits. Their last state was worse than their first.

French policy in Catalonia was dominated by military considerations; they
now had a base in Spain, to be used primarily for striking into Aragon and
Valencia. They appointed a French viceroy and packed the administration
with known friends of France. They insisted on the Catalans' billeting, supplying and paying the French troops, who looked increasingly like an army
of occupation.[34] Catalonia became merely one of the various French theatres
of war. In 1642, with the conquest of Rosellón and the capture of Monzón
and Lérida, it was a successful theatre. But in 1643–44 Philip IV's armies began
to strike back, recovering Monzón and Lérida where, in July 1644, the king
took a solemn oath to observe the Catalan constitutions. Between 1646 and
1648 the French were held to a stalemate in Catalonia; when the Peace of
Westphalia deprived them of their Dutch allies and the Fronde began to

---

[31] Quoted in Elliott, *op. cit.*, p. 504.
[32] Domínguez Ortiz, 'La movilización de la nobleza castellana en 1640', *Anuario de Historia del
Derecho Español*, xxv (1955), 799–823.
[33] Vilar, *op. cit.*, i, 633.
[34] Sanabre, *op. cit.*, p. 148.

occupy their attentions at home, Catalonia ceased to figure prominently in French calculations.

France exploited Catalonia economically as well as militarily. French merchants poured grain and manufactured goods into the newly acquired market, and it soon became clear that commercially Catalonia had even less future with France than with Castile.[35] Unlike the Dutch, the Catalans had no colonial trade as a basis for independent growth; and as they constituted no threat to Castile's American monopoly their cause attracted little international interest.[36] The final blow to Catalan fortunes was delivered by the great plague of 1650–54 which caused severe mortality—claiming 36,000 victims in Barcelona alone—among a people already suffering from wartime malnutrition.[37]

The substitution of Louis XIII of France for Philip IV of Spain solved none of Catalonia's problems. All the complaints the Catalans had held against Castile they now held against France, but to a greater degree, and with less understanding from the absolutist government in Paris. Internal divisions endemic in the principality came to the surface once more, and Catalonia was split between the partisans of France and those of Spain, between the few who profited from offices and opportunities with the French and the many who resented the depredations of the French armies and the predominance of French merchants. The growing alienation from France presented Philip IV with the opportunity to make a supreme bid to recover the principality. In mid-1651 the Spanish army under Don John of Austria, Philip IV's bastard son, advanced on Barcelona and began a lengthy siege of the city, while naval forces established a blockade. The French were unable to relieve Barcelona and it surrendered on 13 October 1652, accepting the sovereignty of Philip IV, with Don John as his viceroy, in return for a general amnesty and the king's promise to preserve the constitutions.[38] France still held Rosellón and continued to wage frontier warfare, but its object was now simply to win bargaining counters for the peace table. It had some success. By the Peace of the Pyrenees (7 November 1659) Spain—and Catalonia—lost both Rosellón and Conflent. But Spain had regained the allegiance of Catalonia and the Catalans could argue that they had preserved their laws and privileges. The Catalan ruling class had learnt some lessons. For the maintenance of their status and property and the supply of law and order they needed a superior sovereignty; their country did not possess the resources for independence and it did not wish to be a satellite of France; the best terms they could get were those from Spain.

[35] E. Giralt, 'La colonia mercantil francesa de Barcelona', *Estudios de Historia Moderna*, vi (Barcelona, 1956), 217–78.
[36] Sanabre, *op. cit.*, pp. 354–55.   [37] Nadal and Giralt, *La population catalane*, pp. 42–44.
[38] Sanabre, *op. cit.*, pp. 533–44; Reglà, *Els virreis de Catalunya*, p. 142.

In the course of discovering this they had led their people into bloodshed and deprivation and had inflicted a grievous wound on the rest of Spain. The role of the Catalan revolt in Spain's mid-century crisis is difficult to define with precision. England too had a civil war about the same time and came out of it a major military power. A basic factor in Spain's crisis was the depression in the Indies trade from 1629.[39] The collapse of maritime defences, the decay of Spanish shipping, the dwindling of trade with America and the decreasing returns therefrom, all caused a profound crisis in the Spanish Atlantic from which Spain never really recovered in the seventeenth century. Once she had lost her last remaining asset, the wealth from America, she was in serious trouble. The crisis in colonial trade not only hit the crown's revenues directly but also reduced the influx of private capital into Castile and thus damaged all sectors of the economy. This was a permanent shock and would have reduced Spain's power regardless of the revolt of Catalonia. But the depression in the Atlantic sector was one of the reasons why the crown had to look elsewhere—including Catalonia and Portugal—for additional revenue, and this was one of the causes of the alienation of these provinces. At this point the Catalan revolution played a crucial role. It prevented Spain from exploiting France's internal instability, and embroiled her in a disastrous and costly civil war at the very moment when she needed all her diminished reserves of money and manpower for campaigns abroad; these reserves now had to be diverted to Catalonia, thus precipitating Spain's collapse. At the same time the Catalan revolt provided an example and an opportunity to the Portuguese and encouraged them to make their own bid for independence. This in turn worsened the crisis in the Atlantic sector.

3. THE SECESSION OF PORTUGAL

Catalonia was a small part of the Spanish imperium, a country orientated towards the Mediterranean and the past. For Spain there was a great security problem in its revolt but not much at stake economically. Portugal was an even greater security risk, for Portugal was more valuable, being an Atlantic power with an overseas empire.

Portugal, like Catalonia, presented a fiscal problem to Castile. It supplied no regular revenue to the central treasury, and its Iberian defences had to be subsidised by Castile, which was also expected to come to the periodic defence of Brazil. Olivares therefore planned to press Portugal too into his Union of Arms, and to the Portuguese, as to the Catalans, he wished to offer improved status and opportunities within the Monarchy.[40] Continuing a

[39] Chaunu, *Séville et l'Atlantique*, viii, 2, 2, pp. 1793–1851.
[40] Marañón, *op. cit.*, pp. 317–18, 441–42.

policy begun by Lerma, though with hardly more success, he first tried to infiltrate the Portuguese administration; in 1634 Princess Margaret of Savoy was sent to govern the country, with a group of Castilian advisers who caused great resentment among the Portuguese bureaucracy. He then attempted to tax Portugal by introducing a regular contribution of 500,000 cruzados a year towards its own defence. In the period 1619–30 Lisbon had already made extraordinary contributions of one kind or another, some of them voluntary offerings, most of them forced loans, to the amount of 1 million cruzados.[41] New demands only increased the irritation of the Portuguese merchant class. They also led to tax riots in 1637 in Evora and other towns; but as these were essentially lower-class convulsions, from which the Portuguese leaders held aloof, they were put down without difficulty. Class divisions within Portugal gave the Spanish government a certain source of strength. While the lower sectors of society, and the lower clergy, traditionally resented Spanish rule, the aristocracy were reconciled to it by the greater opportunities available to them in a larger empire. By 1640, however, the Portuguese aristocracy too were alienated. The cause of their resistance was overtly the issue of military service. For in addition to money Olivares wanted troops from Portugal. Some 6,000 troops were impressed for service in Italy, but the revolt of Catalonia caused them to be diverted to the army recruited for the Catalan front. Olivares was even more anxious to mobilise the Portuguese nobility, with the duke of Braganza at their head, in order that they should be employed in putting down revolution in Catalonia instead of fomenting revolution at home. But the Portuguese nobility, sensing that the time for action had arrived, refused to be lured out of the country; and in the autumn of 1640 some of them began to plan revolution.

Summons to military service was the occasion rather than the cause of Portuguese resistance. In a country which still remembered past independence there was bound to be latent resentment at the loss of sovereignty involved in the union of the crowns. But why did the Portuguese nobility, hitherto supporters of the union, withdraw allegiance in 1640? Olivares's attempt to press Portugal into the Union of Arms was too diffident to provoke a revolution. The revolt of Catalonia gave the Portuguese a model and an opportunity rather than a motive. The real cause of Portuguese alienation must be sought elsewhere, in an area of opportunity which the Portuguese particularly valued and in which they had a vital stake, the Iberian overseas empire. Olivares argued that as Castile helped Portugal in her attempts to recover Brazil then Portugal should help Castile to recover Catalonia. But what was Castile's record in Brazil? If the Portuguese ruling class ceased to find any advantage in union with Spain, was it because the transatlantic interests

[41] Mauro, *Le Portugal et l'Atlantique*, pp. 468–69.

which bound Portugal to Spain in 1621 were no longer effective in 1640?

Portugal's loss of her Asian empire was not a valid test of Iberian collaboration. A trading empire in which Portugal had virtually no commodities to trade was not viable economically; and the Portuguese did not seriously regard Spain as responsible for its defence.[42] In any case loss of the spice trade was more than counterbalanced by the growth of a second Portuguese empire in Brazil. Brazilian sugar became one of the most spectacular growth industries of the early seventeenth century. By 1627–28 there were 200 sugar-mills in Brazil, most of them in the north-east; and an average of 300 sugar-ships left the colony every year, carrying between 70,000 and 80,000 chests of sugar, worth some 4 million cruzados when landed in Portuguese ports.[43] Although this trade had been penetrated by the Dutch, it represented a major investment for Portugal and it yielded valuable returns. Its defence was therefore a vital test of the Iberian partnership. The most serious threat came from the Dutch West India Company, whose ships intercepted large numbers of Portuguese merchant vessels in the South Atlantic and appropriated their rich cargoes. Suggestions were frequently made that a convoy system on the lines of that operated by Spain's transatlantic shipping would provide the best defence against Dutch attacks; and in 1628 Philip IV instructed the Council of Portugal to investigate the possibility.[44] But the idea foundered on the established organisation of the Brazil trade, which was not canalised through monopoly ports, and on the opposition of the sugar producers, merchants and shippers, who were either unable or unwilling to invest the capital needed for the provision of bigger and better armed escorts. Spain, therefore, could hardly be held responsible for the state of Portugal's maritime defences.

The Dutch not only attacked the sugar trade at sea, they also sought to appropriate it at its source. Their first conquest in Brazil drew swift retaliation; and Spain made a large contribution to the relief expedition which recaptured Bahia in 1625.[45] But in 1630 the Dutch West India Company, investing its windfall from the capture of the Mexican silver fleet in 1628, dispatched a second expedition which occupied Olinda and Recife. Within a few years the Dutch had laid the framework of a new colony in north-east Brazil based on the rich province of Pernambuco; there they remained for a quarter of a century and came to appropriate almost half of the sugar trade. Unless the Iberian powers could send a relief expedition and a fleet capable of contesting Dutch sea power in the South Atlantic, there was a distinct possibility that the enemy would conquer the whole of the Brazilian littoral and begin to penetrate Spanish America.

[42] See above, pp. 55–61.   [43] Boxer, *Salvador de Sá*, pp. 178–81.
[44] *Ibid.*, pp. 182–84.   [45] See above, pp. 71–72.

Olivares appreciated that the union of the crowns was on trial. The restitution of Pernambuco became an indispensable Spanish condition for any peace with the Dutch, badly though Spain needed peace. By 1635 Olivares was even prepared to offer the Dutch Breda, 200,000 ducats, and the right to close the Scheldt, if they would return Pernambuco. But the Portuguese wanted more than diplomacy: they wanted military and naval assistance. This too the Spaniards were willing to provide, but they could not provide it quickly. It took over six years to organise a relief expedition, and it was September 1638 before a joint force sailed from Lisbon. Don Fadrique de Toledo, the victor of 1625, declined its command on the gound that it was under strength; the expedition's 41 vessels and 5,000 troops did in fact compare unfavourably with the force dispatched in 1625, a further sign of deterioration in Spain's resources, but reinforcements from Buenos Aires and Rio de Janeiro brought its strength up to 86 sail and 10,000 troops and gave it a clear numerical superiority over the Dutch. In the event the expedition failed not because of the insufficiency of the force but because of the incapacity of its commander, the Portuguese conde da Torre, who was unearthed only after a fruitless search for talent and proved to be totally unqualified for the task. He kept his armada immobile in Bahia for almost the whole of 1639, thus presenting the Dutch with a perfect opportunity to prepare for battle. He finally moved his fleet to Pernambuco; there, in January 1640, he was outfought by a Dutch fleet under half his strength, and after a few days fighting he weakly withdrew, leaving the greater part of his fleet to disperse to the West Indies.[46]

By 1639, therefore, the Iberian partnership had ceased to function effectively. Although the Portuguese themselves conspicuously neglected their imperial defences, Spain as the senior partner had to bear the odium of failure. If Spain failed Portugal it was not through infirmity of will but through poverty of resources. In the Portuguese view Spain was overcommitted elsewhere to the neglect of more vital interests. There had ceased to be any value in the union. Spain could bring to it in the 1630's much less power than in the past. And the Portuguese resented their losses in Brazil from 1630 much more than they had resented their losses in Asia from 1600.[47] Their resentment was aggravated by the fact that they were also in the process of losing one of the greatest advantages accruing from Brazil, their foothold in Spanish America.

At the height of the Brazil trade between 200 and 300 vessels left Portugal annually to cross the South Atlantic; these included many vessels from northern Europe, without counting those which sailed directly from Amsterdam.[48]

[46] Boxer, *Salvador de Sá*, pp. 116–20.   [47] Chaunu, 'Autour de 1640', *Annales*, ix (1954), 44–54.
[48] Chaunu, *Séville et l'Atlantique*, viii, 2, 2, pp. 1328–29, 1833–34.

As Portugal was not a manufacturing country it was obvious that these vessels were exporting merchandise from outside Iberian sources, and on a scale which far exceeded the capacity of the Brazilian market. They were in fact exporting to Spanish America, circumventing the legal route via Panama and Peru, and competing on very favourable terms—these goods were untouched by Spanish taxes—with authorised Spanish exports. Brazil, therefore, became an entrepôt for a vast re-export trade which possibly took half of the Spanish South American market.[49]

The most important point of Portuguese penetration of Spanish America from about 1600 was the Río de la Plata. Merchants from Brazil, the *Peruleiros*, made their way across the pampas, through Tucumán and over the Andes into Upper Peru, where they sold their goods for the coveted silver of Potosí.[50] Across the same route there was a flourishing contraband trade in slaves from Angola, the supply of which the Portuguese virtually monopolised. In addition to trading illegally in Spanish America the Portuguese also settled there, with tacit if not formal permission. Some acquired land, like Salvador de Sá, who married a wealthy creole heiress in Tucumán and thus became the owner of estates strategically placed on the route to Potosí.[51] Others sought and obtained offices. In Peru the Portuguese were prominent in maritime occupations as pilots and owners of vessels; some settled in towns and ports as resident traders, acquiring among other things a virtual monopoly of the export of vicuna wool; others became small landed proprietors.[52] They were also to be found in Mexico, where most of them had improved their prospects as small independent farmers and traders or as wage employees; in the province of Tulancingo, for example, they constituted from 10 to 15 per cent. of the adult male Europeans.[53] This Portuguese invasion of the Spanish Indies was one of their most valuable assets under the union of the crowns. In this sector, at least, Olivares's offer of opportunities was temporarily vindicated; it was not the Castilians who penetrated the Portuguese empire, but the Portuguese who penetrated the empire of Castile.

Inevitably there was a reaction. From about 1630 Spaniards began to resist the Portuguese invasion of their empire. Merchants and colonists, Mexicans

---

[49] Chaunu, 'Autour de 1640', *op. cit.*, p. 53; Canabrava, *O comércio português no Rio da Prata, 1580–1640*, pp. 20–28. Spaniards alleged that 14–18 vessels a year entered Buenos Aires, carrying as much cloth as the *flota* took to Tierra Firme; officials were presumably being bribed into compliance.

[50] Boxer, *Salvador de Sá*, pp. 77–79; Canabrava, *op. cit.*, pp. 96–131; Georges Scelle, *La traite négrière aux Indes de Castille* (2 vols., Paris, 1906), i, 382–484.

[51] Boxer, *Salvador de Sá*, pp. 96–110.

[52] María Encarnación Rodríguez Vicente, *El Tribunal del Consulado de Lima en la primera mitad del siglo XVII* (Madrid, 1960), pp. 70–73, 173, 264–65, 268–69.

[53] Woodrow Borah, 'The Portuguese of Tulancingo and the Special *Donativo* of 1642–1643', *Jahrbuch für Geschichte von Staat, Wirtschaft und Gesellschaft Lateinamerikas*, iv (1967), 386–98.

and Peruvians inundated the imperial government with protests against the ubiquitous Portuguese, intruders who took the fruit from the mouths of Spaniards. According to one memorial, 'the Portuguese are increasing in the Spanish Indies, and go on every fleet, while they are careful to keep the Castilians out of the East Indies'; another claimed that Portuguese Jews controlled the trade of Lima 'from the vilest African Negro to the most precious pearl'.[54] Many, though not all, of the Portuguese who traded with and settled in Spanish America were indeed New Christians, and therefore suspect as judaisers as well as interlopers. From 1634 the Lima Inquisition intensified proceedings against them and increased its confiscation of their property.[55] The state too began to tighten the screw, taxing the Portuguese and their property with growing severity.

The Portuguese now had an added resentment. At the very moment when they looked to the Spanish empire to compensate for losses in their own, Spaniards reasserted their traditional exclusivism in the Indies. They were moved not merely by national and religious emotions but also by a distinct awareness that the Spanish Indies were themselves contracting economically, particularly from 1629, when the trend of prices and of trade went into reverse and when a period of easy profits gave way to one of acute difficulty. Between the 1580's and the 1620's, during its last phase of expansion, the Spanish empire had easily absorbed Portuguese immigrants; but now that there was less cake to share the guests were unwelcome.[56] Harassment of the Portuguese mounted throughout the 1630's and when, early in 1641, news of the revolt of Portugal reached Spanish America colonial officials were already poised to punish the immigrants by fiscal discrimination, property confiscation, and in some cases expulsion.[57]

By 1640 the Portuguese had reasons, convincing to themselves if not to Spaniards, to reject the union with Spain. They also had the opportunity. Naval losses in the battle of the Downs (October 1639) and at Pernambuco (January 1640) had stripped Spain's Atlantic defences and deprived her of a naval arm against Lisbon; now the revolt of Catalonia pinned down the remnants of her military forces. Richelieu had already promised the Portuguese French assistance in the event of a revolt, and they hoped that the Dutch would ease the pressure on their colonial territory if they declared their independence of Spain. The Portuguese had another asset in the person of Dom John, 7th duke of Braganza, who, weak and vacillating though he was, could claim dynastic rights to the Portuguese throne and was a symbol of

---

[54] Quoted in Boxer, *Salvador de Sá*, pp. 77–81.
[55] Rodríguez Vicente, *op. cit.*, p. 75.
[56] Chaunu, 'Autour de 1640', *op. cit.*, p. 54.
[57] Borah, 'The Portuguese of Tulancingo', *op. cit.*, p. 394.

national unity. He had been pressed for some time by a group of influential nobility to proclaim himself king, and when Olivares attempted to lure the nobility out of the country both he and his supporters were forced to commit themselves. They did so on 1 December 1640 when the duke of Braganza was proclaimed king John IV of Portugal in Lisbon.[58] Although there was some attachment to Spain among elements of the nobility, higher clergy and merchants, there was no real opposition to independence, and it was received with positive enthusiasm by the mass of the people. It also had the influential support of the Portuguese Jesuits, who played an important role in the movement and perhaps a decisive one in rallying Brazil to the cause in the early months of 1641.[59]

As long as the Catalan front absorbed Spain's energies within the peninsula she had no chance of recovering Portugal. For the moment therefore she had to remain on the defensive against the Portuguese until she were free to reduce them. Equally the Portuguese were not in a position to wage offensive war on Spain, even had John IV so wished. They had to give priority to the defence of Brazil, for it was the sugar trade which chiefly financed their independence and their armed forces. The major threat to their colonial life-line came from the Dutch, not from Spain. The Dutch concluded a ten-year truce with Portugal in June 1641, but far from helping her against the common enemy they exploited her difficulties. In August 1641 they occupied Luanda, the base of the Angola slave trade, thus threatening to starve Portuguese Brazil of its plantation labour.[60] Dependent now on their own initiative, the Portuguese began to fight back. In 1648 they reconquered Luanda; in 1654 they recovered Recife and expelled the Dutch from Brazil. Now they were free to focus on Spain. With the death of John IV (6 November 1656) and the regency of his widow, Doña Luisa de Guzmán, they adopted a more belligerent policy, if only to show France their value as allies and to dissuade her from making a separate peace with Spain.[61] While Spanish sea power was tied down in war with Cromwell's England, the Portuguese invaded Spain in 1657 and seriously threatened Badajoz; in January 1659 they themselves were invaded but inflicted a shattering defeat on the Spanish

[58] On the Portuguese independence movement see Peres, ed. *História de Portugal*, v–vi; Virginia Rau, *D. Catalina de Bragança* (Lisbon, 1941).

[59] Boxer, *Salvador de Sá*, pp. 142–47. Although in South America the Spanish crown had been an ally of the Jesuits in their conflict with the Paulista slave-hunters, in the Far East it had followed a policy more sympathetic to the missionary methods of the Dominicans than to those of the Jesuits; see Chaunu, 'Autour de 1640', *op. cit.*, p. 55.

[60] Boxer, *Salvador de Sá*, pp. 168–70, 248–92.

[61] On Portuguese diplomacy in this period see Eduardo Brazão, *A restauracão. Relações diplomáticos de Portugal de 1640 a 1688* (Lisbon, 1939); on Luso–French relations see Edgar Prestage, *The Diplomatic Relations of Portugal with France, England and Holland from 1640 to 1668* (Watford, 1925), pp. 1–98.

army at Elvas. France deserted Portugal at the Peace of the Pyrenees in 1659 and hardly compensated by allowing the dispatch of volunteers under count Schomberg. It was the English alliance of 1661 which rescued Portugal from her diplomatic isolation; she now secured the support of English sea power and the assistance of an English military contingent.

For Spain the war was a story of unrelieved disaster. After forty years of warfare the Spanish people had not the stomach for more; they could produce neither enthusiasm, nor an army, nor suitable officers. Philip IV had to rely on German and Italian *tercios*. Even with these Don John of Austria, the victor of Catalonia, was unable to make an impression on the Portuguese, and he was defeated by Schomberg at the battle of Ameixial in June 1663. Another army was laboriously assembled under the command of a veteran soldier, the marquis of Caracena; this too was defeated, at Villaviciosa on 17 June 1665, a few months before the death of Philip IV. By now the war had become his war alone; with his rigidly dynastic view of sovereignty he had stubbornly clung to the belief that the Portuguese were rebel subjects, to be reduced at all costs. The government which succeeded him had neither the will nor the resources to continue. On 13 February 1668 Philip's widow, the regent Mariana of Austria, recognised the independence of Portugal.

4. AFTER OLIVARES

The revolts of Catalonia and Portugal reduced the count duke's policy to dust. Olivares was a victim of economic circumstances as well as of political illusions. Between 1638 and 1641 the vital transatlantic trade suffered an emphatic collapse; if there was an ultimate turning point in Spain's economic power this was it.[62] State revenue and credit inevitably suffered. In 1640 no treasure arrived from the Indies. In 1641 the Tierra Firme fleet brought the crown only half a million ducats, to be followed by an equally meagre consignment in the New Spain fleet.[63] In each instance the crown confiscated half the private returns and compensated the merchants with vellon. The policy was self-defeating. Sequestration of private silver, combined with the rising costs of convoy defence, encouraged yet greater recourse to fraud, aggravated the crisis in the Indies trade, and thus reduced the pickings available to the crown. From 1640 state finances were in chaos; the public had been taxed dry; and there were two new fronts to be supplied.[64] Vellon issues were recklessly increased but these so drove up the premium on silver

---

[62] Chaunu, *Séville et l'Atlantique*, viii, 2, 2, pp. 1797–1848.
[63] Domínguez Ortiz, 'Los caudales de Indias y la política exterior de Felipe IV', *op. cit.*, pp. 358–60.
[64] Domínguez Ortiz, *Política y hacienda de Felipe IV*, pp. 62–64.

that advances from the bankers became impossibly expensive. In September 1642, therefore, the government was forced to deflate by 25 per cent.; this constituted in effect an unscrupulous form of taxation and was a further blow to private savings.[65]

These sacrifices might have been tolerable had they produced proportionate results. But the campaigns in Catalonia and Portugal revealed crass incompetence in the administration and inability to plan for predictable events. Although Olivares had always regarded war as an essential instrument of policy, he had done nothing to give Spain a military machine adequate to its needs. The professional troops were already deployed in Italy, Germany and the Low Countries. But there was virtually no organisation for raising a national army in Castile. Recruits unfortunate enough to be pressed into service resembled nothing so much as a feudal host, untrained, inexperienced, and led by amateurs. As Spain came apart at the seams, Olivares worked feverishly to repair the damage, but his time was running out. In September 1642 Perpignan was lost to France. The royal army so frequently announced and so laboriously assembled, the army on which Olivares pinned all his hopes, now moved unsteadily from Aragon towards Lérida, the key to Catalonia. There it was firmly defeated and lost 5,000 men.[66] In retreat as in attack disorder was complete, and pitiful survivors reaching Zaragoza, to find neither food nor lodgings nor medicine, were visible victims of gross failure of leadership.

Failure made Olivares vulnerable. He had long been hated by the Castilian aristocracy, who resented his monopoly of power and patronage. Some, like the duke of Híjar and the duke of Sessa, welcomed his difficulties in Catalonia and sought to exploit them. Others went further. In 1641 the duke of Medina Sidonia, a cousin of Olivares and brother of the new queen of Portugal, headed a conspiratorial movement to oust Olivares and make Andalucía an independent kingdom. The opposition of most of the nobility, however, took less eccentric forms. First they ostracised Olivares, staging in the last years of his rule a veritable *huelga de grandes* in which they abandoned court and king.[67] Then, in 1642, while Olivares was absent in Aragon, they focused their opposition more precisely and seem to have brought pressure on the king. The movement was organised by the count of Castrillo, a member of the Haro family, who was inspired as much by personal as by political motives. For Olivares had alienated the Haros, who were closely related to him, by legitimising a bastard son, Enrique Felípez de Guzmán, and giving him right of succession to his titles and estates.[68]

---

[65] Hamilton, *American Treasure and the Price Revolution in Spain*, p. 86.
[66] Sanabre, *op. cit.*, pp. 211–12.
[67] On the 'strike of the grandees' see Marañón, *op. cit.*, pp. 89–100. [68] *Ibid.*, pp. 285–301.

Olivares appreciated that his political career could not survive the disasters of 1640–42 and he was ready to go. Philip IV arranged his resignation honourably and without recrimination; on 17 January 1643 he gave him formal permission to retire on the grounds of ill-health. The count duke left Madrid for his house at Loeches, fought a brief propaganda campaign in defence of his reputation, and was then exiled to his sister's house at Toro. There, deranged in mind and broken in body, he died on 22 July 1645.

Superficially the new regime repudiated the rule of Olivares and all its manifestations. Yet it had the same problems, the same enemies, and basically the same system of government. For Olivares was succeeded in the *valimiento* by his nephew, Luis de Haro, a discreet and modest man, then aged forty-four, whose rise to power was less flamboyant than that of Olivares but just as inexorable.[69] On the departure of the count duke Philip IV professed to be shocked by what he discovered of the state of his kingdoms; and he resolved that he must never again abdicate responsibility. In July 1643, on his way to the Aragon front, he met the celebrated mystic, Sor María de Agreda, with whom he corresponded for the next twenty-two years. Sor María was a highly politicised religious and from her convent she directed a flood of advice to the king on the affairs of the Monarchy. She assured him that royal decisions were good, ministerial decisions usually bad; she inveighed against Olivares and denounced *validos*. Her nagging pen, naive though it was, further stirred Philip's conscience, and he decided to work more and delegate less, 'seated in this chair, with papers before me and pen in hand, working on all the consultas sent to me and the despatches from abroad'.[70] He seemed determined not to appoint another *valido*. In the decree which announced the retirement of Olivares he stated: 'The moment is opportune to inform the Council that such a good minister must be replaced only by me myself, since our present difficulties require all my personal attention for their remedy'.[71]

Philip's resolution lasted only a few months. He had been a friend of Haro since childhood and he admired his qualities. Soon he was not only taking his advice but accepting his decisions. By mid-1643 Haro was recognised by observers as undoubtedly the successor of Olivares. Philip was too ashamed and Haro too discreet to acknowledge the fact, and they avoided the terms *valido* and minister. The king guiltily reassured the disapproving Sor María: 'I have always refused to give him the character of minister, in order to

[69] For a character sketch of Haro see Deleito y Pinuela, *El declinar de la monarquía española*, pp. 150–59.
[70] Philip IV to Sor María de Agreda, 30 January 1647, in Valiente, *Los validos en la monarquía española del siglo XVII*, p. 183.
[71] 'Comunicación del Rey al Consejo de la Cámara', 24 January 1643, in Marañón, *op. cit.*, p. 464.

avoid previous mistakes'.[72] Nevertheless by 1647 Haro had acquired almost as many functions as Olivares. He was assisted by a *junta de estado*, which met in his own house as his uncle's had done. Although he was not a member of the Council of State he directed its affairs from outside; and he controlled state papers and their distribution between councils in much the same way as previous *validos*. In general he had the same power as Olivares, though perhaps there was a new division of labour between king and *valido*, with the king attending to more business than he had previously done. Haro had no official titles and did not even use the personal ones he inherited from his uncle. But by the late 1650's Philip was referring to him in state papers as his *primer ministro*; in the Treaty of the Pyrenees he spoke of him as his *primer y principal ministro*.[73] Although the title was a general and occasional one, Haro was in fact first minister and remained such until his death in 1661. Philip IV did not replace him. In the last five years of his reign, either because he found no one to trust or because the call of duty now appealed more than the pleasures of the flesh, he retained personal direction of government, taking advice from many, giving power to none.

If the new regime brought few governmental innovations, it did little to re-orientate Spain's foreign policy. The replacement of Olivares could not work miracles. The war continued to devour men and money, and Castile still bore the brunt. Subsidies from the cortes, forced loans, sale of offices, manipulation of the currency, all the devices favoured by the old regime were also practised by the new. The only difference was that where Olivares ranted Haro reasoned. As long as the demands of war were paramount, however, reason had its limits; there was no opportunity to stop and re-organise public finances. By the beginning of 1644 the crown's income was pledged up to 1648. *Asientos* contracted for 1644 amounted to 5·3 million escudos—over 2 million for the Low Countries, the remainder for Germany, Italy and internal administration. But a further 3 million was needed for the armies on the Catalan and Portuguese fronts and for the royal household. It was therefore decided to sell in the form of *juros* the recent 1 per cent. increase in the *alcabala* tax. Corregidores were instructed to seek the consent of the towns represented in the cortes but not to assemble the *cabildos* until they were sure of getting a favourable vote; if the *cabildos* were not persuaded by the state of the treasury then they were to be told that the king ordered the measure by virtue of his rights under divine and human law.[74] Spanish constitutionalism was as defunct as ever.

The situation in 1645–46 was more or less the same and Haro continued to raise extraordinary revenue by executive measures. The estimate of pro-

[72] See note 70.   [73] Valiente, *op. cit.*, pp. 20, 185–86.
[74] Domínguez Ortiz, *Política y hacienda de Felipe IV*, pp. 64–68.

St. Thomas of Villanueva, archbishop of Valencia, distributing alms to the poor

Facing p. 119

jected expenditure in 1647 was 12·7 million ducats, while available revenue was 7 million short of this. All essential foodstuffs were already overtaxed; forced loans were bringing diminishing returns; and it was not known when the Indies fleets would arrive. Before 1646 was out the Spaniards at great cost forced France to raise the siege of Lérida, but in the Low Countries they lost Dunkirk, and in 1647 there was a revolution in Naples. Available revenue for the next four years was already assigned to bankers and there was nothing with which to make immediate *asientos*. So the crown had to declare the second bankruptcy of the reign, twenty years after the first. By suspending payments and freeing pledged income the crown at once procured some 10 million ducats. The *asentistas*, who were indemnified with *juros*, suffered great losses, particularly the Portuguese and the Genoese; but the four royal factors—Spinola, Imbrea, Centurión and Palavesia—were exempt in order not to deprive them of the means of making further *asientos*.

5. WAR AND PEACE

The political and financial disasters of the 1640's, not the fall of Olivares, forced Spain eventually to re-think her foreign policy and reduce her commitments abroad. There was no thought of retreat from basic objectives, and Philip IV was determined that his subjects should fight on until these were achieved. But there was a readjustment of priorities and a renewed search for peace. First the Spaniards accepted what they had long suspected, that the Habsburg alliance was obsolete. As the Thirty Years War dragged on the rift between Madrid and Vienna became wider. By the early 1640's they no longer had the same war aims. For Spain the principal danger came from France and the United Provinces; for the emperor the main enemy was Sweden. Spain resented her precious subsidies being absorbed by the Swedish war and from 1640 she drastically reduced them. She also resented the emperor's failure to support her position in the Palatinate and his readiness to sacrifice her interests there to conciliate France and Sweden, as he did in 1648.

The Habsburg alliance had been expensive to Spain and had brought her few returns. She could now concentrate what resources she had on the French and Dutch fronts. Unfortunately, owing to the collapse of the Spanish–American trade from 1638, the Spanish forces in the Low Countries could no longer count on the treasure of the Indies.[75] In 1643 the army under Francisco de Melo, Portuguese governor of the Spanish Netherlands, went into action against the French without adequate cavalry, because horses were too expensive. On 19 May at Rocroi it was defeated and routed by the young French commander, the duke of Enghien, and suffered 14,000 casualties

[75] Chaunu, 'Seville et la "Belgique" (1555–1648)', *op. cit.,* p. 277.

I

in dead and wounded; although the mercenaries turned and fled, the Spanish veterans fought to the death. Rocroi has acquired a legendary reputation as the greatest defeat ever suffered by the incomparable Spanish infantry, and it is often taken to mark the end of Spain's military power. But one battle in a war which had already lasted twenty-five years and still had another fifteen to run could not have transcendental significance. There was still plenty of fight left in Spain. Her military effort in the Low Countries did not slacken and although she suffered further reverses, including the loss of Dunkirk, she managed to maintain her position in the southern Netherlands. Overseas the Dutch still found Spanish colonial defences impenetrable, and their expedition to Chile in 1642 was a conspicuous failure.

But the Spanish government was reluctantly forced to conclude that it could not fight the United Provinces and France simultaneously, and when, in 1648, the Peace of Westphalia brought the Thirty Years War to a close Spain took the opportunity to make a separate peace with the Dutch. It was a logical step to take. The greatest threat to her peninsular security came from France; and Mazarin's demands, including a proposal to send auxiliaries to the Portuguese rebels across Spanish territory, were plainly intolerable.[76] By January 1648 the Spanish government had reached agreement with the Dutch on the general terms of a peace treaty, and these formed the basis of the Treaty of Munster of 24 October 1648. Spain recognised the United Provinces as a sovereign, independent state; she procured neither the opening of the Scheldt nor official toleration for Roman Catholics, two of her more important peace aims; and she explicitly recognised the right of the Dutch to conquer all the Portuguese colonial territory to which they laid claim, although in Spanish eyes the Portuguese were still subjects of Philip IV.[77] Spain retained the southern Netherlands, and detached the Dutch from the French alliance. It seemed a meagre result from a war of eighty years.

The recognition of Dutch independence, though galling to Spain, was merely a recognition of long-standing facts. It was designed to isolate France at a time when that country was also weakened by domestic instability. In the event Spain was unable to exploit the anti-Mazarin Fronde, as she did not have the resources for a major effort. But at least she recovered Dunkirk and began the recovery of Catalonia. The war called for further sacrifices from Castile. The crown seized 1 million ducats of private returns from the Indies, anticipated revenue up to 1655, and in November 1651 increased vellon to the level of the pre-1642 deflation.[78] The subsequent price rise was

[76] On Spanish policy at Westphalia see Fraga Iribarne, *Don Diego de Saavedra y Fajardo y la diplomacia de su época*, pp. 564–91.

[77] Boxer, *The Dutch Seaborne Empire*, p. 27.

[78] Domínguez Ortiz, 'Los caudales de Indias y la política exterior de Felipe IV', *op. cit.*, pp 366–68, and *Política y hacienda de Felipe IV*, pp. 68–75.

aggravated by poor grain crops; in Andalucía there were serious disturbances, and Seville was at the mercy of the mob for several days. In 1652 the government deflated again, but by now vellon was utterly discredited and monetary disorder could hardly be worse. Estimated expenditure for 1653—11·3 million ducats—was far in excess of the revenue from ordinary taxation, forced loans and sale of offices. So the government decreed yet another suspension of payments. At this point, if Spain had been able to finance a supreme war effort, she could probably have won a favourable peace, before France recovered from political instability and agricultural distress and before she was joined by England. As it was, Spain barely had the resources to maintain her positions on the various fronts. In the cortes of 1655 the speech from the throne stated that it had not been possible to reach a general peace; it enumerated the positions recovered in Italy, the Low Countries and Catalonia; and it pointed out that insurrections in Sicily and Naples had also been overcome. Defence costs from 1649 to 1654 had totalled 66·8 million escudos, and these had been met without imposing new taxes, 'whatever other means his majesty has been forced to use with his prerogative'. In preference to new taxes the king requested 'a universal means which would yield the same yet would fall on those with personal fortunes and not on the poor beggar, the labourer, the artisan and other people who can only support themselves with their labour'. The cortes, of course, was the last institution from which to expect support for such a tax; it simply voted a renewal of previous subsidies, with an additional 2 million ducats in sale of offices, and financial reform was left for another day. Yet the demands of war drove the crown to impose one fiscal innovation which had social significance. In 1657 it imposed a *media anata* tax (a sum equal to half a year's income) on all grants, pensions and annuities bestowed by Philip IV and his predecessors, exempting only those serving in the armed forces, their dependants, and disabled ex-servicemen. This was the kind of tax which the gentry-dominated cortes had always opposed; it was used frequently by Philip IV and his successor, though the nobility exerted their influence to procure exemption, and it yielded progressively lower returns.[79]

While Spain did not have the means for a major offensive, she was still capable of defending herself, and it is a comment on the alleged waning of her military power that she fought France to a stalemate. At this point, however, the military balance was tipped against Spain by the entry of England into the war. The Spanish government had reason to expect a more propitious outcome from its English policy, which was determined by pragmatism not ideology. In the 1640's Philip IV followed a policy of strict neutrality towards the English civil war, and he showed little sympathy for the Stuart

[79] Domínguez Ortiz, *Política y hacienda de Felipe IV*, p. 74.

cause. He quickly recognised the new republic and, appreciating its threat to the balance of power, was prepared to buy its alliance, or at least neutrality, at almost any price. But Cromwell's price was too high. He wanted an explicit statement of religious toleration towards Englishmen resident in Spain and the admission of English merchants to direct participation in the Spanish colonial trade. These were gratuitous demands: the religious problem had been dealt with in previous treaties and Englishmen had an indirect trade with the Spanish Indies through re-exports from Seville. Indeed the demands were so provocative that they were presumably designed to be rejected. As if to emphasise the point, Cromwell raised them still higher, to include the cession of Calais and Dunkirk.

Cromwell seems to have decided on war with Spain as early as April 1654; from August he was planning a marauding expedition and in December, without declaration of war, this was dispatched with instructions 'to assault the Spaniard in the West Indies'. The operation was ill-planned and badly executed; its commanders failed to overcome Spanish defences at Hispaniola, the principal target, and had to be content with the capture of Jamaica.[80] Meanwhile another English squadron patrolled off Cadiz, waiting to intercept the silver fleets. Philip IV was incredulous. In June 1655 he dismissed warnings from the duke of Medina Sidonia that defence measures were needed: 'It is unbelievable that the English would break public faith and the peace which exists between the two nations; it is therefore unnecessary to take major defensive measures'.[81] He was even ready to overlook—for the time being at least—the conquest of Jamaica if that would facilitate peace with England. But Cromwell did not want peace.

It was Spain's ultimate misfortune, after a long and gruelling war, to be suddenly confronted by a new military power whose foreign policy was dominated by motives of gain and godliness and who seized upon Spain as the most likely target for both. Philip IV was forced into a war with England which he did not seek. In September 1655 an embargo was placed on English property in Spain and in December it was decided to apply the proceeds from its sale to naval defence. The need was urgent, for Spain's maritime communications were now vulnerable to English naval power. In September 1656 a detachment of Blake's squadron intercepted the returning Tierra Firme fleet almost within sight of Cadiz, captured the *capitana* and a merchantman, took booty estimated at 2 million pesos, and sank other valuable

[80] On Cromwell's 'Western Design' see I. A. Wright, ed., *Spanish Narratives of the English Attack on Santo Domingo* (*Camden Miscellany*, xiv, London, 1926); J. M. Incháustegui, *La gran expedición inglesa contra las Antilles Mayores. Tomo I: El plan antillano de Cromwell, 1651–1655* (Mexico, 1953).

[81] Quoted in Domínguez Ortiz, 'España ante la Paz de los Pirineos', *Hispania*, xix (1959), 548. In fact the 1655 silver fleet got through safely.

units. The New Spain fleet was forewarned and took refuge in Santa Cruz de Tenerife; there, on 30 April 1657, it too was sought out by Blake and almost totally destroyed, with the loss of its cargo and treasure.[82] For two years therefore no silver fleet reached Spain, while her foreign trade was paralysed by the enemy blockade of the peninsula and control of the English channel. Spain was now completely isolated, with two major enemies and not a single ally. Yet in 1656 there was a distinct opportunity of peace with France; Catalonia had now been recovered and the French promised not to assist the Portuguese. Against the advice of his ministers Philip IV refused to negotiate, insisting on conditions as unreasonable as those which Cromwell demanded of Spain.[83] Spain was severely punished for his folly. In June 1658 a combined French and English army overwhelmed the Spaniards at the battle of the Dunes and took Dunkirk. The Spanish Netherlands, their subsidy already cut from 3 to 1 million escudos a year, were now seriously exposed. And in the peninsula the Portuguese, by their victory at Elvas, added to Spain's retribution.

As the country reeled under these successive blows, Philip IV's ministers urged him to end the agony; Don John of Austria in the Netherlands, the councils in Madrid, Haro, the primate of Spain, all gave the same advice.[84] As for his subjects, from the aristocracy to the poorest peasant, they had long ceased to believe that the war bore any relation to their interests, and they had lost their military vocation. The final campaigns, even within the peninsula, were fought mainly by Italian conscripts, with Irish and German mercenaries. Want of money to pay for these various armies was reason enough for peace. Mazarin was seeking a solution, and the English government, reluctant further to assist France, was not averse to one. But even now Philip IV was loath to negotiate, and if France had not modified her demands he would have ordered his subjects to fight on. He was eventually moved, not by the sufferings of his people much less by financial distress, but by yet another illusion—that peace with France and England would enable him to isolate and reduce the Portuguese. He therefore agreed to an armistice in May 1659 and the Peace of the Pyrenees was signed on 7 November. The treaty provided for the marriage of Philip IV's daughter, María Teresa, to the king of France. Spain ceded to France territory in the Netherlands and, more significantly, Cerdagne and Roussillon in Catalonia. Further cessions, among them Artois, marked the end of Spanish control over the imperial

[82] See C. H. Firth, *The Last Years of the Protectorate, 1656–1658* (2 vols., London, 1909), ii, 260–61, who, however, exaggerates the significance of the disaster; the transatlantic trade had suffered so many reverses in the last two decades that one year's loss could hardly be decisive.
[83] F. J. Routledge, *England and the Treaty of the Pyrenees* (Liverpool, 1953), p. 9.
[84] For the advice of the *junta de estado* see ibid., p. 17.

route from Milan to the Netherlands.[85] In its territorial provisions, however, the treaty was not a disaster for Spain. Its principal defect was that it came years too late.

Experience taught Philip IV no lessons, and the political philosophy which informed his decisions remained unaffected by the events of 1640–59. He had no conception of a national monarchy transcending dynastic interests. Although he professed a love of his subjects and a desire to alleviate their miseries, he saw himself primarily as the representative of the Habsburg dynasty, charged with the preservation of its possessions. These he regarded essentially as an estate entailed in perpetuity, and he shrank from the responsibility of alienating or losing any part of his sacred inheritance. It never occurred to him to ask whether the continued possession of the Netherlands or Portugal was of any benefit to his Spanish subjects. His only criterion was his legal rights. This accounts for his almost total subordination of domestic to foreign policy and for his stubborn commitment to war in defence of Habsburg property. In 1648 he reluctantly abandoned the war with the Dutch in order to concentrate on that with France. Six years later, still at war with France, he acquired a second enemy, England. Now, in 1659, he ended Spain's forty years war simply to fight another one, against Portugal. Again he miscalculated, for the Portuguese quickly escaped from their isolation and secured an alliance with England which enabled them successfully to defend their independence. The Portuguese war dealt the death blow to the crown's tottering finances. The campaign cost an estimated 5 million ducats a year. From 1660 to 1665, in a final orgy of taxation, the government wildly employed every unsound device known to Habsburg administration —taxes on *juros*, currency manipulation, increase of the *alcabala*, further taxes on foodstuffs, anticipation of revenue and, in 1662, yet another suspension of payments.[86] By 1664 the crown's total indebtedness amounted to 21·6 million ducats. Philip IV bequeathed to his successor an empty treasury, a discredited currency, and a multitude of new taxes already alienated to financiers. And Portugal remained independent.

Philip IV died on 17 September 1665. The last months of his life were marred by acute melancholia. His subjects too had little cause for rejoicing. The political future looked unpromising, for Philip left, if not a succession problem, at least a problem successor, his son Charles, a child of his old age, who was destined to be the most degenerate of all the Spanish Habsburgs. Spaniards would look in vain for new leadership. Economic prospects were also bleak. Spain had been at war for almost half a century. The people had

---

[85] *Ibid.*, pp. 67–70, 81; see also Juan Reglà, 'El tratado de los Pirineos de 1659', *Hispania*, xiii (1953), 101–66.

[86] Domínguez Ortiz, *Política y hacienda de Felipe IV*, pp. 81–85.

been taxed and conscripted beyond endurance, the population ravaged by epidemic disease, and the colonial life-line badly frayed. Excessive investment in war did not bring comparable returns. Some assets remained. The Spanish colonial empire was still intact, territorially at least. And Spain's military power, though badly eroded, was not extinct. It had taken the combined efforts of France and England to force her to the peace table in 1659 and neither could have done it alone. But basically Spain had nothing to show for her efforts in northern and central Europe. The Habsburg alliance was dead, imperial communications were meaningless; and if Spain retained the southern Netherlands it was less because of her military presence than because the other powers could not agree on an alternative sovereignty.

Nations can recover from the consequences of war and renew their life. But Spain's prostration was so prolonged that it points to a deeper malaise. War and taxation merely placed additional burdens on a society already carrying a dead-weight of privilege and on an economy already weakened by structural defects.

CHAPTER VI

SOCIETY AND ECONOMY

I. POPULATION AND PESTILENCE

A T the end of the seventeenth century there were fewer people in Spain than there had been at the beginning. By the 1590's the demographic upswing of the sixteenth century had spent itself. The population was then about 8,485,000. A century later it was 7 million.[1] The rest of Europe too suffered demographic recession, or at least stagnation, in the seventeenth century, but nowhere did reverses begin so early, last so long, or attain such proportions as they did in Spain.[2] How can we explain this catastrophe? War, famine and pestilence were not exclusive to the seventeenth century; birth control, though not unknown, was hardly practised; and the birth-rate was normally high in Spain, in spite of the incidence of celibacy. A deficit of 1½ million, most of it in the first half of the century, could only be the result of an exceptional concurrence of adversities.

The secular demographic trend was not the same in every part of Spain. Most of the non-Castilian regions suffered stagnation rather than loss. In Valencia the expulsion of the moriscos reduced the population from approximately 450,000 to 300,000; by mid-century the vacuum had still not been filled when the province was struck by plague. At the end of the century Valencia probably had between 350,000 and 400,000 inhabitants.[3] Catalonia, like other parts of Spain, suffered from plague and famine; the principality was a battlefield from 1640, losing Rosellón in 1659; and French immigration, which had previously boosted its numbers, was much reduced in the second half of the century. In 1700, therefore, the population of Catalonia was between 400,000 and 450,000, no larger than it had been in 1600.[4] Aragon, where the moriscos were less numerous than in Valencia, recovered more quickly from their expulsion, but poor economic conditions caused a down-

[1] A careful discussion of the sources and methods for the study of Spanish demographic history in this period, and the best estimates, are provided by Domínguez Ortiz, *La sociedad española en el siglo XVII*, pp. 53–157; see also Javier Ruiz Almansa, 'La población de España en el siglo XVI', *Revista Internacional de Sociología*, no. 4 (1943), 115–36, and *La población de Galicia* (1500–1945), vol. I (Madrid, 1948).

[2] See Karl F. Helleiner, 'The Population of Europe from the Black Death to the Eve of the Vital Revolution', *The Cambridge Economic History of Europe*, iv (Cambridge, 1967), 1–95.

[3] Lapeyre, *Géographie de l'Espagne morisque*, pp. 30, 203–5; see above, pp. 45–48.

[4] Nadal and Giralt, *La population catalane de 1553 à 1717*, pp. 19–23, 337.

ward demographic trend after 1650. The relative immunity of Navarre and the Basque provinces from the great plagues was counterbalanced by their primitive economy which forced many younger sons to emigrate, and here too the population remained stationary, roughly 350,000 throughout the century. In the 1590's the population of the non-Castilian regions totalled some 1,785,000. A century later it was probably slightly less than this.

The greatest blows were reserved for Castile, and within Castile for its heartland. The periphery provinces—Galicia, Asturias, Andalucía and Murcia—escaped the worst incidence of depopulation. The most vulnerable region was the arid and infertile central plateau, and it was this which bore the brunt of the 1½ million deficit; Old Castile, New Castile, and Extremadura all suffered grievous losses. Disaster was absolute. No doubt there was some shift of population towards less depressed regions and overseas; but most of the missing Castilians died of hunger or disease or in war, and adverse economic conditions retarded their replacement. Disaster was also sudden. It began in the 1590's, and sixty years later the worst was over. At the beginning of this period the population of Castile was about 6,700,000. Between 1591 and 1614 severe epidemics and the expulsion of the moriscos reduced this number by 600,000–700,000, or about one-tenth. In 1630–32 plague and famine caused further heavy losses. From 1640 civil wars combined with the famine and epidemics of 1647–52 reduced the population of Castile to its lowest point, and it was now that Andalucía suffered its worst catastrophe. In 1665 the population of Castile was little more than 5 million, which was also the figure yielded by the censuses at the beginning of the eighteenth century. After the damaging years 1677–83, when disease and climatic adversity again struck Castile, the population tended to level off, with perhaps a slight tendency to rise.[5]

Spaniards were at the mercy of disease and the elements. The basic cause of demographic recession was an abnormally high mortality-rate, and the chief killer was epidemic disease.[6] Small-pox, typhus, dysentery and other malignant diseases all played their part in pushing up the death-rates. But the greatest enemy was plague, principally bubonic plague carried by flea-infested rats. The virulence of disease was enhanced by two conditions endemic in Spanish life. Periodic subsistence crises, the fate of a people who neglected arable farming, caused extreme malnutrition and lowered resistance to infection. And excessive urbanisation, leading to overcrowding, working-class slums and neglect of hygiene, made Spanish towns breeding-grounds of disease.

[5] Domínguez Ortiz, *La sociedad española en el siglo XVII*, graph facing p. 112.
[6] *Ibid.*, pp. 67–81; see also Luis Sánchez Granjel, 'Las epidemias de peste en España durante el siglo XVII', *Cuadernos de Historia de la Medicina Española*, iii (Salamanca, 1964), 19–40.

The outbreak of 1596–1602, the first major epidemic of the period, devoured northern and central Spain and Andalucía, accounting for perhaps 500,000 victims.[7] Its successor, the great plague of 1647–52, struck chiefly eastern Spain and Andalucía. It first penetrated Valencia—perhaps from Algiers—and killed 30,000 people. From there it spread relentlessly to Andalucía and finally swept through Aragon and Catalonia. Andalucía was devastated. On the coast Málaga alone lost 40,000 people. Seville neglected quarantine measures and was contaminated in 1649; entire streets, whole districts were emptied of their inhabitants, and the city was brought to a standstill. Seville and its rural environs probably lost a quarter of their 600,000 people; the economy suffered a permanent shock.[8] Altogether Spain lost about 500,000 people in this monstrous epidemic. Twenty-five years later, between 1676 and 1685, the country was again visited by lethal disease, and again Valencia and Andalucía were the foci of infection. The poor harvests of 1682–83 caused famine conditions, weakening resistance and prolonging the crisis. This, the final great plague of the seventeenth century, claimed about 250,000 victims, and brought the total epidemic losses for the century to at least 1,250,000.

The spectre of death haunted Spain in the seventeenth century. Compared with disease other adversities were of minor significance, but they mounted in conjunction a further assault on human resources. The expulsion of the moriscos varied in its effects from region to region. The total deficit was in the order of 275,000.[9] Castile's share of this was relatively small; but Aragon lost 20 per cent. of its population and Valencia 25 per cent. Repopulation of Valencia was slow, incomplete, and chiefly at the expense of other parts of the province, for harsh seigneurial conditions were a deterrent to new colonists. Castilians would be more likely to emigrate to America than to Valencia. How many of them did so is open to speculation. Contemporaries had the impression that shoals of emigrants crossed the Atlantic every year, leaving in their wake an empty Castile. But the impression was misleading. Surviving evidence indicates that 150,000 emigration permits were issued during the entire colonial period; of these the seventeenth century would account for perhaps 40,000, or an average of 400 a year.[10] The figure is manifestly too low: the documentation itself is incomplete, and of its nature it fails to

[7] See above, pp. 6–7.

[8] A. Domínguez Ortiz, *Orto y ocaso de Sevilla. Estudio sobre la prosperidad y decadencia de la ciudad en los siglos XVI y XVII* (Sevilla, 1946).

[9] This is the estimate of Lapeyre; Domínguez Ortiz would raise the figure to 300,000; see above, pp. 44–48.

[10] For discussion of the evidence see Domínguez Ortiz, *La sociedad española en el siglo XVII*, pp. 86–91, and G. Céspedes del Castillo, 'Las Indias en el siglo XVII', in J. Vicens Vives, ed., *Historia social y económica de España y América* (5 vols., Barcelona, 1957–59), iii, 497; see also *Spain under the Habsburgs*, i, 149; and below, p. 161.

record the large number of illegal emigrants. A mixture of calculation and guess-work produces an estimate of 4,000 to 5,000 emigrants a year, an insignificant number in a population of 7 million.[11] But most of them probably came from Castile, and they were a further drain on the region's resources.

The demographic consequences of war cannot be precisely computed. As a warrior nation Spain obviously suffered heavy casualties: in the first half of the seventeenth century she was engaged in almost continuous warfare. But war was not total; the mass of the people were not in the firing-line, nor were they at first conscripted. Spain had forces fighting in the Low Countries, Germany, Italy, and on the French frontier. These were professional troops, with a hard core of volunteers and large numbers of foreign mercenaries. Her naval forces too consisted of professionals. The balance of naval warfare was moving against Spain, and her seamen, particularly in major defeats like the battle of the Downs (1639), suffered heavy casualties in the course of the century. All these, however, could be regarded as the normal hazards of the regular services. From 1635 the situation changed. War with France forced the government to extend the range of its recruitment, to mobilise nobility, gentry, and their retainers, to call up town militias, to take a quota of conscripts from each community. From 1640 the peninsula itself became a theatre of war, and Castile's conflict with Catalonia and Portugal assumed the character, if not of total war, at least of war to the death, with large-scale pillage and devastation, killing of prisoners, and heavy conscription. For the Catalan front the government aimed at drafting 12,000 men a year in Castile by quotas from each district. The burden fell most heavily on the poorer classes, for the nobility and the rich paid for a substitute or bought an office which carried exemption from military service. The war with Portugal was fought at first by a series of skirmishes along the lengthy frontier and was largely a holding operation. Even so it exacted a heavy toll and civilian casualties were large; Galicia in particular was subject to constant conscription. After 1659 the attempt to reconquer Portugal was made with small armies composed largely of foreign troops.

The greatest military effort, therefore, was concentrated in the years 1635–59, and it was in this period that war-time mortality rates were highest. But death came by stealth rather than assault. For war bred disease and famine and then perpetuated them. It is probable that more people died from the secondary effects of war, from pestilence and malnutrition, than from the sword and the bullet. The figures are difficult to calculate, but a reasoned estimate places the average casualty rate (including Catalonia) at 20,000 a

[11] The estimate is that of Domínguez Ortiz, *La sociedad española en el siglo XVII*, p. 90.

year, which gives a total of 288,000 for the crucial twenty-four years.[12] The presumption of heavy casualties is reinforced by the abnormally high proportion of widows registered in the census of 1646; in Mérida, Extremadura, for example, widows constituted one-sixth of the population.

The syndrome of plague, famine and war brought demographic catastrophe to Spain. The government was aware of the crisis, if only through the reports of its tax-collectors and recruiting-sergeants. But it did not have reliable statistics; it regarded war as inevitable; and in matters of public health it was a creature of its age. Standards of sanitation were abysmal, medical resources primitive. The state was more interested in the consequences of depopulation than in its causes. It occasionally tinkered with the problem, to no visible effect.[13] Among the reform plans adumbrated at the beginning of Philip IV's reign was the creation of a *junta de población*, perhaps with the intention of creating industries and attracting foreigners; but as it had no funds it soon ceased activity. And in an attempt to boost the birth rate the government exempted from taxation fathers who begat eight or more sons; these prolific Spaniards were derisively known as *hidalgos de bragueta*.

2. ARISTOCRACY

The polarisation of Spanish society into two sectors, a privileged minority monopolising land and office, and a mass of peasants and workers, continued with greater momentum in the seventeenth century. The basis of this social division was wealth. It is true that function—originally military function—assigned the nobility its social status and honour, and that this was juridically recognised in the *fuero de hidalguía* which exempted the noble from personal taxes and from the normal process of law. But in the ultimate analysis it was money which bought nobility, and money was the motor of social mobility. Class distinction was recognised and reinforced by legislation. The various sumptuary laws, while they were motivated by economic considerations, also served to underline social differences. One such law prohibited the wearing of silk by artisans, labourers, all who worked with their hands, and their wives; another restricted the use of coaches and sedan chairs. Decrees of this kind simply helped to identify status symbols and to encourage social pretensions. But they were welcome to the poor nobility who resented the pretensions of tradesmen, professional people and other urban groups. For its part the crown preserved the nobility, even against itself. Nobles had to get royal permission to marry, to alienate their patrimony, to mortgage their estates, in short to do anything which might weaken their

[12] *Ibid.*, p. 95.   [13] *Ibid.*, pp. 98–99.

class. For the crown regarded the nobility, somewhat naively, as a reserve of talent at the service of the country.

The nobility were also favoured by the educational system. They now monopolised the Colegios Mayores, foundations originally created to finance the studies of clever students from poor families.[14] From these they graduated to automatic preferment in church and state. And for the elder sons of the higher nobility there was a special institution, the Colegio Imperial in Madrid, founded by the Jesuits in the reign of Philip IV with the specific purpose of training an elite. The college justified itself with the claim that

> well-ordered states have usually derived their success from the good education of their youth, and although it would be very appropriate to extend such education to the common people it is much more important to give it to the sons of princes and nobles, because they are the principal part of the state and, for good or for evil, they lead the rest; moreover they subsequently control the government and administration of the kingdom.[15]

Higher education in Spain had become a powerful instrument for perpetuating the social and political dominance of the aristocracy.

In the course of its history the Spanish aristocracy bred its own hierarchy and its own distinctions. This was inevitable in a class which, by the beginning of the seventeenth century, had grown to 650,000 in Castile, or about one in ten of the population.[16] The original *nobleza de sangre* were joined in the sixteenth and seventeenth centuries by masses of *hidalgos*, who bought, earned or proved their noble status. In the face of this invasion the older and wealthier nobility sought to preserve social distinctions by insulating themselves in the ranks of the grandees and *títulos*. This re-grouping of the aristocracy became more pronounced in the course of the seventeenth century, and by the end of the period there was a wide gap between the grandees and *títulos*, who were the real nobility, and the mass of *caballeros* and *hidalgos*, who had little more than a coat-of-arms. The ultimate test was an economic one: some were wealthier than others. As Lope de Vega put it,

> No dudes que el dinero es todo en todo.
> Es príncipe, es hidalgo, es caballero,
> Es alta sangre, es descendiente godo.

At the bottom of the hierarchy swarmed the *hidalgos*, nobles by heredity or recent procurement, but debarred by their poverty or lack of office from

---

[14] J. Sarrailh, *L'Espagne éclairée de la second moitié du XVIIIe siècle* (Paris, 1954), pp. 201–2.

[15] Quoted by Domínguez Ortiz, *La sociedad española en el siglo XVII*, p. 289; see also J. S. Diaz, *Historia del Colegio Imperial de Madrid* (Madrid, 1952).

[16] John C. Salyer, 'La política española en la época del mercantilismo', *Anales de Economía*, no. 31 (1952), 319–21. See also Domínguez Ortiz, *La sociedad española en el siglo XVII*, pp. 189–91.

further advancement. Their principal habitat was northern Castile and the highlands of Cantabria. Some scraped a living from petty estates, others performed work regarded as vile, and not a few were reduced to beggary. These were the classical targets of the satirists. Further south *hidalgos* who possessed any fortune at all preferred the more illustrious designation of *caballero*. The *caballeros* were nobles of middle rank; they lived in town houses, drew most of their income from their estates, and supplemented this by annuities from investments in *juros* and *censos*. They frequently held *regimientos*—seats in municipal councils—which gave them the opportunity of becoming procurators in the cortes and thus of diverting taxation from the property and interests of their class. But *caballeros*, especially the newly arrived, aspired to higher things. To enhance their status they sometimes bought, if they had not already inherited, seigneurial jurisdiction and thus became *señores de vasallos*, of whom there were 254 in Castile at the beginning of the seventeenth century. Above all they craved to be *caballeros de hábito* and *comendadores*, not because the military orders any longer fulfilled a function but because they conferred unimpeachable honour, proof of racial purity, and test of nobility, while the *encomiendas* yielded a useful income.[17] In the seventeenth century, when pressure for *hábitos* increased, Olivares sold them in their hundreds and the government of Charles II further debased their currency.

Armed with a *señorío*, a *hábito* and perhaps an *encomienda*, the *caballero* strove to enter the ranks of the *títulos*. These were distinguished by their position and their wealth, and in popular estimation they were the real nobility. Again the criterion was wealth, especially in the seventeenth century. Those who had enough money to buy land, jurisdiction and vassals, to live a life of ease and ostentation, to advance substantial sums to the treasury, could expect to rise from the rank of simple *caballero* to that of count or marquis. The growth of the *título* class in turn enhanced the value of the *grandeza*, the most exclusive and class-conscious group of all. This constant struggle for preferment, for *caballeros* to become *títulos*, and *títulos* grandees, engendered a kind of social mobility and modified the composition of the nobility. The sixteenth century saw a moderate movement upwards: the original 20 grandees and 35 *títulos* had increased to 99 at the end of Philip II's reign—18 dukes, 38 marquises, and 43 counts. Philip III accelerated the process, creating a further 20 marquises and 25 counts. Philip IV, in a longer—44 years—and more penurious reign, created 67 marquises and 25 counts. Charles II, in a reign of 35 years, sanctioned the creation of as many titles as in the previous two centuries—5 viscounts, 78 counts and 209 marquises.[18]

When, in 1520, Charles V legally defined the *grandeza*, it comprised twenty

[17] *Ibid.*, pp. 200–1.   [18] *Ibid.*, pp. 209–22.

families, among them the dukes of Medinaceli, Alburquerque, Medina Sidonia, Alba, Frías, and Béjar. The first grandees were a select and powerful group; they possessed specific juridical and diplomatic privileges; and to keep them out of politics the early Habsburgs employed them—and their fortunes —in war and diplomacy rather than in central administration. With the accession of the more pliant Philip III the grandees moved more noticeably towards the court, where they negotiated the best appointments in the Council of State and the viceroyalties. Philip IV added lavishly to their number: preferment was a weapon in the hands of Olivares which he used to reward and attract. In 1640 the crown created ten new grandees, each of them undertaking to lead a military contingent to the Catalan front.[19] The older grandees regarded the newcomers with contempt and their patron with suspicion. Olivares returned the antipathy, turning his opponents into declared enemies. Haro treated the grandees more suavely. And under Charles II they reached the apogee of their power.[20] To satisfy their pride and exclusivism further refinements were introduced with the more elaborate distinction between grandees of the first, second and third class. All of them, however, were extremely wealthy men, owners of the greatest fortunes in the kingdom. That was precisely why they were grandees, and that was the basis of their revival in the seventeenth century.

While the grandees and *títulos* looked out from their lofty position, their humbler colleagues had to work hard at being noble. To acquire or confirm the status they had to prove their lineage, their purity of blood—meaning freedom from Jewish ancestry—and their exemption from taxation. Unless a man was of *notoria hidalguía* his claim to nobility would usually involve lengthy and expensive litigation, for it would be contested by his enemies or by remaining taxpayers. Yet the advantages were thought to justify the struggle, and in many cases they probably did. The law dealt more leniently with the noble than with the commoner, and he could not be tortured, sentenced to the galleys, or imprisoned for debt. Nobility was also a card of entry to the bureaucracy. The best public offices were virtually monopolised by nobles, and nobles occupied about half of municipal offices. The Council of State was always dominated by the higher nobility. The other councils had a greater proportion of *hidalgos* and *caballeros* but no commoners. And other important offices, such as that of *corregidor* (district officer) were usually in the hands of *caballeros*. Finally nobility conferred exemption from personal taxation; indeed tax exemption was the crucial test of *hidalguía*. Minor nobles, on the margin of their class, watched the municipal tax registers with acute anxiety, for it was these which separated the *pecheros* (commoners or taxpayers) from *hidalgos*. Fiscal privilege was much eroded in the seven-

[19] *Ibid.*, pp. 218–19.   [20] See below, pp. 232–36.

teenth century by the increase of indirect taxes—principally the *millones*—and other impositions which the crown developed in order to make the nobility contribute, sometimes heavily.[21] But they strenuously resisted personal taxes such as the *servicio ordinario y extraordinario*, for exemption identified their status and had great symbolic value. They also maintained their exemption from certain municipal taxes, including the *sisa* (excise duty); and some towns had special shops for nobles where they could buy food free of purchase tax. The financial advantages of fiscal privilege were not to be despised; but its prestige value was even greater, for it conferred *honor* and social status, and in pursuit of this many Castilians were prepared to sacrifice all.

Nobility was not synonymous with wealth. But the poor *hidalgo* of northern Castile, the object of so much ridicule then and since, was not typical of the whole of Spain. Elsewhere the nobility did more than make ends meet. The source of a noble's wealth, however, was just as important as its size. Could a noble work? The question was much debated in legal and genealogical literature, and the ideal answer was that he should not. In the event impoverished *hidalgos* had to work, and in northern Spain they were driven to occupations which were strictly speaking incompatible with nobility. Apart from these, a number of *títulos* and *caballeros* were involved in industry and commerce, and this was acceptable as long as they did not manage their own enterprises or run them in their own homes. In the trading ports, especially in Seville and Cadiz, where they had the example of uninhibited foreigners before their eyes, Spaniards saw virtually no incompatibility between nobility and commercial enterprise, as long as this was wholesale, successful, and large-scale.

In practice, however, noble entrepreneurs were a rarity. The income of the nobility came primarily from land, secured by primogeniture and entail, and reinforced by *señoríos*. Whether income from agriculture dropped in the seventeenth century is difficult to determine. The fact that a noble had a large estate, or even extended it, did not mean that he was economically motivated. Land was a social rather than an economic investment. Nobles were not normally improving farmers and it would need exceptionally favourable conditions to persuade them to invest in extension of farmland. Agricultural prices dropped in the period 1605–12, failed to rise faster than non-agricultural in 1612–25, and lagged far behind non-agricultural in 1625–65.[22] If nobles were incapable of improving their income from land, this could explain their renewed anxiety to supplement their resources by grants and offices. Those who failed to do so and continued to live exclusively

[21] A. Domínguez Ortiz, 'La desigualdad contributiva en Castilla durante el siglo XVII' *Anuario de Historia del Derecho Español*, xxi–xxii (1951–52), 1222–68.

[22] Hamilton, *American Treasure and the Price Revolution in Spain*, pp. 260–61; Carmelo Viñas y Mey, *El problema de la tierra en la España de los siglos XVI–XVII* (Madrid, 1941), p. 30.

on rural revenue tended to feel the pinch. Their more successful colleagues varied their sources of income.[23]

Income from land was frequently supplemented by seigneurial revenue. The aristocracy had acquired *senoríos* either by virtue of immemorial possession, or by royal grant, or by purchase.[24] The early Habsburgs sold *senoríos* chiefly from disentailed lands of the military orders, but Philip IV, who sold on a much bigger scale, alienated royal jurisdiction to do so.[25] Seigneurial jurisdiction over towns and villages gave a noble vassals, offices, and frequently rents, the most important of which were the *alcabalas*. The noble's gain, therefore, was the crown's loss. It lost income from important taxes, cognisance of many law suits, and revenue from litigation. *Alcabalas* were often sold simultaneously with *senoríos*, and by the mid-seventeenth century more than 3,000 townships and villages in Castile paid their *alcabala* tax not to the crown but to their lords.[26] Paradoxically, as the Habsburgs alienated jurisdiction so they tried to reclaim it, either by decree or more commonly by litigation. In the 1630's and 1640's the fiscal of the Council of Finance, Juan Bautista Larrea, initiated a number of court actions against nobles whose right to possession of *alcabalas* was questionable. But the campaign was not uniformly successful, and the most that Philip IV's government accomplished was to oblige some of the wealthier holders to disgorge a lump sum to the treasury by way of composition. It was not until the eighteenth century that the incorporation of *senoríos* was seriously undertaken.

In the course of the seventeenth century general economic depression accentuated the tendency of the nobility to turn to courtly and urban functions; at the same time their educational opportunities improved through their success in usurping the funds of the Colegios Mayores and thus procuring a free university education. They cornered the embassies and the councils; they filled the *corregimientos*, seats in the cortes, desirable benefices in the church; they held most of the crown revenues which were out on lease, and they had heavy investments in *juros* and *censos*. Like the rest of society, of course, they were vulnerable to economic adversity and state policy. Monetary inflation hurt those who lived on fixed incomes. The aristocracy of Aragon and Valencia were hit by the loss of the morisco labour force from 1609. And from the 1620's they were all scrutinised more closely by finance

[23] Domínguez Ortiz, *La sociedad española en el siglo XVII*, pp. 223–28.

[24] Alfonso María Guilarte, *El régimen señorial en el siglo XVI* (Madrid, 1962), pp. 1–12, 173–201, 285–324; Salvador de Moxo, 'Los señoríos. En torno a una problemática para el estudio del régimen señorial', *Hispania*, xxiv (1964), 185–236, 399–430.

[25] Salvador de Moxo, *La incorporación de señoríos en la España del antiguo régimen* (Valladolid, 1959), pp. 13–18.

[26] Salvador de Moxo, 'Los orígenes de la percepción de alcabalas por particulares', *Hispania*, xviii (1958), 307–39; see also the same author's *La alcabala. Sobre sus orígenes, concepto y naturaleza* (Madrid, 1963).

K

ministers. Philip IV, desperate to expand his revenue, requested more and more benevolences from the nobility and began to demand military service or alternatively purchase of exemption. In October 1632 the duke of Béjar, the duke of Medina Sidonia, and the marquis of Priego were asked to supply 3,000 men each for the royal army, in effect to depopulate their estates. A year later they were asked to raise this to 4,000. Requests of this kind were issued so frequently that in 1638 the duke of Béjar began to object.[27] Many of those who failed to comply were banished from court to their estates, with admonitions to save now and contribute later. This was one of the reasons for the alienation of the nobility, from Philip IV as well as from Olivares, and it required all the tact of Haro to win them back.

The nobles, however, were their own worst enemies. If they were in genuine difficulties in the seventeenth century it was due primarily to personal ineptitude. So inefficiently did they run their estates that without the built-in check of entail they would have begun to sell out. As it was many of them tried to do so. The crown normally refused permission to alienate any part of an estate, but it looked more indulgently on requests to mortgage property, requests which now flooded into the Council of Castile. While they were amateurs in managing their affairs, the nobles were also prisoners of an expensive system. Great nobles had heavy overheads: they had to live in style and maintain a large household; they were expected to be generous almsgivers, supporters of foundations, chantries and hospitals, all of which ate into the income of any self-respecting noble. For one reason or another many nobles, including the highest, were heavily in debt, and any emergency—service to the crown, a daughter's dowry—found them in trouble. Even the Constable of Castile, Bernardino de Velasco, lord of vast territories, had to plead financial difficulties in 1635, claiming that on succeeding to his patrimony he had found it 'mortgaged up to 400,000 ducats, and most of this sum spent on service to the crown'. The estate of the Enríquez, Admirals of Castile, was constantly besieged by creditors, encumbered as it was with vast debts and heavy expenditure. By 1640 the duke of Infantado was paying 30,000 ducats a year in mortgage repayments. In the middle of the century the house of Pastrana had debts totalling 400,000 ducats and the Council of Castile had to take over the administration of its revenues.[28]

As commerce and industry did not appeal to the higher aristocracy, they sought the sustenance of royal *mercedes*. These were not normally outright grants of money, but 'expenses' for services rendered, and offices, especially the lucrative viceroyalties in Italy and the Indies. Philip III was ridiculously generous with nobles and courtiers, and they looked back on his reign as a

---

[27] Domínguez Ortiz, *La sociedad española en el siglo XVII*, pp. 228–32.
[28] For these and many other examples, *ibid.*, pp. 232–42.

golden age. Olivares attempted to cut back on *mercedes*, but Philip IV was a difficult man to restrain and the aristocratic reaction which followed the count duke's fall unleashed a new flood of pensions and grants. In effect the taxpayers were forced to subsidise an expensive aristocracy. Given the depressed condition of Castile, the lavishing of *mercedes* on nobles while poorer people died of hunger was the most pernicious aspect of the bias towards aristocracy in Spanish society. Parasitism could hardly go further.

From various sources, then, the Spanish nobility derived enormous wealth, even though some of them, like the crown itself, had to live on credit. The fact that aristocratic income was used unproductively was bound to have a harmful effect on the Spanish economy. Some of this wealth, no doubt, was invested in pious and charitable works and, in the first half of Philip IV's reign, in service to the state, But most of it was spent in conspicuous consumption and social ostentation, to the neglect of saving and investment and to the detriment of the balance of payments. The aristocratic way of life stemmed from false ideals of honour and reputation which contaminated the whole of society and seriously compromised economic values.

3. 'La Gente Comun'

A minister of Philip IV noted that Spaniards 'each in their station and estate desire above all else honour and esteem, and everyone tries to advance himself, as can be seen in the fact that sons rarely follow the occupation of their father; the son of a shoemaker hates that occupation, the son of a merchant wishes to be a gentleman, and so it is with the rest'.[29] Spain had no law defining estates, and legally speaking there was no third estate, simply a mass of people—some 6 million—of varying fortune who were only defined by their exclusion from the aristocratic and ecclesiastical estates. There was nothing to stop a commoner who got rich and lived *noblemente* from wearing silk, using a coach, and in general aping the consumer pattern of the nobility.

There were various avenues open to a man of ambition. In the countryside an industrious and thrifty farmer might acquire an entail, then make his presence felt in the local municipality, and finally begin proceedings for ennoblement. In the towns a commoner could purchase an office and move on from there. Or he could enter the church and rely on his qualifications for preferment. The way ahead was difficult and already crowded with nobility. But those who persevered could succeed. '*No tener oficio ni beneficio* came to be synonymous with personal incapacity'.[30] The social preferences were obvious: the most highly regarded careers were in the bureaucracy and the church. Trade and industry attracted far fewer candidates.

Spanish society was not devoid of entrepreneurial instincts. It had its

[29] Quoted *ibid.*, p. 47.   [30] *Ibid.*, p. 47.

manufacturers, shipowners, and merchants, especially in the periphery provinces. The transatlantic trade still sustained a number of Spanish businessmen. No doubt their profits were now reduced and increasingly shared by outsiders, but even in the 1640's the great merchants of Seville were capable of assembling loans for the crown. In 1645 a consortium of Seville businessmen provided an *asiento* of 340,000 escudos, one of a number of transactions of this kind.[31] Spanish entrepreneurs, however, were few in number. They did not form a middle class, with the social and economic objectives of a middle class. Indeed they usually aspired to aristocratic status, preferring to invest their profits in a title, a landed estate, a daughter's dowry, or mortgage-type securities. The mania for aristocratic status was also fed by racial prejudice. In the sixteenth century a number of prominent Spanish businessmen were undoubtedly of Jewish extraction. This fostered a bias against the whole entrepreneurial class and caused many of its members, including those with Jewish ancestry, to buy their way out, to procure land and ennoblement, and thus to make their social status impeccable.

Public policy reinforced private prejudice. In Aragon and Valencia urban middle groups were badly hit by the expulsion of the moriscos, for in effect they lost the income from their investment in morisco agriculture.[32] In Castile taxation fell principally on the non-aristocratic sector and inhibited investment in trade and industry, while government support of monopoly practices stifled the spirit of competition. A distinguished *arbitrista*, González de Cellorigo, argued that disproportion in the incidence of taxation was dividing Spanish society into two groups: 'We lack people in the middle who are neither rich nor poor but follow their natural occupation. And the cause of this defect is our inequitable system of taxation'.[33] Cellorigo was no egalitarian. He wanted an equilibrium between the three social groups; for this reason he viewed with dismay the erosion of the middle sector, as some climbed out and others dropped below. Taxation, of course, reflected rather than created the social structure; from the 1630's, moreover, aristocratic immunity was diminished in various ways. Nevertheless the property and interests of nobles remained basically intact, while nothing was done to give tax relief to entrepreneurial activities. Fiscal policy therefore tended to perpetuate social polarisation.

The result could be seen all over Spain. It could be seen in Madrid. Between 1597 and 1617 the capital doubled its population from 65,000 to 130,000. This was an essentially parasitic community, a focus of consumption

---

[31] Domínguez Ortiz, *Política y hacienda de Felipe IV*, pp. 147–54.
[32] Juan Reglà, 'La expulsión de los moriscos y sus consecuencias en la economía valenciana', *Hispania*, xxiii (1963), 200–18.
[33] Quoted by Sureda Carrión, *La hacienda castellana y los economistas del siglo XVII*, p. 168.

not of production. It comprised on the one hand nobles, courtiers and bureaucrats, people who lived on rents and offices, and on the other hand a vast service sector, together with labourers, underemployed or unemployed, and hordes of adventurers and beggars. With its stark contrast between luxury and squalor, between the elegant palaces of the aristocracy and the adobe dwellings of the masses, Madrid was a microcosm of Spanish society.[34] Burgos, on the other hand, a thriving business centre in the sixteenth century, suffered economic and demographic collapse. No doubt its trade with northern Europe was dislocated by war from the 1580's. But adverse trading conditions alone could not be responsible for the fall in the population of Burgos from 25,000 in the mid-sixteenth century to 8,000 at the end of the seventeenth.[35] The majority of the town's businessmen simply abandoned their class. While 119 merchants attended the *consulado* (merchant guild) assembly in 1535, in 1661 the number was reduced to 8 and these were a majority of the guild's members.[36]

The role of entrepreneur, abandoned by Spaniards, was taken over by foreigners.[37] Since the sixteenth century the principal bankers of the crown had been foreigners. By the 1620's Italians, mainly Genoese, dominated the *asiento* business. The Fuggers were now past their peak, but they still possessed two assets, the lease of the *cruzada*, one of the most lucrative revenues in Spain, and the Almaden mercury mine. Whoever they were the foreign *asentistas* were a hated group, popularly regarded as leeches on the Spanish economy, accused of enriching themselves at the expense of the treasury and the taxpayer, charging excessive interest, appropriating the best revenues, and using their right to export silver for the crown as a cloak for private transactions. There was some truth in these allegations, but basically the foreign bankers simply supplied a demand, on a scale far beyond the capacity of Spanish financiers, and with an eye to the customer's unreliability. Eventually, their resources much reduced by the suspension of payments in 1627 and the insatiable demands of Philip IV and Olivares, the Italians were joined by a number of Portuguese financiers.

[34] Domínguez Ortiz, *La sociedad española en el siglo XVII*, pp. 129–36; Ricardo Martorell *Aportaciones al estudio de la población de Madrid en el siglo XVII* (Madrid, 1930); C. Viñas y Mey, 'Notas sobre la estructura social demográfica del Madrid de los Austrias', *Revista de la Universidad de Madrid*, iv (1955), 461–96.
[35] Domínguez Ortiz, *La sociedad española en el siglo XVII*, pp. 143–45.
[36] The number of insurance policies issued in Burgos dropped drastically in the first decade of the seventeenth century; see R. S. Smith, *The Spanish Guild Merchant. A History of the Consulado 1250–1700* (Durham, N.C., 1940), p. 71; see also Manuel Basas Fernández, *El Consulado de Burgos en el siglo XVI* (Madrid, 1963).
[37] A. Girard, 'Les étrangers dans la vie économique de l'Espagne au XVIe et XVIIe siècles', *Annales d'Histoire Economique et Sociale*, xxiv (1933), 567–78; A. Domínguez Ortiz, 'Los extranjeros en la vida española durante el siglo XVII', *Estudios de Historia Social de España*, iv, 2 (1960), 293–426; H. Sánchez de Sopranis, 'Las naciones extranjeras en Cádiz durante el siglo XVII', *Estudios de Historia Social de España*, iv, 2 (1960), 643–877,

The Portuguese *marranos* were convert Jews, some of them descendants of Spanish Jews expelled in 1492. They were prominent in the domestic and international trade of Portugal; they almost monopolised the slave trade; and they handled spices, sugar and other colonial commodities. In Portugal they were vulnerable. The Inquisition suspected their orthodoxy and the populace resented their wealth. So they welcomed the union of the crowns and began to seek new pastures in Spain. In return for a handsome subsidy to the crown they were given the right to emigrate in 1601, and many of them immediately entered Spain. There they extended their business operations, and were soon accused of every misdemeanour from cornering the Indies trade to organising prostitution. The privilege of 1601 was revoked in 1610, but they simply evaded the law. From the beginning of Philip IV's reign they were lessees of royal revenues, notably the inland customs. Olivares, who seems to have been free of racial prejudice, brought them into the *asiento* business, and under his patronage they were allowed freedom of movement within the peninsula and to some extent protected from the attentions of the Inquisition.[38] In addition to the small group of *asentistas*—Duarte Fernández, Simón Suárez, Manuel de Paz, and Juan Núñez Saravia—lesser Portuguese businessmen swarmed into Spain to deploy their enterprise and capital, and particularly to procure a foothold in the Indies trade. By 1640 there were probably 2,000 Portuguese merchants in Seville alone. Not all of these immigrants escaped intact. One of the principal *asentistas*, Juan Núñez Saravia, was accused of judaising and exporting bullion to colleagues abroad, for which he suffered five years imprisonment, while others were subject to fines and confiscations.[39] Yet on the whole the Portuguese in Castile had a good run for their money under Olivares, and even in the first years of the Portuguese rebellion the Spanish authorities shielded most of them from popular hatred. After the fall of Olivares, however, they were more vulnerable; some of them were further hit by the state bankruptcy of 1647; and the Castilian economy became too depressed to offer them easy profits.[40] The mid-seventeenth century, therefore, saw a further flight of merchants and capital from Spain, as the Portuguese went in search of new opportunities in northern Europe, leaving behind from their number only a few administrators of royal revenues.

Meanwhile other foreigners filled the ranks vacated by Spaniards and Portuguese. Spain's overseas trade, especially the Indies trade, drew increasing

[38] A. Domínguez Ortiz, 'Los conversos de orígen judío después de la expulsión', *Estudios de Historia Social de España*, iii (1955), 226–431.

[39] A. Domínguez Ortiz, 'El proceso inquisitorial de Juan Núñez Saravia, banquero de Felipe IV', *Hispania*, xv (1955), 559–81.

[40] J. Caro Baroja, *Los judíos en la España moderna y contemporanea* (3 vols., Madrid, 1962), ii, 68–131; Henry Kamen, *The Spanish Inquisition* (London, 1965), pp. 221–26.

numbers of foreign merchants to her ports as importers, exporters, factors and agents.[41] This was simply another sign of the country's underdevelopment. Spain was a good export market for manufactured goods and a useful source of certain raw materials. As the foreigners had the goods, the capital and the shipping, they could retain in their own hands the whole import–export operation, reducing their Spanish counterparts to little more than commission agents. Many of the foreign merchants became permanent residents in Spain; they were to be found chiefly in Seville and Cadiz, where they could supervise the re-export of their goods to the Spanish Indies. In the course of the seventeenth century the Genoese and Flemings were joined in the ports of Andalucía by growing numbers of non-allied nationals, notably the French, English and Dutch. Spain had a liberal immigration policy and her reputation for religious intolerance was much exaggerated abroad; by the middle of the century the English had developed a working relation with the Inquisition and they were allowed in effect to reside in Spain without harassment; even during wartime, when their position was necessarily more difficult, many of them chose to remain. The actual number of foreigners in Spain at any one time is a matter of speculation. In 1640 Seville had about 12,000, one-tenth of its population; in 1665, after the ravages of the great plague, the city still had 7,000 foreigners. Altogether, in 1650, there were between 120,000 and 150,000 foreign residents in the whole country.[42] These in effect were Spain's entrepreneurial class.

The vast majority of Spaniards, peasants in the fields, labourers in the towns, had no hope of advancement, only the fear that they might fall even lower, into that underworld of Spanish society populated by vagabonds, beggars and bandits, the victims of widespread unemployment. Again, fiscal policy perpetuated social malaise, for it weighed most heavily on the underprivileged. The *alcabala* tax was particularly loaded against the poor; the ultimate consumer bought an article at a price inflated by an accumulation of taxes charged every time it changed hands.[43] From the end of the sixteenth century a new tax appeared, the *millones*, and this fell chiefly on three basic foodstuffs, meat, wine and oil. For the poor this caused an intolerable rise in the cost of living, and one which they were less capable of evading than the nobility. Where towns or districts paid a composition tax, the municipalities, dominated by a wealthy oligarchy, fixed the tax rates to benefit themselves; then they frequently sold the products of their estates with the purchase tax added, passing only a portion to the treasury. The fiscal system accelerated

---

[41] Sánchez de Sopranis, 'Las naciones extranjeras en Cádiz durante el siglo XVII', *op. cit.*, pp. 647–59.

[42] Domínguez Ortiz, 'Los extranjeros en la vida española durante el siglo XVII', *op. cit.*, pp. 389–91.

[43] Sureda Carrión, *op. cit.*, p. 180.

the rural depopulation of Castile. And as some people fled from the tax-collector, the quota for that district fell entirely on those who remained, who in turn would be driven to emigrate. Not a few villages of Castile disappeared from the map in the course of the century, their inhabitants joining the urban proletariat, not because the towns were booming or could offer them work but because there was less likelihood of starving there than in the countryside. Many Spaniards lived more or less below subsistence level, and bitter experience taught them that from those who had least most was taken.

On more than one occasion, in Andalucía in the 1650's and in Valencia later in the century, peasant unrest exploded into violence, but the alliance between crown and aristocracy was too close and the forces of law and order were too solid to leave any opening for social revolution. In the event the mass of the Spanish poor accepted their fate with mute resignation. Their only spokesmen were a few *arbitristas*, though these did not always go to the root of the problem which lay in the maldistribution of agrarian property. Many of them criticised fiscal injustice or, as Jacinto de Alcazar Arriaza put it, 'the inequality in the system of taxes, which the poor pay and the rich enjoy'.[44] Fernández Navarrete denounced tax exemption: 'It is not just that some should be exempt at the expense of others and that the whole burden should fall on the weak shoulders of peasants and labourers'.[45] Padre López Bravo, writing at the beginning of Philip IV's reign, attacked the distribution of property: 'It is highly pernicious that poverty should have its origin in an unjust distribution of wealth, causing the affluence of the few and the depriva-tion of the many. . . . The result is that people abandon the countryside for the towns; the poor become slaves of the rich; and the rich intensify their pursuit of luxury and pleasure'.[46] In the 1620's the Benedectine Benito de Peñalosa y Mondragón recorded the 'extreme misery' of the Castilian peas-ants, their 'simple meals of garlic, onions, low-grade beef, bread of barley and rye'; their rough clothes, 'sandals, loose coats, large hoods, coarse collars, burlap shirts, sheepskin coats preserved with resin'; their miserable dwellings, 'poor cottages and huts with mud walls crumbling or fallen'; and their pitiful possessions, 'ill-cultivated fields, with emaciated and starving cattle, deprived of common lands for pasture'.[47]

The Spanish peasants were hopeless victims of the seigneurial society in which they lived, a society rigid in its structure and undeviating in its ideals. No doubt underdevelopment immobilised this society and prolonged its stagnation. Perhaps economic growth would have raised the living standards

---

[44] Quoted *ibid.*, p. 181.　　　　[45] Quoted *ibid.*, p. 194.
[46] Quoted by J. Reglà, 'La época de los dos ultimos Austrias', *Historia social y económica de España y América*, iii, 272.　　　　[47] Quoted *ibid.*, pp. 325–26.

of the peasants and nurtured a native middle class. But social rigidity was a cause as well as a result of economic depression. The pattern of investment in Spain reflected the structure of society. When it was not hoarded or spent in conspicuous consumption, capital tended to flow into *asientos, juros* and *censos*, that is loans destined primarily to finance state and consumer expenditure, rather than into productive enterprises. One of the reasons was the higher rate of return on these investments—7 per cent. on *censos*, much more on *asientos*—than on those in other undertakings; agriculture, according to the *arbitristas*, yielded a return of only 4 per cent. But the basic reason was to be found in deeply rooted social ideals, which placed greater value on honour and status than on entrepreneurial activity. Even if the consumption level of the upper income groups could have been reduced there was no guarantee that the savings would have been invested in agriculture and industry.

4. Agriculture and Industry

Spain can be divided into two parts, wet and dry. In both these Spains the people had to struggle against adverse topographical or climatic conditions. In the plains of Castile, Extremadura and Andalucía rainfall was erratic and the soil poor; when it rained it rained in torrents on a soil subject to erosion; and in the summer there was drought. The arid terrain of the central plateau discouraged tillage and made it difficult to extend and improve cultivation. In those areas where rainfall was adequate, in Galicia for example, the soil was frequently bad with high acidic content. If there was little investment in agriculture, therefore, one of the reasons was that the land was not good enough to guarantee returns. It would have needed a technical revolution to make it so. Yet while their inheritance was meagre, Spaniards did not endeavour to use it wisely. Although in the course of the seventeenth century there was some extension of new crops, such as the potato and maize, this was not on a scale to produce agricultural change. The area under cultivation did not increase in the course of the century. Land tenure remained inefficient and cultivation backward.[48]

Some parts of Spain had been forced into fertility by irrigation and hard work. Valencia, for example, had been endowed with rich *huertas* (market gardens), and even the arid uplands had been made to yield crops by the industry of the moriscos. The expulsion of the latter adversely affected production, particularly of the basic crops of the region: sugar, rice and grain, so that Valencia, according to a contemporary chronicler, 'which was formerly the most flourishing region of Spain is now reduced to an arid and

[48] Manuel Colmeiro, *Historia de la economía política en España* (first published 1863; 2 vols., Madrid, 1965), ii, 657–717.

neglected desert'.[49] Sugar output had hardly recovered when it was further hit by competition from Brazilian and Caribbean sugar.[50] Rice production no longer yielded a surplus for export, and after 1609 Valencia was dependent on imported grain. Finally, the expulsion of the moriscos caused an even greater concentration of agrarian property, for in the hard times which followed only the biggest and most powerful landowners could survive.

Meanwhile Castile was also losing its labour force. Rural depopulation seems to have reached serious proportions from the late sixteenth century. In 1598 the cortes urged the government to take measures to increase farming and stock-breeding: 'The principal cause of decrease in cultivation is the great dearth of people; many places are visibly depopulated and others have lost almost half of their inhabitants'.[51] Observers pointed specifically to the shortage of labourers, blaming wars, emigration to the Indies, sale of common land, pressure of powerful landlords, and above all fiscal inequality which caused people to flee from the tax-collector.[52] The Duero basin was one of the zones particularly affected; it was estimated that in the first two decades of the seventeenth century the number of labourers in the diocese of Salamanca dropped from 8,345 to 4,135, and more than eighty places had been depopulated. It was probably this region that the count of Gondomar, whose home was in Valladolid, had in mind when he wrote of the depopulation, poverty and misery of Spain, the land which foreigners found more distressing and deserted than any other in Europe.[53]

The evidence from government reports and private memoranda are too consistent to be ignored. Lison y Biedma, member for Granada in the cortes of 1621, recorded:

Numerous places have become depopulated and disappeared from the map, in some provinces as many as fifty or sixty, their churches decayed, houses in ruins, property wasted, and fields uncultivated. The vassals who formerly cultivated them now wander the roads with their wives and children, searching from district to district for a living, and eating herbs and roots to keep alive. Others go to distant provinces which are not so burdened with taxation, with the *millones*, the *alcabalas* and other impositions; for it is the weight of taxation and the oppression of the tax-collectors which are the principal causes of this depopulation.[54]

[49] Quoted by Boronat, *Los moriscos españoles y su expulsión*, ii, 329.

[50] Reglà, 'La expulsión de los moriscos y sus consecuencias en la economía valenciana', *op. cit.* pp. 211–12.   [51] *Actas*, xv, 748.

[52] Reports of corregidores, c. 1600, in Viñas y Mey, *El problema de la tierra en la España de los siglos XVI–XVII*, appendix I.

[53] Gondomar to Philip III, 1619, *Documentos inéditos para la historia de España* (new series, 4 vols., Madrid, 1936–45), ii, 131–46.

[54] Quoted by Domínguez Ortiz, *La sociedad española en el siglo XVII*, p. 119.

Other observers attributed rural depopulation to the sale of *tierras baldías*, or common waste lands. Alienation of the commons, authorised by Philip II and his successors, deprived the poor of the plots which they were supposed to receive in rotation, of pasture for their cattle, sheep and goats, and of firewood from the forests, all of which had been of common usage in the villages. In 1628 the *arbitrista* Barbón y Castañeda remarked: 'If the sale of common land is extended to the rest of Spain then it will experience the same ruin as Old Castile; for it is a truism that the population level of towns and villages depends on the status and treatment accorded to their inhabitants'.[55] By the 1660's, after half a century of war and other adversities, the situation had further deteriorated. According to a memorandum written by a royal minister in 1669:

> This country has now plunged the depths of misfortune and reached a state of prostration unprecedented in our history. In the course of my office I have to visit many places which a few years ago had 1000 inhabitants and now have less than 500, while those which used to have 500 now have barely 100. In all of them there are numerous families who go one or two days without a full meal, and others live on herbs and roots from the fields.[56]

Declarations of this kind, of course, are statistically unreliable, and their authors tend to generalise from a particular district. But their broad conclusions are vindicated by public documents, particularly financial documents. Depopulation reached a point where communities had to request a lowering of the tax quota which they had been set in the registers of 1591–94. The administration only granted a reduction when a community had lost one-half or one-third of its population. Surviving evidence reveals that 156 communities requested, and in most cases procured, a reduction of their tax quota in the course of the seventeenth century, and these communities were only a portion of those which became depopulated.[57] Most of them were in the two Castiles, Extremadura and Andalucía, that is in dry Spain. The zone of maximum depopulation was around Guadalajara and Toledo in New Castile. The inhabitants of these bleak plains and wild *sierras* scraped a living from the cultivation of vines and olives and later from cereal monoculture. Abrupt climatic changes in the second half of the seventeenth century and in particular a series of disastrous frosts ruined this marginal cultivation and caused the mass exodus of its

[55] Quoted *ibid.*, pp. 119–20.
[56] Quoted by Duque de Maura, *Vida y reinado de Carlos II* (2nd ed., 2 vols., Madrid, 1954), i, 396.
[57] Domínguez Ortiz publishes the details in *La sociedad española en el siglo XVII*, appendix I, pp. 325–37.

practitioners, most of whom presumably made their way to nearby Madrid.

Some of the causes of rural depopulation—plague, famine and war—have already been noticed. In addition to these classical adversities, there were certain institutional obstacles to agricultural progress in this period. One of these, though probably the least important, was price control of grain. Throughout the sixteenth century government controls were consistently applied in an effort to counter rising prices. This policy, of course, favoured the consumer against the producer, whose own costs were also subject to inflation, and it was highly unpopular with farmers and peasants. In the first half of the seventeenth century there was a gradual movement towards a free market in grain, in a belated attempt to improve production and alleviate rural distress. Between 1619 and 1628, and again from 1632 to 1650, farmers were free to sell their grain at unregulated prices. By this time agriculture was too stagnant to respond to price de-control alone. But even in its hey-day the policy of control had never been fully enforced and farmers had been driven to devise means of exceeding the ceilings. This factor, therefore, was not a major cause of agricultural depression.[58]

Taxation was one of the greatest obstacles to farming in Spain. Burden after burden was imposed on the Castilian peasant, until the weight became more than he could bear. First he paid dues to his lord. Then he paid tithes to the church, and these were one of his heaviest outgoings, some ten to twenty times higher than seigneurial dues. Next he paid taxes to the crown, the *servicios* and *millones* on basic consumer goods. Finally he paid rent to his landlord and instalments on his mortgage. At the end of the sixteenth century these accumulated obligations consumed more than 50 per cent. of a peasant's product in New Castile.[59] In other words more than half of the crop so laboriously farmed by the New Castilian peasantry went to enrich non-peasant classes. And from the pittance that remained to him the peasant farmer had to live, support his family, pay his labourers, renew his equipment and buy his seeds. Little wonder that many of them abandoned the struggle in despair.

The peasant farmer was caught between the tax-collector and the big landowner. The concentration of landed property in the hands of the higher nobility was difficult to break and easy to extend. Established in their vast latifundia, secured by entail, and fortified by seigneurial power, the aristocracy were in an impregnable position which only their own improvidence could subvert. And they were well placed to make further conquests. As they dominated the higher administration and municipal government they could

[58] Hamilton, *American Treasure and the Price Revolution in Spain,* pp. 254–56.
[59] Noël Salomon, *La campagne de Nouvelle Castille à la fin du XVIe siècle d'après les Relaciones topográficas* (Paris, 1964), pp. 212–51.

appropriate common land with impunity and without too much expense. They also absorbed farms previously owned by small proprietors who could not keep up with their overheads, their taxes, and their mortgage repayments. The *censos*, or mortgage system, offered only a short-term escape for the small farmer and he tended to ruin himself by it.[60] The time came when many of them were forced to redeem their mortgages at the expense of their property and sell out to their more powerful neighbours, who were anxious to round off their estates. Many aristocratic proprietors were absentee landlords who regarded their estates as a status symbol rather than an investment. The great estate was a social not an economic institution. It was wasteful of land and rarely became an efficient unit of production. It was a further obstacle to rural change.

Depressed by taxation and the agrarian structure, agriculture was then kept prostrate by the traditional bias towards livestock farming in Castile.[61] The Mesta, the organisation of migrating herdsmen, had already won the struggle for access to commons, waste lands, fallow strips adjoining tilled fields and other town lands; the notorious law of *posesión*, by which a Mesta member was granted permanent tenancy of any field he had occupied, continued to operate; and Philip II and his successors reinforced previous legislation in favour of pastoral and against arable farming.[62] The cumulative effect of this policy was to prevent the extension of arable lands in central and southern Castile and to accelerate rural depopulation. Yet in the second half of the sixteenth century the power of the Mesta had begun to wane. Its flocks of sheep and its wool production ceased to expand; its profits were eroded by heavy taxation; and its legal position was gradually subverted. In a series of important law-suits Mesta members lost a number of pasture privileges. Their opponents were towns and local agrarian interests, fighting for possession of common lands. But this was not a victory for arable farming: the new enclosers were simply the sedentary branch of the pastoral industry, enclosing for ox pastures, swine fields and non-migratory sheep grazing. By the end of the seventeenth century, under pressure of independent landowners, farmers and peasants, the Mesta had further retreated, but so had arable farming.[63] The consequence of this was that Spain continued to suffer periodic subsistence crises and to depend on the import of foreign grain. Valencia needed imports from the Mediterranean area, Andalucía from northern Europe. In 1635, during the war with the United Provinces and France, when trade with the enemy was prohibited, San Sebastián complained

---

[60] *Ibid.*, pp. 245–47.

[61] See *Spain under the Habsburgs*, i, 17–19, 115–16, 143.

[62] J. Klein, *The Mesta. A Study in Spanish Economic History*, 1273–1836 (Cambridge, Mass., 1920), pp. 93–94, 322.

[63] *Ibid.*, pp. 279, 337–43.

that Guipúzcoa was suffering from severe grain shortage, because its normal suppliers, the Dutch and the French, were excluded from Spanish ports.[64]

Thwarted on every side, agriculture yielded progressively less in the course of the seventeenth century, especially on small farms. There was no technical progress to enable farmers to expand production and cut costs. As the *arbitrista* Pérez del Barrio noted in 1697: 'We still follow the ancient method of scratching at the top-soil with a plough, then letting it lie fallow for three or four years, without ever asking the real causes of sterility but attributing everything to lack of water'.[65]

Agriculture was the key which locked the door to economic growth in Spain. Without agrarian reform there was no prospect of raising the living standards of the mass of the people, and without this there was no possibility of industrial development. Peasants living at subsistence level were not regular consumers of manufactures; and urban workers had to pay too much for food to have anything left for consumer goods. Inhibited by the mediocrity of the market, industry was also frustrated by the pattern of consumption and investment in Spain. The small luxury market preferred foreign goods, which were a drain on domestic capital; what was left was invested in state and consumer loans rather than risked in industrial enterprise.[66] Industry was also depressed by the fiscal policy of the state which penalised production by heavy purchase taxes.[67] But this was not all. Internal customs barriers impeded the free movement of materials and goods. There were customs posts between Castile, the Basque provinces, Navarre, the Aragonese provinces, and Andalucía; and royal customs, usually at 10 per cent., were accompanied by numerous municipal and seigneurial tolls, which further encumbered the transit of goods.[68] It was frequently cheaper to import foreign manufactures by sea than to place orders within Spain. As Gondomar pointed out in 1616:

It would be better for Spain to remove all internal customs and to increase those at the ports, where foreigners would pay and not the natives who

[64] A. Domínguez Ortiz, 'Guerra económica y comercio extranjero en el reinado de Felipe IV', *Hispania*, xxiii (1963), 94–95.

[65] Quoted by Reglà, 'La época de los dos últimos Austrias', *Historia social y económica de España y América*, iii, 342.

[66] For a different interpretation of the failure of Spanish industry see E. J. Hamilton, 'American Treasure and the Rise of Capitalism, 1500–1700', *Economica*, ix (1929), 338–57. According to Hamilton, the lag of prices behind wages in Spain gave insufficient profits to manufacturers and deterred investment in industry, while there was no technical progress to reduce costs; but it has still to be shown that wages of industrial workers in Spain were in general higher than those of workers in industrialising countries. See the same author's 'The Decline of Spain', *Economic History Review*, 1st ser. viii (1938), 168–79.

[67] Salvador de Moxo, *La alcabala. Sobre sus orígenes, concepto y naturaleza* (Madrid, 1963).

[68] J. Carrera Pujal, *Historia política y económica de Cataluña*, ii, 459.

trade within the country ... It is more convenient at the moment for consumers in Galicia, Asturias, Vizcaya, Navarre, Aragon, Valencia, Catalonia, Andalucía and Portugal to get their cloth from London than from Segovia.[69]

Virtually every sector of Spanish industry was depressed in the seventeenth century, though the depression was more serious in the major sectors—textiles, metallurgy and shipbuilding—than in light industries supplying local markets. The worst victim was the once-booming textile industry, embracing the woollen cloth of Segovia, Toledo and Cuenca, and the silks of Granada, Malaga, Seville and Toledo.[70] While none of these centres actually ceased production, all of them suffered severe recession, unemployment, and loss of export markets. Their individual performance cannot be charted with any precision, but their collapse is to be seen in its consequences. Between 1591 and 1700 the population of Segovia dropped from 25,000 to 8,000, that of Cuenca from 15,000 to 5,000. Toledo's failure was spectacular. Measured in the number of looms in operation, its woollen output fell by three-quarters in the first two-thirds of the seventeenth century; in the 1660's thousands of silk looms closed down, and by 1685 there were only 600 in active operation; and its population fell from 60,000 in the late sixteenth century to 20,000 in 1691, by which time Toledo was a town of churches and convents.[71] The depopulation of these industrial centres further reduced the demand for consumer goods, while the loss of skilled labour worsened the prospects of revival; subsequent attempts to rebuild the textile industry invariably involved the employment of foreign craftsmen or management. To some extent Spanish textiles failed to adapt themselves to changes in consumer tastes. They lost the home market to competition from English cloth: England possessed a quasi-monopoly of long-staple light-weight wool, especially suitable for wear in Mediterranean countries, and it was partly this which enabled English worsted manufacturers to dominate the Spanish market in the seventeenth century.[72]

Spain had formerly possessed a small but active metallurgical industry, centred in the northern provinces of Vizcaya and Guipúzcoa. By the 1550's this consisted of some 300 iron-works, powered by large water-driven hammers, and producing about 300,000 quintals (3,300 tons) of iron and steel

[69] Gondomar to Philip III, 1616, in Sureda Carrión, op. cit., pp. 123–24.

[70] On Spanish industry in the seventeenth century see Colmeiro, op. cit., ii, 783–97; J. Carrera Pujal, Historia de la economía española (5 vols., Barcelona, 1943–47), i–ii; Santiago Rodríguez García El arte de las sedas valencianas en el siglo XVIII (Valencia, 1959).

[71] Domínguez Ortiz, La sociedad española en el siglo XVII, pp. 136–39.

[72] P. J. Bowden, 'Wool supply and the woollen industry', Economic History Review, 2nd ser., ix (1956–57), 44–58.

goods a year.[73] Two-thirds of this output consisted of arms, ships' parts, and general hardware, while the rest was in the form of ingots. Defence orders obviously provided a stimulus to the metallurgical industry and indeed exceeded its capacity. In the first decades of the seventeenth century Spanish firms were still supplying all types of arms but no longer on the scale with which they had supplied the Armada of 1588. By this time output of iron and steel manufactures seems to have dropped to some 100,000 quintals a year. A report of 1634 estimated that 80,000 quintals of iron and steel a year, about three-quarters in the form of manufactured products, were being shipped through Bilbao for other parts of Spain, for the colonies, and for export abroad.[74] The industry could no longer meet domestic requirements. As early as 1619 the *arbitrista* Sancho de Moncada claimed that although iron ore was exported the country had to import some 2 million ducats' worth of iron and steel manufactures every year. These included arms. The most famous centre for swords and daggers had been Toledo, but by the 1650's its forges had almost ceased production; Vizcaya still produced a few but they were extremely expensive.[75] In the second half of the seventeenth century the country depended for its hardware on England and France, who also supplied much of its military equipment. Spain, a military power for so long, no longer even possessed an adequate arms industry.

The shipbuilding industry had experienced a boom in the sixteenth century, stimulated by orders for the Indies trade and defence requirements.[76] Now orders were less frequent and more difficult to meet. The Barcelona shipyards, rescued from stagnation by Philip II's naval war against Islam, did not sustain their performance in the seventeenth century; shippers tended increasingly to purchase or hire vessels in Italy.[77] The shipyards of northern Spain were more active than those of Catalonia. Although they had come to depend heavily on imports of timber and naval stores from the Baltic, they had so far survived the attempts of Spain's northern enemies to cut these vital supplies. In the best years of the sixteenth century there were orders totalling 15,000 *toneladas* under construction at one time in the shipyards of Bilbao.[78] Production continued, though on a reduced scale, in the first decades of the seventeenth century, and vessels were still built for the navy, the merchant marine,

---

[73] T. Guiard Larrauri, *Historia del Consulado y Casa de Contratación de Bilbao y del comercio de la villa (1511–1880)* (2 vols., Bilbao, 1913–14); J. Caro Baroja, *Los Vascos. Etnología* (San Sebastian, 1949), pp. 255–71.   [74] Guiard, *op. cit.*, i, 526.

[75] Antoine Brunel, 'Voyage d'Espagne' (1655), *Revue Hispanique*, xxx (1914), 119–376.

[76] See *Spain under the Habsburgs*, i, 117–19.

[77] Carrera Pujal, *Historia política y económica de Cataluña*, ii, 333–69.

[78] Gervasio de Artíñano de Galdárano, *Historia del comercio con las Indias durante el dominio de los Austrias* (Madrid, 1917), pp. 247–48; see the same author's *La arquitectura naval española (en madera)* (Madrid, 1920).

Las Hilanderas

Facing p. 150

including transports for iron, and the fishing industry. It was reported by the *consulado* of Bilbao in 1630 that 40 galleons, many of 600–700 tons, had been constructed in the port's shipyards during the previous twenty years. In 1640 there were four large vessels under construction, and in 1662 there were ten.[79] In 1677–79 five vessels were built in the various yards of Guipúzcoa. One of the leading shipbuilders in the first half of the century was Pedro de Colima who undertook to construct 12 galleons of 800 tons in 1638 and 6 galleons of 850 tons the following year in the shipyards of San Sebastian, Ubursil and Osorno.[80]

While the Basque shipbuilding industry survived in the seventeenth century it was only a shadow of its former self. It suffered in the first place from the recession in the Indies trade from the 1620's which seriously reduced investment in new ocean-going vessels.[81] It was, moreover, heavily dependent on foreign-based service industries for the supply of masts, tar, hemp and sail. Spain could not furnish appropriate timber in sufficient quantity, and she produced virtually no naval stores; these had to be imported from the Baltic, and as war material they were a particular target of the Dutch blockade. Shortage of naval stores raised their price; shipbuilding costs were also raised by shortage of skilled labour which inflated the industry's wages bill. Tomás Cano, a former captain, calculated in 1612 that a vessel of 500 tons, which in the mid-sixteenth century cost 4,000 ducats, now cost 15,000.[82] Yet adverse conditions were not the only enemy of the Basque shipbuilding industry. It was also a victim of its own technical failure. In the period 1614–22 the number of Basque-built vessels in the Indies trade fell dramatically; in the next three decades it fell further, and Basque vessels came to constitute less than one-third of those operating on the transatlantic run, losing place to foreign vessels (more than one-third) and even to American-built vessels (about one-third).[83] Shippers at Seville and Cadiz no longer merely tolerated foreign vessels: they preferred them, and one of the reasons was their superior quality. In the first quarter of the seventeenth century a series of losses at sea cast serious doubts upon the adequacy of Spanish-built ships and caused many shippers to complain of their technical inferiority. As more and more foreign transports entered the Indies trade the government made several attempts by decree to impose on the Basque industry new standards of construction and new proportions in vessels for the

[79] Guiard, *op. cit.*, i, 531; see the same author's *La industria naval vizcaína. Anotaciones históricas y estadísticas* (Bilbao, 1917).

[80] José de Veitia Linage, *Norte de la contratación de las Indias Occidentales* [1672] (Buenos Aires, 1945), p. 667. The price contracted for was 30 ducats a ton.

[81] Chaunu, *Séville et l'Atlantique*, viii, 2, 2, pp. 1046, 1520–21, 1597.

[82] *Arte de Navegar*, 1612, quoted in Braudel, *op. cit.*, p. 399.

[83] Chaunu, *Séville et l'Atlantique*, vi, 1, pp. 114–67; viii, 2, 2, pp. 1563, 1682, 1757–58, 1831.

L

transatlantic run.[84] Yet by 1640 little progress had been made. A treatise published in that year focused on two weaknesses of the industry.[85] It was starved of naval stores and other raw materials, and these were only available at prices well above the general price-level. The industry also lacked technical proficiency, and was impervious to change; it still produced huge and ponderous galleons, floating castles which were years behind the vessels of northern Europe in manoeuvrability and adaptability.

While textiles, metallurgy and shipbuilding were all in serious trouble in the seventeenth century, import-substitution industries seemed to have fared better. In Barcelona and Valencia the manufacture of ceramics and glass, drawing on local raw materials, maintained its performance, and output was probably adequate for the home market, though this was not large as glass was less used for windows in Spain than elsewhere in Europe. Leather manufacture at Córdoba (shoes), and Ciudad Real and Ocana (gloves), seems to have diminished but still supplied the home market. Soap manufacturing was continued in establishments at Triana (Seville) and Valencia, and even succeeded in exporting some of its product. Paper mills, on the other hand, while continuing production at Segovia, Gerona and Cuenca, could not meet domestic demand, and Spain depended heavily on paper imports throughout the seventeenth century.[86]

The evidence is too scanty to permit a quantitative assessment of Spanish industry in the seventeenth century, and the most that it yields is a general impression. Two conclusions may be justified. The traditional picture of universal and utter collapse has been overdrawn. A number of light industries, fed by local raw materials and catering for the home market, stayed in business and effectively substituted for imports. But in three of the European growth industries of the period—textiles, metallurgy and shipbuilding—Spain suffered serious recession and lagged far behind her rivals in northern Europe. She lost her export markets, of course, but she also lost a large part of her domestic and colonial markets; she lost them to the English, the French and the Dutch.

Contemporary proposals for remedying the situation were based on mercantilist assumptions.[87] A typical example was the submission made by

[84] See A. P. Usher, 'Spanish Ships and Shipping in the 16th and 17th centuries', in *Facts and Factors in Economic History. Essays presented to Edward Francis Gay* (Cambridge, Mass., 1932), pp. 189–90.

[85] 'Diálogo entre un viscaíno y un montañes sobre construcción de naves', 1640, summarised in Chaunu, *Séville et l'Atlantique*, v, p. 369; on the neglect of naval architecture in Spain see Veitia Linage, *op. cit.*, p. 665.   [86] Colmeiro, *op. cit.*, ii, 783–97.

[87] On contemporary economic thought see E. J. Hamilton, 'Spanish Mercantilism before 1700', in *Facts and Factors in Economic History*, pp. 214–39; Robert S. Smith, 'Spanish Anti-mercantilism of the Seventeenth Century', *Journal of Political Economy*, xlviii (1940), 401–11; J. Larraz, *La época del mercantilismo en Castilla*, 1500–1700 (2nd ed., Madrid, 1944).

the University of Toledo in a memorandum drafted by one of its professors, Sancho de Moncada. It was argued that countries which produced only primary products were poor and had a trade deficit, for the unit value of their exports was less than that of countries which exported manufactured goods; it followed that Spain should industrialise, and this was also essential for defence needs and to supply the colonies; and industry should be given protection by outright prohibition of foreign manufactured goods. The policy of import prohibition was frequently canvassed and occasionally adopted. A decree issued in the celebrated *Pragmática de Reformación* (10 February 1623) forbad under pain of fine and confiscation the import of textile, leather, and other manufactures for the consumer market, on the grounds that these competed with Spanish products, put Spanish factories and artisans out of work, and impaired the balance of payments.[88] Amidst a chorus of protest from foreign exporters and native importers, the government was forced to concede so many exemptions that the decree became irrelevant. Prohibition simply caused a diminution of trade or, more likely, an expansion of contraband, from both of which the treasury suffered. The basic reason for the failure of this policy was that Spain either took foreign imports or went without manufactures altogether. For the removal of competition could not in itself revive Spanish industry. The mercantilists never explained where the factors of production were to come from. Who was to supply the capital, the entrepreneurial skills and the technical expertise for industrial expansion? And would not industrialisation simply divert resources which could be better used to expand the production of wool, agricultural and other primary products already assured of export markets? Even as an exporter of raw materials Spain's performance was not impressive.

5. FOREIGN TRADE

Spain's commodity exports were limited to a few primary products— wool, wine, olive oil, iron, and cochineal (a re-export from America). Against these she imported textiles, linens, hardware, naval stores, paper, and grain. Large foreign payments also had to be made for defence purposes. The deteriorating balance of payments was bridged by export of gold and silver, when they were available.

Wool continued to be the most important Spanish export commodity. By the end of the sixteenth century the quality of Spanish wool in fineness was accepted as superior to English and it was doing much better than its rival in continental wool markets.[89] Spanish wool maintained its reputation

[88] Domínguez Ortiz, 'Guerra económica y comercio extranjero en el reinado de Felipe IV' *Hispania*, xxiii (1963), 71–110.
[89] Bowden, 'Wool supply and the woollen industry', *op. cit.*, p. 48.

until well past the middle of the seventeenth century. In the meantime it had secured a good market in England. English manufacturers began to increase their import of fine Spanish wool from the 1620's; it was this wool which enabled the West Country to develop the production of a new type of cloth, called Spanish or medley cloth, a high quality product which sold well in northern Europe.[90] In 1667, at the time of the Anglo-Spanish commercial treaty, it was estimated that Spain exported 36,000 to 40,000 bags of wool a year, with 8 *arrobas* of wool in each bag; Holland and Hamburg took 22,000 bags, England between 2,000 and 7,000 bags.[91] While Spanish wool was of good quality it was also expensive. This was due not only to inflationary tendencies in Spain but also to government taxes on wool exports. By 1667 these had reached a level which caused the *consulado* of Bilbao to complain that they were almost equivalent to the value of the commodity taxed.[92] An English estimate in 1680 claimed that fine Spanish wool was 'always near twice as dear as our finest English wool'.[93]

Following the collapse of Burgos, the wool trade was almost entirely handled by the merchants of Bilbao. Bilbao also exported iron, a high quality ore from its hinterland, for which there was a fairly constant demand. In 1680 it was complained in England that the great increase in the import of Spanish iron was detrimental to native iron works.[94] Between wool and iron Bilbao enjoyed some prosperity in the seventeenth century. While the account books of *consulado* income are not a valid index of trade, they give perhaps a general picture of commercial activity. The *consulado* of Bilbao's average annual income was some 607,000 maravedis in the period 1590–96; 565,000 in 1600–25; 725,000 in 1626–51; 1,850,000 in 1651–77; 2,555,000 in 1677–1701.[95] From this it would appear that Bilbao maintained some activity in maritime commerce, and did not suffer the fate of other commercial centres in Spain. The volume of Bilbao's shipping in this period can be deduced from the evidence of the charity tax on each vessel entering and clearing the port. An average of 209 vessels a year paid the tax in the period 1601–26; 184 in 1626–51; 211 in 1651–75; 213 in 1675–1700.[96]

In the first half of the seventeenth century Spanish foreign trade had to operate in conditions of almost permanent warfare. Yet war never caused a complete cessation of trade, even with the enemy. In the long war with

[90] *Ibid.*, pp. 56–58.
[91] Jean O. McLachlan, *Trade and Peace with Old Spain, 1667–1750* (Cambridge, 1940), pp. 8–9.
[92] Klein, *op. cit.*, p. 46; Smith, *The Spanish Guild Merchant*, pp. 74–75.
[93] 'Discourse of Trade', 1680, in J. R. McCulloch, ed., *Early English Tracts on Commerce* (Cambridge, 1954), p. 322.
[94] *Ibid.*, p. 418.
[95] Smith, *The Spanish Guild Merchant*, p. 89.
[96] *Ibid.*, pp. 89–90.

England to 1604, and with the United Provinces to 1609, Spain had to allow her enemies to bring grain and manufactured goods into the peninsula, for she needed these imports and did not have the shipping to handle them; for the rest of her northern trade she had to rely on Hansa shipping. The route between Cadiz and northern Europe, therefore, was still active. Following the renewal of war between Spain and the United Provinces in 1621, the Dutch continued to trade with Spain by various means, inserting their goods via France and Portugal. The trade was so active that the Council of Castile complained in 1624: 'The Dutch buy merchandise from the English, export it here, and take out gold and silver, with which they then finance their rebellion against us'.[97]

The Spanish government attempted to fight back on the commercial front. In October 1624 it created the *Almirantazgo de Sevilla*, a kind of trading company whose function was to provide armed convoys for trade with northern Europe, to attack Dutch shipping, and to keep it out of the peninsula.[98] The company was therefore instructed to maintain an armada of 24 warships and merchant vessels, financed from prizes, condemnations, and a 1 per cent. tax on goods from Andalucía to northern Europe. In view of the difficulty experienced in maintaining armed convoys for the Indies trade, it is not surprising that the *almirantazgo* failed to function in this form. It soon became simply a bureaucratic institution, based on Madrid, which maintained a network of agents for the confiscation of enemy goods entering the penin-sula.[99] The English during the war of 1625–30, and the French during the war of 1635–59, suffered from its attentions. And so, until 1648, did the Dutch. Indeed they were the particular target of this type of economic warfare, but they were skilful enemies. They devised various means of evading the em-bargo; a favoured method, in collaboration with Spanish merchants, was to exchange goods for silver a few miles from the coast.

Spanish merchants complained bitterly against the *almirantazgo*, alleging that it fulfilled none of its positive functions but simply restricted valuable trade. They argued that obstacles to imports not only caused shortages and drove up prices but also harmed Spanish exports, to such an extent that the wine and olive producers of Andalucía were in serious difficulty. Seville merchants were particularly resentful, for they were deprived of their usual supplies for the American trade, and this in turn reduced the sale of re-exports from America; according to the *consulado* of Seville, the price of

---

[97] Quoted by Domínguez Ortiz, 'Guerra económica', *op. cit.*, p. 75; see also Mauro, *Le Portuga et l'Atlantique au XVIIe siècle*, p. 342.

[98] A. Domínguez Ortiz, 'El Almirantazgo de los Países Septentrionales y la política económica de Felipe IV', *Hispania*, xxvii (1947), 272–90.

[99] Domínguez Ortiz, 'Guerra económica', *op. cit.*, pp. 78–81, 85.

cochineal, indigo, and ginger dropped by 25 per cent.[100] Yet the government of Olivares continued to prohibit trade with the enemy, in the belief that prohibition deprived the enemy of wealth. A decree of 16 May 1628 further defined illegal trade: it included enemy and neutral goods carried in enemy vessels, and enemy goods carried in neutral vessels. The list of prohibited goods indicates the type of imports on which Spain normally relied: textiles headed the list, followed by furniture, watches, books, pictures, needles, combs and musical instruments.

Although these measures ceased to apply against England after the Anglo-Spanish peace of 1630, they were intensified against France, especially from the outbreak of full-scale war in 1635. But total closure was never effected. French linens always found a ready market in Spain, chiefly for re-export to the Indies; and shippers relied on the import of French sails for equipping the Indies fleets.[101] The frontier provinces of north-east Spain were also dependent on trade with France, in their case for food imports as well as consumer goods. In these circumstances prohibition was evaded by various devices, ranging from outright contraband to the use of neutral vessels—mainly Hansa and English—which endeavoured to conceal the origins of their cargo. The government itself recognised the need for French imports, from which it could also derive a revenue. It therefore sold licences: in 1638 revenue from licences yielded 255,460 ducats, indicating a substantial trade with France, for the licencees usually exceeded their quotas. In any case, the government could not control climatic conditions and it had to allow the entry of French grain. The Cantabrian region continued to import French grain, and in 1647, a year of poor harvests, Andalucía was allowed to do the same. In 1648 the government believed that peace with Holland would enable it to tighten up on the French trade, as it now had an alternative trading partner. In fact the Dutch simply took the opportunity to carry French merchandise into Spain, as the English were already doing.

By 1650 it was appreciated even in official circles that measures against French trade were ineffective. Yet the policy of prohibiting trade with the enemy continued to be applied, and, by decree of 8 April, it was extended to a new enemy, Cromwell's England. In 1657 the Council of Castile debated its efficacy. A minority group argued that the policy was ineffective and harmful, ineffective because corrupt customs officials connived at evasion, harmful because it deprived the treasury of revenue. Yet the majority of councillors favoured prohibition as a weapon of war and believed that it could be made effective if the Portuguese lessees were removed from the customs houses.

---

[100] Memorandum of the consulado of Seville, 1627, *ibid.*, pp. 85–86.

[101] In the years 1636–37 there was a spurt of demand in the Indies trade which reinforced the need for French goods; see Chaunu, *Séville et l'Atlantique*, v, p. 237; viii, 2, 2, p. 1757.

In the event the weapon was as harmless against England as it had been against France. English goods continued to reach Spain, frequently in Dutch vessels, and to be re-exported to the Spanish Indies.

During war Spain was a target as well as a market for her enemies. Normally the Indies fleets were too strongly defended to offer easy prizes to privateers, and by this time there were very few Spanish vessels on the trade routes of western and northern Europe. Enemy privateering, therefore, was directed essentially against neutral vessels trading in war commodities to Spain. The English took a much stricter view of war contraband than the French and the Dutch, who were prepared to deal in most commodities, including naval stores. English privateers crowded the Channel and sought to cut communications between Spain and northern Europe, at least in respect of vital war supplies. During the war of 1625–30 they were particularly active off the north-west coast of Spain and kept Galicia virtually in a state of siege.[102] In the war of 1655–60, on the other hand, the privateers tended to trade with the enemy, and it was the English navy that conducted operations against Spanish shipping. Spain herself did not develop a privateering industry: there were very few Spanish candidates for licences, and foreign captains could not be trusted. When, after 1648, a number of Dutch captains procured Spanish privateering licences for use against French shipping, they simply traded with France, took the merchandise to the Spanish Indies, and sold it as an alleged prize of war. Basque captains did the same. In 1651 it was alleged that 12–14 vessels were operating in this way.[103] Normally, however, Spain did not issue privateering licences, for she was fearful of massive retaliation.

By the mid-seventeenth century Spain's balance of payments difficulties had worsened. Her export performance was poor: wool output was not increasing, and wine, oil, raisins and other agricultural products were earning little. Bullion had to be expended on Portuguese sugar and spices, on grain from northern Europe and the Mediterranean, and on manufactured goods, arms and naval stores from England, France, Holland, Denmark and Sweden. As an English observer remarked in 1680, 'The exporting of treasure [is] prohibited in Spain under the highest penalties; and yet because Spain is overbalanced by consumptive importations, foreigners continually carry it away'.[104]

Yet peace was hardly more propitious than war. As Spain did not win her prolonged war against Holland, France and finally England, she was forced to concede favourable trading terms to her former enemies, to the Dutch in

---

[102] Domínguez Ortiz, 'Guerra económica', *op. cit.,* pp. 96–98.
[103] *Ibid.,* pp. 99–100.
[104] 'Discourse of Trade', 1680, in McCulloch, *op. cit.,* pp. 390–91.

1648–50, to the French in 1659, and to the English in 1667. The Dutch were acknowledged to have complete freedom to transport merchandise of all countries, including those at war with Spain. By the Treaty of the Pyrenees France procured a most-favoured-nation clause, giving her all the privileges the Dutch had already acquired; and French merchants spent the rest of the century exploiting the treaty.[105] Customs duties were limited; merchants' accounts and warehouses were free from inspection; consuls were appointed in Andalusian towns; and eventually a Judge Conservator was appointed to hear cases involving Frenchmen. Under favourable conditions French trade to Andalucía—chiefly Rouen linens and Lyons silks—expanded rapidly and acquired a large stake in the Indies trade.

The pattern of Spanish trade with England was already established.[106] The chief import was cloth, especially the new worsted fabrics. Fish was another important item, worth perhaps £500,000 a year to England. Spain also took lead, tin, wax, wheat, butter and cheese. She exported oil, wine, dried fruit, iron ore and above all two basic commodities for the English cloth industry, wool and dyeing materials, the latter chiefly American cochineal.[107] England's considerable exports to Spain, and her command of the carrying trade between the two countries, earned her a surplus in bullion with which she financed her trade to other parts of the world. As English merchants wryly remarked, the only advantage Spain possessed was the ability to place an embargo on English property in the event of war: 'In time of free trade with Spain the subjects of England have seldom less in that country than one million pounds sterling besides the great number of ships . . . and in England the Spaniards have no estate to answer such an adventure'.[108]

The Anglo-Spanish treaty of 1667 improved the conditions of trade between the two countries, to the greater benefit of the more powerful partner.[109] It gave the English advantageous terms for important branches of their trade, including the carrying trade and the fishing industry. Without abolishing customs duties, it limited the number of customs officers who might visit an English ship and left the actual level of duties vague enough to enable English merchants to negotiate with compliant officials. And individual merchants came to enjoy the protection of a Judge Conservator

[105] A. Girard, *Le commerce francais à Séville et Cadix au temps des Habsburgs. Contribution à l'étude du commerce étranger en Espagne aux XVIIe et XVIIIe siècles* (Bordeaux, 1932), pp. 133–86.
[106] See Ralph Davis, 'English Foreign Trade, 1660–1700', *Economic History Review*, 2nd ser., vii (1954–55), 150–66.
[107] McLachlan, *Trade and Peace with Old Spain*, p. 10.
[108] 'The Humble Complaint of Merchants', 1660–64, in J. O. McLachlan, 'Documents illustrating Anglo-Spanish trade between the commercial treaty of 1667 and the asiento contract of 1713', *Cambridge Historical Journal*, iv (1932–34), 299–311; see particularly p. 303.
[109] On the treaty of 1667 see *ibid.*, pp. 304–8, and the same author's *Trade and Peace with Old Spain*, pp. 20–22.

who, among other things, prevented inspection of their books. Armed with this treaty, the English developed their trade to Spain in the last decades of the seventeenth century. Spain, on the other hand, continued to suffer a large trade deficit. In 1697–98 the value of Spanish imports from England totalled £580,499 and her exports to England £354,165; in 1698–99 imports totalled £574,628 and exports £469,903; in 1699–1700 imports totalled £610,912 and exports £545,056. The balance against Spain was normally in the region of £100,000 to £200,000.[110]

In the eighteenth century Spanish economists and officials blamed the commercial treaties for Spain's trading adversities.[111] But the treaties did not create economic conditions; they simply reflected Spain's inferiority in manufactures, capital resources, and shipping. Contemporaries were particularly impressed by the 'drain' on Spain's bullion supplies. Ultimately these supplies were the returns which Spain earned from her investment in the Indies, an integral part of the Spanish economy. They were normally re-invested not in domestic production—shipbuilding perhaps excepted— but in foreign trade. Yet as long as Spain earned sufficient profits in America to bridge her trade gap in Europe she could be said to be paying her way. In the course of the seventeenth century, however, returns from America dwindled to a trickle. The crisis in the Indies trade caused severe dislocation in the Spanish economy and contributed to its prolonged depression; the Indies trade was also a victim of that depression.

[110] McLachlan, 'Documents illustrating Anglo-Spanish Trade', op. cit., pp. 310–11, and Trade and Peace with Old Spain, graph 1.
[111] A. Christelow, 'Great Britain and the trades from Cadiz and Lisbon to Spanish America and Brazil, 1759–1783', Hispanic American Historical Review, xxvii (1947), 2–29, and the same author's 'Economic Background of the Anglo-Spanish War of 1762', Journal of Modern History, xviii (1946), 22–36; see also Reglà, 'La época de los dos últimos Austrias', Historia social y económica de España y América, pp. 348–50; Girard, Le commerce français à Séville et Cadix, pp. 115–34.

CHAPTER VII

AMERICAN TRADE: CONTRACTION AND CRISIS

1. The Monopoly: Seville and Cadiz

FTER a century of almost unbroken expansion Spain's American trade first contracted then collapsed. The great upswing of 1562–92 was followed by a plateau from 1593 to 1622 and a downward swing from 1623 to 1650; the trade did not recover until a century later. This profound crisis in the *carrera de Indias* had its roots within the trade itself and the colonial economies which fed it; but it was aggravated by challenge and violence from without which relentlessly eroded the Seville monopoly.

The ideal of a Castilian and more particularly an Andalusian monopoly survived into the seventeenth century.[1] It drew its strength from the capital resources of the Seville merchants, seconded by foreign colleagues, first the Genoese and Portuguese, then the French, Dutch and English; from the network of interests which bound together the merchants and shippers of the *consulado* of Seville and the officials of the *Casa de Contratación*, the government body which regulated the trade; from another network, more obscure but no less powerful, between these same merchants and the great territorial magnates of Andalucía, of whom the count duke of Olivares was the most striking representative; and from the slavish devotion to routine of the Spanish bureaucracy which, having devised an effective means of delivering goods to America and receiving silver in return, was content to maintain the apparatus even when circumstances changed and even when foreign interests began to appropriate it.

The doors of American trade were more effectively closed to Spanish nationals than to foreigners. Yet the exclusion of Aragonese and Catalans from the *carrera de Indias* was due less to Castilian prejudice than to the facts of economic life. The peoples of eastern Spain did not have the resources to contribute to trade and colonisation in America; and had they been allowed to do so they might well have become yet further agents of foreign penetration. In any case we have to distinguish between emigration and trade. In law non-Castilians were free to enter America; this was made clear by the decree of 1596 which stated that Aragonese, Catalans and Valencians were

[1] On the monopoly and its organisation see *Spain under the Habsburgs*, i, 151–59.

not classified as foreigners and could reside in the Indies.[2] In 1619 the ordin-
ances of the *consulado* of Lima, describing the qualifications needed by the
guild's thirty electors, specifically included subjects of the crown of Aragon.[3]
The great jurist, Juan de Solórzano, writing probably under the influence of
the Catalan revolt of 1640, remarked in his *Política Indiana* (1647) that subjects
of the crown of Aragon 'appeared' to be classified as foreigners in relation
to the Indies; but he also admitted that force of custom allowed them in.[4] The
Recopilación of 1680, the general coding of the Laws of the Indies, had no such
doubts; it simply repeated the decree of 1596. Castile therefore possessed no
monopoly of emigration. If few Aragonese and Catalans actually went to
America it was for other reasons than legal ones.[5]

Commerce was a different matter. Andalucía was better endowed for
transatlantic trade than any other region of Spain.[6] In the early years of
colonial enterprise the Catalans showed not the slightest interest in America.
Belatedly, in 1522, they requested permission to trade and were refused.[7]
But every businessman in Europe knew that you did not need to cross the
Atlantic to get your hands on American treasure. All you needed was a
foothold in Seville or Cadiz. These ports were as open to Catalans as they
were to foreigners, and in the sixteenth century they were to be found there,
selling their goods in the transatlantic trade; by mid-century three-quarters of
their textile exports to Castile were probably re-exported to the Indies.[8] But
eastern Spain could not sustain even this modest effort. Aragon was excluded
by its economic recession and stagnation which culminated in the expulsion
of the moriscos.[9] Catalonia spent its commercial energies, before and after the
revolt of 1640, in attempting to restore its first life-line, the Mediterranean
trade. It was not until the last decades of the century that modest economic
recovery brought Catalonia within striking distance of transatlantic operations. Its merchants then evinced a new interest in America and advocated the

---

[2] *Recopilación de leyes de los reinos de las Indias* [1680] (3 vols., Madrid, 1943), IX, xxvii, 28. The
law of 1596 simply legitimatised existing practice and echoed similar enactments of 1564 and
1591; see Artíñano, *Historia del comercio con las Indias*, p. 118.

[3] '. . . y no han de ser extranjeros de los Reinos de España, y se entiende no serlo los de la
Corona de Aragon . . .'. See R. Konetzke, *Colección de documentos para la historia de la formación
social de Hispanoamérica 1493–1810* (3 vols., Madrid, 1953–62), ii, 294; María E. Rodríguez Vicente,
El tribunal del consulado de Lima en la primera mitad del siglo XVII (Madrid, 1960), p. 319.

[4] F. Rahola, *Comercio de Cataluña con América en el siglo XVIII* (Barcelona, 1931), p. 13.

[5] C. Bermúdez Plata, *Catálogo de pasageros de Indias durante los siglos XVI, XVII, y XVIII* (2
vols., Seville, 1932–40) gives the official figures for the first few decades, inadequate though they
are: in 1509–38 out of a total of 13,399 there were 89 Aragonese, 48 Valencians and 38 Catalans;
see J. Rodríguez Argua, 'Las regiones españoles y la población de América (1509–1538)', *Revista
de Indias*, viii (1947), 698–748.

[6] *Spain under the Habsburgs*, i, 151–53.

[7] Carrera Pujal, *Historia política y económica de Cataluña*, i, 298–99, 303–4.

[8] *Ibid.*, i, 321–24; Vilar, *La Catalogne dans l'Espagne moderne*, i, 537.

[9] Chaunu, *Séville et l'Atlantique*, viii, 1, pp. 249–50.

formation of a trading company; and in the first half of the eighteenth century their economic resources enabled them to overcome the law and break into the colonial trade. The Basques, too, sought permission for direct trade with America, especially after the independence of Portugal prevented them from using Lisbon as an entrepôt.[10] But it was 1728 before they proved their point and procured for the Basque-financed Caracas Company the privilege of trading with Venezuela.

Seville's desperate defence of its monopoly in the seventeenth century reflected shift of power as well as depression of opportunity in the trans-atlantic sector. Seville, of course, had never possessed the entire monopoly. It was an Andalusian monopoly of which Seville was the commercial, financial and administrative centre. Between 1506 and 1650 Seville had 60 per cent. of registered trade to America, and was followed in order of importance by Cadiz, San Lucar de Barrameda, the Canaries and Lisbon.[11] In the course of the seventeenth century, however, Seville suffered an accumulation of adversities which weakened its economy. Its population was ravaged by plague and dropped from a peak of 150,000 in 1588 to 85,000 a century later.[12] Its merchants bore the brunt of royal taxation and forced loans. And its location became a serious liability. For Seville was an inland port, access to which steadily deteriorated in proportion to the heavy increase in tonnage of trans-atlantic vessels—the average size rose from 70 tons in 1504 to 391 tons in 1641–45. From the early seventeenth century navigation of the Guadalquivir and the bar at San Lucar became increasingly hazardous. Seville's loss was Cadiz's gain. As a sea port Cadiz was more accessible and more successful in procuring foreign vessels at a time, especially from the 1630's, when Indies shipping, like its contents, ceased to be Spanish.[13] Cadiz, moreover, was preferred by foreigners who wished to evade the administration in Seville and found the bay of Cadiz more suitable for contraband than the riverine port. Finally, Cadiz had advantageous customs rates, as its customs lessees pur-posely sought to attract foreign merchants to their constituency. By 1650 Cadiz had successfully challenged the supremacy of its rival, and in the second half of the century its victory was complete. As trade moved towards Cadiz so did people: its population grew from some 2,000 in 1600 to 40,000 by 1700.[14]

The rivalry between Seville and Cadiz in the seventeenth century was symptomatic of the growing crisis in the Indies trade. The days of peace and

[10] Guiard Larrauri, *Historia del Consulado y Casa de Contratación de Bilbao*, i, 445–50.
[11] Chaunu, *Séville et l'Atlantique*, viii, 1, pp. 228–33.
[12] Domínguez Ortiz, *La sociedad española en el siglo XVII*, pp. 140–42.
[13] Chaunu, *Séville et l'Atlantique*, viii, 1, pp. 294–329; Domínguez Ortiz, *Orto y ocaso de Sevilla*, p. 89.
[14] Domínguez Ortiz, *La sociedad española en el siglo XVII*, pp. 142–43.

plenty were over, and the remnants of prosperity were bitterly contested. The crown too fought for its share of dwindling returns, with the advantage that it could make its own rules.

2. Fraud: the Response to Taxation

A monopoly trade was an easy trade to tax. All traffic between Spain and America was subject to registration, and the outgoing register was checked at destination. Taxation was directed at the trade itself and at the colonial economies. On the former there were two major impositions, the *avería* and the *almojarifazgo*.

The *avería*, an *ad valorem* duty charged through the register, was paid by the trade to procure its own defence. It was therefore governed by two factors, the cost of defence and the value of cargo, and it varied from year to year according to the size of the fleets and of their escorts.[15] From 1562 the *avería* was let out by contract to the *consulado* of Seville; it eventually became a millstone round its neck. Enemy attack, or more often simply threat of attack, forced the convoys to increase their naval escorts, especially from 1621 when the Dutch mounted a new offensive. The gross tonnage of the escorting *armadas* increased from 20,128 tons in 1601–5 to 30,362 in 1636–40; it then plunged to 16,575 in 1640–45, to 16,560 in 1646–50.[16] During the crisis years of 1620–30 the tonnage of the *armada de la guardia* amounted to 37 per cent. of the total tonnage of the fleets, compared with 12 per cent. in 1601. The *avería* thus became a tax which devoured the trade it was designed to defend. The rising cost of defence, of naval stores and of shipbuilding, coincided from 1608 with the contraction and depression of transatlantic trade. As defence costs rose and the trade became less capable of meeting them, merchants took refuge in fraud, and the *avería* disintegrated. Fraud was less a cause than a consequence of crisis. For the *avería* penalised those who obeyed the law. Spanish merchants suffered in relation to foreign contrabandists who shipped their goods on the fleets unregistered and untaxed. Inevitably Spanish merchants too sought to save their returns from a diminishing trade by evasion and fraud. The development of fraud further restricted the taxable material, reduced the yield of the *avería*, weakened the escorting *armadas*, and invited further enemy attack. This was the vicious circle in which the transatlantic trade was entrapped. Between 1602 and 1630 the *avería* was levied at the rate of 6 per cent.; in 1631 it rose to 35 per cent., clear evidence of the absolute fraud which killed the system. Although the *consulado*

---

[15] Guillermo Céspedes del Castillo, *La avería en el comercio de Indias* (Seville, 1945); Chaunu, *Séville et l'Atlantique*, i, 169–237.

[16] *Ibid.*, i, 204; vi, tables 183–84.

renewed the contract on various occasions up to 1628, in fact it cut down on effective defence and used the *armadas* as merchant vessels. Between 1628 and 1660 the *ad valorem* duty was gradually abandoned; from 1641 the *consulado* refused to renew the contract; the state had now to administer the *avería* itself, make good its deficiency, and in effect subsidise defence of the trade.

The *almojarifazgo* was an *ad valorem* customs duty charged on merchandise at Spanish and American ports. Up to 1660 total customs on outbound traffic (exit and entry) amounted to 15 per cent., on the eastbound trade 17½ per cent.[17] The duties exacted in America were based on prices in the American market. Merchandise shipped from Spain to Peru, for example, paid *almojarifazgo* first on appraised value at Portobello, and on arrival at Callao 5 per cent. of the increase in value which had accrued in transit from the isthmus. This rule held good for all the Indies, covering European commodities reshipped from one colonial port to another. Some commodities received special fiscal attention. By 1616 cochineal imported into Spain was taxed at 50 ducats an *arroba*, its selling price being 126 ducats. Taxation on this scale simply diverted the trade into contraband: registered imports of cochineal fell from 7,673 *arrobas* in 1607, to 2,000 in 1614, to 859 in 1615, though it was known that in the latter year 4,000 *arrobas* left New Spain alone.[18]

The colonial economies themselves were subject to a variety of taxes, the *quinto* (the royal fifth on bullion), proceeds of the sale of mercury, Indian tributes (a personal assessment of 6 pesos), the *cruzada*, and the *alcabala*. Out of these the treasuries of Mexico and Peru had to defray local administrative and defence costs, subsidise their dependent colonies, and remit the surplus to Spain. At the end of the sixteenth century the surplus from Mexico amounted to about 1 million pesos a year, a peak from which it subsequently fell; Peru provided greater returns, for its superior silver production yielded a greater *quinto*.[19] To supplement this revenue the crown levied various extraordinary taxes. One of these was the Union of Arms imposed in 1627 as part of Olivares's call for assistance from all provinces. America was assessed at 600,000 ducats a year for fifteen years, 250,000 from New Spain and 350,000 from Peru, on the understanding that it would be applied to naval defence of the transatlantic route. The contribution was raised by doubling the *alcabala* from 2 to 4 per cent., and it was subsequently renewed so that it became a permanent tax with little relevance to its declared object.[20]

[17] C. H. Haring, *Trade and Navigation between Spain and the Indies in the time of the Hapsburgs* (Cambridge, Mass., 1918), pp. 83–86.

[18] Chaunu, *Séville et l'Atlantique*, iv, 571–72.

[19] Domínguez Ortiz, 'Los caudales de Indias y la política exterior de Felipe IV', *Anuario de Estudios Americanos*, xiii (1956), 314.

[20] *Ibid.*, pp. 317–19.

Further sums were raised from loans and *donativos* (voluntary gifts), often overtly for imperial defence but invariably diverted to expenditure in Europe. Between 1613 and 1655 the *consulado* of Lima raised 277,000 pesos in *donativos*.[21] But they were bargains rather than gifts. While colonial merchants rarely got the naval defence they were promised, they received other valuable concessions, such as 'pardons' for past fraud and above all honours and titles of nobility. The *donativo* was one of the ways by which colonial merchants improved their social status. Another means of acquiring security and respectability was by purchase of office. This too the crown exploited as a money-raising device; sale of office had been practised in the sixteenth century, but in the reign of Philip IV, especially in the 1640's and 1650's, it acquired new dimensions, and was extended to financial and judicial offices, with pernicious results.[22]

By extending imperial taxation the crown sought to squeeze the last drops from an empire whose mineral wealth was either drying up or being diverted to other channels. In spite of increased fiscal pressure the crown's revenue from America fell from about 2 million pesos a year in the reign of Philip III to 1 million a year and less in the reign of Philip IV. To counter the downward trend the crown resorted increasingly to a last desperate expedient, confiscation of private bullion returns. Silver sent from Mexico and Peru to pay for last year's merchandise and gain credit for the next was taken over by the crown, and merchants were compensated in vellon currency or in *juros* at 10 per cent., later reduced to 6·3 per cent. In 1620 Philip III took one-eighth of registered private treasure. Philip IV took much more—in 1629 1 million ducats, in 1635–37 2 million ducats (forcibly exchanged for vellon), in 1637–38 500,000 ducats, in the 1640's varying amounts culminating in 1 million ducats in 1649.[23] This was the most harmful of all fiscal devices. Its immediate effect was to deprive the trade of vital capital, for merchants reacted by consigning less bullion in the following year. They were also driven to large-scale fraud to protect their investments. The combined result of withdrawal and fraud was to reduce registered trade to the point where the crown's own customs revenue was seriously damaged. But the greatest victim was the *avería*, which was assessed on registered returns. As the latter decreased, the *avería* rate increased and became a further incitement to fraud; the time came when the crown had to subsidise the *avería* in order to maintain a semblance of transatlantic defence. By its new folly,

[21] Rodríguez Vicente, *El tribunal del consulado de Lima*, pp. 144–47.
[22] J. H. Parry, *The Sale of Public Office in the Spanish Indies under the Habsburgs* (Berkeley and Los Angeles, 1953), pp. 48–58.
[23] Domínguez Ortiz, 'Los caudales de Indias y la política exterior de Felipe IV', *op. cit.*, pp. 342–52; Rodríguez Vicente, *El tribunal del consulado de Lima*, pp. 149–50.

therefore, the crown not only undermined long-term confidence and invest-ment in the Indies trade but also subverted its own financial position. The consequences were most apparent in the 1640's. In 1642, with the connivance of the fleets' commanders, the greater part of private silver returns was not declared, thus evading not only confiscation but also the *avería* and other taxes.[24] The Council of the Indies regarded confiscation of private treasure as one of the greatest abuses afflicting the transatlantic trade, and it recommended in 1643 'that on no account and for no reason should Your Majesty lay hands on private silver consignments from the Indies, but should give orders that in future when the fleets arrive from Peru and New Spain their consign-ments should be immediately handed to their owners'. The crown remained unrepentant. In 1649 it confiscated 1 million pesos of private returns. At the beginning of 1652 government agents descended on Seville to compute sequestrations in advance of the fleets, and in addition to buy up merchandise (tobacco, cochineal and indigo) then held by the merchants of Seville at imposed prices and in vellon for immediate shipment to Flanders.[25] This was the last straw. In the face of acute resentment and opposition the govern-ment was forced to cancel the projected confiscation, and indeed made no more. But by now it was too late; the habit of fraud was too deeply en-grained and the trade too depressed to respond to official reform.

The crown was not the only parasite on the American trade and colonies. The wealth of the New World was regarded as fair game by hordes of place and pension seekers, many of whom had never crossed the Atlantic. *Mercedes* to courtiers and favourites, pensions to widows and orphans, dowries to ladies-in-waiting, grants of various kinds were frequently charged on the colonial treasuries, especially in the second half of the seventeenth century. Many *mercedes* were granted on *indios vacos*, that is on *encomiendas* (grants of Indians who paid tribute in labour and/or money) which had fallen vacant. Viceroys and colonists protested in vain that *encomiendas* which should have been reserved for descendants of the conquerors were going instead to people who had never left Castile. Some of these *encomiendas* were granted in anticipation of their becoming vacant and meanwhile the grants were charged on the colonial treasuries. The recipients were usually courtiers and higher nobility. A few examples will suffice.[26] To doña Leonor Moscoso on the occasion of her marriage in 1653 a grant of 3,000 ducats a year on a vacant *encomienda*, valid for two lives; to Juan de Palafox y Cardona, son of the marquis of Ariza and nephew of bishop Palafox, 2,000 ducats a year on vacant *encomiendas* in Guatemala; to doña Antonia de Mendoza, countess of

[24] Domínguez Ortiz, 'Los caudales de Indias y la política exterior de Felipe IV', *op. cit.*, p. 362.
[25] *Ibid.*, pp. 370–72.
[26] Domínguez Ortiz, *La sociedad española en el siglo XVII*, pp. 246–47.

Prospecto del Cerro de Potosí

Benavente and lady-in-waiting to the Infanta, 6,000 ducats in 1665 on vacant *encomiendas*; to doña Antonia María de Toledo, widow of the count of Priego, 2,000 ducats in 1666 on vacant *encomiendas* to improve her financial position. Many a wretched Indian scraping a living in the Peruvian *sierra* was working in fact for distressed gentlefolk in Castile.

Plunder and parasitism made fraud and contraband a way of life. The monopoly system and high prices induced market conditions propitious for contraband; taxes and confiscations incited it; impecunious officials connived at it; naval authorities co-operated in it. The close alliance between the merchants of Seville and officials of the *Casa de Contratación* made customs control one of the weakest points of the monopoly.[27] Contents of merchandise were assessed at their declared not their verified value, and volume was declared in general categories; naturally they were falsely declared and undervalued in order to evade customs.[28] On the outward voyage the object was to avoid displaying the Seville register at the port of entry in the Indies, on the return voyage to avoid registration on leaving the Indies so that there would be no check on the accuracy of declarations at Seville. Both ways meant underpayment of taxes. Another device was to use the warship escorts for merchandise and thus avoid registration altogether, in connivance with the naval commanders who might also permit vessels to unload at unauthorised ports.

Contraband in silver returns from the Indies was also highly developed and took two main forms, evasion of the royal *quinto* at the mining base, and evasion of registration at port. Again, the methods were various, ranging from suborning ships' captains, to declaring ingots under their real weight, to loading at the last minute and thus avoiding close inspection. A favoured device in Peru was to consign registered silver to non-existent persons in Panama, where the consignment nominally remained and was marked off the register; this silver would then be transferred across the isthmus to the fleet waiting in Portobello for the return journey to Spain. The object of fraud in silver consignments was not merely to avoid paying the *avería*, but also to have free silver to trade with, for this was a much more valuable trading commodity than registered silver. In the first place it was not in danger of confiscation; secondly it was easier to re-export abroad from Spain to buy the foreign goods so much in demand in the Indies trade. At Portobello Spanish merchants would lower the prices of their goods by 10 or 15 per cent. in order to get their hands on unregistered silver.[29] There is, of course, no way of measuring the volume of contraband; but in 1651 a

[27] See *Spain under the Habsburgs*, i, 155–56.
[28] Chaunu, *Séville et l'Atlantique*, i, 88–121.
[29] Rodríguez Vicente, *El tribunal del consulado de Lima*, pp. 262–63.

M

Peruvian estimate, for what it is worth, claimed that 25 per cent. of the silver shipped from Callao was unregistered.[30] In any case fraud was not constant throughout the history of the Indies trade: it increased from 1590 and even more from 1620.[31] This makes it difficult to estimate accurately silver returns from America, public and private.

Total treasure receipts dropped from the peak of 35·1 million pesos in 1591–95, to 34·4 million in 1596–1600, to 24·4 million in 1601–5.[32] Then followed a period of fluctuation, an upswing to 31·4 million pesos in 1606–10, down to 24·5 million in 1611–15, and up again to 30·1 million in 1616–20. After this date receipts diminished irretrievably, from 27 million pesos in 1621–25, to 11·7 million in 1646–50, to 3·3 million in 1656–60. There was therefore a marked recession in the period 1601–30, and a precipitate drop in 1631–60. Crown receipts began to fall earlier and continued to fall more quickly than private receipts. From the peak of 10·9 million pesos in 1596–1600, they fell to 6·5 million in 1601–5, rose to 8·5 million in 1606–10, and fell again to 7·2 million in 1611–15. From that date they fell disastrously, to 4·3 million pesos in 1616–20, maintaining themselves at about that level until 1646–50 when they fell to 1·6 million; after a slight rise to 2·2 million in 1651–55, they collapsed to 606,524 pesos in 1655–60.

What were the causes of the decrease in American treasure? Economic depression, or shift, in the colonies between the late sixteenth and mid-seventeenth centuries lowered their returns to the metropolis.[33] The fall in the Indian population reduced the yield of encomiendas and of silver mines and made Mexico in particular much less profitable to Spain. Moreover the colonies were absorbing more of their own revenue in administrative and defence costs; appropriations for garrisons, fortifications and naval forces progressively reduced public returns to the crown. Enemy action accounted for very few losses among the treasure fleets; but the convoys always needed escorts, and the mere threat of attack was enough to swell defence expenditure, raise the avería and thus augment fraud. These were the reasons why the actual amount of royal treasure from the Indies rarely equalled its reputation. It never represented more than one-tenth of Philip IV's total revenue, and in many years not even one-twentieth. But this income had an importance beyond its quantity. The very fact that it was a fortuitous income, both in the date of its arrival and in its volume, prevented it from suffering the fate of other royal revenues which were assigned in advance to bankers and juristas

[30] Ibid., p. 259.
[31] Chaunu, Séville et l'Atlantique, viii, 2, 1, p. 398.
[32] Hamilton, American Treasure and the Price Revolution in Spain, pp. 34–38; these are official figures based on registered imports; they do not account for treasure which evaded control at the mining centres, for unregistered treasure, for treasure which financed the trans-Pacific trade.
[33] See below, pp. 199–200, 204–12, 215–18, 221–24.

and permanently lost to the treasury. When it arrived it was ready cash, immediately available for use; and in a period of debased currency an income in silver was particularly valuable to the crown for its overseas payments and to businessmen for foreign trade. If the silver fleets were delayed the premium on silver soared, foreign trade was hit, and supplies for the armed forces abroad were unobtainable.

While much bullion escaped official channels before it could reach Spain, much also was syphoned off after it arrived. Although the export of bullion was prohibited by law, the law was ignored, because the Spanish market and the Indies trade itself needed foreign manufactures. The amount of bullion smuggled out of Spain is a matter of speculation. Between 10 and 30 per cent. of *registered* bullion, which was supposed to be transferred directly from the fleets to the *Casa de Contratación* before being distributed to its owners, in fact left Spain illegally.[34] Unregistered bullion, of course, was designed precisely for smuggling. Professional smugglers, the *metedores*, acting on behalf of the owners, took it from the Indies fleets and loaded it on the foreign ships waiting in Cadiz bay to convey it northwards.[35] Unable to prevent the loss of bullion the Spanish government sought to compensate itself by selling *indultos*, or pardons, to those who admitted to bullion frauds. The proceeds from *indultos*, however, did not satisfy the government's own need for precious metals in an age of rising defence expenditure and falling silver returns. It was at this point that it reached out to take possession of private silver consignments, and thus completed the vicious circle of further fraud and loss of revenue.

3. FOREIGN PENETRATION

Foreigners had two ways of penetrating the Indies trade and appropriating its returns. They could sell their merchandise by contraband, either in Seville–Cadiz or in the Indies themselves; or they could actually settle in the Indies. By law emigrants had to be Spaniards or naturalised Spaniards, and they had to have a licence. By decree of November 1607 ships' captains were threatened with the death penalty and generals and admirals of fleets with loss of rank if they carried unlicensed passengers. By the 1670's, however, the punishment had been reduced to a fine and the order was widely disregarded.[36] Forging passports was a profession in Seville. Foreigners travelled on the official fleets, or they entered by the back door, the Río de la Plata. In Peru three groups could be identified. A number of foreigners had settled in the

[34] Hamilton, *American Treasure and the Price Revolution in Spain*, p. 37.
[35] Haring, *Trade and Navigation between Spain and the Indies*, p. 112.
[36] *Ibid.*, p. 103.

interior and acquired modest property holdings. Others were to be found in maritime occupations, as pilots and seamen, profiting from the shortage of skilled personnel; in 1619 foreigners—Italians, Frenchmen, and above all Portuguese—were owners and in many cases masters of eighteen vessels in the Peruvian merchant marine.[37] But the biggest group were merchants, officially transient but in fact resident, in the ports and towns. By 1630 the Portuguese dominated the retail trade of Lima. Others were active in the transatlantic trade itself, using Spanish agents as front men as was done in Seville; they had contacts with contrabandists in Andalucía who exported goods without paying duties and undersold their rivals. Following its normal practice the Spanish crown taxed what it could not prevent: foreigners were granted permission to trade if they had twenty years' residence in Peru, were married to a Peruvian, had property valued at not less than 4,000 ducats, and paid a composition tax to the crown.[38] The Portuguese also favoured Cartagena, an important staging post in the Indies trade. So numerous did they become there after 1610 that they even acquired administrative offices; they also received the attentions of the Inquisition, for they included a number of Jews, and from 1640 of course they were harassed and in some cases expelled.[39]

It was common knowledge, however, that a foreign merchant could tap the American trade without going to America; he could concentrate on its metropolitan base in Andalucía. Here too the law was explicit enough. To engage in transatlantic commerce a merchant had to be a native Spaniard; this precluded foreigners from trading with the colonies either on their own account or through Spanish intermediaries.[40] But the law could be evaded, either by simple contraband, or by use of Spanish cover-men, or by acquiring naturalisation. The latter gave the greatest security, but there were certain legal requirements: the successful applicant had to have twenty years' residence in Spain, at least ten of them in a furnished house, he had to be married to a Spanish wife, and he had to possess at least 4,000 ducats' worth of property. More and more foreigners began to take advantage of naturalisation. In the last quarter of the sixteenth century only 25 foreigners acquired naturalisation rights to trade with the Indies—17 Portuguese, 5 Flemings and 3 French.[41] During the reign of Philip III (1598–1621) the number rose to 59, comprising 21 Flemings, 17 Portuguese, 11 Italians, 4 French and, among the

---

[37] Rodríguez Vicente, *El tribunal del consulado de Lima*, p. 71.

[38] *Ibid.*, pp. 73–74.

[39] Manuel Tejardo Fernández, *Aspectos de la vida social en Cartagena de Indias durante el seiscientos* (Seville, 1954). On the Portuguese in Mexico, see above, pp. 112–13.

[40] Haring, *Trade and Navigation between Spain and the Indies*, pp. 107–8.

[41] A. Domínguez Ortiz, 'La concesión de "naturalezas para comerciar en Indias" durante el siglo XVII', *Revista de Indias*, xix (1959), 227–39.

small groups, one Englishman. In the first decade of Philip IV's reign naturalisation rights for trade with the Indies were given even more liberally: between 1621 and 1630 there were 77 successful applicants. Many of these did not possess the legal qualifications, but they made up for this by handsome payments to the crown; in effect the crown sold certificates of naturalisation, again making money out of lawbreakers. The scale on which Philip IV's government issued certificates caused such resentment among Spanish merchants and their allies in the *Casa de Contratación* that the policy was strongly attacked in the 1630's and 1640's.[42] For the growing demand from foreign merchants was essentially an attempt to eliminate Spanish intermediaries in order to sell direct to the Indies from their own merchant houses in Andalucía. Under pressure from monopolist interests in Seville the crown began to tighten up on eligibility from about 1645. Later in the century, however, particularly from the early 1680's, naturalisation policy was again relaxed. By the end of the century the majority of the merchant aristocracy of Cadiz, with legal status in the Indies trade, consisted of foreigners, without counting the many foreigners who traded through Spanish intermediaries.[43]

The use of intermediaries was well developed. They are often called mere commission agents, and perhaps some of them were, passing foreign goods through inspection and registration, loading them under their own name, and watching the returns going direct to the owner.[44] But some of them were more than agents. They were part of the triangular trade between Europe, Andalucía and the Indies. The foreigners brought their manufactures to Andalucía and there they bought Andalusian products, wine, oil and fruits. This left the Spaniards with a large trade gap which had to be bridged by the Indies trade. Many Seville merchants shipped to America on their own account Spanish and foreign goods, and from the returns they balanced their foreign payments, making very good profits, or commissions, from all these transactions. In the course of the seventeenth century it became less necessary for foreigners to use the official channels as more of the actual loading and unloading of the fleets was transferred from Seville to Cadiz and its satellite ports.[45] Here, away from the immediate surveillance of the *Casa de Contratación*, the *metedores* could load merchandise direct from foreign vessels on to the fleets after the last inspection had been completed.[46] Foreign merchants could thus escape registration, customs duties and the *avería*, and undersell their Spanish competitors in the American market. So Spaniards too had to

[42] Chaunu, *Séville et l'Atlantique*, v, 413.

[43] Raimundo Lantery, *Memorias de Raimundo de Lantery, mercader de Indias en Cádiz, 1673–1700.* Publícalas Alvaro Ricardo y Gómez (Cadiz, 1949).

[44] Girard, *Le commerce français a Séville et Cadix au temps des Habsbourgs*, p. 87.

[45] See above, p. 162.

[46] Chaunu, *Séville et l'Atlantique*, iv, 536; v, 368.

smuggle to survive. The government reacted by applying its classic seven-teenth-century formula: it sanctioned lawbreaking and taxed the offenders; foreigners were included in the sequestrations imposed on Andalusian merchants and in the fines levied for past frauds.

Foreigners supplied not only merchandise for the American trade but also capital and shipping. As the Dutch, the French and the English came to earn increasing returns from the Indies, they also began to plough back some of their profits. In the first half of the seventeenth century the trade did not depend entirely on foreign capital; it also received large injections of American capital. But its dependence on foreigners was enough to alarm some Spanish merchants. At the prompting of the *consulado* of Seville the crown issued a decree in 1608 prohibiting foreign merchants from selling their goods on credit to Spanish shippers against payment in the Indies.[47] But this decree, like many others, was a mere formality. As Spanish merchants rarely possessed sufficient capital for their purchases they were forced to rely on a degree of foreign finance to keep the trade going.

The law closed the Indies trade not only to foreigners but also to foreign shipping. But again what the law forbad conditions encouraged. The growing impoverishment of the Spanish merchant marine forced the government to accept the need for foreign vessels in the Indies trade. It tried to insist that these should be owned by Spaniards and should carry Spanish crews.[48] But in the reign of Philip IV, especially from the 1630's, even this became a formality; the government had to allow the hiring of foreign-owned vessels and to accept the fact that their crews contained aliens as well as Spaniards.[49] The freighting of foreign vessels, of course, increased the opportunities of fraud; it was also resented by the owners and builders of Spanish ships. Under their pressure foreign-built ships were excluded from the Indies trade by decree of July 1642. The decree, which was intended to stimulate Spanish shipbuilding, simply revived previous prohibitions; the only difference was that the condition of the Spanish shipbuilding industry in the 1640's made its application even less likely than before.[50] In any case foreign vessels were particularly vital for carrying specialised cargoes such as naval stores, for which there was constant demand from Spain's other competitors, the ship-yards of the New World. In the circumstances the most that the *Casa de Contratación* could do was to give preference to Spanish vessels when they were available.

The extent of foreign penetration of the American trade is impossible to

[47] *Ibid.*, iv, 393.
[48] Girard, *op. cit.*, p. 21.
[49] On the number and origin of foreign vessels see Chaunu, *Seville et l'Atlantique*, v, 342, 364, 390, 404–8, 432–37.
[50] Haring, *Trade and Navigation between Spain and the Indies*, pp. 258–61; see above, pp. 150–52.

compute, granted its devious ways.[51] In 1628 the *consulado* of Seville—an interested party prone to exaggeration—explained to the government that the Indies trade needed each year more than 6 million ducats' worth of foreign goods; American and Spanish products sold in return covered barely half of this; it was therefore impossible to comply with a recent decree insisting that foreign payments should be met entirely by merchandise and not by bullion.

> Foreign imports to the value of even 6 million ducats are barely adequate to satisfy demand; shortage and high prices are notorious, especially in woollen goods. . . . The New Spain fleet which sailed from Cadiz on 15 July this year is a good example. Its cargo would have been confined to wines, had not the French vessels arrived in time with their merchandise; and although they provided cloth it was only half the amount required by New Spain. It is to be feared that if the Indies are not supplied in the normal way then our enemies will supply them illegally and the colonists will admit them out of necessity.[52]

Throughout most of the seventeenth century relations between foreign merchants and the Indies trade were regulated more or less by the free play of supply and demand.[53] Most foreigners found conditions in Andalucía suitable for their operations. But some, as the *consulado* of Seville implied, were tempted to tap the wealth of the Indies nearer its source, in the Caribbean and the Pacific.

4. Imperial Defence: the Atlantic

In the course of the sixteenth century Spanish seamen perfected the technique of maintaining regular communications between Andalucía and America by means of two large fleets a year, each sailing in convoy, one to Tierra Firme, the other to New Spain.[54] They sailed from Cadiz or San Lucar, the New Spain fleet in May (if it was ready) and the Tierra Firme fleet in August. First they headed southwest to the coast of Africa and then proceeded to the Canaries; from the Canaries the route was west by southwest until they caught the trade winds which took them due west to Deseada or one of the other Leeward islands. From there the *galeones*, as the Tierra

[51] Some of it moreover was based on the Portuguese trade to Brazil and its re-export through the Río de la Plata.

[52] Quoted by Domínguez Ortiz, 'Guerra económica y comercio extranjero en el reinado de Felipe IV', *Hispania*, xxiii (1963), 92–93; the decree in fact was suspended.

[53] On foreign participation in the late seventeenth century see below, pp. 191–92.

[54] There are two classical 'institutional' accounts of the *carrera*, both valuable repositories of source material: José de Veitia Linage, *Norte de la contratación de las Indias Occidentales* [1672] (Buenos Aires, 1945) by a treasurer of the *Casa de Contratación*; Rafael Antúñez y Acevedo, *Memorias históricas sobre la legislación y gobierno del comercio de los españoles con sus colonias en las Indias Occidentales* (Madrid, 1797).

Firme fleet was called, steered southwest to Cartagena and Portobello (4,300 miles and 8 weeks from Cadiz), while the *flota* took a northwesterly direction to Hispaniola, Cuba, and Vera Cruz (4,860 miles from Cadiz). The return course for Spain was via Cuba and through the Bahama channel, the most dangerous passage of the whole voyage; having negotiated its hurricanes and reefs, the fleets headed northeast to pick up strong northerly winds, then east to the Azores and so to San Lucar.[55]

Predictable though the route was, the fleets suffered few losses from enemy action. They drew strength from the convoy system; the merchantmen carried armament; and they had their naval escort, usually eight galleons for the Tierra Firme fleet (the famous *armada de la guardia de la carrera de las Indias*) and two for the Mexican. These defences may not have been completely adequate, but the enemy could rarely assemble anything more powerful. In September 1628 a numerically superior Dutch fleet—31 vessels, 700 cannon, 3,000 men—attacked the Mexican *flota* of some 20 vessels off Matanzas in Cuba, destroyed it and took its enormous treasure, some 6 million pesos according to the Dutch. This disaster was due in part to an unwonted failure of intelligence about the enemy's movements, but above all to failure of leadership; the Spanish commander, General Juan de Benavides, paid for his negligence on the gallows.[56] In 1656 an English squadron from Blake's fleet took the *capitana* and another galleon of the Tierra Firme fleet as it approached Cadiz, capturing some 2 million pesos. The English then sought out the Mexican fleet which had taken refuge in the Azores; there, in April 1657, they almost completely destroyed it, and the Spaniards managed to save only a portion of its treasure.

These were the only major disasters to the *carrera de Indias* at the hands of enemies. The fleets suffered much more from the elements. Harassed by the close schedule of the turn-round, delays to trade and silver supplies, the expense of wintering in the Indies, and a government impatient for its bullion, fleet commanders often took excessive risks in sailing out of season. In 1622 five merchantmen and three galleons of the Tierra Firme fleet sank in storms with heavy loss of treasure. In 1624 the same fleet lost three galleons through shipwreck, with 433,770 ducats of the crown's silver and 1 million belonging to private merchants. In 1631 the New Spain fleet left Veracruz late in the season and was struck by hurricane off the coast of Yucatán; the *almiranta* went down with all its silver, and most of the merchantmen were sunk or ran aground, a disaster which Olivares lamented as 'beyond words'.[57] In 1641 the New Spain fleet, again sailing late in the

[55] Haring, *Trade and Navigation between Spain and the Indies*, pp. 201–30.
[56] Fernández Duro, *Armada española*, iv, 97–106.
[57] Domínguez Ortiz, *Política y hacienda de Felipe IV*, p. 283.

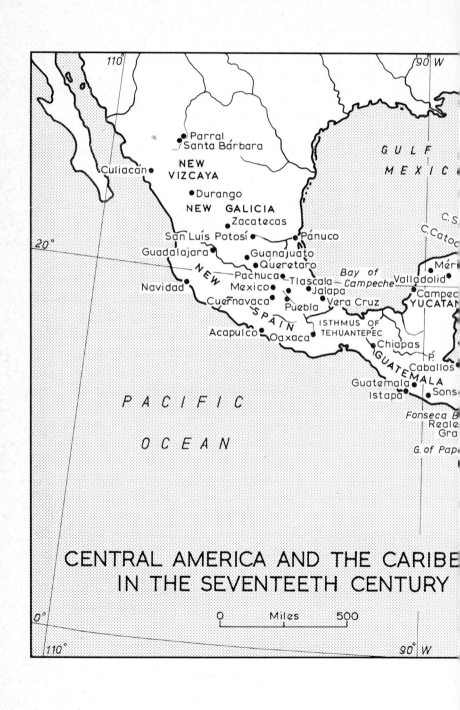

CENTRAL AMERICA AND THE CARIBE

IN THE SEVENTEETH CENTURY

season, was devastated by hurricane on leaving the Bahama channel; the *almiranta* made its way to Santo Domingo where it sank; and the *capitana*, having survived the crossing, went down at the bar of San Lucar; between them they lost 770,000 pesos for the king and 1,070,000 for merchants, though most of the *capitana*'s cargo was subsequently salvaged.[58]

The activities of pirates and privateers were puny compared to hurricanes in the Bahama strait. An international pirate community infested the Caribbean from bases like Tortuga, attacking local trade and pouncing on undefended Spanish settlements. But these were petty operations, even after their increase from the early seventeenth century. Nor was privateering particularly successful, confined as it was to the less prosperous and less defended parts of the Spanish empire. The returns from English privateering were so low that they hardly covered investment. Englishmen preferred contraband to privateering, though even this was second in importance to trade with Seville. From about 1625, however, the French, English and Dutch came to the lesser Antilles as settlers as well as interlopers, trading with Venezuela and the offshore islands, selling cloth and Negroes against tobacco and cacao, and syphoning off much of the local trade.[59]

The opportunities for contraband trade in the Caribbean, called by the Spaniards *rescate*, were becoming more numerous. Constant surveillance of the whole area was out of the question. The fleet system was geared to the supply of large markets in Mexico and Peru. Smaller settlements remote from the main routes were starved of trade. They were allowed *permiso* vessels which detached themselves from the fleets and made their way unescorted to a few ports of call; but these single vessels were favourite targets of corsairs and they tended to be withdrawn. Jamaica was one of the victims of such neglect; direct links between the island and Spain had virtually ceased by 1634, twenty years before its loss to England.[60] Settlements like Jamaica and Venezuela were also low on the list of Spanish defence priorities, preference being given to Hispaniola and Cuba which had greater strategic importance. The poor relations of the Indies trade were thus extremely vulnerable to commercial penetration by foreigners and less amenable to Spanish trade on the rare occasions when it arrived. The main zone of contraband was the coast of Tierra Firme from Trinidad to Maracaibo.[61] Here the economy was based on tobacco and cacao; as these had insufficient outlet in the annual fleets the trade fell into the hands of foreigners, the English, Dutch and Portuguese, who also supplied the Negro slaves needed on the

[58] Artíñano, *Historia del comercio con las Indias*, p. 346.
[59] Haring, *Trade and Navigation between Spain and the Indies*, pp. 118–22.
[60] Chaunu, *Séville et l'Atlantique*, viii, 1, p. 570; see also Francisco Morales Padrón, *La Jamaica Española* (Seville, 1952).
[61] Chaunu, *Séville et l'Atlantique*, viii, 1, p. 626.

coastal plantations. This trade, of course, was on the periphery of the Spanish empire and it did not tap the major sources of wealth, Mexico and Peru. But it was yet another breach of the monopoly, and it was conducted from bases which threatened Spain's imperial communications.

The foreign colonies which proliferated in the lesser Antilles from 1625 were dangerously close to the route by which the fleets entered the Caribbean. Even more dangerous were the English settlements in the islands of Santa Catalina and Tortuga. This movement towards the heart of the Spanish empire, closer to the routes of returning silver fleets, was regarded as a grave threat to security. No power could possibly have provided military and naval defence for every part of this vast empire. Spain's first reaction to foreign aggression, therefore, was to establish an order of priorities, abandoning those settlements regarded as of little value and concentrating defence on Mexico and Peru and on the staging posts thereto. This might be called a strategic withdrawal, first from the lesser Antilles, later from Jamaica. It was a rational enough policy and in pursuing it Spain lost nothing of value. She also devised certain substitutes for defence. Occasionally the warships escorting the trade fleets were diverted from convoy duty to eject foreign intruders. In 1629 the galleons of don Fadrique de Toledo were used to expel English and French settlers from the islands of Nevis and St. Kitts.[62] The risk attached to these operations—the fleets were left exposed—meant that they were confined to those foreign bases which were potential threats to the main trade routes and ports. One of these was the Dutch stronghold of St. Martin which was cleared in 1633. Another was Santa Catalina, occupied by the English from 1630 and called by them Providence; after the failure of two small expeditions from Cartagena in 1635 and 1640, the galleons of don Francisco Díaz Pimenta overcame the settlers in 1641 and left a Spanish garrison.[63] Finally, as a substitute for defence from the metropolis, the colonies themselves were encouraged to take the initiative. Their resources were usually adequate for immediate self-defence: the Dutch were repulsed at Puerto Rico in 1626, the English at Santo Domingo in 1654. But they were incapable of taking the offensive against intruders.[64] An expedition from Santo Domingo cleared the island of Tortuga in 1635, but the English and French soon returned, as they had already returned to St. Kitts. These mopping-up operations did not succeed in stemming the tide. A permanent naval force was needed. This was recognised by the metropolis, though the latter short-sightedly preferred to channel resources to northern Europe.

[62] Fernández Duro, *op. cit.*, iv, 109.

[63] D. Rowland, 'Spanish Occupation of the Island of Old Providence or Santa Catalina, 1641–70', *Hispanic American Historical Review*, xv (1935), 298–312; Fernández Duro, *op. cit.*, iv, 338.

[64] R. D. Hussey, 'Spanish Reaction to Foreign Aggression in the Caribbean to about 1680', *Hispanic American Historical Review*, ix (1929), 286–302.

At the eastern end of the transatlantic route defence was provided by the *Armada del Mar Océano* which operated out of home waters, protecting the Atlantic approaches for the returning fleets and performing general defence duties in western Europe. Its strength fluctuated considerably: in the early 1620's it consisted of 46 vessels, but it gradually diminished in the course of the century and by the last decade it was down to about 20. For Caribbean defence there were sporadic attempts to maintain an *Armada de Barlovento*, or Windward Squadron, charged on the colonial treasuries.[65] This was first dispatched—six frigates and other craft—in 1598, but it was soon diverted to convoy duty; from 1606 it was kept in Spanish waters and the money provided by the colonies for its maintenance was absorbed in European expenditure. In 1640, after five years' discussion, a new *Armada de Barlovento* consisting of eight galleons was assigned to anti-corsair operations and escort duties in the Caribbean.[66] In 1641 it escorted the New Spain fleet from Havana to Vera Cruz, back to Havana and from there to the Bahama channel. Again, however, it was soon diverted to transatlantic convoy duty: in 1643 it escorted the New Spain fleet from Vera Cruz to Spain, and also provided the escort for its outward voyage in 1644. From then until 1647 it continued to perform escort and transport duties across the Atlantic, becoming in effect a substitute for the *armada de la guardia*, evidence that defence of the fleets was now being subsidised by the colonies themselves. Yet they were not even getting value for their money, for in 1648 the *Armada de Barlovento* was incorporated in the *Armada del Mar Océano*, and between then and 1667 there was no permanent defence squadron in the Caribbean. In 1665 the *Armada de Barlovento* was re-formed; it consisted of eight vessels, four of them specially built in Holland, and was immediately assigned to European duties. Two years later five of its units were dispatched to the Indies; two were quickly diverted to transatlantic duties, and the remainder were destroyed by Henry Morgan and his buccaneers at the entrance to Lake Maracaibo. In 1672 a revived *Armada de Barlovento* entered service; it consisted of five vessels with subsequent additions from Caribbean resources, and in more or less this form it survived for the rest of the century.

Meanwhile military fortifications had also received some attention. In the 1620's and 1640's defence installations in Cuba and other major bases were reconstructed and extended. The English capture of Jamaica in 1655 stimulated further defence programmes. 'By the last quarter of the seventeenth century most harbors important for trade or military strategy possessed strong forts and fair garrisons'.[67]

This defence record was not unimpressive. No major possession was lost and no foreign colony was allowed to remain a danger. Had the metropolis properly used all the funds which the colonies appropriated to defence, instead of diverting them to Europe, even more could have been accomplished. As it was, resources were not sufficient to recover Jamaica and Curaçao, or to defend the most desirable islands in the Antilles against foreign occupation. From the mid-seventeenth century, with a growing sense of realism, Spain began to accept the inevitable. Foreigners, too, wanted peace in order to consolidate their possessions and extend their trade. There resulted a series of treaties recognising the existing situation in terms of effective occupation. In 1648 the Treaty of Munster gave the Dutch all the territory they actually occupied in America—this was not very much—in return for a promise not to trade with Spanish domains. In 1670 the Treaty of Madrid sanctioned Britain's retention of its existing possessions in the West Indies and America, against a promise to refrain from illegal trade. Meanwhile the hordes of independent pirates, the buccaneers, had also become an international nuisance, and by 1680 the English, French and Dutch, as well as the Spaniards, were taking action against them. Defence policy in the Caribbean therefore lost its urgency. And Spain could not reverse the economic trend which made contraband trade, in spite of treaty promises, an extensive and lucrative practice, widening the breach of the monopoly which had already been made at Cadiz.

5. Pacific Defence

The fleet system was designed to supply all the southern continent by way of the isthmus of Panama, thence down the Pacific to Peru and Chile, and inland to Upper Peru and the Río de la Plata. The Tierra Firme fleet transferred its cargo at Portobello; it was then transported in mule trains across the isthmus to Panama where the Pacific fleet, which had already brought up the silver consignments from Peru, was waiting to ship it to the southern markets.

To preserve this monopoly route and prevent the escape of Potosí silver the Spaniards closed the Río de la Plata to trade and shipping. For the same reason they also had to maintain Buenos Aires, fortified and populated, as a key defence point. But how could they attract settlers to this distant possession and at the same time enforce a closed-port policy which made it impossible for settlers to survive? To solve this dilemma Spain tried to do

[67] Hussey, 'Spanish Reaction to Foreign Aggression in the Caribbean', *op. cit.*, p. 295.

two things at once, to maintain her trade system and to relax it in the smallest possible degree in favour of Buenos Aires. A decree of 1618 re-defined the restrictions on the maritime trade of Buenos Aires; the port was allowed two licensed vessels a year to Seville and back, though the licences became ever more irregular and insufficient. And to seal off Buenos Aires from the silver province of Upper Peru an inland customs house was established in Córdoba, at the foot of the eastern cordillera; operating from about 1622, it charged 50 per cent. duties on goods moving inland.[68] This policy restricted the economic prospects of the Río de la Plata without greatly restricting contraband trade. Through the pampa route to Upper Peru the Portuguese directed a traffic which at its peak in 1600–20 may have taken returns amounting to 20 or even 25 per cent. of Potosí's silver production.[69] Spanish countermeasures reduced this traffic but did not eliminate it.

The Portuguese 'route to Potosí' was successful not because it was a superior route but because Potosí was an insatiable market. The Pacific provinces of the subcontinent were best supplied via Panama. This was the shortest route to the heart of Spanish South America, which, because of the location of silver deposits and labour supply, was nearer to the Pacific than the Atlantic. The transfer of merchandise at the isthmus was economically much less onerous than would have been the routing of trade across the vast and empty pampas of the Río de la Plata, devoid of inhabitants, water, and defences against marauding Indians. And navigation across the South Atlantic was extremely vulnerable to attack from Brazil, especially from the 1620's when the Dutch had a base there and from 1640 when the Portuguese were enemies of Spain. Pacific trading routes, on the other hand, had certain built-in advantages.

The principal trading route in the Spanish Pacific was that between Panama, Callao (the port of Lima) and Arica (the port of Potosí), which was simply an extension of the transatlantic route. There were also two secondary routes, Acapulco–Callao for trade between Mexico and Peru, and Acapulco–Manila for trans-Pacific trade. The targets most favoured by the enemies of Spain were the silver fleets from Arica to Panama and the Manila galleons. Yet the Pacific was effectively sealed to large-scale enemy penetration without too much effort by Spain. After the severe lessons taught by the English marauders in the late sixteenth century, the isthmus complex was now a focus

[68] Ricardo Levene, *Investigaciones acerca de la historia económica del virreinato del Plata* (1st ed., 1927–28, 2nd ed., 1952 reprinted by Academia Nacional de la Historia, *Obras de Ricardo Levene 2*, Buenos Aires, 1962), pp. 141–84; Mario Rodriguez, 'The Genesis of Economic Attitudes in the Río de la Plata', *Hispanic American Historical Review*, xxxvi (1956), 171–89; Raúl A. Molina, 'Una Historia Inédita de los primeros ochenta años de Buenos Aires. El "Defensorio" de D. Alonso de Solórzano y Velazco, Oidor de la Real Audiencia (1667)', *Revista de Historia de América*, no. 52 (1961), 429–97.   [69] Chaunu, *Séville et l'Atlantique*, viii, 1, p. 1182.

of defence which could not easily be breached. Access to the Pacific by sea round the Horn was limited by the navigational possibilities of the time. Spain never dominated the Straits of Magellan; shipping found it difficult to survive the unpredictable winds and the shallow waters of the narrowest straits, and the victims of shipwreck were likely to die of hunger and exposure in this cruel region. The same conditions prevented Spain's enemies from maintaining constant pressure via Cape Horn, and in the seventeenth century it remained an exceptional rather than a regular route.

In these circumstances the defence problem in the Pacific was not to stem a continuing wave of intruders but to have sufficient force to repulse rare attacks when they occurred. This did not require constant patrolling of the coast from Acapulco to the Straits. All that was needed was an efficient early-warning system and an *armada* based on Callao. The former was supplied by intelligence from Spain, which usually identified all hostile expeditions leaving Europe, and from warnings relayed up the Pacific coast once the enemy had navigated the Straits of Magellan. Naval power was provided by the *armada de la mar del Sur* operating out of Callao. From the late sixteenth century this consisted, when at full strength, of five galleons, built in the shipyards of Guayaquil from funds supplied by the *alcabala* revenue.[70] Its purpose was to transport silver, guard the silver route and escort merchant convoys between Arica, Callao and Panama. It was divided into two flotillas, each consisting of two galleons and a patache, one operating to the south, the other to the north, if necessary as far as Mexico, while the fifth galleon was held in reserve in Callao.[71]

For some years after the English intrusion in the sixteenth century the Spanish Pacific enjoyed a period of calm. This was disturbed by the coming of Dutch raiders, known to Spaniards as *Pechelingues*, a word corrupted from the name of the island port of Flushing. The first major expedition was dispatched by the Dutch East India Company in August 1614, during the period of truce with Spain. It consisted of four large and heavily armed warships and two smaller vessels, and it was commanded by Admiral Joris von Speilbergen, a German in the company's service. Its ultimate object was to trade and reinforce Dutch naval power in the Moluccas, but it was equally intended to attack the Spanish empire on the way.[72] The expedition entered

[70] Marie Helmer, 'Le Callao (1615–1618)', *Jahrbuch für Geschichte von Staat, Wirtschaft und Gesellschaft Lateinamerikas*, ii (1965), 145–95; Chaunu, *Séville et l'Atlantique*, viii, 1, p. 1107.

[71] The Peruvian convoy system was never as rigorous as the transatlantic one; merchants preferred to trade out of convoy, as the danger from pirates was intermittent and they wished to evade registration; see Helmer, 'Le Callao', *op. cit.*, pp. 174–76.

[72] See Peter Gerhard, *Pirates on the West Coast of New Spain 1575–1742* (Glendale, 1960), pp. 108–21, a work which goes beyond its title and gives the most comprehensive and authoritative account of attack and defence in the Spanish Pacific.

the Pacific through the Straits of Magellan in May 1615 and as it moved up the coast warnings went ahead. Just south of Callao the way was barred by a Spanish squadron of eight ships (the southern flotilla reinforced by merchant-men) under Rodrigo de Mendoza; but in a sharp engagement on 17–18 July the Spaniards were soundly defeated, losing two warships and 450 men. With the whole west coast lying open, the Dutch ignored Callao, missed the northern *armada*, and sailed to Acapulco where they obtained provisioning facilities in exchange for return of Peruvian prisoners. In December they left Mexican waters to cross the Pacific and missed the Manila galleon.

After this uncomfortable experience the Spaniards began to look to their defences. The viceroy of New Spain began the construction of a fortress at Acapulco, and in Peru naval defences were improved. These were in the capable hands of viceroy the marquis of Esquilache, who brought the *armada* up to strength, increased its firepower and manpower, and formed militia units. But his programme was highly expensive and ate into Imperial revenue, including the royal *quinto*; remittances to Spain were reduced, which was thought to be extremely inconvenient on the eve of the Thirty Years War, and so Esquilache was recalled. Colonial defence was sacrificed to policy in Europe.[73]

Yet Esquilache was right. In 1616 the Dutchman Jacob Le Maire discovered a new though hardly less dangerous or shorter passage into the Pacific south of Tierra del Fuego through the strait which still bears his name. This heralded a new series of raiders. In April 1623 the so-called Nassau fleet left Holland; consisting of 11 vessels, heavy armament, and 1,637 men under the command of Admiral Jacob L'Heremite, its object was not only to attack Spanish ports and shipping and impose contraband trade but also to challenge Spanish sovereignty in the Pacific by establishing a Dutch military and trading post in Peru or Chile in alliance with disaffected Indians.[74] The expedition entered the Pacific through the Le Maire Strait in February 1624 and arrived off Callao on 8 May, just five days after the viceroy, who had been forewarned, had dispatched to Panama the treasure fleet carrying two years' silver, some 9 million pesos.[75] At this point L'Heremite died and his successor, the young and inexperienced Hugo Schapenham, lost his chance through indecision. An ill-managed attack on Callao was repulsed, and the Dutch then spent over four months on the coast of Peru, accomplishing little apart from the destruction of Guayaquil and acquiring a bad reputation for killing prisoners. The expedition reached the coast of Mexico in October; but now Acapulco had its fortress and it refused provisions; at other points on the coast the Dutch

[73] Helmer, 'Le Callao', *op. cit.*, pp. 153–57.
[74] Gerhard, *op. cit.*, pp. 123–29; Chaunu, *Séville et l'Atlantique*, v, 74–79.
[75] Fernández Duro, *op. cit.*, iv, 35–38.

were harried, and in November they abandoned their wait for the Manila galleon and left to cross the Pacific. This expedition was a failure, and the Spaniards had now evened the score.

Spanish defence forces now rested on their laurels. Viceroy Esquilache had tried to create a new and larger *armada de la mar del Sur* to patrol the coasts of Mexico, Central America, Peru and Chile. From 1624 to 1635 the idea was shuttled back and forth between Peru and Spain, based on a requirement of 10 galleons and 7,000 men at an estimated cost of 1 million pesos.[76] The idea was eventually abandoned, not because Peru lacked the money but because the crown wanted that money in Europe. Apart from some minor military and naval improvements, Spanish authorities continued to rely on the natural invulnerability of the Pacific. For the moment they were probably justified. After the fiasco of 1624 the Dutch confined their hostilities to the Atlantic side of America. Their last serious effort to penetrate the Spanish Pacific was the expedition of Hendrick Brouwer under the auspices of the Dutch West India Company. This was another attempt to establish a trading colony. The Dutch squadron arrived off the island of Chiloe in May 1643. Although Brouwer died a few months later, his men stayed on at Valdivia, built a fort, and attacked the Spaniards. But they found the land inhospitable and the Indians aloof; and they left in October 1643. So in the event the Dutch made little impact in the Spanish Pacific: the chief consequence of their activity was to raise the defence expenditure of the Lima treasury— 200,000 pesos in 1624, 948,000 pesos in 1643.

In the second half of the seventeenth century, however, new enemies penetrated the Pacific, this time from the Caribbean. These were the buccaneers, the international gangsters of the Indies. From the 1640's to the 1670's, in alliance with the Indians of the Mosquito Shore, the buccaneers asserted control over the largely uncolonised east coast of Central America and made periodic raids inland. The San Juan River of Nicaragua offered access to the Pacific coast in spite of Spanish fortifications. In 1660 Henry Morgan led a raid on Costa Rica, though he was driven off. He returned to capture Portobello, which he held for a while in the summer of 1668. In January 1671 Morgan led an expedition across the isthmus of Panama, defeated a Spanish force 2,000 strong, held the city for a month, attacked other coastal settlements, and departed in March with substantial booty.[77] This was a pointer to his colleagues.

The isthmus of Panama was the vital link between the silver route from Peru and the transatlantic route from Spain. It had always been protected by distance. Now, after the English capture of Jamaica in 1655, its protection

[76] Chaunu, *Séville et l'Atlantique*, v, 75–79.
[77] Gerhard, *op. cit.*, pp. 139–41.

was removed. It needed military and naval security. After Morgan's raid Portobello and Panama were re-fortified, their garrisons were increased, and the silver route across the isthmus was strongly guarded. But a few miles east of Panama, in the province of Darien, swamp and jungle country, inhabited by Indians hostile to the Spaniards, offered another means of access to the Pacific. This jungle route became 'an inter-oceanic highway for the buccaneers'.[78]

In April 1680 English pirates launched a major invasion of the Pacific. First they took all the shipping in the Gulf of Panama. Then, after raiding, pillaging and capturing a silver transport in the vicinity, they sailed south along the Pacific coast under the command of Bartholomew Sharp; for over a year they raided the west coast of South America, including the silver port of Arica, and took two valuable prizes loaded with bullion. Eventually they left via Cape Horn and reached Barbados in February 1682. This was the most serious attack yet on the Spanish Pacific. The Spaniards estimated the damage to shipping and ports at over 4 million pesos; their merchant marine lost 25 ships; and they suffered more than 200 fatal casualties.[79] And there was more to come.

The largest buccaneer invasion of the Pacific began in March 1684 with the entry of three English ships, two through the Straits of Magellan, the third round Cape Horn.[80] They made their way to Central America where they were joined by other pirate gangs who had crossed the isthmus of Panama. In June 1685 in the Gulf of Panama they attacked a Spanish silver fleet from Callao; the Spaniards first landed their treasure and then beat off the pirates.[81] The invaders escaped to create immense havoc up and down the coast. They attacked coastal settlements in Nicaragua, careened in the Galápagos Islands, took a few prizes off Peru, raided Central America and Mexico, looted Guayaquil, but missed the Manila galleon; eventually the various groups left via Cape Horn or across Central America in the course of 1686–87. This was the last large-scale invasion of the Pacific. In May 1690 Captain John Strong entered through the Straits of Magellan on a contraband mission and disposed of most of his cargo in Peru; but this, like one or two other foreign incursions of the time, was a trading, not a piratical, expedition, and it heralded the French break-through into the Pacific in the early eighteenth century.

Meanwhile from the 1680's the Spaniards renewed their defences. The *armada de la mar del Sur* had been allowed to run down to two galleons and a patache. It was adequate enough for escorting silver fleets, as it showed in

[78] *Ibid.*, p. 146; see also G. Céspedes del Castillo, 'La defensa militar del istmo de Panamá a fines del siglo XVII y comienzos del XVIII', *Anuario de Estudios Americanos*, ix (1952), 235–75.

[79] Artíñano, *Historia del comercio con las Indias*, p. 225.

[80] Gerhard, *op. cit.*, pp. 154–94.

[81] Fernández Duro, *op. cit.*, v, 300–1.

N

1685, but for nothing more. From 1692 it acquired new vessels and was brought to a strength of three galleons and two pataches, with 144 cannon and 1238 men.[82] In addition Mexico was at last provided with a small defence flotilla of its own.[83] Military fortifications at Valdivia, Callao and above all Panama were improved and their garrisons strengthened—but at heavy cost to the Lima treasury and its remittances to Spain.[84] This was the classical story of imperial defence. The metropolis lost more in defence expenditure than in enemy action. The remedy was more painful than the disease.

6. The Collapse of American Trade

In the sixteenth century the Indies trade underwent two long phases of expansion, from 1504 to 1550 and from 1562 to 1592, separated by a mid-century recession of twelve years. This was followed by a reversal of the major trend between 1593 and 1622, and the great depression from 1623 to 1650.[85] The movement of vessels between Spain and America quadrupled between 1506 and 1620, from 226 sailings (outbound and inbound) in 1506–10 to 867 in 1616–20. The number of sailings reached three quinquennial peaks, 874 in 1546–50, 886 in 1586–90, and 965 in 1606–10; but they dropped to 366 in 1646–50, and the average in 1641–50 was practically the same as in 1521–25. Gross tonnage (outbound and inbound) increased from 15,680 tons in 1511–15, to 273,560 in 1606–10; between then and 1646–50 it suffered a 60 per cent. drop, to 121,308 tons. The whole period may be divided into (a) a long wave of expansion, culminating in 1608, and (b) a prolonged period of contraction, interrupted by short upturns.

[82] Céspedes, 'La defensa militar del istmo de Panamá', *op. cit.*, pp. 250–51.

[83] Gerhard, *op. cit.*, p. 198.

[84] See below, pp. 223–24.

[85] The trends have been identified and the estimates computed by Chaunu. Valuable reviews of this great work are provided by H. G. Koenigsberger, *English Historical Review* (1961), 675–81; C. H. Haring, 'Trade and Navigation between Spain and the Indies: a Re-view—1918–1958', *H.A.H.R.*, xl (1960), 53–62; Robert S. Smith, 'Seville and the Atlantic; Cycles in Spanish Colonial Trade', *Journal of Economic History*, xxii (1962), 253–59. It has received a more critical reception from W. Brulez, 'Séville et l'Atlantique: quelques réflexions critiques', *Revue Belge de Philologie et d'Histoire*, xlii (1964), 568–92. Lacking production statistics, Chaunu assumes that tonnage statistics—the carrying capacity of vessels leaving and returning to Seville—measure general economic activity. Doubtless there are margins of error caused by fraud, arrivals and departures at other ports than Seville–Cadiz, the failure of some vessels to fill their cargo capacity and the tendency of others to overfill, and the loss of vessels on voyage. But Chaunu is aware of almost every possible contingency, and in particular he has anticipated criticisms concerning the relation between tonnage and the volume of merchandise carried, by showing that shippers bought or chartered vessels of a particular tonnage according to the state of the trade; Spanish shippers were not so devoid of economic instincts as to underutilise their vessels over a long period. Finally, Chaunu does more than measure an exclusively Spanish commercial activity; his Atlantic is the European Atlantic, for it is incontrovertible that most European merchants preferred to trade via Seville rather than in the Indies themselves.

Until the seventeenth century the trade of Tierra Firme (mainly Peru) and New Spain was more or less balanced, rather more than 40 per cent. of the trade going to Tierra Firme, rather less than 40 per cent. to New Spain, the remainder to the Caribbean islands. Until about 1570–80 exports to America were dominated by grain, oil and wine. But from then, when the colonists had settled for home-produced meat, wheat and maize, and their own wine production had increased, foodstuffs gave way to textiles and hardware. To about 1580–90 Spanish products dominated the trade; subsequently the products of northern Europe and France eroded the Spanish monopoly. Imports from America were dominated by precious metals; in value they constituted more than 90 per cent. of returns.

At the beginning of the seventeenth century the outbound fleets carried wine, oil, mercury, iron and hardware, textiles, books and paper. But the export pattern of the colonies was changing, evidence of a shift in the American economies. In 1594 precious metals formed 95·62 per cent. of total imports from America.[86] In 1609 they were down to 84 per cent., the remainder being agricultural and colonial products, mostly Mexican. In this period Mexico sent back silver, cochineal, hides, indigo, wool, dyes, dye-woods, medicinal plants and, especially in the years 1600–20, Chinese silks, re-exports from Manila.[87] In 1609 Mexico exported to Spain 3·3 million pesos of precious metals (public and private); non-treasure exports totalled 1·8 million pesos, or about 35 per cent. of the value of cargo.[88] Mexico's non-treasure exports became progressively more important as the colony diversified its economy. The Peruvian economy on the other hand, more 'colonial' in its structure, was more closely tied to mining, and Peru exported little but silver to Spain.

The years 1592–1622 form a plateau between expansion and contraction, a high plateau to be sure, with continuing signs of prosperity but equally distinct signs of hesitation which indicate a reversal of the previous trend.[89] At the end of this period sailings (outbound and inbound) dropped by 10 per cent., from 867 in 1616–20 to 775 in 1621–25. The relative roles of Tierra Firme and New Spain also began to fluctuate. Between 1581 and 1590 Tierra Firme had contributed the major part in trade and in silver to the great expansion of those years. But between 1596 and 1620 the high plateau was sustained by increasing contributions of trade from New Spain. After 1620 New Spain flagged again, leaving Tierra Firme to sustain the plateau. Prices and the Indies trade fluctuated in more or less regular periods, and did so in

[86] Hamilton, *American Treasure and the Price Revolution in Spain*, pp. 33–34.
[87] François Chevalier, 'Les cargaisons des flottes de Nouvelle Espagne vers 1600', *Revista de Indias*, iv (1943), 323–30.
[88] *Ibid.*, p. 329.
[89] Chaunu, *Séville et l'Atlantique*, viii, 2, 2, pp. 852–1525.

statistical correlation. The end of expansion corresponded to the reversal of the major trend of prices about 1605, followed by the depression of real prices in 1609–12. Subsequent inflation was artificially induced by monetary debasement, especially from the 1620's, which was not healthy for the Indies trade or for any trade.

The great inflation of the sixteenth century had been engendered in large part by treasure imports. These now began to drop, from 35·1 million pesos in 1591–95, to 24·4 million in 1601–5, to 17·1 million in 1631–35. Crown receipts dropped almost 40 per cent. from 10·9 million pesos in 1596–1600 to 6·5 million in 1601–5; there was a long plateau from 1616 to 1645 when they scarcely rose above 4 million in any quinquennium, followed by a further drop to 1·6 million in 1646–50, to 606,524 in 1656–60.[90] The depression of public treasure receipts was a further sign of a changing empire, for it represented to some degree an increase in the cost of colonial administration and defence, a kind of state investment in the Indies. The reversal of the major trend of private treasure receipts occurred rather later than that of public receipts. Although they fell from 25·1 million pesos in 1591–95 to 17·8 million in 1601–5, they rose again to 25·7 million in 1616–20; they then dropped to 20·3 million in 1626–30, to 12·3 million in 1631–35; after this the fall was irretrievable, to 10·1 million in 1646–50, 5 million in 1651–55, and 2·7 million in 1656–60.

What was the relation of treasure, prices, and trade? What was the effect of the 16,887 tons of silver and 1,813 tons of gold—or perhaps double this amount if allowance is made for contraband—delivered from America to Spain between 1501 and 1650? This massive importation of treasure directly affected prices, which in turn stimulated trade, or, when imports levelled off and fell, depressed it. Treasure returns gave merchants the capital for further investment; when treasure diminished, trade was starved of finance. But the more the American trade expanded in the second half of the sixteenth century, the greater the amount of treasure it needed to keep it going. For treasure induced inflation, which meant that the yield of mining in effect progressively diminished: the very success of American mining caused the value of its yield to decrease.[91] In the course of the sixteenth century prices in Spain quadrupled; in the same period the value of gold and silver, as mer-

[90] Hamilton, *American Treasure and the Price Revolution in Spain*, pp. 34–38. It is difficult to correlate treasure receipts and trade performance, for treasure was the commodity most susceptible to fraud. Hamilton suggests a 10 per cent. margin of error through contraband, but this is too low; from about 1630 the amount of treasure escaping control of the *Casa de Contratacion* may have exceeded the amount registered. Unregistered bullion was most likely to go abroad as immediate returns to foreigners, while most of the registered bullion remained in Spain and was re-invested in the Indies trade. The statistics therefore have some value; see Chaunu, *Séville et l'Atlantique*, viii, 2, 2, p. 902.

[91] See the acute analysis by Chaunu, *Séville et l'Atlantique*, viii, 2, 2, p. 917.

chandise, decreased by about three-quarters. To prolong the expansion, to sustain the purchasing power of gold and silver, mining production had to grow faster than prices and trade. This could only be done by constant extension of the mining area or great improvement of technology. By about 1590, however, the Spaniards had exhausted the immediately available mineral wealth of America without renewing their methods. With the primitive production techniques of the colonists, the Spanish American economy had reached the limits of its expansion; it was also seriously affected by labour shortage caused by the depopulation of the Indian sector. Simultaneously the colonists were beginning to supply their own needs and becoming less dependent on European imports; the growing self-sufficiency of the empire was a basic factor in the crisis of the Indies trade. Up to 1622 the curve of prices and trade remained roughly level. But in the meantime Spain's own economy had been seriously weakened by an extraordinary rise in wages caused by acute labour shortage after the plague of 1599–1600 and the expulsion of the moriscos in 1609.

Even in this period, however, the Indies trade was still capable of striking performance. The year 1608 was the 'year of all the records'.[92] The previous year had seen the worst recession yet; outward sailings dropped from 98 in 1606 to 37 in 1607 (62 per cent.), and tonnage from 23,286 tons to 9,783 (57 per cent.).[93] In 1608 massive convoys totalling 202 ships and 54,093 tons were dispatched to America, an increase of 445·9 per cent. in vessels and 452·9 per cent. in tonnage. This was 50 per cent. better than the previous peak in 1596, and it was never equalled again. Indeed 1608 was a flash of lightning out of surrounding gloom, a year of fragile prosperity made at the expense of subsequent years. In 1609 the trade returned to the secular norm—138 ships and 32,536 tons outwards.[94] There were serious fears in Seville that the Mexican market had reached saturation point. And there were other signs of trouble. The Tierra Firme fleet of this year brought to Seville a horde of *Peruleros*. These, as their name implies, were factors of creole business houses in Peru. They were not to tied to monopolistic trading practices as were the merchants of Seville; they brought with them large supplies of capital for use in Europe; and they were, if anything, even more serious competitors than the foreigners.[95] The presence of the *Peruleros* in Seville, their employment of American capital in a trade which was theoretically the monopoly of Spain, was a further sign of the re-orientation of the empire and of its growing economic independence. The normal reaction of the monopolists to crisis was to restrict trade, induce shortage and raise prices. The *Peruleros* resisted this practice. In 1610, in opposition to the *consulado* of Seville, they insisted on

---

[92] *Ibid.*, viii, 2, 2, p. 1276. [93] *Ibid.*, viii, 2, 2, p. 1236.
[94] *Ibid.*, viii, 2, 2, p. 1299. [95] *Ibid.*, viii, 2, 2, pp. 1330–32; see below, p. 196.

dispatching a fleet. Peru itself was advancing and demanding more trade, including naval stores for its shipyards; the growth of American shipping and its competition with Spanish trade and navigation were yet further signs of the shift of power from Andalucía.

In 1611 recession was manifest. Traffic (outbound and inbound) fell from 201 to 159 sailings (21 per cent.), tonnage from 65,713 to 41,684 tons (36·6 per cent.). The volume of traffic to New Spain in 1611 was almost 50 per cent. less than in 1609, and by 1620 outbound traffic was down to 47 vessels; the colony's withdrawal into itself was now irreversible.[96] Many of the vessels in the transatlantic fleets were no longer Spanish. From 1614 Biscayan predominance in Indies shipping became a thing of the past. Instead of replacing stock by new orders from Basque shipyards, Spanish shippers relied more and more on foreign, Portuguese, and American vessels.[97] Difficulties were aggravated by the shortage of seamen and the high level of wages. Seville's response to recession was to reduce tonnage and ship only the most expensive and lucrative goods; these were necessarily foreign manufactures, a development which favoured the drift of trade from Seville to Cadiz, the port preferred by foreigners. The crisis of 1619–23 was all the more ominous as it was not a war-induced crisis of a type familiar to Spanish trade—the years 1609–21 were ones of exceptional peace—but a crisis caused by structural failings within the Indies trade.

From 1623 the trend was sharply and irretrievably downwards, both in prices and in the volume and value of trade. The great depression had begun, and it continued until, by 1650, the American trade in its classical form and dimensions was almost totally destroyed. In traffic and tonnage the depression was in the order of at least 50 per cent.: sailings (outbound and inbound) dropped from 965 in 1606–10 to 366 in 1646–50; gross tonnage dropped from 273,560 tons in 1606–10 to 121,308 in 1646–50.[98] The depression gathered momentum between 1621–25 and 1626–30, total sailings dropping from 775 to 588 (about 24 per cent.). The trend was most evident in the outward traffic to New Spain; its portion of total trade moved from 43·19 per cent. in 1621–25, to 28·58 per cent. in 1626–30, to 29·82 per cent. in 1631–35, while Tierra Firme climbed up to 51·23 per cent.[99] Peru was now the most important sector of the transatlantic economy and it attracted relatively more trade. The balance in favour of Peru can also be seen in the origin of treasure imports.[100] Between 1586 and 1625 Mexico supplied 36 per cent. of total treasure imports, Peru 64 per cent., evidence not only of major depres-

---

[96] *Ibid.*, viii, 2, 2, pp. 1336–45, 1499.   [97] *Ibid.*, viii, 2, 2, pp. 1415–17.
[98] *Ibid.*, viii, 2, 2, pp. 1541–43.   [99] *Ibid.*, viii, 2, 2, pp. 1534–35.
[100] Again these are the official figures of registered treasure, but assuming that contraband was roughly the same for both sectors they give the relative position.

sion of Mexican mining but also of the fact that Mexico was diversifying its economy more rapidly than Peru. Mexican consignments decreased to 21 per cent. of total treasure receipts in 1626–30, while those from Peru rose to 79 per cent. And while the actual amount from Mexico fell from 10·8 million pesos in 1621–25 to 5 million in 1626–30, Peru's contribution rose from 16·2 million pesos in 1621–25 to 19·5 million in 1626–30. There was therefore some correlation between the recession in trade and treasure. It was evidently in the 1620's that the collapse of New Spain's first economy became most pronounced. This was the major factor behind the crisis in the American trade.

New Spain was the sick man of the transatlantic economy from the 1620's to the 1650's. Depopulation of the Indians deprived the colony of a sufficient labour force to keep its economy at its former level, and it was not until the second half of the seventeenth century that there were signs of demographic recovery. In the absence of significant technological change or the discovery of new mineral resources, there was no possibility of Mexico's renewing its contribution to transatlantic trade before the eighteenth century.[101] Basic change in the Mexican economy, therefore, disrupted the Atlantic trade and the Pacific trade between Acapulco and Manila, which also suffered recession in the 1620's.[102] But the crisis was aggravated by other factors. The correlation between treasure, prices, and trade was again significant. The precipitous drop in royal treasure returns was one of the reasons why the crown had recourse to monetary inflation by debasement, which was highly damaging to commercial transactions, especially from the 1620's. The slump in Spanish shipping was another factor. In the course of the depression of 1623–50 Biscayan shipping dropped to less than one-third of the vessels employed on the transatlantic run. More than one-third were now foreign vessels, principally English and Dutch; while American vessels, the products of Havana shipyards, contributed the remaining third.[103] In terms of shipping, therefore, Spain was losing control of her imperial communications. Here the state also played a part, for it preferred large galleons for war-time *armadas* and convoys. This again favoured Cadiz against Seville, and had further repercussions on the other side of the Atlantic. It meant that many of the island and coastal settlements of the Caribbean, where navigation was difficult for heavy galleons, were virtually abandoned; this neglect of the poor relations of the empire precipitated their economic independence and widened the breach for foreign interlopers; these increased their pressure from 1620, still

---

[101] For a more detailed discussion of Mexico's crisis see below, pp. 200–12.
[102] Pierre Chaunu, *Les Philippines et le Pacifique des Ibériques* (Paris, 1960), pp. 96–97, 100–1, 202–3, 222–23.
[103] Chaunu, *Séville et l'Atlantique*, viii, 2, 2, p. 1563.

further from 1630.[104] Finally, the Indies trade, stripped of its resources, was all the more sensitive to renewed warfare; the enemy was now a constant menace, especially the Dutch who from the 1620's obtained a foothold in Brazil. In 1628, at the hands of the Dutch, the *carrera* suffered a crushing defeat at Matanzas, its first real defeat. Apart from the loss of vessels and the grievous loss of seamen, the trade was deprived of almost a year's returns from New Spain, estimated at 36–40 per cent. of its working capital.[105] Matanzas was also a profound psychological shock which heightened the nervous tension within the *carrera* and hastened its breakdown.

The American trade paid for Matanzas in the period immediately following. The years 1629–31 were catastrophic.[106] The presence of the Dutch in Brazil undermined the confidence of investors. It also forced the *carrera* to increase its defences, a burden which the enfeebled trade could not bear. The *avería* was no longer sufficient to finance even minimum defence requirements, and could only cover 50 per cent. of the cost of the *armada de la guardia*. The ever growing shortage of seamen, and their cost, reached a point where the navy was reduced to augmenting crews with slaves. Traffic (outbound and inbound) fell from 143 sailings in 1630 to 79 in 1631 (44 per cent.), gross tonnage from 59,025 tons to 22,367 (60 per cent.).[107] In 1635 the war with France caused the government to divert some of the transatlantic galleons to the home fleet; their places were taken by more foreign vessels, together with their crews and masters.[108] In the years 1637–38 Spanish vessels almost disappeared from the Indies trade and those that remained were old and unseaworthy. Altogether this was a depressing decade for Seville and Cadiz.

The catastrophe of 1629–31 was repeated in 1639–41.[109] In the period 1632–41 the annual average of sailings (outbound and inbound) was 94; in 1639–41 it dropped to 69. The trade was starved of capital: private receipts of American silver, which had totalled 25·7 million pesos in 1616–20, fell to 12·3 million in 1631–35, and to 11·6 million in 1636–40. In 1639 the fleet to New Spain was cancelled in order to concentrate available resources on that to Tierra Firme. From now the cost of the *armadas* fell more and more on the royal treasury, for the *consulado* of Seville, which in 1640 undertook a three-year *avería* contract, was forced to declare itself bankrupt. The weakened fabric of trade was further torn by the political crisis of 1640. True, the revolt of Catalonia had no direct repercussions in Seville, nor did it visibly

[104] *Ibid.*, viii, 1, pp. 224–28.
[105] *Ibid.*, viii, 2, 2, p. 1645.
[106] *Ibid.*, viii, 2, 2, pp. 1653–84.
[107] *Ibid.*, viii, 2, 2, p. 1677.
[108] Chaunu refers to 'l'importation massive de navires anglais et hanseates' in 1635–38, *ibid.*, viii, 2, 2, pp. 1757, 1796.
[109] *Ibid.*, viii, 2, 2, pp. 1793–1851.

affect the Indies trade.[110] But the revolt of Portugal was a different matter. Portugal was an important sector of the Spanish Atlantic; its alienation from Spain was a consequence of economic depression and of the attendant restraint on Portuguese in the Spanish empire; and its revolt heightened the sense of uncertainty in Seville and directly affected investment.[111] Military conflict in the peninsula, moreover, forced up the government's defence budget and launched the wildest vellon inflation to date, a severe handicap for any trade to bear. On top of everything came a major calamity at sea in 1641 which revealed in microcosm the whole Atlantic crisis. The returning New Spain convoy was shattered by hurricane in the Bahama channel and lost ten vessels totalling 5,000 tons.[112] This was not a random disaster. The ships themselves were in a pitiable state to start with; they had been further impaired when the sluggishness of the market caused them to be immobilised at Vera Cruz for more than a year, exposed in the warm seas of the tropics to the *broma*, that deterioration of hulls and cordage dreaded by seamen; and the fleet did not command the financial resources to refit. It then left Havana over three weeks after the last date (20 August) set by meteorological observation as the margin of safety before the hurricane season. To ignore the experience of a century and a half of Atlantic navigation was inviting disaster, for the sake moreover of a cargo which was at best mediocre. The whole episode was a sign of the times.

The depression continued unabated for the rest of the decade. In 1650 traffic (outbound and inbound) totalled only 51 sailings, gross tonnage 14,022 tons.[113] The convoys were sailing without their full complement of escorts, as European defence needs diverted warships to other duties. American vessels now outnumbered those built in Spain, a further stage in demonopolisation and a further shift towards American control of the trade, first heralded by the appearance of the *Peruleros*. The Mexican sector continued to contract; its contribution to total colonial exports fell from 40 per cent. in 1636–40 to 22 per cent. in 1646–50, while that of Tierra Firme rose from 60 to 78 per cent. Silver returns from Peru thus maintained themselves, while those of New Spain collapsed.

After 1650 the Atlantic trade decayed even further. The golden days of Seville were now over and Cadiz took the remnants of former prosperity. English naval operations in 1656–57 brought a new period of insecurity, accounting for a substantial part of the Tierra Firme fleet at Cadiz in 1656 and the New Spain fleet in the Azores in the following year.[114] In 1659 the

---

[110] *Ibid.*, viii, 2, 2, pp. 1831–32.
[111] On the reaction against the Portuguese in the Spanish empire see above, pp. 112–13.
[112] See above, pp. 174–75.
[113] Chaunu, *Séville et l'Atlantique*, viii, 2, 2, pp. 1867–68, 1876, 1952.
[114] See above, pp. 122–23, 174.

Tierra Firme fleet carried copious remittances, the accumulation of three years. It was diverted to Santander to avoid a repetition of 1656, but Santander lacked even the modest machinery of control possessed by Seville and Cadiz, and the opportunities for fraud were unlimited. The New Spain fleet of 1661 was diverted to La Coruña, with similar results. A *consulta* of the *junta de guerra* testified to the Spaniards' helplessness.[115] It reported that numerous foreign vessels lay in wait at Cadiz to syphon off the silver from the returning fleets. In 1659 and 1661 they simply transferred to Santander and La Coruña in the company of the fleets and there continued operations. It was thought too dangerous to take rigorous counter-measures, for fear of provoking armed attack which Spain did not have the means to repulse. The report even justified the situation by arguing that foreigners had legitimate rights to bullion in return for their considerable exports to America.

The fleet system continued for the rest of the century, though not on an annual basis, and tonnage remained a fraction of former levels.[116] Spaniards continued to trade with the Indies, but they had to share the returns with foreigners. A few examples are available.[117] In 1670 the New Spain fleet brought 8·5 million pesos; of this the Genoese took 1·5 million, the French 1·3 million, the Dutch 700,000, the Germans 500,000, and the English 300,000. In the same year the Tierra Firme fleet brought 22 million pesos, of which France alone took 3·4 million, or 15·67 per cent. Between then and the 1680's the French normally appropriated from 12 to 16 per cent. of the silver shipments; to this should be added the quotas of the other nations represented at Cadiz.[118] And these were only the official returns, not counting contraband.

The disintegration of the American trade could be seen in the collapse of its defence tax, the *avería*. From 1641 the *consulado* of Seville, which had gone bankrupt on its contract of 1640, refused to handle the tax, and the state had to resume its administration. As the amount of registered trade diminished through fraud, so did the yield of the *avería*.[119] The parlous condition of the Spanish marine and the rising costs of ship-building drove the state to

[115] Sept.–Oct., 1661, cited by Domínguez Ortiz, 'Los caudales de Indias y la política exterior de Felipe IV', *op. cit.*, p. 376.

[116] Veitia Linage, *op. cit.*, pp. 534–35.

[117] Girard, *op. cit.*, pp. 323, 414, 445–55.

[118] According to a French memorandum of 1691, the French exported every two years 20 million livres of goods to Cadiz, of which 12 million were re-exported to America; of the latter 6 or 7 million went on account of the French themselves, the rest on account of the Spaniards and others who bought from the French. Profits on goods sold in the Indies were generally 40 to 50 per cent. Of this trade the French appropriated 25 per cent.; Genoese 21 per cent.; Dutch 19 per cent.; Flemish 11 per cent.; English 11 per cent.; Germans 7·6 per cent.; and Spaniards only 3·8 per cent. These figures, of course, cannot be taken literally, and may represent only one exceptional year. See Haring, *The Spanish Empire in America*, p. 295, n. 1.

[119] Chaunu, *Séville et l'Atlantique*, i, 224–37.

desperate expedients in fulfilment of its defence obligations. The government had no credit abroad; to procure warships for the convoys from foreign sources it had to make expensive contracts each year with private merchants whose credit was better than its own. When it tried to recoup its losses by raising the *avería* it simply encountered more fraud. The point was eventually reached when the government preferred to demand from merchants a fixed contribution and to abandon the system of taxation. By decree of 11 March 1660 it was declared that private treasure and merchandise shipped from the Indies would no longer be subject to the formalities of registration nor the payment of *ad valorem* taxes of *avería, almojarifazgo* or any other import duty. Instead a fixed quota was imposed on the fleets, to be paid by the merchants of Andalucía and the Indies, for the expenses of convoys and *armadas*. The new system was designed to raise 790,000 ducats, distributed as follows: Peru 350,000 ducats; New Spain 200,000; New Granada 50,000; Cartagena 40,000; the royal treasury 150,000.[120] The total sum was supposed to correspond to the costs of an *armada de la guardia* for the Tierra Firme fleet and two armed escorts for the New Spain fleet. This arrangement, too, underwent vicissitudes in the course of the century, but it was better than an unrealistic *avería*. Although Andalucía was not apparently assessed, in fact it paid the New Spain quota. The *consulado* of Seville therefore suggested a reassessment which was accepted in 1667: royal treasury 150,000 ducats; Peru 350,000; Andalucía 170,000; New Spain, 90,000; Cartagena and New Granada 30,000; total 790,000.

It is tempting to attribute the great depression of the American trade to the collapse of the colonial economies. But it was a consequence of shift rather than collapse. If the colonies no longer fed the trade as of old, it was largely because they were employing their capital at home, in public and private investment. More than this, they even absorbed Spanish and European capital. By the 1640's more and more merchants were leaving their bullion returns in America, especially in Peru, either as loans or investments, thus avoiding the risk of sequestration in Spain. Even if this was only a temporary expedient, it suggests that there was a profitable use for capital in America and is evidence of economic vigour and autonomy. The crisis in the *carrera de Indias* occurred not because the American economies were collapsing but because they were developing and disengaging themselves from their primitive dependence on the mother country. This was the first emancipation of Spanish America.

[120] *Ibid.*, v, 415–16; Céspedes, *La avería en el comercio de Indias*, pp. 89–96.

CHAPTER VIII

SPANISH AMERICA: A CHANGING EMPIRE

1. The Hispanic World: A New Balance of Power

In the prime of empire Spain held her colonies in leading strings.[1] Spanish bureaucrats supplied their government, Spanish merchants their material needs. Manufactures, equipment, even foodstuffs were so apportioned from Spain as to yield the maximum return for the minimum outlay. Payment was demanded in precious metals, virtually the only commodity of interest to the metropolis. The foci of empire were therefore the silver colonies of Mexico and Peru, whose societies and economies were orientated around mining production. Other settlements were assigned inferior status and given the minimum support compatible with imperial defence. The system was paternal, benevolent, but essentially exploitative. And the balance of power was firmly weighted towards the metropolis.

This primitive imperialism could not endure. Mineral wealth was a wasting asset, and invariably engendered other activities. American societies gradually acquired an identity and a life of their own, developing further sources of wealth, reinvesting in production, improving their subsistence economies in foodstuffs, wine, oil, and cloth. As the first mining cycle came to an end in Mexico, the colony rebuilt its economy around agriculture and livestock and began to supply some of its own needs in manufactured goods. Peru still had considerable mining capacity and remained less 'developed' than Mexico; but Peru, too, diversified its economy, exploited its natural resources, and absorbed its own wealth. As the inequity, shortages and high prices of the Spanish monopoly system became more flagrant, the colonies extended economic relations between themselves, and inter-colonial trade developed a buoyancy of its own, independent of the transatlantic network. Economic growth was accompanied by social change, by the formation of a creole elite of landowners and merchants whose interests did not always coincide with those of the metropolis, least of all in their pressing claims to property

---

[1] On the Spanish empire in America there are two fine works, C. H. Haring, *The Spanish Empire in America* (New York, 1952), and Bailey W. Diffie, *Latin American Civilization: Colonial Period* (Harrisburg, 1945); and two distinguished recent accounts, J. H. Parry, *The Spanish Seaborne Empire* (London, 1966), and Charles Gibson, *Spain in America* (New York, 1966).

and labour. While the colonial aristocracy never acquired formal political power, it was a force which bureaucrats could not ignore, and Spanish colonial government became in effect a compromise between imperial sovereignty and settler interests.

The new balance of power was reflected in the diminution of treasure returns to Spain.[2] This was a consequence not merely of recession in the mining industry but also of redistribution of wealth within the Hispanic world. It meant that the colonies now appropriated more of their own production, and employed their capital in their own administration, defence, and investment. Living more for itself, America gave less to Spain and shared less in Spain's European commitments. Spain's recession was America's growth.

Shift of power from the peninsula was also noticeable outside the mining colonies. At the beginning of the seventeenth century, particularly towards 1620, new plantation economies appeared, self-sufficient in their development, outside the *carrera de Indias*, and beyond the control of Spain. Unlike the mines, the plantations did not work for Spain; they sold their products directly to foreigners or to other colonies; and they employed a type of shipping which the monopoly trade no longer possessed—small, mobile vessels, plying singly or in flotillas, with a rapid turn-round. Tobacco plantations brought modest prosperity to the forgotten coasts of eastern Tierra Firme and its adjacent islands, to Trinidad, Cumaná, Caracas, Río de la Hacha, Maracaibo, and Margarita.[3] By 1621 Trinidad was producing 6,000 arrobas of tobacco a year, Cumaná 12,000. An active contraband trade developed; the Portuguese, English and Dutch were soon involved; and slave ships were found to serve a double purpose, taking labour in and products out. Many of these slave cargoes, licensed by the Spanish crown for Peru and Mexico, were in fact diverted from their official markets by growing demand in the new plantations, ready to expand their investment and compete for labour with the older colonies. By the early 1620's the Portuguese virtually monopolised the tobacco trade, shipping the commodity direct to Europe. When, in 1621, the Spanish government was alerted and tried to impose a state monopoly in tobacco, it was too late; producers preferred the more regular traffic and the better prices of the contrabandists. The tobacco cycle was succeeded by cacao. Plantations of cacao were developed in the central valleys of Venezuela towards the end of the sixteenth century, and by 1630 there were half a million trees in the various centres of production. Cacao gave rise to a creole aristocracy of plantation owners, the *grandes cacaos*, who invested in Negro slaves, extended their holdings, and grew rich

---

[2] See above, pp. 168, 186, 190.
[3] Chaunu, *Séville et l'Atlantique*, viii, 1, pp. 602–12.

from a lucrative export trade. Cacao was exported not to Spain but to Mexico, earning for Venezuela a growing share of Mexico's silver.[4]

The expansion of economic activity in the colonies denoted an investment pattern—American capital in the American economy—which though modest in its proportions was outside the transatlantic sector. There was also a certain flow of capital into America from outside; Spanish merchants and royal bankers often preferred to have their loans to the government repaid on the American treasuries and to employ their capital in America, removed from sequestration and from the heavier taxes of the peninsula. Finally, Americans began to export their capital and to employ it in Europe. This was the significance of the *Peruleros*, who made their presence felt in Seville from the early seventeenth century.[5] The *Peruleros* brought silver from Peru to employ it directly in Spain, either on their own account or more often as factors of Peruvian capitalists. They disrupted the commercial practices of the *carrera de Indias*, for they were not content to buy at the American end of the trade but preferred to do their business in Europe, competing with the Spanish monopolists. The latters' resentment bore more than a trace of anti-Americanism. The *contador*, Antonio de Rojas, reported on the intruders to Olivares in 1623:

> There ought to be a law against the so-called *Peruleros* who come from Tierra Firme to do business in Spain and cause notorious damage to our own trade. . . . They are the drones in the hive of Spanish commerce with the Indies; they devour it and deprive Spaniards of profits. They are not the owners of the capital they employ but merely factors. They assemble all the silver from Peru, silver which ought to be employed in purchasing from the fleet at Portobello; but they do not in fact employ it there, with the result that there are no buyers for Spanish merchandise and it has to be sold off at a loss. Instead the *Peruleros* bring their capital to Spain and buy up merchandise here, sending up prices and ruining the market.[6]

The Seville merchants could not compete with these American capitalists, who made direct contact with foreign suppliers and if necessary employed their capital outside of Spain. They represented the determination of Peruvian merchants to dictate the terms of trade, to break the grip of Spanish monopolists on the most valuable market in America, and to give the developing colony the supplies it wanted. And the Peruvians operated from a position of strength, for the *carrera* needed their capital; this was why they received preferential treatment from the crown, especially in the matter of sequestrations, from which they secured either exemption or repayment in silver.

[4] See below, pp. 227–28.
[5] See above, p. 187.
[6] Domínguez Ortiz, *Política y hacienda de Felipe IV*, p. 294, n. 6.

The transatlantic trade came to rely not only on American capital but also on American shipping. By the 1640's American-built vessels comprised at least 40 per cent. of the fleets; they shared first place with foreign vessels, and were much more numerous than Spanish. This new inroad into the Spanish monopoly tipped the balance still more towards America. It was made possible by the development of a shipbuilding industry in America, one of the soundest growth industries in the New World and another outlet for American and Spanish capital.

Havana was the greatest centre of American shipbuilding, producing about 75 per cent. of American vessels employed in the transatlantic trade.[7] Cuba was favoured by local abundance of raw materials, including excellent timber; the island was also a strategic base of Caribbean defence and of the homeward-bound silver fleets, for which it offered repair facilities. The first major stimulus to Cuban shipbuilding was the conquest and occupation of Florida (1565–74), for which it provided most of the vessels; between 1572 and 1590 Cuba built a great number of frigates. It then graduated to heavy galleons, and in the period 1608–30 orders multiplied, placed partly by Spanish merchants for their transatlantic fleets and partly by the state for the escorting *armadas*. From about 1620 Cuba had to import timber from neighbouring islands and the mainland to supplement its own resources. For naval stores—iron, nails, rigging, pitch, tar and hemp—its shipyards relied on imports from Europe via Seville. In the course of the seventeenth century, however, Cuba came to procure these supplies direct from northern Europe.[8] The Spanish government, now relying more on American than on Spanish shipyards, had to open breaches in the monopoly to expedite the supply of naval stores to America. In 1608, for example, having placed orders in the Havana yards for galleons for the *Armada de Barlovento*, it concluded a contract with prominent Antwerp businessmen, Denis and Jacob Lhermit, for the supply of naval stores direct from the Baltic to Havana; in return for this they received the right to trade with Havana, from which apparently they profited beyond all permission.[9]

While other American shipyards did not achieve the Atlantic stature of Havana, they built for local trade and navigation and thus contributed to the growth of an independent American economy. Maracaibo developed a shipbuilding industry precisely because its shores were neglected by transatlantic shipping which found them difficult to navigate; local shipyards were established in the sixteenth century to cater for local needs, producing small vessels suitable for coastal navigation in the Caribbean. Maracaibo had

---

[7] Chaunu, *Séville et l'Atlantique*, viii, 1, p. 667.
[8] *Ibid.*, viii, 1, p. 566, n. 3.
[9] *Ibid.*, i, 205–6; v, 1622 A, n. 2.

good access to supplies of pitch in its hinterland and to timber in the hills of Mérida. It profited from the growth of the tobacco and cacao trades, which brought in further capital for investment in a merchant marine. Its vessels increased in size and by the late 1630's it was building up to 180 tons, specialising in a Dutch rather than a Spanish type of vessel; one which was extremely navigable, and combined great cargo capacity with shallow draught. Cartagena was another secondary centre of shipbuilding. Its yards developed in the second half of the sixteenth century primarily for repair work on the Tierra Firme fleet and small defence contracts, such as construction of galleys for anti-corsair patrols. But its real growth began in the early seventeenth century, again in response to the recession in Spanish shipyards. It now built large galleons for the transatlantic run, and by mid-century was producing vessels of over 600 tons.[10]

These developments did not go unnoticed. In Spain there was considerable prejudice against American shipbuilding, and jaundiced comments on its high costs, its poor quality, and above all its danger as an instrument of economic independence. The first criticism was exaggerated, the second untrue. But the third was accurate enough—the balance of Atlantic shipbuilding had now moved decisively from east to west, from Spain to America.

Isolated from transatlantic shipping, Pacific navigation necessarily depended on local shipyards. These built vessels of a Spanish Atlantic type, generally smaller but including galleons—three-masted vessels with high sides and seaworthy features. Panama had shipyards almost from its foundation, and by the 1530's the industry had reached sizeable proportions, profiting from local supplies of timber and the demand of the Pacific coastal trade. At the beginning of the seventeenth century it was building small vessels between 45 and 130 tons. Realejo in Nicaragua had even better reserves of raw materials. It could draw on a variety of suitable timber from forests near the coast; it had access to adequate deposits of *brea* (pitch); and local *pita* and *cabuya* fibres were manufactured into cables and cordage on the nearby island of Puna.[11] By the mid-sixteenth century Realejo had outstripped Panama and was producing vessels up to 700 tons for the trans-Pacific run to Manila.[12]

But the best, the largest and the most numerous vessels on the Pacific coast came from Guayaquil. By the beginning of the seventeenth century the yards on the River Guayas became one of the most active shipbuilding centres in the Hispanic world, stimulated by defence contracts, the needs of the

[10] *Ibid.*, viii, 1, pp. 1033, 1037–38.
[11] Woodrow Borah, *Early Colonial Trade and Navigation between Mexico and Peru* (Berkeley and Los Angeles, 1954), p. 5.
[12] *Ibid.*, pp. 65–66.

Pacific coastal trade, and the demand for galleons for the trans-Pacific route. Guayaquil, a town of about 200 Spaniards, had exceptional resources. In the tropical forests of its hinterland there were vast reserves of timber, linked to the coast by a labyrinth of navigable rivers; at nearby Piura deposits of *copey* yielded tar and pitch to supplement imports from Nicaragua; at Porto Viejo the *cabuya* fibre provided a good substitute for hemp; from the inland river port of Chimbo came sail cloth; and copper was imported from Chile. At Guayaquil therefore Spanish technique worked almost entirely on American material. The only supplies which its yards had to import from Spain were hardware, nails and anchors, for no iron-ore deposits were then exploited in America; these were a major item in the industry's costs but one which it could afford.[13] From about 1610, in response to Dutch penetration of the Pacific, Peru increased its defence expenditure, and Guayaquil received a series of substantial contracts for large warships. In the course of 1616–20 the Lima treasury placed orders amounting to 25·8 million maravedis, the equivalent of 12·3 per cent. of government funds remitted to Spain; from that date the figures remained fairly constant; in 1641–45 naval orders amounted to 36·2 million maravedis, 8 per cent. of remittances to Spain.[14] In the second half of the century, however, Peruvian investment in defence increased still further and ate more ruthlessly into remittances to Spain.[15] Shipbuilding at Guayaquil therefore became a major industry, absorbing state as well as private capital, and stimulating the local economy.

Investment in shipbuilding, however, was only one aspect of America's self-sufficiency in defence. Military and naval defence in Mexico and Peru were financed out of the local treasuries; this involved heavy expenditure on fortifications, garrisons, warships and crews. In addition these two viceroyalties were responsible for the defence costs of the rest of America, in the form of *situados* (subsidies, primarily for defence) assigned to those parts of the empire which were strategically important but lacked the resources to provide for themselves. Peru was responsible for defence in the *mar del Sur*, and also subsidised Chile, Panama and distant Cumaná. New Spain provided the *situados* for the coasts and islands in the Caribbean from Florida to Paria, and also for the Philippines. In 1664, for example, Lima was instructed to provide 105,150 pesos a year for the military defences of Panama; in 1673 this was raised to 275,314 pesos. A subsidy of 212,000 ducats a year for the army in Chile was also charged on the viceroyalty.[16] New Spain had equally heavy obligations; by the mid 1630's it already supported defence charges of

[13] A Guayaquil-built galleon cost 300,000 pesos, rising to 500,000 in the later seventeenth century; see Emilio Romero, *Historia económica del Perú* (Buenos Aires, 1949), p. 151.

[14] Chaunu, *Séville et l'Atlantique*, viii, 1, pp. 1089, 1168–69.

[15] See below, pp. 222–23.

[16] See below, pp. 223–24.

O

more than 400,000 pesos, and this steadily increased in the course of the century.

America was more than self-sufficient in defence. It also contributed to Atlantic defence. The *Armada de Barlovento*, overtly a Caribbean squadron, was charged on the New Spain treasury and subsidised by the *consulado* of Mexico. But in fact, as has been seen, it was invariably diverted to convoy duty between Spain and America, and on more than one occasion was assigned for long periods to the home fleet.[17] This simply meant that Seville would not or could not provide the revenue for convoy defence, and America had to come to its rescue, paying three-quarters of the cost of defending transatlantic communications.[18] This was further evidence of the shift of economic power within the Hispanic world. The merchants of America, who already controlled the Pacific trade between Acapulco and Manila, were becoming increasingly dominant in the Atlantic route.

Defence expenditure is not normally regarded as an instrument of great economic growth. But it can have vital importance for developing countries; it amounts in effect to a form of economic aid from the metropolis to its dependencies. This is roughly what happened in Spanish America: imperial defence contracts went to the colonies not to Spain. These contracts, of course, had a peculiar feature, for they were financed from capital which America itself created through its bullion production. They were another example of American capital being invested in the American economy. And they were a stimulus to growth, activating not only shipyards, copper-foundries, and arms workshops, but also secondary supply bases servicing these industries. They provided increased employment in the various sectors, and indirectly they gave a boost to agriculture, for workers, crews and garrisons had to be fed as well as clothed and paid.

2. Mexico: From Mining to Agriculture

The Mexican economy was never exclusively orientated towards mining. The colony began a balanced economic development with the first generation of settlers, and by 1540–60 it was enjoying a boom in the rapid expansion of European agriculture and the growth of industry. European-type production, especially in raising sheep and silk, weaving of textiles, and manufacture of furniture and clothing, gave the colony a wide base of prosperity. Production was modest in its proportions, but it met much of the local demand and helped to keep prices low by competing with imports from Spain. There was even a surplus for export in sugar, textiles, clothing, furniture and

---

[17] See above, p. 177.
[18] Chaunu, *Séville et l'Atlantique*, v, 420.

household articles, and other manufactures. Compared with other colonies, including Peru, this development involved a much larger Spanish population, with more farmers and craftsmen, and it brought more of the Indian population into European-type production. Between 1531 and 1580, for example, silk raising, especially in the Mixteca, expanded rapidly and gave rise to a silk manufacturing industry in centres like Mexico City, Puebla and Antequera, producing for the home market and for export to Peru.[19] By the early seventeenth century, however, silk raising, like other sectors of the Mexican economy, was in severe recession, hit by competition from Chinese silks, by the government's policy of restricting competition and economic independence in the interests of Spain, and above all by the decrease of the Indian population.[20]

The white population of Mexico steadily increased, from 63,000 in 1570 to 125,000 in 1646.[21] In Mexico City the growth was relatively greater, from 18,000 to 48,000; whereas in 1570 the capital's white population comprised 28·5 per cent. of that of the whole colony, by the 1640's it was 38·4 per cent., evidence of the growth of a great European-style city, a centre of production but above all of consumption. The upper ranks of the white population formed a colonial aristocracy which was drawn from two groups, *encomenderos* and merchants. The *encomenderos* were descendants of the conquerors and others who had earned royal favour; they lived on the income from tribute or labour supplied by the Indians who had been commended to them. By the end of the sixteenth century many of them had begun to supplement possession of Indians with the other great mark of nobility, possession of land, and to associate their *encomiendas* with *haciendas*. These were the classical aristocracy. They were joined by many who made their fortunes in Atlantic and Pacific trade, men like Simon de Haro, prior of the *consulado* of Mexico in 1650, whose fortune was estimated at 600,000 pesos.[22] Capital earned in commerce was often invested in agrarian property, for the Mexican merchant, like his Spanish counterpart, sought social status in landowning. And some capital found its way into mining. The actual mining proprietor was not normally a wealthy capitalist or at the summit of the social hierarchy. There was wealth in mining, of course, but this wealth did not go exclusively to mineowners and prospectors; much of it went to those who supplied labour and finance, and who were to be found among the colonial aristocracy, once or twice removed from actual operations.

[19] Woodrow Borah, *Silk Raising in Colonial Mexico* (Berkeley and Los Angeles, 1943), pp. 32–38.

[20] *Ibid.*, pp. 85–101; see below, p. 225.

[21] Woodrow Borah, *New Spain's Century of Depression* (Berkeley and Los Angeles, 1951), p. 18.

[22] Chaunu, *Séville et l'Atlantique*, viii, 1, p. 733; on the social structure of the colony see L. N. McAlister, 'Social Structure and Social Change in New Spain', *H.A.H.R.*, xliii (1963), 349–70.

While the white population was increasing, the Indians were vanishing. The Indian population of central Mexico, which may have been as high as 25 million in 1519, decreased from 16,871,408 in 1532, to 2,649,573 in 1568, to 1,372,228 in 1595, to 1,069,255 in 1608.[23] In the Valley of Mexico alone the native population fell from 1,500,000 on the eve of the conquest to 325,000 in 1570, to 70,000 in the mid-seventeenth century.[24] This demographic calamity, 'one of the great catastrophes in the history of the human race', was the result of a number of factors, chief among which was epidemic disease, particularly the scourges of 1545–48 and 1576–81. The Mexican Indians were victims of imported diseases against which they had no immunity; the greatest killers were smallpox, measles, typhus and typhoid, though malaria and influenza also took their toll. Indian resistance to disease, however, was weakened by the shock of conquest and subjugation, by ecological changes attendant on the disruption of their economy, and by deteriorating food supplies. The native inhabitants lost some of their land and water resources to the Spaniards; the latter imported cattle and sheep which swarmed over the land left vacant by the diminishing Indians, and often invaded the reserves of land needed by the native system of field rotation; finally the diversion of scarce water supplies to Spanish farms, ranches and flour mills greatly handicapped Indian agriculture.[25] If the Indians abandoned the land to seek a livelihood elsewhere, in mines and *obrajes* (factories), inhuman conditions wrought havoc on bodies and spirits already enfeebled by destitution. Leaderless and increasingly landless, the Indians were reduced to a subordinate position, payers of tribute and suppliers of labour. They sought refuge in alcohol: 'few peoples in the whole of history were more prone to drunkenness than the Indians of the Spanish colony'.[26] Conditions improved but slowly. After the great demographic tragedy, the downward trend was reversed about 1650, and the Indian population began to increase again in the second half of the century.[27]

Human losses on this scale were bound to affect the economic structure of the colony. A growing settler population encountered fewer Indians to

[23] Woodrow Borah and Sherburne F. Cook, *The Aboriginal Population of Central Mexico on the Eve of the Spanish Conquest* (Berkeley and Los Angeles, 1963), pp. 4, 88; Cook and Borah, *The Indian Population of Central Mexico 1531–1610* (Berkeley and Los Angeles, 1960), p. 48; Borah and Cook, *The Population of Central Mexico in 1548: A Critical Analysis of the Suma de visitas de pueblos* (Berkeley and Los Angeles, 1960). See also A. Rosenblat, *La población de América en 1492* (Mexico 1967).

[24] Charles Gibson, *The Aztecs under Spanish Rule. A History of the Indians of the Valley of Mexico 1519–1810* (Stanford and London, 1964), pp. 136–41.

[25] Lesley Byrd Simpson, *Exploitation of Land in Central Mexico in the Sixteenth Century* (Berkeley and Los Angeles, 1952).   [26] Gibson, *The Aztecs under Spanish Rule*, p. 409.

[27] See however José Miranda, 'La población indígena de México en el siglo XVII', *Historia Mexicana*, xii (1962–63), 182–89, who conjectures that the reversal of the downward trend began in the 1620's and 1630's.

work for its needs, especially after the precipitous population fall during the epidemic of 1576–81. Labour shortage affected all sectors of the economy—agriculture, mining and manufacture. Fewer hands meant harder work and ruthless competition for those who remained; and new forms of labour recruitment had to be devised. Meanwhile, from the 1570's to about the middle of the seventeenth century, while the colony adjusted itself to its profound labour crisis and until the Indian population began to increase, New Spain endured a prolonged economic crisis.[28]

Mexico can be broadly divided into two parts, the humid south and the dry north, with the frontier between the two some 100 miles north of Mexico City. This was also more or less a demographic division: the south had a relatively dense population of mild and sedentary Indians, while the tribes of the north were scattered, nomadic, wild and indomitable. Northern Mexico was the mining zone; the south was agricultural.

The Puebla region specialised in production of grain and maize, supplying the transatlantic fleets and the Mexico City market. Cuernavaca was one of the principal sugar zones; sugar production in Mexico never attained the importance of the industry in Hispaniola, but two cycles can be identified, the first to 1570, followed by recession induced by the diversion of diminishing labour supply to the mining boom, and a second period of growth from about 1618.[29] Cuernavaca was also the centre of indigo production, radiating to other parts of Mexico. The Mixteca, with its relatively large Indian population, produced salt, cotton and maize. But it was also the chief centre of raw silk, and of cochineal which, after silver, was the second most important export of the colony. Further south still, in Oaxaca, was the territory of the Marquesado del Valle, the immense fief granted to Cortés. European crops and livestock had been quickly introduced by the agents of the Cortés estate, and maize was also cultivated. Oaxaca, like the Mixteca, produced cochineal for export. This, in brief, was the economy of the south. It was severely disrupted by the Indian depopulation. Shortage of labour caused a steady fall in food production; the urban centres, foci of the growing white population, suffered decrease in supplies and, from the 1570's, serious shortage.[30] In 1595 Viceroy Velasco reported gloomily to Philip II: 'All supplies are becoming scarce and are rising in price so fast that before many years this land will experience as great a dearth and want as now exists in Spain'.[31] The measures adopted to meet the crisis constituted in effect an attempt to impose a system of rationing. After 1595 the failure of crop production to keep pace

[28] This is the brilliantly argued hypothesis of Woodrow Borah, *New Spain's Century o Depression*.

[29] François Chevalier, *La formation des grands domaines au Mexique. Terre et société aux XVIe–XVIIe siècles* (Paris, 1952), p. 96.

[30] Borah, *New Spain's Century of Depression*, pp. 22–26. [31] *Ibid.*, p. 23.

with a still rising white population brought down living standards and reduced the poor whites to the margin of subsistence. And agriculture had to
compete for labour with mining.

Mexico's mining zone lay substantially in the north, in New Galicia,
which included the most important mines of all, notably Zacatecas and San
Luis Potosí, and New Viscaya, whose principal settlements were Durango
and Santa Barbara, supplemented by a later strike at Parral.[32] These settlements were remote islands in a sea of hostile and rebel tribes. The mining
zone was a frontier, whose expansion promoted pacification and colonisation,
it is true, but only with great difficulty and at heavy cost. For the further
north the mining frontier advanced the more hostile the Indians became. San
Luis Potosí, the richest strike of all after Zacatecas, was only worked relatively
late, in 1591, after the viceroy had negotiated a truce with the Chichimecs;
this permitted the establishment of a colony of friendly Tlaxcalans to begin
operations. When, after 1600, northern expansion opened up new mines,
these were expensive to sustain, and they invariably suffered from shortage of
troops and arms. In the northernmost mining district of Parral a case of
cannibalism was reported in 1652 when the rebellious Chichimecs were
alleged to have eaten a Jesuit missionary.[33]

Mexican silver production reached its peak in the 1590's. After this the
boom was over; many mineowners found returns insufficient to cover
labour and equipment costs, and they were forced to cut back on investment.
By 1630 even Zacatecas was failing; by 1635 San Luis was also in depression.
The days of great mining fortunes were past; new bonanzas were rare, and
after the 1650's there were no major strikes until the following century. By
about 1690 depression had settled over almost the whole of the industry,
though a few places like Parral, which had enjoyed a late boom from 1630,
survived longer than others.[34] In the course of the century a number of mines
were completely abandoned, and miners retreated into their rural estates or
sought alternative income from purchase of office.[35] Although the first
signs of depression were already evident in the late sixteenth century, actual
mining output increased up to about 1600. There was then a slow recession to
about 1630, with booms at Zacatecas and San Luis compensating for setbacks
elsewhere; after 1630 output deteriorated rapidly, and even the late bonanza
at Parral could not offset the great depression at Zacatecas and San Luis.[36] The

[32] Robert C. West, *The Mining Community in Northern New Spain: The Parral Mining District*
(Berkeley and Los Angeles, 1949), pp. 10–14.
[33] Chaunu, *Séville et l'Atlantique*, viii, 1, p. 776.
[34] Modesto Bargalló, *La minería y la metalurgia en la América Española durante la época colonial*
(Mexico, 1955), pp. 210–12; West, *op. cit.*, pp. 12–14.
[35] Chevalier, *La formation des grands domaines au Mexique*, pp. 178–80.
[36] Borah, *New Spain's Century of Depression*, p. 43.

crisis of Mexican mining was reflected in the colony's silver exports to Spain and its contribution to transatlantic trade; both of these diminished, especially from the early 1620's.[37]

The key to mining performance was manpower. The recruitment and feeding of workers, in a zone which was largely semi-desert, were perennial problems for Mexican mining, and account for the relatively small labour force employed in the industry.[38] But mining was a heavy consumer of labour. The appalling conditions of work, lack of safety precautions, foul air, high temperatures, heavy carrying tasks, and mercurial poisoning, all caused the physical deterioration of workers—or absenteeism. The crown acceded to the colonists' demands for Indian labour by sanctioning *repartimiento* (forced wage labour), which was applied to mining as well as agriculture. But this could only supply a rotating and unskilled labour force, whereas from the 1570's the industry was confronted by greater technical problems associated with drainage, deeper shafts, and the amalgamation process, all of which required skilled and permanent labourers. Moreover, the richest mines—Zacatecas, San Luis, Durango, Guanajuato, Parral—were situated in northern territory where the nomadic and hostile Indian population was quite un-adaptable to *repartimiento*. The northern mines, therefore, always tended to prefer free labour, tempted from central and southern Mexico by higher wages and then frequently held to employment by debt peonage.

These difficulties were worsened by the demographic catastrophe which overtook the Indians, especially from the 1570's. The depleted task force was now spread more thinly over the various sectors of the economy, and sub-jected to relatively greater demands. The mines at Pachuca in central Mexico, for example, which before the great epidemic of 1576 had a *repartimiento* quota of 1,108 Indians a week, had only 57 in 1661.[39] The crown was forced to impose a policy of labour curtailment and rationing, with priority to essential sectors such as agriculture and mining.[40] Decrees of the late sixteenth century prohibited the use of Indians in certain industries considered particu-larly detrimental to their health, notably sugar processing and cloth produc-tion. And attempts were made to prevent the transfer of Indians over long distances, which ruled out the northernmost areas. The policy was not entirely consistent and could be circumvented, and mining simply competed as best as it could with the labour demands of agriculture, public works and building.

[37] See above, pp. 188–89.
[38] Even Zacatecas in 1570 only had 300 Spaniards, 500 slaves; in 1605 it had about 1,000 Euro-peans; see J. H. Parry, *The Audiencia of New Galicia in the Sixteenth Century* (Cambridge, 1948), p. 186.
[39] Borah, *New Spain's Century of Depression*, p. 26.
[40] *Ibid.*, pp. 34–36.

The poor technical performance and now the utter decrease of *repartimiento* labour forced miners to turn to other sources of supply. One of these was Negro slaves. Between 1519 and 1650 Mexico imported at least 120,000 slaves, two-thirds of all the Africans shipped to Spanish America.[41] The Negro population grew from 20,000 in 1570 to 35,000 in 1650 with 100,000 mulattos and zambos. This was in direct response to Indian depopulation. The Negroes were directed to plantations and ranches, to sugar refineries and textile factories (where Indian labour came to be prohibited), and to the service sector of the towns. Some of them also went to the northern mines, though not in great numbers. Slaves were a heavy capital investment; at the beginning of the seventeenth century a Negro slave cost 400 pesos, the equivalent of about eight months' wages for a *repartimiento* Indian.[42] They had already suffered physical deterioration since leaving Africa, and they were unfitted for work in the dry, cold climate of the northern plateau; in any case they hated mining and fiercely resisted it.[43] For these reasons Negro slaves never formed more than a small percentage of the mining labour force: at the beginning of the seventeenth century they composed only 6 per cent. of the total labour force at Zacatecas, and 10 per cent. at Pachuca.[44] There were other slaves, too, the so-called *gente de guerra*, rebellious Indians captured in war, and these probably outnumbered Negroes in the mining industry, though again they were not numerous.

The mines, therefore, relied more and more on free labour, Indians from central Mexico, mulattos and mestizos, attracted by the high salaries and even more perhaps by assurance of food and clothing. Free labourers were more expensive—4 reales a day compared with the 1 real paid to *repartimiento* Indians— but their technical performance was better and the miners preferred them, frequently holding them by debt peonage. By 1600 they outnumbered *repartimiento* Indians in most mines, and by 1650 they had almost displaced them. At Zacatecas the entire Indian labour force consisted of free workers, and at Parral almost all wage earning workers were freely hired.[45] The employment of free labour, of course, could not solve the problem of diminishing labour supply. It merely meant that the mines were competing more keenly for what labour was available, particularly against agriculture, which had to feed a growing white population and also drew heavily on the free labour market.

[41] Gonzalo Aguirre Beltrán, *La población negra de México*, 1519–1810 (Mexico, 1946), pp. 199–222; see also Rolando Mellafe, *La esclavitud en Hispanoamérica* (Buenos Aires, 1964).

[42] Gibson, *The Aztecs under Spanish Rule*, p. 244.

[43] David M. Davidson, 'Negro Slave Control and Resistance in Colonial Mexico, 1519–1650', *H.A.H.R.*, xlvi (1966), 235–53.

[44] West, *op. cit.*, p. 53.

[45] Borah, *New Spain's Century of Depression*, p. 37; West, *op. cit.*, pp. 48–51.

The effects of labour shortage were more pronounced as they coincided with other difficulties besetting the mining industry, particularly the upward trend of costs. Whereas miners received a fixed price for their bullion—1 peso an ounce—they were faced with rising costs for labour, food and equipment. They had campaigned successfully to get the *quinto*, the royal tax on silver, reduced to a tenth; they then sought to evade even the reduced taxation. To get their profits quickly and to avoid taking their product long distances to the nearest *caja real* for stamping and assaying, miners adopted the practice of selling their silver at the mine direct to merchants, often under price. Outside capitalists thus came to exert a powerful control over the industry, for they also handled supplies to the mines and frequently advanced loans to the miners against future yield. With the product in their grasp merchants kept back a portion from registration and taxation and so retained a highly valuable trading commodity. The profits from mining, therefore, were largely escaping the control of the miners themselves, with the result that they had insufficient margin for reinvestment at a time when operations were posing new problems.

By the beginning of the seventeenth century, the amalgamation process of refining silver, which had first been adopted in the 1550's, was employed in most mines, and about two-thirds of the Mexican product were thus processed. Amalgamation revolutionised mining, for it forced a yield from low-grade ores, precisely when these were becoming more frequent.[46] But amalgamation needed additional equipment and labour, and it depended on a number of ingredients, particularly mercury, which were scarce and expensive. The exhaustion of rich ores near the surface led to deeper mining—down to 400 feet—for lower-grade ores, a development encouraged by the amalgamation process. But as mining went deeper costs increased, and so did technical difficulties. Shaft reinforcement, illumination, ventilation, and haulage operations all became more complicated and more expensive. The greatest problem was flooding, for drainage technique was primitive in the extreme; and some miners found drainage so expensive that they preferred to abandon their mines. Finally, amalgamation demanded finely ground ores; grinding machinery, and the numerous mules needed to drive it, became an additional expense. In short, mining now required heavy capital investment for an end product whose yield was steadily diminishing.

Costs were further inflated by the expense of procuring supplies. To some degree mining settlements were self-sufficient units, for the industry stimulated local stock ranching and grain farming as proximate bases of supply.[47] The northern plateau provided a favourable environment for livestock,

[46] Bargalló, *op. cit.*, pp. 107–33, 203–14.
[47] West, *op. cit.*, pp. 57–91.

which multiplied enormously in the period 1560–1620. Local ranches, some-times owned by miners as an additional investment, supplied mules for motor-force, hides and tallow for mining operations, and meat for the labourers.[48] But farming did not keep pace with ranching, and some settle-ments had to import grain supplies. And they all relied on imports for tropical products such as sugar, for wine, textiles, hardware, and other manufactures. Trade between Mexico City, the entrepôt for European imports and locally produced goods, and the northern mining settlements was one of the principal commercial activities of the colony. According to an estimate of 1673, some 600,000 pesos' worth of merchandise was sent annually from the capital to Parral.[49] The mines had to compete at a long distance with other sectors for these supplies, not all of which were abundant; and they were faced with heavy transport costs, for the northern settlements were two to three months' journey from the capital.

But it was mercury which posed the greatest supply problem. World sources of mercury were—and remain—few in number. Through a striking coincidence of circumstances Spain possessed not only the greatest silver mines in the world but also two rich and workable deposits of mercury, the mines at Almadén in the peninsula and Huancavelica in Peru. The Mexican mines required about 5,000 to 6,000 quintals of mercury a year; consump-tion grew from 263 quintals a year in 1559, to 1,387 in 1569, to 6,557 in 1589, and varied between 3,000 and 3,700 in 1597–1606.[50] Up to about 1580 they were supplied from the total production of both Almadén and Huancavelica; subsequently, owing to the increasing demand of Peru's own silver mines, Mexico had to rely on the sole product of Almadén. In some years Mexico even had to compete for Almadén's exports with Peru; yet Zacatecas alone, in 1612–18, when its output was still forging ahead, consumed 1,180 to 2,330 quintals of mercury a year.[51] Mexico's mining fortunes were linked to Almadén at a time when the latter's production had passed its peak of sus-tained growth. Output fluctuated from 4,526 quintals in 1622, to 6,936 in 1624, to 4,797 in 1631; by the 1670's it was averaging only 2,000 a year.[52] According to miners, the high price of mercury—its distribution and sale were a state monopoly—was a major item pushing up their costs. Chrono-logically, however, the problem of mercury supply was a relatively late factor in the mining depression; it simply placed an additional burden on an already enfeebled industry.

[48] Chevalier, La formation des grands domaines au Mexique, pp. 167–68.
[49] West, op. cit., p. 85.
[50] Chaunu, Séville et l'Atlantique, viii, 2, 2, pp. 1958–80.   [51] Bargalló, op. cit., p. 273.
[52] Chaunu, Séville et l'Atlantique, viii, 2, 2, p. 1973; on the reasons for Almadén's difficulties, linked to the waning fortunes of the Fuggers, see Domínguez Ortiz, Política y hacienda de Felipe IV, pp. 144–46.

As Mexico's first mining cycle drew to a close, the colony's economy was re-orientated towards agriculture for subsistence purposes, and to a lesser extent manufacturing for the home market. And Mexican society was re-integrated around an institution which was to dominate it for three centuries to come, the *hacienda*, the great landed estate, the characteristic base of a new colonial aristocracy. The *hacienda* emerged in a period of economic crisis when the Indians could no longer support the *encomenderos* or the towns. It was a means of escape from direct dependence on the weakened Indian communities for food supplies. The estates, of course, still relied on the Indians for labour, but the Indians could be better organised for commercialised food production on estates under Spanish supervision than when they were left to produce food in their own communities.[53]

The origin of the *hacienda* can be traced back to the land grants which the Spanish crown made to the conquistadores and their offspring for services rendered. These grants were limited in size, but the grantees tended to ignore the limitations. From the 1570's they began to occupy land vacated by the vanishing Indians, with or without title from the crown; they also began to encroach on areas still being worked by Indian communities, and to add to their territorial wealth by Indian land procured through extortion or purchase.[54] The process was hastened by the demands of the mining settlements for food supplies; each *real de minas* needed its tributary stock ranches and grain farms in close proximity, and the ranch–mine complex became the typical unit of settlement in northern Mexico. Then, when the first mining cycle ended, the miners themselves were forced to look to the land for a living, and many of them became *hacendados*. The formation of great estates was further promoted by the tendency of *encomenderos* to transfer their *encomiendas*, which were strictly speaking not land grants, into farms, especially when their income from tribute decreased with the depopulation of the Indians.[55] Finally, the growth of the great *hacienda* was stimulated by a motive which lay deep in the Iberian mentality: Spaniards and creoles alike wanted large estates for the sake of size alone and the social prestige that accrued therefrom, for landownership was linked with nobility and 'purity of blood'.[56] Thus, by one means or another, by the middle of the seventeenth century a very large part of Mexico was in the hands of the *latifundistas*.

[53] Borah, *New Spain's Century of Depression*, p. 32.
[54] Gibson, *The Aztecs under Spanish Rule*, pp. 274–76; Chevalier, *La formation des grands domaines au Mexique*, pp. 113, 127–28.
[55] Lesley Byrd Simpson, *The Ecomienda in New Spain: The Beginnings of Spanish Mexico* (Berkeley and Los Angeles, 1950).
[56] Chevalier, *La formation des grands domaines au Mexique*, p. 231. This fine and readable work on the formation of the latifundia has also been published in English: *Land and Society in Colonial Mexico. The Great Hacienda*, trans. Alvin Eustis, ed. Lesley Byrd Simpson (Berkeley and Los Angeles, 1963).

The growth of the large estate, of course, could not in itself solve the basic question of labour. So fierce was the competition from agriculture and other sectors for the diminishing supply of *repartimiento* labour that employers turned to another means of securing workers—free, or ostensibly free, wage labour.[57] Under this system the worker hired himself out to an employer for wages and could leave at any time. In practice such labour had a tendency to turn into debt bondage, the worker being bound to serve by advances of money, food and clothing, and unable to leave the employer until he had worked out his debt. But the new labour system also had compensations from which the Indians benefited. Competition for labour in a free market resulted in higher wages and better living conditions; this accounts perhaps for the higher survival rate among the remnants of the Indian population in the later seventeenth century, and for the eventual reversal of the demographic trend.[58] Moreover, in some aspects the *hacienda* was a benevolent institution, a refuge, a means of livelihood, and an instrument of credit. In later colonial times debt peonage in the Valley of Mexico affected fewer than half the workers on *haciendas*, and there was relative freedom of movement among workers as they went in search of yet bigger advances, attempting 'not to escape but to enlarge the indebtedness'.[59]

The *hacienda* involved not only increasing white domination over land and labour but also over agriculture.[60] On their own land the Indians preferred maize. But Spaniards wanted wheat, and Indian resistance to wheat cultivation simply accelerated the Spanish acquisition of land. In the Valley of Mexico the transition to large-scale enterprise in wheat occurred in the late sixteenth century. Between 1563 and 1602 the number of wheat farms increased about four times and the amount of grain sown about twelve times. In its next stage of advance, between 1580 and 1630, Spanish agriculture moved into Indian crops; large-scale enterprises began commercial production of maize and *pulque* (an intoxicating drink obtained from maguey), competing with Indian production and acquiring control of the markets.

In tropical Mexico the *hacienda* quickly adapted itself to its environment. Indigo production, especially in Yucatán, made great strides and was an important export commodity in the seventeenth century. Sugar cane was even more important. In the sixteenth century the sugar industry underwent an excessive boom, eating into land needed for other crops and ruthlessly consuming Indian labour.[61] Government policy added its weight to natural

[57] Borah, *New Spain's Century of Depression*, pp. 36–42.

[58] Lesley Byrd Simpson, 'Mexico's Forgotten Century', *Pacific Historical Review*, xxii (1953), 113–21, especially p. 120.

[59] Gibson, *The Aztecs under Spanish Rule*, p. 255.   [60] *Ibid.*, pp. 323–34.

[61] Fernando B. Sandoval, *La industria del azúcar en Nueva España* (Mexico, 1951), pp. 23–44, 45–51.

restraints to cut back the industry. Official preference granted to Caribbean sugar virtually closed the Spanish market to the Mexican product by the end of the sixteenth century. And pressure to restrict the use—or abuse—of Indian workers culminated in a decree (24 November 1601) forbidding even free Indian labour in the refineries and permitting it only in the fields. Although Mexican sugar did not develop into a good export commodity, its domestic performance was highly successful in the seventeenth century and provided further evidence of the colony's self-sufficiency. The principal zones of production were the Cuernavaca basin, Michoacán, the Marquesado del Valle, and Jalapa. Sugar was an industrial as well as an agricultural enterprise. It needed large tracts of fertile land, ample water supply, and expensive equipment. Each *hacienda* employed hundreds of Indians and Negroes, to be fed as well as employed, and they became in effect self-contained units of production. Sugar therefore required heavy capital investment; normally it attracted an ample flow of capital, from private sources and religious institutions, usually in the form of mortgage-type loans at 5 per cent. interest.[62]

Yet the typical Mexican *hacienda* was not the farm, nor the sugar estate, but the cattle ranch. In the vast, unpopulated, and semi-arid territories of the north, stock farming was obvious adaptation to environment. To some extent, as has been seen, it expanded with the advance of the mining frontier, and new ranches were established along highways to silver mines, particularly in the environs of Zacatecas and Querétaro.[63] By the early 1580's some 200,000 sheep, 100,000 cattle, and 10,000 horses were grazing on ranges a few miles south of Querétaro. Stock raising was cheaper and needed less Indian labour than crop raising. And it needed vast estates: certain stockmen in the region of Valles had 150,000 cattle, and 20,000 were considered a mere trifle.[64] Each *hacienda* aimed to be self-sufficient. As well as pasturage for their herds and flocks, the cattle barons would try to acquire fertile valley land for raising subsistence crops, and further extend their estates to control water supply from rivers or streams. Stock raising on this scale could be risky for there was always a danger of glut. But normally the rancher had two principal outlets—hides were a good export commodity, and wool was in demand by the colony's own textile industry.

With the collapse of the silver boom, therefore, land became virtually the sole source of income in Mexico. The *hacienda* became a microcosm of Mexico's economic self-sufficiency and of its growing independence. But the *hacienda*

---

[62] *Ibid.,* pp. 114–23.

[63] William H. Dusenberry, *The Mexican Mesta. The Administration of Ranching in Colonial Mexico* (Urbana, 1963), pp. 35–39.

[64] Chevalier, *La formation des grands domaines au Mexique,* p. 141; Dusenberry, *op. cit.,* pp. 174–91.

could generate further activity, for it needed to import some consumer goods and it provided raw materials for the colony's own production. If the new economy denoted 'stagnation' after boom, it was a relatively high plateau of stagnation. While government revenue is not a proof of economic performance, it can be a useful indicator. The revenue of the central treasury in Mexico from taxes and other sources rose steadily to 2·3 million pesos in 1609 and over 3 million in 1623. It fell after 1625 but not substantially.[65] This creates a presumption in favour of sustained economic activity which is not easy to reconcile with a hypothesis of absolute depression. Moreover, an increasing proportion of government income in Mexico remained in the colony or its dependencies for administration, defence and public works, which meant that Mexico's wealth now sustained Mexico rather than Spain. The *almojarifazgo* tax, an index of maritime trade, increased steadily until about 1600, after which there was a slight drop; it spurted again in the period 1626–38, before dropping after 1640. The *alcabala*, an index of internal trade, increased until 1638, to be followed by a slight drop. Public remittances to Spain, it can be inferred, diminished, but this was not simply because of depression; it was because Mexico retained more public revenue for its own purposes, and also because its subsidies to the Philippines grew, from 100,000 pesos a year in 1590 to 500,000 a year by the mid-seventeenth century. These official indices of activity point to a transition from one economic structure to another, from a mining economy to one more widely based. The period of transition was a critical one for the Mexican economy, but it was a crisis of change rather than stagnation.

3. PERU: SILVER COLONY, SILVER METROPOLIS

Peru, a wealthy and powerful kingdom, with rich mines of silver, gold, mercury, lead, tin and copper. A land endowed with every kind of food, abundant in livestock, agriculture, birds and fish. A land of moderate climate, free of poisonous snakes and wild beasts. A land of many herbs and medicinal plants'.[66]

The anonymous Iberian Jew, writing in the early seventeenth century for his Dutch masters, was aware of his priorities and their implications. In the eyes of the world Peru was a producer of silver, virtually its only export commodity, the monopoly of Spain, the envy of other powers. Yet this was not the whole story. Peru also possessed the resources to service its mining sector and to achieve a high degree of autonomy. And the colony's developing economy began to absorb more of the mining product.

[65] Chaunu, *Séville et l'Atlantique*, viii, 1, pp. 753, 759–67, 799–802.
[66] *Descripción del Virreinato del Perú. Crónica inédita de comienzos del siglo XVII*. Ed. Boleslao Lewin (Rosario, 1958), p. 19.

SOUTH AMERICA
IN THE
SEVENTEENTH
CENTURY

0   Miles   800

Facing p. 212

Peru's white population increased more rapidly than that of Mexico but remained much smaller—25,000 in 1570, 70,000 in 1650.[67] In the same period the colony's Negroes, mestizos and mulattos increased from 60,000 to 130,000. Meanwhile the Indian population diminished, though far less disastrously than in Mexico. The Peruvian Indians, who may have numbered some 2 million on the eve of the conquest, decreased to 1,500,000 in 1570, to 1,400,000 in 1650.[68] Peru was spared the relentless and devastating epidemics that struck Mexico, and the explanation for the Indian demographic recession must be sought in other factors—the social disruption caused by the conquest, the heavy mortality suffered in rebellion in the 1530's, the subsequent massive dispersals, especially after 1570, and the *mita*, the forced recruitment for mining and other tasks which, although it affected relatively few Indians, caused many more to flee from Spanish jurisdiction.[69] Yet the shock of conquest was less traumatic for the Peruvian Indians than for their Mexican counterparts. They were already conditioned to imperial domination and to working for sovereign masters; and they had a well-developed agrarian economy capable of sustaining workers. It is difficult to measure the relative demands of the Incas and the Spaniards on the working population.[70] Work in the mines was new, at any rate on the scale demanded by Spaniards. It was also very punishing. But so had been the almost superhuman architectural tasks imposed by the Incas. Whereas before the Peruvian Indians had toiled to build temples of the Sun, now they laboured to satisfy the bullion demands of the world economy.

The conquerors and their descendants, as in Mexico, were assigned Indians in *encomienda*, which gave them title to tribute and in effect to labour. The *encomienda* conferred, if not nobility, social status and prestige, and it was regarded as a mark of natural aristocracy, to be secured if possible in perpetuity. In the course of the seventeenth century, however, the Peruvian *encomenderos* entered a period of crisis. To counter the feudal implications of the institution, the crown tended to refuse requests for grants in perpetuity, to

[67] These figures exclude Upper Peru, for which the same source gives 7,000 in 1570, 50,000 in 1650; for source see note 68.
[68] Angel Rosenblat, *La población indígena y el mestizaje en América* (2 vols., Buenos Aires, 1954), i, 59, 76–77, 88, 225. David N. Cook, however, gives a total of 6 million in 1531, 350,000 in 1750, in *América colonial. Población y economía* (Rosario, 1965).
[69] George Kubler, 'The Quechua in the Colonial World', *Handbook of South American Indians* (6 vols., Washington, Smithsonian Institute, Bureau of American Ethnology, Bull. 143, 1946–50), ii, 331–410, especially pp. 334–40.
[70] See however John Howland Rowe, 'The Incas under Spanish Colonial Institutions', *H.A.H.R.*, xxxvii (1957), 155–99, a key, though perhaps partial, study, which concludes that Spanish rule over the Peruvian Indians carried 'economic exploitation and personal degradation ... to an extreme'; for a good account of Spanish government over the Indians at district officer level see Guillermo Lohmann Villena, *El corregidor de indios en el Perú bajo los Austrias* (Madrid, 1957).

seek the reversion of *encomiendas*, and to diminish their economic benefits by heavier taxation.[71] Far from keeping up with inflation, income from *encomiendas* decreased in value and in security. The *encomenderos* were driven to seek an alternative source of income, in land, office, or even commerce. While the original aristocracy became less disdainful of commerce—their participation was usually indirect and dissimulated—merchants acquired aspirations to nobility. Commerce, as long as it was wholesale, was no more an obstacle to social status in Peru than it was in Spain. The *consulado* of Lima, unlike that of Seville, extended its jurisdiction to retail as well as wholesale merchants; but it was the latter who provided the prior and consuls and monopolised voting rights.[72] An income acquired from large-scale maritime trade was socially respectable. It could also be invested in further advancement. Such was the crown's need for money, especially in the reign of Philip IV, that it sold *hábitos* and titles of nobility for hard cash; in the late seventeenth century the price of a title was 30,000 pesos, somewhat less if it was for one life only.[73] Merchants were more likely to have this amount of capital than were *encomenderos* or landowners. According to an observer in the early seventeenth century, 'There are merchants in Lima who have fortunes of a million pesos, many with 500,000, and very many with 100,000. Very few of these wealthy people have retail shops. They export their capital and employ it abroad, in Spain, Mexico and other places. Some of them trade with China. And many merchants have an income from land'.[74] Wealth of this kind broke through social barriers, and promoted further fusion between landed and merchant classes in Peru by means of marriage alliances, which was another way for descendants of rich merchants to ennoble themselves and for the aristocracy to revive its fortunes.

The ultimate source of merchant wealth, as of all wealth in Peru, was silver mining: this was the market merchants supplied and the industry they financed. But the Peruvian economy also had to provide for the sustenance of mining and its secondary industries. And it had to feed Lima, capital of Peru and of the mining industry, a city of 10,000 whites, 10,000 Negroes, and

[71] Manuel Belaunde Guinassi, *La encomienda en el Perú* (Lima, 1945), pp. 218–49; Marvin Goldwert, 'La lucha por la perpetuidad de encomiendas en el Perú virreinal, 1550–1600', *Revista Histórica* (Lima), xxii (1955–56), 336–60, xxiii (1957–58), 207–45; Guillermo Céspedes del Castillo, 'La sociedad colonial americana en los siglos XVI y XVII', in J. Vicens Vives, ed., *Historia social y económica de España y América*, iii, 388–578, especially pp. 518–24; the latter work is a fine synthesis of the economic and social history of Spanish America to 1700.

[72] Rodríguez Vicente, *El tribunal del consulado de Lima*, pp. 40–41, 51, 56, 69, 75–76.

[73] Richard Konetzke, 'La formación de la nobleza en Indias', *Estudios Americanos*, iii (1951), 329–57; Guillermo Lohmann Villena, *Los americanos en las órdenes nobiliarias*, 1529–1900 (2 vols., Madrid, 1947); on the entrepreneurial activities of the colonial aristocracy, see Hans Pohl, 'Zur Geschichte des adligen Unternehmers im spanischen Amerika (17./18. Jahrhundert)', *Jahrbuch für Geschichte von Staat, Wirtschaft und Gesellschaft Lateinamerikas*, ii (1965), 218–44.

[74] *Descripción del Virreinato del Perú*, p. 59.

Mexico City

Facing p. 214

5,000 Indians.[75] North and south of Lima, in the valleys of coastal Peru, a Mediterranean-type economy was created as the region developed its centres of food production, commercial crops, and raw materials.[76] In the immediate vicinity of Lima some 200 well-irrigated *chacras* (farms or small estates) supplied the capital with wheat, maize and animal fodder. These were supplemented by supplies brought down the coast by sea. The region to the north of Lima—Guanbacho, Lasma and La Barranca—sent the products of the fertile valleys of Callejón de Huaylas, where many Lima residents had landed property, producing wheat, maize, wine, vegetables, fruits, poultry, goats, pigs, mules, tallow, hides, charcoal and firewood. The coastal plantations supplied cotton and sugar, products which at Chancay, where the Jesuits had property, were developed on a highly commercial basis. Everywhere along the coast labour was in great demand; there were complaints that *mita* Indians (*mita* being the Peruvian form of *repartimiento*) were diminishing, further evidence perhaps of an expanding agricultural economy. Further north the region of Trujillo also had its irrigated valleys, worked by Negroes and Indians, and rendered more productive by the use of guano as a fertiliser. Here wheat and maize were excellent investments, yielding returns of 500 per cent. and 200 per cent. respectively. Trujillo also produced cotton and sugar, wines and olives, as well as a variety of fruits; it had a number of flour, sugar and cotton mills; and it exported its products north to Panama and south to Lima.

To the south of the capital the outstanding product was wine, which became second in importance to silver—though well behind—as a motor of the Peruvian economy.[77] In the sixteenth century vines from Andalucía, notably from Málaga, were exported with official blessing to Peru, where they were cultivated by Negro slave labour in the valleys of Pisco, Ica and Nozca, producing high quality wines and a local variant known as *pisco*. Output was abundant and sold beyond the confines of Peru: it was exported to Chile, New Granada, Tierra Firme, Central America and Mexico, where it was traded against Mexican silk. Soon the days when the Tierra Firme fleet brought 150,000 casks of wine from Andalucía were a thing of the past. The metropolis became anxious. From about 1569 it was official policy to restrict the Peruvian wine industry, not merely because it competed with imports from the peninsula but also because it engendered economic independence.[78] In the 1590's Viceroy Cañete reported that Peru was peopled with Spaniards, born in the colony who had no attachments to the mother country;

[75] Helmer, 'Le Callao (1615–1618)', *op. cit.*, p. 151, n. 12; Rosenblat, *op. cit.*, i, 225, gives much higher figures for Lima's population in 1630, taking perhaps a wider district—25,000 whites, 30,000 Negroes, 5,000 Indians.
[76] Romero, *Historia económica del Perú*, pp. 115–29.   [77] *Ibid.*, 124–27.
[78] Borah, *Early Colonial Trade and Navigation between Mexico and Peru*, p. 124.

P

that the colony was virtually self-sufficient in foodstuffs, including wine and sugar, and in coarser textiles; that the Philippine trade supplied it with silks and linens; all this to the ruin of Spanish trade and to the detriment of colonial dependence on the metropolis.

Agricultural development was associated with the formation of great estates, though not on the same scale as in Mexico. *Estancias de pan llevar* (wheatland), relying on native labour services and sometimes associated with *encomiendas*, made their appearance from the late sixteenth century. The origins of these medium-sized estates were varied: some were granted to settlers by *cabildos* from Inca government land; others were based on land bought or usurped from Indians fleeing *mita* service; and periodic government reviews of land titles, notably that of 1634, provided good opportunities for consolidating or extending land claims.[79] As the possibilities of agriculture became more appreciated—it sometimes yielded 500 per cent. and rarely less than 50 per cent. returns—and as commercialised products like sugar and wine assumed more importance, there was a tendency to accumulate land and to group *estancias* into great *haciendas*. These depended on much greater labour and water supplies; so *hacendados* had to be influential enough to acquire *mita* or *encomienda* Indians, wealthy enough to invest in slave labour, and powerful enough to usurp precious water resources. This tended to force out small proprietors or to reduce them to dependency on larger units.[80]

Products like wine and sugar, for which there was a wider market throughout Spanish South America, lent themselves to commercialised production. Not all Peruvian estate owners responded to this challenge. Among those who did were the Jesuits, and they set the pace of commercial farming in Peru. Jesuit estates were distributed between the coast and the *sierra*, and were managed according to strict specialisation, grain and livestock in the central *sierra*, sugar and wine on the coast. Property was accumulated from a number of sources—gifts of land from friends and devotees, purchases with funds donated to the Society, reinvestment of profits from existing enterprises, mortgage borrowings, and in some cases usurpation of marginal land.[81] The Jesuits tended to buy neglected *haciendas* and develop them, rounding off their boundaries, building sugar mills, investing in Negro slave labour, and making the whole into an efficient unit of production. Sugar

[79] Rowe, 'The Incas under Spanish Colonial Institutions', *op. cit.*, pp. 179–83; see also José María Ots Capdequí, *España en América. El régimen de tierras en la época colonial* (Mexico, 1959), and John Preston Moore, *The Cabildo in Peru under the Habsburgs* (Durham, N.C., 1954).

[80] Romero, *op. cit.*, pp. 112–14.

[81] Pablo Macera, *Instrucciones para el manejo de las haciendas jesuítas del Perú (ss. XVII–XVIII)* (*Nueva Corónica*, vol. ii, fasc. 2, Lima, 1966), pp. 16–23; this is a collection of instructions to managers of Jesuit estates, preceded by a striking editorial introduction.

plantations comprised about 50 per cent. of Jesuit holdings, and these were the nucleus of the colony's export industry in sugar. Production was concentrated in coastal Peru, principally in the valleys of Santa and Rímac.[82] It was a demanding enterprise and depended on several concurrent factors. It needed abundant water supply for irrigation and for driving the *ingenios* (water-driven mills). It required extensive land, for the plantations were worked on a rotation system to avoid soil exhaustion; land was also needed to service sugar production, particularly for the provision of *alfalfa*, the fodder for the oxen that ploughed the fields and drove the *trapiches* (animal-driven mills), and for transport animals. Sugar also demanded heavy capital investment, in mechanical installations, and above all in slaves, the latter representing 25–40 per cent. of total capital outlay. The high cost of slave labour meant that it was reserved almost exclusively for the commercialised plantations of coastal Peru. General agriculture, livestock and grain, which the Jesuits practised in their *sierra* estates, employed servile Indian labour and frequently developed debt peonage.

The greatest markets for the produce of the plantations, for sugar, wine and cotton, were the mining settlements of Upper Peru. In one way or another the whole of Peru worked for Potosí and profited from its wealth. To supply the mining settlements, the colony created an agricultural economy which developed parallel to the mines. If its returns were less spectacular than those from mining, it was more stable and more durable. A kind of agricultural capitalism emerged, modest enough in its proportions but sufficient to engender a prosperity of its own. Peru never became so self-sufficient in manufactures as it did in agriculture. It had its European craftsmen, of course, but their operations were on a small scale; and Indian manufactures did not appeal to Europeans.[83] Nevertheless, numerous workshops, the notorious *obrajes*, employing forced *mita* labour and owned by the state or by individual Spaniards, produced for the lower-class market or for particular needs. *Obraje* operations underwent some expansion in the seventeenth century, at the expense of the sweated labour employed there, and maintained a fairly high level of output in woollen and cotton cloth, cordage, sandals, leather goods, and gunpowder.[84] For the rest Peru did not necessarily rely on imports from Spain: she had surplus capital and a merchant

---

[82] *Ibid.*, pp. 32–49.

[83] There was, however, a distinct Peruvian class of craftsmen and artisans in the colonial period, including Indians, mestizos and Negroes; these have been well documented by Emilio Harth-Terré, *Artífices en el virreinato del Perú* (Lima, 1945), *El indígena peruano en las bellas artes virreinales* (Cuzco, 1960), and, with Alberto Harth-Terré, *Márquez Abanto. Perspectiva social y económica del artesano virreinal en Lima* (Lima, 1963).

[84] Romero, *op. cit.*, pp. 131–47; Rowe, 'The Incas under Spanish Colonial Institutions', *op. cit.*, pp. 177–79; F. Silva Santisteban, *Los obrajes en el virreinato del Perú* (Lima 1964).

marine, and she could satisfy many of her consumer needs within America, particularly from Mexico, and from the Far East.[85]

The Peruvian merchant marine consisted of 52 vessels plying the longer distances to Panama, Mexico and Chile, and 23 working the local coastal trade.[86] Their owners were Lima merchants, Jesuits, Potosí miners, and in some cases the Spanish, Genoese and Portuguese captains. These 75 vessels were in active operation; at least one vessel left or entered Callao every day, linking some twenty ports along the Pacific coast. They carried copper, tallow and hides from Valparaiso, wine from Pisco, grain and sugar from Trujillo, tropical woods, cotton and cacao from Guayaquil.[87] At Arica they unloaded supplies and merchandise for Potosí and collected its silver exports; at Panama they linked up with transatlantic traffic. The whole of this trade, local and transatlantic, was controlled by the merchants of Lima, who supplied the *avio* (advances) to cover mining overheads in Potosí and there sold most of their merchandise. And it reflected the increasing development of Peru: coastal and intercolonial trade was much more buoyant than the traffic to Panama, a sign of the colony's gradual disengagement from transatlantic trade. The Peruvian economy was self-sufficient; it expanded independently of the Spanish economy in the seventeenth century, and it was able to survive without the massive production of silver demanded by Spain. It possessed its own motors of trade, of which silver was only one; and even in the mining sector, Peru was beginning to keep more of the product for itself.

Potosí was a Spanish not an Inca creation. Situated high in the Andes, its extraordinary elevation made mining at once possible and tragic, possible because it obviated the difficulties of flooding and draining, one of the greatest problems in New World mining, tragic because the effort of labour in an atmosphere rare in oxygen—the *cerro* of Potosí rose to a height of 16,000 feet above sea level—was too great even for the plateau Indians, who were forced to work at altitudes beyond their physical capacity. On the foundations of its dearly extracted silver Potosí became the greatest city in America and in the whole Spanish world, with a population which grew from 120,000 in 1580 to 160,000 in 1650.[88] In the eyes of moralists Potosí was a monstrous Babylon of the New World, catering for large-scale vice as well as for Europe's bullion demand. And many of its people were indeed parasites, living on credit and on their wits: as one observer wrote to Philip II in 1595, 'there are 3,000 Europeans, including Spaniards, Portuguese and other

---

[85] See below, pp. 224–26.

[86] Helmer, 'Le Callao (1615–1618)', *op. cit.*, pp. 160–62.   [87] *Ibid.*, pp. 171–72.

[88] Lewis Hanke, *The Imperial City of Potosí. An unwritten chapter in the history of Spanish America* (The Hague, 1956), pp. 1, 3; on Potosí see also the monumental chronicle by Bartolomé Arzáns de Orsúa y Vela, *Historia de la Villa Imperial de Potosí*. Ed. Lewis Hanke and Gunnar Mendoza (3 vols., Providence, Rhode Island, 1965), with important introductory studies by the editors.

nationalities, 2,000 of them idle delinquents, who have no other occupation than gambling, drinking, fornication, robbery and assassination'.[89] Here, as in Mexico, the greatest profits from mining went not so much to actual mineowners as to those who could finance labour and operational costs, and these were mainly the capitalists of Lima.

Unlike Mexico, where the *real de minas* was a closely knit complex of mines, farms and ranches, the Peruvian mining settlements, owing to their high elevation, cold climate and arid soil, lacked the natural basis for the growth of satellite supply bases in the immediate vicinity.[90] Food and supplies had to be brought in from outside, often over great distances. The *mita* Indians brought their own staples, *chuño* (dried frozen potatoes) and coca. For the rest, food supplies and mine timbers had to be transported from the distant Yungas valleys, especially Cochabamba, or from agricultural areas on the western slopes of the Andes such as Arequipa. Mules for work in the mines were driven from north-western Río de la Plata; Tucumán and Santa Cruz de la Sierra also sent wheat, fruits and cotton; from the distant pampas came hides and tallow, which were also supplied by Chile and northern Peru. For the import of Peruvian, American and European products, including vital mercury supplies, Potosí relied on the port of Arica, 400 miles away, and on the transport controlled by Arica—2,000 mules and 12,000 llamas, on whose backs were carried the incoming mercury and merchandise and the outgoing silver; and Arica developed in its vicinity a thriving agricultural sector providing fodder for the pack animals.

Potosí's silver production reached its peak towards the end of the sixteenth century. Registered exports to Spain quadrupled from 4·6 million pesos in 1571–75 to 19·1 million in 1581–85, and in 1591–95 they reached 23·9 million. After the 1590's production levelled off, though the level was fairly high, until about 1650. In the second half of the century, output dropped considerably. Mining recession in Peru, therefore, occurred later and remained much less severe than in Mexico. The factors affecting production were similar in both colonies, but less oppressive in Peru. First, operational problems were mounting. Exhaustion of accessible deposits led to deeper mining, presenting greater technical problems which the industry was not equipped to solve; from the deeper galleries came a type of ore which needed more sophisticated treatment to make it yield all its silver, and this was

[89] Quoted by Marie Helmer, 'Luchas entre vazcongados y "vicuñas" en Potosí', *Revista de Indias*, xx (1960), 185–95, an expert analysis of social conflicts in Potosí through review of Alberto Crespo Rodas, *La guerra entre vicuñas y vascongados, Potosí, 1622–1625* (Lima, 1956), and Gunnar Mendoza L., *Guerra civil entre vascongados y otras naciones de Potosí. Documentos del Archivo Nacional de Bolivia, 1622–1641* (Potosí, 1954).

[90] Gwendolin B. Cobb, 'Supply and Transportation for the Potosí Mines, 1545–1640', *H.A.H.R.*, xxix (1949), 25–45.

beyond the geological competence of the Peruvian miners. In conditions of technical stagnation output could only be maintained by extension of the mining area; discovery of rich deposits at Oruro in 1608 compensated for Potosí's performance, until the new mines too were overtaken by similar problems. Deeper mining, therefore, meant rising costs for fewer returns. To this was added the problem of labour supply.

Potosí's mineworkers were forcibly recruited from 119 Indian villages in the highland area between Cuzco and Tarija. This, the notorious *mita de Potosí*, provided some 4,000 labourers who worked for four months at a time, or some 12,000 a year, out of a reserve of 86,000.[91] This was a crushing burden on the designated area. Admittedly it affected only a limited part of the total Indian population, and it required from a given individual only four months' mine work once in seven years. But it was an appalling experience while it lasted, ravaging bodies already weakened from malnutrition. After toiling underground—where they were sometimes kept continuously from Monday to Saturday—in an atmosphere rare in oxygen, rich in carbonic gas, hot and humid, the Indians staggered sweating into outside temperatures below freezing point. Mine work in Potosí played its part in depopulating the recruiting area; and its reputation did the rest, causing a flight of *mitayo* Indians beyond reach of the law. Some who remained found the means to buy themselves out; this they could do by paying the employer to whom they were assigned the equivalent of the wage of a free worker. In a period of rising costs and diminishing returns many owners preferred to leave their mines unworked and to live on the income from their *indios de faltriquera* as they were called.[92] This accounts for the determination of mineowners to retain their quota of *mitayos*, which in turn prevented the distribution of labour according to the needs and performance of actual mines.

Finally, mining output was affected by mercury supply. The great expansion of silver production at the end of the sixteenth century was made possible by the adoption of the *patio*, or amalgamation, process at Potosí about 1580, an innovation which was itself stimulated by the successful performance of Peru's own mercury mine at Huancavelica.[93] Between 1559 and 1660 Huancavelica produced 21·8 million tons of mercury, compared to 15·1 million tons imported into America from Europe (principally from Alma-

[91] Alberto Crespo Rodas, La 'mita' de Potosí (Potosí, 1959); Jorge Basadre, 'El régimen de la mita', *Letras*. Universidad Mayor de San Marcos, tercer trimestre, no. 8 (1937), 325–64; Rowe, 'The Incas under Spanish Colonial Institutions', *op. cit.*, pp. 170–79.

[92] About 1660 miners' income from *indios de faltriquera* was estimated at 600,000 pesos a year, compared with royal *quinto*'s 400,000; see Rubén Vargas Ugarte, *Historia del Perú. Virreinato, siglo XVII* (Buenos Aires, 1954), pp. 305–6. On labour problems at Potosí see Guillermo Lohmann Villena, *El Conde de Lemos, virrey del Perú* (Madrid, 1946), pp. 245–77.

[93] Guillermo Lohmann Villena, *Las minas de Huancavelica en los siglos XVI y XVII* (Seville, 1949).

dén).[94] Only in its crisis years of 1606–10, 1621–25, 1626–30, 1631–35, did Huancavelica's output fail to surpass European imports, and even on these occasions it was not far behind. But the silver mines of Upper Peru needed at least 6,000 quintals of mercury a year, 5,000 for Potosí, the remainder for small mines. And from about 1595 production at Huancavelica began to fluctuate. Some of its problems were peculiar to mercury mining: the miners were small operators who depended on prompt payment for their product; purchase and sale of mercury was a state monopoly, and the state was some-times years in arrears in its payments, which forced miners to cut back on production. Otherwise the industry's problems simply mirrored those of silver mining—mounting technical difficulties, rising costs, and, inevitably, the erosion of labour supply by mortality, absenteeism, and competition from other sectors. Work at Huancavelica had special hazards, notably mercurial poisoning, and a *mita* Indian was lucky to be alive after a stint in its subterranean galleries.[95] Brutal exploitation of Indian workers occasionally drew the attention of officials, churchmen and humanitarians. Although their interventions were transitory and, on the whole, unsuccessful, they sometimes affected short-term production, as they did in 1591–1610, when, largely as a result of Viceroy Velasco's reforms, output dropped by 50 per cent.[96] In the second decade of the seventeenth century production revived; and although it dropped again in 1626–30, it subsequently maintained itself; with the exception of the years 1651–60; however, it never repeated the peak of the late sixteenth century, and after the 1650's it further diminished.

Potosí survived its crisis of technology, labour, and mercury much better than did the mining industry in Mexico. But it never repeated its massive performance of the late sixteenth century. Silver registered at Potosí dropped from 4·4 million pesos in 1602 to 3·5 million in 1608; between then and 1624 it did not drop below 3 million, nor below 2·8 million in the period 1625–40.[97] The yield from the royal *quinto* fell from 850,000 pesos in 1616 to 650,000 in 1619.[98] In default of better technology the only hope of recovery

[94] Chaunu, *Séville et l'Atlantique*, viii, 1, p. 118.

[95] Whereas 1,300 *mita* Indians were employed at the face at Huancavelica in 1596, there were scarcely 620 a century later, indicating considerable depopulation; see Bargalló, *op. cit.*, p. 257, and Arthur P. Whitaker, *The Huancavelica Mercury Mine. A Contribution to the History of the Bourbon Renaissance in the Spanish Empire* (Cambridge, Mass., 1941), p. 15.

[96] Lohmann Villena, *Las minas de Huancavelica*, pp. 180, 207.

[97] These figures are taken from an estimate by a treasury official in Potosí, reproduced in Haring, *Trade and Navigation between Spain and the Indies in the time of the Hapsburgs*, Appendix VI, pp. 333–35; they are not, of course, a measurement of actual production, for they do not account for fraud; unregistered and unquinted silver may have amounted to 70,000 or 80,000 pesos a year; see reference in note 98.

[98] Carmen Bancora Cañero, 'Las remesas de metales preciosos desde el Callao a España en la primera mitad del siglo XVII', *Revista de Indias*, xix (1959), 35–88, especially pp. 44–53; for different figures see Helmer, 'Le Callao (1615–1618)', *op. cit.*, p. 179.

lay in new strikes; in 1636 the working of new veins at Potosí enabled output to revive and pushed up the *quinto* from 600,000 pesos in 1635 to 870,000
in 1636. By 1640, however, it was back to 600,000, and dropped to 500,000
in 1650.[99] Potosí's downward trend was subsequently countered by new
strikes at Chocaya and Caylloma, but these, like Oruro, soon exhausted their
richest and most accessible ores.

The mining districts, chiefly Potosí, provided up to 80 per cent. of the
revenue of the central treasury in Lima; and out of this revenue a surplus had
to be sent to Spain.[100] The surplus was inexorably reduced by falling output
at Potosí, local defence expenditure, administrative costs, and fraud. According to Viceroy Esquilache (1615–21), the royal treasury income in Peru, from
all sources, was theoretically 3,200,000 pesos a year; of this, 1,500,000 was
spent in Peru on administration, purchase and shipment of mercury, and
defence; the rest was sent to Spain.[101] Between 1600 and 1621, however,
there was a fairly continuous downward trend in public remittances to
Spain, from 2·4 million pesos to 686,195. In the period 1622–39 the trend was
halted, and there was an irregular rise from 1·1 million in 1622 to 2·4 million
in 1639, the result of unprecedented fiscal pressure. The period 1640–50 was
one of fluctuation, the highest points being 2·6 million pesos in 1641 and 2·7
million in 1650, the lowest 1·7 million in 1645 and 956,000 in 1648.[102] In
general Spain's loss was Peru's gain. An increasing proportion of silver
in Peru, as in Mexico, was absorbed by the viceroyalty in its own administrative and defence costs, and therefore indirectly in its own economy. While
public remittances to Spain between 1621 and 1650 slowly decreased, the
contributions of the Lima treasury to the needs of Chile and Peru, to coastal
defence and naval construction, increased and multiplied. By 1650 defence
costs alone absorbed about 20 per cent. of total viceregal revenue.[103]

The shift of economic activity was further reflected in the performance of
the *almojarifazgo* and *alcabala* taxes. Jointly these represented only 5 per cent.
of total viceregal revenue, but their relative yield was an index of economic
change. Roughly speaking the *almojarifazgo* represented imperial trade, the
alcabala local trade; and of the two it was the latter which grew more
regularly and more significantly.[104] The fall in the *almojarifazgo* from 1630
and still more from 1640 denoted a fall in commerce with Spain; the growth

[99] Bancora Cañero, 'Las remesas de metales preciosos', *op. cit.*, pp. 56–57.

[100] Chaunu, *Séville et l'Atlantique*, viii, 1, pp. 1129–35, 1168–69.

[101] 'Relación del virrey Esquilache', in Ricardo Beltrán y Rozpide and Angel de Altolaguirre,
eds., *Colección de las memorias y relaciones que escribieron los virreyes del Perú* (2 vols., Madrid, 1921–
30), i, 275.

[102] Bancora Cañero, 'Las remesas de metales preciosos', *op. cit.*, pp. 85–86.

[103] Chaunu, *Séville et l'Atlantique*, viii, 1, pp. 1129–35, 1168–69.

[104] For figures see *ibid.*, viii, 1, pp. 1133–35, 1140–69.

of the *alcabala* meant that local trade was buoyant, that Peruvian money was being spent in Peru, that the colonial economy was increasingly independent.

These trends were accentuated in the second half of the seventeenth century. Up to 1650 the crown fought to maintain its income from Peru by exploiting every device in the tax-gatherer's repertoire. Now it had to give up the struggle. The total income of the Lima treasury from all sources dropped from 5·9 million pesos in 1651 to an annual average of 1·5 million in 1664–66. It then rose to 3·1 million in 1678, dropped again to 2·4 million in 1685, and reached an annual average of 3 million in 1686–90.[105] These fluctuations were due, as in the first half of the century, to the irregular performance of mining and of transatlantic commerce.

Mining output continued to suffer from exhaustion of accessible deposits, and from the technical difficulties and prohibitive costs of going deeper. The sufferings of the *mitayo* Indians were incalculable; and labour shortage was not arrested until 1690 when the *mita* quota was doubled by extending it to new provinces. Mercury supply was still limited by crude production techniques and by the state's failure to pay for the product—by 1661 it owed miners 400,000 pesos. The discovery of new veins led to some improvement in the 1670's, but by the end of the century Huancavelica was stagnant again with output showing a tendency to drop.[106] Transatlantic trade was now in full depression and yielded little in taxes. In the 1650's the Callao fleets sailed to Panama every year. From 1663 they maintained regularity, but only every three years and sometimes four. From about 1682 the intervals became longer, until sailings were exceptional—in 1685, 1690 and 1696.

Remittances to Spain, however, were conditioned not only by Peruvian revenue but also by Peruvian expenditure. While public returns to Spain were going down, expenditure on defence and *situados* was going steeply up. This included defence of the *mar del Sur*, naval construction, and fortifications at the Straits of Magellan, Valdivia, Lima, Callao, and above all at Panama, which was the focal point of corsair activity in the last decades of the seventeenth century. The *situado* for Panama was increased from 105,000 pesos in 1670 to 406,000 in 1690.[107] Defence expenditure in the 1680's was enormous; it reached a peak of 6·5 million pesos in 1686–90, when only 749,277 pesos were remitted to Spain. Between 1651 and 1739 the income of the Lima treasury totalled 178·9 million pesos. Of this sum 55·2 million, or 30 per cent., was invested in defence of the viceroyalty and its dependencies; a

---

[105] María E. Rodríguez Vicente, 'Los caudales remitidos desde el Perú a España por cuenta de la Real Hacienda. Serie estadísticas (1651–1739)', *Anuario de Estudios Americanos*, xxi (1964), 1–24, a valuable contribution.

[106] Lohmann Villena, *Las minas de Huancavelica*, pp. 354–60.

[107] Céspedes, 'La defensa militar del istmo de Panamá a fines del siglo XVII y comienzos del XVIII', *op. cit.*, pp. 263–64.

further 49·4 per cent. was expended on viceregal administration, salaries, pensions, grants, and above all purchase of mercury; and only 20·6 per cent. (36·9 million pesos) was remitted to Spain. The bulk of Peruvian public revenue, therefore, was spent in Peru. The colony had become in some degree its own metropolis.

4. INTER-AMERICAN TRADE

The shift of the Spanish American economy and its mounting independence of Spain, the decrease of remittances to the metropolis and the growth of investment in the colonies themselves, all gave rise to a flourishing trade between the various parts of Spanish America, which further stimulated independent growth. The main routes of inter-American trade and navigation were between Mexico and Peru, and between Mexico and Venezuela.

By the beginning of the seventeenth century the Peruvian economy had begun to turn away from Spain towards Mexico. Transatlantic trade was too rare and too expensive to meet the demands of the growing colony. The Peruvian cycle of production and export, depending as it did on the seasonal activity of the mining industry, was difficult to synchronise with the arrival of the annual fleet at Portobello. The Spaniards too found it impossible to maintain the official timetable; transatlantic navigation became increasingly irregular, and between 1600 and 1650 Tierra Firme received only 29 fleets.[108] To the inconvenience of transatlantic trade was added the insecurity of the capital invested in it. Sequestration of private silver remittances to Seville simply encouraged Lima merchants to divert their capital to inter-colonial trade, which was in any case less heavily taxed; it was also less subject to enemy attack and therefore less burdened with defence costs.[109] For all these reasons merchants' shipments from Peru to Spain moved from 14 million pesos in the two-year consignment of 1626 to 3,680,000 in 1635, to 5 million in 1645, to 4·3 million in 1650.[110]

Trade between Mexico and Peru began in the sixteenth century, and consisted in the movement of manufactured and luxury goods from Mexico, whose economy was more developed, and the return of silver from Peru, where mining was more productive and prices higher. Peru thus imported textiles, clothing, furniture, jewelry, toilet and household goods, leather goods and books from Mexico, and paid for them in silver, later also in wine and in some years mercury.[111] By the end of the sixteenth century the trade

[108] Manuel Moreyra y Paz-Soldán, Estudios sobre el tráfico marítimo en la época colonial (Lima, 1944), pp. 67–87.
[109] Borah, Early Colonial Trade and Navigation between Mexico and Peru, p. 125.
[110] Rodríguez Vicente, El tribunal del consulado de Lima, pp. 227–28.
[111] Borah, Early Colonial Trade and Navigation between Mexico and Peru, pp. 80–95.

was buoyant and never short of finance. The drift of capital from Spanish to colonial trade was reported by the viceroy of Peru in 1592; he attributed it to the shortage and delays of shipments from Spain, the slow returns on capital, taxation and sequestration; whereas trade in Peruvian products and the import of goods from Mexico enjoyed a quick turnover and steady prosperity in safer conditions.[112]

From the 1570's the trade received a new injection—Chinese goods, procured in the Philippines, shipped across the Pacific in the Manila galleons, and sold for silver in Mexico.[113] Chinese damasks, satins, silks, chinaware, porcelain, perfumes and jewelry began to pour into Acapulco and found a ready market. For the Philippine trade offered a supply of luxury goods, and even vital necessities such as spices, iron and copper, at prices far below imports from Spain or even the cheaper—and cruder—products of the Mexican *obrajes*. In the 1590's Chinese textiles sold for perhaps one-ninth of the price of Spanish cloth in Peru. The opening of the Manila–Acapulco trade coincided with the steep rise of Potosí's silver output, which immediately acted as a magnet. Peruvian merchants were forbidden direct access to the Orient. With their greater silver resources, however, they could outbid the Mexicans for Chinese imports in the Acapulco market, and these they re-exported to Peru in enormous and increasing volume. By the 1590's the value of the Mexico–Peru trade, including re-exports of Chinese goods, amounted perhaps to 2 or even 3 million pesos a year.[114] It had grown even larger by 1602 when the *cabildo* of Mexico City claimed that 5 million pesos a year went from Acapulco to the Philippines and thence to the Chinese. Most of this money came from Peru, which took the greater part of the cargoes and supplied perhaps some 3 millions of the returns. By this time Mexico was merely an entrepôt for the re-export of Oriental goods to Peru, and Mexican manufactures—many of which Peru could now produce for itself—amounted to no more than about one-tenth in value of the trade. Indeed one Mexican activity, silk raising and manufacture, was a victim of Chinese competition, which, combined with Indian labour shortage and crown policy, helped to ruin the industry.[115]

The very prosperity of the new trade brought retribution. The imperial government was conscious of Peru's economic independence and alarmed at the escape of silver to the Far East. Spanish monopolists resented the competition and the shrinking market. Peninsular interests therefore combined to curtail the Philippine trade and to stop re-export to Peru.[116] Their reaction

---

[112] *Ibid.*, pp. 95, 121.   [113] William Schurz, *The Manila Galleon* (New York, 1939).
[114] Borah, *Early Colonial Trade and Navigation between Mexico and Peru*, pp. 116–24.
[115] Borah, *Silk Raising in Colonial Mexico*, pp. 85–101.
[116] Borah, *Early Colonial Trade and Navigation between Mexico and Peru*, pp. 124–27.

was part of the desperate attempt of Spanish merchants, in a period of contracting trade, to preserve Peru, the most valuable market, for themselves. Simultaneously they were also attempting to close another gap in the monopoly's defences, Buenos Aires and the pampa route to Peru.[117] In 1593 shipment of Chinese goods to all colonies other than Mexico was forbidden. Trade between Mexico and the Philippines was restricted to two ships; Chinese goods from Manila could be imported to the value of 250,000 pesos a year, and returns in silver to Manila up to 500,000 pesos. This legislation simply diverted the Mexico–Peru trade to contraband channels. These flowed so freely that the crown tried to impose further restrictions. In 1604 it reduced the size of the two Manila galleons from 300 to 200 tons; trade between Mexico and Peru was limited to three ships of 300 tons each a year; these might carry products of Mexico and Peru for exchange, but no specie, and they were restricted to the ports of Acapulco and Callao. In spite of heavier penalties, the contraband trade continued to flourish.[118] Further decrees reduced navigation between Mexico and Peru to two vessels a year, then to one a year, and in 1620 the export of Peruvian wine to Mexico was forbidden. Finally, the logical conclusion of this policy was reached in 1631 when, under pressure of the *consulado* of Seville, the crown forbad all trade and navigation between Mexico and Peru, a prohibition which was renewed in 1634 and endured for the rest of the century and beyond.

These prohibitions were not taken seriously. Peruvian ecclesiastics argued that they were unjust and not binding in conscience; and local officials could not resist the pressure, or the temptation, to turn a blind eye.[119] In any case there were too many contraband outlets to permit strict control. One loophole was Peru's legal trade with Nicaragua, a source of vital supplies of pitch; this provided cover under which Chinese goods, transported from Mexico to Realejo and Sonsonate, could be loaded on Peruvian vessels. Another method was to divert to Acapulco silver consignments nominally registered to Guatemala and Nicaragua; returning shipments could be landed at Paita or other minor ports north of Callao. And there was always the well-tried device of rendezvous and transfer of silver off the Peruvian coast. Guayaquil was a favourite base of contraband, for it possessed weaker customs machinery than Callao; and vessels from Central America coming to its shipyards for repair did not normally arrive empty. The source of contraband, the Philippine trade itself, outgrew its legal confines; the value of shipments varied between 200,000 and 1·5 million pesos at Manila, worth two or three times that amount in Mexico and Peru; and contraband trade sometimes raised the final value to more than 10 million pesos.

[117] See above, pp. 178–9.   [118] Chaunu, *Séville et l'Atlantique*, viii, 1, p. 759.
[119] Rodríguez Vicente, *El tribunal del consulado de Lima*, pp. 244–52, 270.

The other great route of inter-colonial trade was that linking Venezuela and Mexico. Venezuela's chief product and export commodity was cacao, and its principal market was Mexico, where returns were quick and secure. Chocolate was in wide and popular demand; it was a favourite creole beverage, and Venezuela's product had a reputation for quality.[120] In the course of the seventeenth century production in the province of Caracas expanded strongly, and by the 1690's there was an exportable surplus of some 13,000 fanegas a year.[121] Regular traffic between Venezuela and Mexico began in 1622 when one vessel shipped 60 fanegas of cacao; in Mexico it earned good prices, paid in silver, which enabled producers to invest further in cacao production. From then onwards the Mexican market became far more important to Venezuela than that of the metropolis, both in the regularity of traffic and its value. In the period 1620–50 Venezuela exported to Mexico 35,512 fanegas of cacao, to Spain only 289. In 1651–1700 the Mexican market consumed 322,264 fanegas of Venezuelan cacao, while Spain took only 71,306. Up to about 1670 Spain provided a modest market for Venezuelan hides and tobacco, but these were trifling in value compared to cacao. Venezuela lived on colonial trade and had decreasing contact with Seville. By 1630 Mexican purchases had risen to 112,560 reales, while Spain's purchases (all products) stood at 136,177. In 1640 Mexican purchases of cacao amounted to 321,792 reales, and those of Spain (all products) dropped to 44,400. In 1660 Venezuelan exports to Mexico were valued at 572,720 reales, those to Spain only 61,650. Although after this date cacao exports to Spain increased, they increased even more to Mexico. In the period 1661–1700 Mexico imported 273,763 fanegas of Venezuelan cacao, a 200 per cent. increase over the previous forty years.[122] Between 1684 and 1720 Mexico was virtually the only market for Venezuela, for trade with Spain dwindled to a trickle, not only in cacao but also in hides and tobacco, which the Dutch were now carrying direct to Europe. In the last decade of the seventeenth century, while Mexico consumed 108,801 fanegas of Venezuelan cacao valued at about 17 million reales, Spanish purchases in all products hardly reached 2 million reales.[123]

The only competition for Venezuela could come from Guayaquil, whose cacao production expanded about the same time. But Venezuela won the struggle for dominance in the Mexican market, thanks in part to the support

[120] Eduardo Arcila Farías, *Economía colonial de Venezuela* (Mexico, 1946), pp. 87–98; see also Antonio Arellano Moreno, *Orígenes de la economía venezolana* (Mexico, 1947), and Federico Brito Figueroa, *La estructura económica de Venezuela colonial* (Caracas, 1963).

[121] Eduardo Arcila Farías, *Comercio entre Venezuela y México en los siglos XVII y XVIII* (Mexico, 1950), 51–61, 72–73.

[122] *Ibid.*, pp. 106, 134–35.

[123] *Ibid.*, p. 56.

of Spain. It was the policy of the crown, within the limits of its actual power, so to regulate inter-colonial trade that there was an apportioning of activities and markets and no monoculture colony was left completely out. Just as it deterred sugar exports from Mexico, which had alternative activities, in order to protect the Caribbean islands, so it discouraged cacao exports from Guayaquil in order to favour Venezuela.[124] In so doing the crown furthered Venezuela's growth until it had little need of Spain. The colony then developed its modest economy independently of the metropolis, earning Mexican silver for reinvestment in its plantations and merchant marine, and generating enough public revenue to pay for its own administration and defence. Venezuela, like the larger colonies, helped to create a second Spanish empire, whose societies and economies had emancipated themselves from their primitive dependence on Spain.

[124] *Ibid.*, 195–216, 249–78.

CHAPTER IX
GOVERNMENT AND SOCIETY IN THE REIGN OF CHARLES II

1. Privilege and Power: The Rule of Aristocracy

CHARLES II was the last, the most degenerate, and the most pathetic victim of Habsburg inbreeding. When, on 17 September 1665, he succeeded his father, Philip IV, he was only four years old, a sickly child, retarded by rickets, and mentally subnormal. During the whole of his thirty-nine years he suffered chronic ill-health, serious psychological disturbances, and frequent attacks of acute melancholia; these he tried to exorcise by spiritual means, which earned him the name of *el Hechizado*, the bewitched. Living his life under the shadow of death, he was incapable of exercising government. He was also incapable of producing children, and his two marriages remained, if not unconsummated, at least unfruitful. Monarchy therefore now suffered from two mortal afflictions—a weak incumbent and a succession problem.[1]

Royal sovereignty was totally eclipsed by the only alternative power base, the aristocracy. Charles II was no more than a cipher, a shadow king. Government was first controlled by his mother, the queen regent, and then by a succession of favourites and ministers, the former destroyed, the latter created by the aristocracy. Orders and decrees were issued in the king's name, but they were seldom submitted to him for signature, and official documents of the reign usually bore only a facsimile of the royal hand. In the unhappy, neurotic person of Charles II Spanish monarchy was reduced to a mockery of its former grandeur. Into the vacuum moved the aristocracy, who now reached their greatest—and their final—fulfilment. The only challenge to them came from the church. While the aristocracy deposed royal favourites and promoted their own leaders, the church provided the royal confessors

---

[1] The outstanding work on the reign of Charles II is by the Duque de Maura, *Vida y reinado de Carlos II* (2nd ed., 2 vols., Madrid, 1954). This year-by-year chronicle of the political events of the reign is almost unreadable, but it is based on a lifetime of study, and on original documentation described in the preface. The peculiar form in which the work is cast is due in part to the fact that the author's entire collection of books, transcripts and notes was destroyed in the Civil War. Two previous works on the reign are much inferior: Julian Juderías, *España en tiempo de Carlos II el Hechizado* (Madrid, 1912); Ludwig Pfandl, *Carlos II* (Madrid, 1947) Spanish translation of German edition published 1940.

who moved assiduously along the corridors of influence if not of power. Premier and priest, these were the two manipulators of power in the reign of Charles II. But if there was any conflict between the two estates it was an argument between allies, not between alternatives. They had much in common. They were the privileged sectors of society; between them they virtually monopolised land; and the hierarchy of the church was almost an aristocratic preserve.

Against the general demographic trend of the seventeenth century, the ecclesiastical population seemed to be increasing. In the absence of exact statistics, estimates are largely guess-work; contemporary guesses varied between 100,000 for the 1620's and 180,000 for the 1660's.[2] Most of the *arbitristas* complained of the excessive number of clergy. According to Sancho de Moncada, 'a third of the Spanish population is made up of ecclesiastics, if we include religious and nuns, secular clergy, tertiaries, hermits, and people who have taken a vow of chastity'. While the ecclesiastical population grew in numbers, it did not grow in wisdom, knowledge, or even piety. No doubt there was much anonymous sanctity and charity in the Spanish church, but for many of its clergy it was simply a career. The higher clergy, sons of the aristocracy, shared the ideals and the background of their class. The mass of the lower clergy, the majority of humble origin, had little hope of preferment; but many of them had entered the priesthood in order to escape the winds of destitution outside the cloister, and in this at least they succeeded. The church drew its wealth essentially from its own land and from other people's labour, that is from rents and from tithes. The extent of landed property controlled by ecclesiastical institutions is difficult to determine; in the mid-eighteenth century it amounted perhaps to one-seventh in area of the two Castiles and León, and one-fourth in rent collected.[3] In addition to land owned directly in mortmain, the church also possessed *señorío eclesiástico*, which gave it seigneurial jurisdiction and revenue in the towns and lands under its lordship. Finally, as a last line of defence, the church possessed its own *fuero*; this endowed the clergy with substantial immunity from civil jurisdiction and enabled them to defend their interests—and their property—by reference to ecclesiastical law and in ecclesiastical courts.[4]

The omnipresence of the clergy, their economic security, and their extensive *fuero*, all engendered a certain anti-clericalism in the rest of society and provided material for conflict with the state. In the cortes of 1621 Mateo Lison, deputy for Málaga, denounced the 'disadvantages of so many religious

[2] Reglà, 'La época de los dos últimos Austrias', in J. Vicens Vives, ed., *Historia social y económica de España y América*, iii, 267.

[3] A. Domínguez Ortiz, *La sociedad española en el siglo XVIII* (Madrid, 1955), p. 128.

[4] See Quintín Aldea, S. J., *Iglesia y Estado en la España del siglo XVII (Ideario político-eclesiástico)* (Comillas, 1961).

Charles II

Facing p. 231

foundations and chantries, and the excessive accumulation of landed property by the ecclesiastical estate'. In 1626 the cortes complained of ecclesiastics who 'by endowments, confraternities, chantries, or simple purchase, are gradually possessing themselves of the whole kingdom', and it requested the crown to halt the accumulation of property in mortmain, particularly as it was exempt from taxation. Criticism of this kind became even more common in the reign of Charles II. Reporting on the state of Valladolid, in 1683, at a time of great economic difficulty, a minister of the crown claimed that

> the most important part of the inhabitants consists of the ecclesiastical chapters and other clergy, infinite in number, from the University, College, Chancellery, and Inquisition, and from the 53 convents of religious that there are, besides 17 parishes and other oratories, all of which employ people solely for the service of their ministers. . . . It seems that this city is made up principally of consumers only.[5]

Valladolid of course was an exceptional centre of ecclesiastical activity; and it was easy to blame the church for problems which the administration could not solve. Nevertheless, the number of clergy in a country which notoriously lacked producers inevitably drew the attention of ministers seeking solutions to economic distress. In its concern the government of Charles II took an unprecedented step and in 1689 addressed a circular letter to all the bishops of Spain asking them temporarily to suspend ordinations to the priesthood:

> The number of those admitted to minor orders in recent years is so great that many places have hardly a batchelor left who is not a cleric. And many older men, now widowers, also enter orders. The object of most of them is to procure clerical immunity, to live with greater ease, to enjoy exemption from taxes, and other worldly motives.[6]

The church in fact was not completely exempt from taxation. Its services were indispensable for raising the *cruzada*, whose annual yield in the peninsula alone was 800,000 ducats in silver. And the church itself paid the *tercios reales*, a portion of its income from tithes; the *subsidio*, an annual tax on real property, yielding 420,000 ducats; and the *excusado*, a type of tithe, producing 250,000 ducats.[7] The papacy also conceded a number of special taxes on the Spanish clergy, the *décimas eclesiásticas*, assigned to defence needs from time to time and amounting to some hundreds of thousands of ducats.

---

[5] Quoted by Henry Kamen, 'The Decline of Castile: the last crisis', *Economic History Review*, 2nd ser., xvii (1964–65), 63–76, see especially p. 70.

[6] Quoted by Maura, *op. cit.*, i, 510.

[7] Domínguez Ortiz, *Política y hacienda de Felipe IV*, pp. 193–232.

Q

Finally, the clergy were liable, much to their resentment, to the *millones*, though this too was subject to the periodic permission of the papacy, not always granted with enthusiasm. In 1656 there was a kind of clergy revolt led by Archbishop Pedro de Tapia of Seville and Bishop Juan de Palafox of Osma, aroused by constant demands for revenue and by government accusations that the clergy were not contributing to national needs. In the reign of Charles II the archbishop of Toledo utterly refused to allow his clergy to be taxed for the *millones*. By this time the church was even better positioned to defend itself, for the archbishop of Toledo and the royal confessors occupied important positions in the counsels of government.

Yet the church could not compete in privilege and power with the secular aristocracy, who now reached their political majority, if not maturity. The monarchy of Charles II was a kind of aristocratic republic, where the grandees assembled to make or break a government regardless of the royal will. Numerically the higher aristocracy expanded in this reign, as more and more nobles, some of them recently created, were promoted to the ranks of the *grandeza*. Whereas in 1627 there were only 41 grandees, in 1707 there were 113.[8] This movement upwards served to heighten the intolerance and exclusivism of the older aristocratic houses, but it also augmented the power and the wealth of the group as a whole. For the new grandees were wealthy men who openly bought their rank. Wealth, after all, was the ultimate test of *grandeza*. The grandees had the greatest fortunes in the kingdom, some of them 100,000 ducats a year, most of them not less than 40,000 to 80,000. At the beginning of the seventeenth century the income of grandees and *titulos* in the whole of Spain was computed at 5 million ducats, not counting the value of their property; at mid-century it was estimated at 7 million ducats, compared to 1·7 million received by 11 archbishops and 55 bishops.

The extravagant expenditure of many nobles outstripped their capital resources. For them the rule of Charles II came as manna from heaven. The heavy financial demands of Philip IV and Olivares had wounded the pride and hurt the pockets of numerous noble families and alienated them from the crown; further resentment was caused when older houses, struggling with creditors, saw upstart *hidalgos*, well placed in the higher ranks of the administration, getting rich and buying *senoríos* and titles. Political power could be employed in defence of property. In the reign of Charles II the crown was too weak to stand up to the nobility; they could divert taxation away from their class, refuse with impunity to give *donativos*, and increase their demands for *mercedes*. The request for a *donativo* in 1667 drew only paltry returns from some and a curt refusal from others; many nobles stated quite firmly that they had already given more than enough to Philip IV. In

[8] Domínguez Ortiz, *La sociedad española en el siglo XVII*, pp. 219–21.

the last decades of the century the administration had to reconcile itself to requesting only limited *donativos* from the nobility. By then severe economic depression had affected even big estates. To a decree of 1680 conceding four months' delay to cattle owners for payment of the *hierbas* tax, the duke of Béjar replied that the rent from his pasture land was 'almost the only capital he has, so depopulated are his estates; he has lost a fortune in the Portuguese wars; he has to pay 30,000 ducats a year to run his house in Valladolid, and 6,000 for other establishments; he has lost 30,000 ducats through devaluation, and he owes 120,000 to his creditors'.[9] If this was the situation of one of the greatest magnates in Castile, the middle and lower ranks of the nobility were even worse off, for they could expect less by way of *mercedes*.

Lacking entrepreneurial instincts or experience, the nobility were incapable of remedying their fortunes by economic methods alone. In the second half of the seventeenth century the financial affairs of some of the greatest families of Castile were in chaos.[10] The estates of the Enríquez, the Admirals of Castile, were encumbered by vast debts and besieged by creditors; the dukes of Osuna, the house of Pastrana, the Constables of Castile, and many other members of the higher nobility were in similar difficulties. Nevertheless they continued to live up to their rank and to remain the largest spenders in the community. How did they do it? Partly by mortgaging their property. The crown was reluctant to allow this, regarding it as almost as bad as disentailing. But permission could be procured, especially under Charles II, and especially for pretexts such as dowries; this explains the immense dowries of the time—they were a means of freeing property and getting hands on liquid capital. By one means or another the nobility maintained their personal income. And one of the means was royal grants.

The aristocratic reaction which followed the fall of Olivares, combined with the indolence and generosity of Philip IV, opened the gates for a new outflow of pensions and grants. This became a deluge in the reign of Charles II. Access to *mercedes* was at once a motive and a consequence of aristocratic dominance. Indeed so accessible did public funds become, including colonial *encomiendas* and revenue, that the treasury virtually ran a welfare service for the aristocracy, and many nobles regarded an income from *mercedes* as a convenient alternative to working their estates. It was estimated that *mercedes* and other benefits consumed some 3 million ducats a year, an enormous burden for a treasury already tottering under its many obligations. The Council of Finance attempted to stem the flood, not out of principle but because it could not find the funds. It did not have much success. In some cases, perhaps, royal grants were justified because of services rendered.

[9] Quoted *ibid.*, p. 231.
[10] See above, pp. 135–36.

Embassies were financial tombstones for their incumbents; and they were only given to those who had personal fortunes, for cost-of-living allowances only covered part of the heavy outlay. But these were not the appointments most sought by the aristocracy. The richest prizes were the viceroyalties in Italy and the Indies. These were so profitable that even after living in extraordinary splendour and making princely gifts to the king, viceroys still had enough to restore their estates and build great mansions. Nobles like the marquis of Mancera brought back immense riches from the Indies. These viceroyalties were so valuable that the ministers of Charles II auctioned them off to the highest bidder. In 1695 the viceroyalties of Mexico and Peru were so disposed of; the former went to the count of Cañete for 250,000 escudos.[11]

Offices, court appointments and *mercedes* were all supplementary to the nobles' basic income which came from land, *señoríos*, and royal revenue alienated to them. This complex of property rights enabled the aristocracy to monopolise power at a local level, and gave Spanish provincial life an essentially feudal character. By virtue of *señorío* jurisdiction a lord had the right to name judges and local officials, receive seigneurial dues, and in some cases possess the revenue from *alcabalas*. This meant that in a large part of Spain the king was not sovereign. In the province of Salamanca, for example, only 30·5 per cent. of territory and 33·7 per cent. of population came under royal jurisdiction; 63 per cent. of territory and 60·4 per cent. of population lay within secular *señoríos*; and the rest belonged to *señorío eclesiástico*.[12] Other provinces of Old Castile presented similar features, the chief cities being in royal jurisdiction but all the major towns and villages in the hands of the aristocracy. By the eighteenth century 17 cities and one-third of the towns and villages of Spain belonged to secular *señoríos*. The proportion was highest in the two Castiles, Extremadura, western Andalucía and Valencia.[13]

This primitive feudalism seriously inhibited royal administration. For the territorial preponderance of the nobility was paralleled by their control of political and social life. The greatest cities of Castile—Toledo, Avila, Ciudad Real, Seville—were dominated by aristocratic families, who spread out a network of influence throughout the land. Vassals served them, corregidores deferred to them; and delinquents, if they were relatives or clients, could shelter under their protection. A chronicler of Jérez recounts that in 1664, after violent riots in the town, a special judge, Sebastian Infante, was sent to restore law and order; one of his first actions was to initiate proceedings against the corregidor, Rodrigo Dávila Ponce de León. At this point the duke of

[11] Domínguez Ortiz, *La sociedad española en el siglo XVII*, p. 249.
[12] See María Dolores Mateos, *Salamanca*, in Miguel Artola, ed., *La España del Antiguo Régimen* (Salamanca, 1966).
[13] Richard Herr, *The Eighteenth-Century Revolution in Spain* (Princeton, 1958), p. 95; G. Desdevises du Dezert, *L'Espagne de l'ancien régime* (3 vols., Paris, 1897–1904), i, 130.

Arcos arrived one night in his coach outside the lodgings of the judge, and seeing the latter's clerk in the porch called out from his coach, 'Listen, where is don Sebastian?'. 'He is inside sir, I'll call him'. 'Just tell him that the corregidor of Jérez belongs to my family, that's all'. The clerk immediately informed the judge, who came rushing out, pulling on his clothes and running after the coach, but the duke, although he heard him calling, did not stop.[14]

The territorial power of the aristocracy in the *señorío* was complemented by their political power in the *municipio*. The Castilian nobility tended to live in towns rather than on their uncomfortable estates, the higher aristocracy in Madrid, the rest in the provinces. Excluded by the earlier Habsburgs from a political role at the centre, the majority of the nobles had made their base of influence in the towns. In the course of the seventeenth century most towns came to be dominated by proprietory *regidores*; these were almost always nobles of the middle rank, the *caballeros*. In some of the principal towns of Castile—Valladolid, Avila, Toledo, Alcalá de Henares, Plasencia, Ciudad Real, Trujillo, Córdoba, Seville, Madrid itself—the nobility had a legal monopoly of municipal offices, which they often exercised through deputies or rented out for money. But the majority of Castilian towns practised the system of *mitad de oficios*, that is an equal distribution of offices between nobles and commoners, a system still favourable to the nobles as they were a minority.

What did commoners think of government by aristocracy? In Valencia, where seigneurial jurisdiction was particularly savage, anti-aristocratic feeling exploded into rebellion.[15] In Castile on the other hand there was virtually no challenge to the existing structure. The larger cities had long lost the right to elect their representatives; and provincial interests saw some advantage in having proprietory *regidores*, independent of the central government. In smaller towns the system of *mitad de oficios* was a compromise solution, though it did not entirely preclude conflict between nobles and commoners. The towns of northern Castile were so prolific in *hidalgos* that there could be no successful challenge from below. In the south the nobles were a small minority, but of greater substance, and urban opposition movements simply substituted one noble leader for another. But in the towns of central Castile there was a balance of estates and fierce competition for power, issuing sometimes in popular revolt on a small-town scale. Violence was ruthlessly suppressed; in the absence of a police force the nobility itself controlled the enforcement of order and dominated the local militia. Yet there is no evidence of basic anti-aristocratic sentiments in society at large or of any real threat to the social structure. The close and mutual alliance

[14] Domínguez Ortiz, *La sociedad española en el siglo XVII*, p. 221.
[15] See below, pp. 258–60.

between crown and aristocracy presented a united front to the rest of society.

For most of the Habsburg period the relation between aristocracy and crown was based on a compromise: the nobles were left undisturbed in their provincial strongholds, while the king exercised undisputed sovereignty at the centre. Under a strong monarchy like Philip II the equilibrium was tipped towards the crown; under Charles II the equilibrium was destroyed. The grandees first made it clear that they would not tolerate ministers who came from outside their ranks; they then assessed the weakness of the queen mother and her son and decided they were amenable to force; and they finally ousted plebeian *validos* and replaced them by aristocrats. But these interventions were purely factious and destructive, and embodied no political programme. The nobles failed to co-operate with their own chief ministers or even to sustain them. As soon as they entered politics they exposed their ineptitude and parasitism. It is not surprising that under a new dynasty they were quickly demoted.

2. The Last 'Validos'

Spanish government needed a prime minister: this had now been recognised by kings and political theorists alike. Unfortunately the office emerged in association with the *valido*, the favourite, who monopolised the king's confidence and patronage as well as his political duties. It therefore attracted the prejudice of moralisers and the suspicion of the aristocracy, who regarded the *valido* as a barrier between themselves and the crown. In his last years Philip IV succumbed to these prejudices and ruled without a prime minister. And he so disposed in his will that there would be no place for a *valido* after his death. He appointed the queen mother, Mariana, regent and guardian of the heir to the throne, the young Charles, until he should reach the age of fourteen. She was authorised to deal with state papers and to remit them to the deliberations of a *Junta de Gobierno*, formed under the terms of Philip's will. This was to be composed of the president of the Council of Castile, the vicechancellor of Aragon, the archbishop of Toledo, the inquisitor general, a councillor of state, and a grandee to be nominated. Thus although the queen mother was in a sense the chief executive she did not have sovereign power, for she had to act with the advice of the Junta, which was instructed to assemble daily.[16] The thinking behind Philip's will is clear enough. Mariana was an unstable, ignorant and obstinate woman, unfitted to rule a vast and complex empire. On her own she was ready made for recourse to a *valido*. The solution as Philip saw it was to assign power in advance not to a single person—admittedly there were few outstanding candidates for a premiership

[16] Valiente, *Los validos en la monarquía española del siglo XVII*, p. 21.

—but to an institution representing the higher bureaucracy, the church and the grandees. This was intended to take the place of a *valido* and prevent one emerging. But in the event the Junta was not incompatible with favouritism, for there was nothing to prevent it being subverted from within.

And subverted it was.[17] At first the queen worked exclusively with her official advisers. But she soon began to prefer more personal support. As she was weak of character and scrupulous of conscience she inevitably took counsel of her confessor, not only on faith and morals but also on matters of government. Her confessor was John Everard Nithard (or Neidhard), an Austrian Jesuit who had accompanied Mariana to Spain on her marriage to Philip IV. He was a good divine, pious and ascetic, but inexperienced in politics and unqualified for office. Mariana trusted him and now promoted him. From the confessional he moved to the Council of State, the office of inquisitor general, membership of the Junta de Gobierno, and finally in effect prime minister. Like all previous *validos*, Nithard was first friend and confidant of his royal patron, then, with the latter's total support, head of government. Observers watched the process with incredulity. As an anonymous memorial said of the new favourite: 'From favour he passed to confidence, then to arrogance, and from all this to command of a universal empire'.[18]

Yet Nithard was unlike any previous *valido*. An essential difference lay in his personal qualifications. As these did not conform to the social structure of power in Spain they virtually ruled him out as a serious candidate for leadership. He was not a member of the Castilian aristocracy. He was moreover extremely unpopular, being regarded as an obscure Jesuit of modest origins, and a foreigner to boot. As if this were not enough there were two political impediments to his progress, the will of the dead king and the opposition of Don Juan José de Austria. The will of Philip IV was difficult to ignore, for it possessed a kind of 'constitutional' appeal. The queen did not dare to flout it openly. She sought instead to preserve the appearance of constitutionalism by preserving the Junta de Gobierno, and then included Nithard in it at the first opportunity. It was not enough to appoint him to the Council of State, for there he was simply one of its members, with no more status or voting power than the others. In the course of 1666, therefore, the queen procured Spanish naturalisation for Nithard; this she did by appeal to the votes of the cities represented in the cortes, though five of them, under the influence of a hostile aristocracy, abstained from voting. She then got the necessary papal

[17] For a contemporary account of Spanish politics, 1665–75, see 'Relación histórica de la menor edad de Carlos II y estado de la monarquía durante este período', *Colección de documentos inéditos para la historia de España*, lxvii, 3–68.
[18] Quoted by Valiente, *op. cit.*, p. 23.

permission for Nithard as a Jesuit to accept high ecclesiastical office, and on 22 September 1666 appointed him inquisitor general.[19] He was now *ex officio* member of the Junta de Gobierno, and it was at this point that the settlement of Philip IV was subverted. The Junta itself, representing different factional interests, was not homogeneous enough to resist the placing of a *valido* within its ranks. And opinion at court was divided: some wanted to reinforce the power of the Junta, others wanted to give power to Don John of Austria.

This dark, handsome prince, the illegitimate son of Philip IV and the actress María Calderón, was deeply sensitive of his second-class status in the royal family. Touchy and conceited, he seemed to attract the extremes of admiration and aversion. His father was frankly outraged by his blatant political ambition and in his last years refused to have him in his presence. Don John attributed the estrangement to the malice of his stepmother, and his distrust of Mariana gradually hardened into hatred. He enjoyed some popularity of a demagogic kind. He had fought in every theatre of Spain's recent wars—Naples, Catalonia, the Low Countries, and Portugal. Although his various commands had not been crowned with conspicuous success, he embodied what military virtues existed in Spain at the time; and his patriotic career, combined with a reputation as a womaniser, gave him some place in popular estimation. At all events he contrasted vividly with the sombre Nithard. The political vacuum left by Philip IV sharpened Don John's political ambitions. Now aged thirty-seven, he resented his exclusion from the Junta de Gobierno, and refused to be fobbed off with peripheral assignments. In his own eyes at least, he was no longer a mere general.

In 1667 Louis XIV launched the War of Devolution to enforce his spurious claim to the Spanish Netherlands. Amidst the political uncertainties of the time, war at least was a familiar landmark, and the Spanish government went through the well-tried motions of raising money and troops for dispatch northwards. Don John was appointed commander-in-chief and governor of the Netherlands. He had previous experience of a similar appointment; and now, as an inducement to leave Spain, he was given unprecedented powers—authority to make war and peace, to confer titles of nobility, to dispose of 1 million pesos in cash and 780,000 escudos in letters-of-credit. He was assigned a personal emolument of 600,000 escudos; reinforcements were ready and a naval squadron was waiting at La Coruña. Anxious for a confrontation with Nithard, Don John declared all this insufficient and raised his demands impossibly high, including the right to sell commercial privileges to the English and to enter into financial arrangements with the Dutch. When these terms were inevitably rejected, he

[19] Maura, *op. cit.*, i, 87–89.

claimed that the government had 'closed all roads for employing my life in the service of the crown'; and he declined the appointment.[20] The Junta recognised the latent threat to their own position, and so did the administration. With unwonted vigour they abandoned the traditional procedure of posting opponents to lucrative offices in the periphery, and instead went on the offensive. Don John was replaced as governor of the Netherlands by the Constable of Castile and was ordered to be confined at Consuegra in New Castile, where he was prior of the military order of San Juan. And a number of his partisans, such as the duke of Pastrana and the count of Castrillo, were removed from office.

Yet the unity of the Junta and the councils which advised it was more apparent than real. Don John had his supporters within their ranks, nobles who referred to him as 'the son of our lamented monarch' and who thought he embodied the qualities of monarchy, at a time when there was no Infante and the shadowy figure of the boy king inspired little confidence for the future. Meanwhile the rule of Nithard, if such it was, earned little credit from its handling of the war. The Triple Alliance of England, the United Provinces and Sweden brought Louis XIV to the peace table in 1668, but Spain, after heavy defeats in the Netherlands, had no cards to play. In return for recovering Franche-Comté she had to give up a number of strategic points in the Low Countries. At home, whatever his qualities of integrity and dedication, Nithard was totally lacking in credibility and the kind of prestige which counted in Spain; he was not a noble, he had no faction or political following, and his position depended solely on the support of the queen, whose own power was not sovereign. Mariana might regard Nithard as prime minister, but the administration refused to view him as anything other than a *valido* whose influence on the queen was secret and sinister. In 1668 the Council of Castile addressed a *consulta* to the queen requesting her to choose 'a person through whose hands would pass matters of government'. The 'person' tacitly proposed was undoubtedly Don John. But the Council was not unanimous: four councillors expressed a minority view arguing that Philip IV knew what he was doing in establishing the existing form of government and purposely avoided giving total power to one man. This of course was an argument against Nithard as well as against Don John. And on this occasion the queen leaned towards the minority report and sought to maintain more of an equilibrium between the Junta and the *valido*.

The lowest common denominator among government opinion was opposition to Nithard. Was this enough to win power for Don John? He thought it was. In October 1668 he resumed his conspiratorial activities with more determination. The Junta got wind of these and ordered his arrest. But the

[20] *Ibid.,* i, 111–12.

military were reluctant to co-operate and a leak from the Junta forewarned Don John. He was able to escape to Aragon and Catalonia, denouncing 'the tyranny and execrable evil of Father Nithard', and rallying some support in the eastern kingdoms. These events were evidence of a split in Junta solidarity and of support for Don John within its ranks. The Council of Castile refused to initiate legal proceedings against him, and by the end of 1668 the other councils were moving away from the queen and her *valido*. The tendency within the administration was not so much to back Don John as to wait and see. What they saw was threat of violence. In January 1669 Don John moved out of Aragon towards Madrid and refused to disband his forces until the queen dismissed Nithard. The menace was sufficient to persuade the Junta de Gobierno and the Council of Castile to advise compliance; and the queen, reluctantly but with no alternative, dismissed the *valido* and sent him out of the country.[21]

The programme of Don John and his aristocratic faction, as expounded by an assiduous propaganda machine, was impeccably reformist—reorganisation of the treasury and fiscal relief; just distribution of *mercedes*; improvement of the army, 'the right arm of monarchy'; good administration of justice; careful education of the king; replacement of Nithard's creatures; and a promise that never again would the royal confessor have control of government.[22] This sounded more like a charter for the aristocracy than a new deal for the common people. In any case it remained no more than a promise. Having removed Nithard, the only point on which there was unanimity, Don John did not reach the premiership. He professed not to want it: 'I have never had civil ambition or thought of seizing power; indeed I would expect to be regarded the most unworthy of creatures the day I was seen to seek or procure it'.[23] In fact he could not get it. Political opinion was not yet ready for a military *golpe de estado*, nor did Don John know how to implement one. After a few months of uncertainty he seemed to lose his nerve and took the easy way out, accepting appointment as vicar-general of Aragon and Catalonia and taking up residence in the archiepiscopal palace in Zaragoza. As for his supporters they did not form a compact opposition capable of replacing the senior ministers and the conciliar personnel, so these continued to serve their constitutional superiors. From mid-1669 to 1673 the queen mother governed under the advice of the Junta de Gobierno and with its collaboration. The will of Philip IV appeared to have been vindicated.

Yet this system of government was still as vulnerable as before. The semi-coup of 1669 had shaken the queen mother but not changed her. Don John

[21] *Ibid.*, i, 139–50; Valiente, *op. cit.*, pp. 25–26, 61–62; Antonio Cánovas del Castillo, *Bosquejo histórico de la Casa de Austria* (Madrid, 1911), p. 337.

[22] Maura, *op cit.*, i, 153–54.   [23] Quoted *ibid.*, i, 151.

had failed to follow up his negative success. And the aristocracy, while they could agitate, had not yet grouped themselves into an opposition capable of controlling government developments. So by 1673 political observers had identified a successor to Nithard. The new *valido*, Fernando Valenzuela, proved at least that in seventeenth-century Spain success was open to a certain type of talent. Valenzuela was an adventurer. Born in 1636, the son of an obscure army officer, he began life in the service of the duke of Infantado. After an unsuccessful military career in Italy he returned to Madrid at the age of twenty-three, an elegant, uneducated young man, hanging around the fringes of the court, without office or prospects.[24] In 1661, through marriage to a maid of honour at the palace, he obtained an appointment as equerry to the queen, and acted unofficially as a kind of factotum in the night life of Philip IV. He survived in the new court in the service of the queen and Nithard, and was rewarded with the *hábito* of Santiago in 1671. Rumours began to circulate, chiefly from the pen of the archbishop of Toledo, that Valenzuela's relations with the queen were sexual; this was certainly untrue and, in Mariana's case, out of character. What she needed was a government adviser to lean on. She was an ignorant and bewildered woman, unable to cope alone or to confront an institution like the Junta de Gobierno without personal support; so she relied on Valenzuela for information about people and affairs and for reassuring advice. In 1673 he was appointed chief equerry and superintendent of works at the palace; this gave him unrestricted access to the royal household. In 1674 he was promoted to the Council of Italy, though this was an income rather than an office. In fact Valenzuela, unlike Nithard, received no major political appointment at this stage. He was simply the closest confidant of the queen; while this made him influential, it did not enable him to handle matters of government directly. But he reinforced his position by self-advertising activity in the realm of patronage: he was associated with a number of court hand-outs, bread and bull fights for the populace of Madrid, *mercedes* and offices for the aristocracy, contracts for bankers and merchants.[25]

Influence over the queen and in matters of patronage were not the only factors in Valenzuela's meteoric rise. He was also helped by the poor performance of the Junta de Gobierno, an effete and supine body both collectively and, with the possible exception of the archbishop of Toledo, individually.[26] The count of Peñaranda was decrepit, the count of Villaumbrosa indolent, don Melchor de Navarra incompetent, the Constable

---

[24] On Valenzuela see *ibid.*, i, 185–90, 194–201, 225–42, 244–52, 257–61.
[25] For contemporary material on Valenzuela see 'Documentos referentes a D. Fernando de Valenzuela, primer marqués de Villasierra', *Colección de documentos inéditos para la historia de España*, lxvii, 135–457.
[26] Maura, *op. cit.*, i, 178–82.

semi-illiterate and as lacking in scruple as in ability, and don Diego Sarmiento de Valladares was one of the worst presidents of Castile in recent memory, solely concerned with keeping himself in office. If the aristocracy were to be judged by these representatives they had already failed the country. In these circumstances it was not surprising that a clever, bold and self-confident creature like Valenzuela should have come to monopolise the counsels of the queen. And new developments soon gave him a more positive political role.

On 6 November 1675 Charles II attained his majority at the age of fourteen. His reign lasted another twenty-five years, during which he was always ailing, often close to death, and increasingly neurotic in his behaviour. Now that the king had come of age the Junta de Gobierno should have automatically terminated. This was probably one of the reasons why Don John had withdrawn from political activity, in the expectation of being called to power by constitutional means. He now returned to court, confident that his time had come. And again he was disappointed. As Charles II was obviously incapable of ruling alone, the existing team of ministers sought to share power by retaining the previous system, ignoring its obvious vulnerability to favouritism. On 7 November the Councils of State and Castile advised in *consulta* that the king should now sign decrees, but these should be supervised for two more years by the Junta de Gobierno under the presidency of the queen; Don John should be sent to Italy, and Valenzuela banished from court.[27] Don John left to re-think his tactics. As for Valenzuela he only went through the motions of complying. As a gesture he was nominally appointed ambassador to Venice; but the queen was only waiting for the dust to settle. Within a few months, in April 1676, he returned to court and, as Charles was dominated by his mother, soon became *valido* of the king as well as of the queen. Under their joint patronage he was loaded with appointments. He acquired offices such as master of the horse, governor and general of the coast of Andalucía, the title of marquis of Villasierra, and in particular the two things he most sought, elevation to the *grandeza* and appointment as *primer ministro*, with authorisation to lodge in the royal palace. If Valenzuela was not the first *valido* to be described as prime minister, he was the first to receive specific appointment as such. As a consequence of this a decree was issued in September 1676 dissolving the Junta de Gobierno; Valenzuela was given the right to attend all sessions of councils; and the presidents of councils were ordered to present themselves before him for regular conference on matters of government. Valenzuela was now at the height of his power, prime minister as well as *valido*.[28]

[27] *Ibid.*, i, 211–26.
[28] *Ibid.*, i, 235–42; Valiente, *op. cit.*, 28–30, 103–5; Cánovas, *op. cit.*, p. 347.

In a sense this was constitutional development. The prime minister had at last acquired a single public title, with unequivocal superiority over the presidents of councils and other ministers. But it was a frustrated development. In the first place, Valenzuela did not do much actual governing: he was more interested in patronage than policy. Secondly, his position was politically untenable. The higher nobility were outraged, regarding this as the last straw. As their existing representatives in the government were manifestly incapable of controlling events, the aristocracy began to plan concerted action outside the government.

3. THE REVOLT OF THE GRANDEES

Most of the royal ministers complied with the decree ordering them to confer with Valenzuela; but they did so reluctantly, and two of them, the duke of Osuna and the count of Peñaranda, refused to conform and openly joined the faction of malcontents. These were the higher nobility of Castile, offended in their social values by the dominance of the upstart Valenzuela; to them it was intolerable that their interests should be at the disposal of a vulgar outsider. Their candidate for office was Don John, a man of royal blood, acceptable on class grounds, and popular at large. And Don John became their spokesman. The aristocracy now met together, grouped themselves into a solid opposition, and declared themselves.

On 15 December 1676 they issued a manifesto signed by 24 leading nobles, among them Don John, the dukes of Alba, Osuna, Medina Sidonia, Arcos, Gandia, the duchess of Infantado, and the counts of Benavente and Monterrey. This *documento de la grandeza* attributed the country's disorder and discontent to 'the evil influence of the queen mother . . . and particularly the abominable promotion of don Fernando Valenzuela'.[29] It demanded that the king 'remove the queen mother totally and permanently from his presence, imprison don Fernando Valenzuela, and establish permanently at his side the Lord Don John of Austria'. The signatories undertook upon their 'honour, faith, and word as *caballeros*' to employ all effective means to secure these objectives 'without any reserve whatsoever', and to serve with their 'persons, houses, estates, rents and retainers'. The grandees were not completely unanimous. One of their number, Pedro de Aragon, refused to sign because he had been promised high office; others, like the duke of Medinaceli and the count of Oropesa, held aloof because they did not like the political implications of the document. And in the event the persons, estates and retainers of the grandees were not sufficient, or not sufficiently mobilised, to make a civil coup d'etat.

[29] For a summary of the text see Maura, *op. cit.*, i, 244–45.

It also needed the intervention of the army, the conspiratorial activity of Don John, and the support of the regions.

Don John had a base of power in Aragon, a region which he had culti-vated for some time, posing as the defender of its *fueros* and the representative of its interests. Aragon was behind him and ready to move. He also had much support in Catalonia. There he was remembered as the general who had helped to drive out the French, the negotiator of favourable terms after the Catalan revolution, the viceroy who had mediated between Catalonia and Madrid. Following his subsequent visit in 1668 Don John had patronised the principality and built up a following. Catalans who believed in economic growth and saw their hopes frustrated by Madrid looked upon Don John as a champion who would win further victories for their *fueros* and open new channels for their trade.[30] Although he did not have a specifically regional support elsewhere in Spain, he had the aristocracy behind him. From Anda-lucía and the two Castiles the government received news that the grandees were arming their vassals and preparing to join Don John. Finally, in addition to regional and aristocratic support, Don John had the sympathy of two important institutions. The military regarded him as one of their own, a patron who would look after their careers; and his friends among the senior officers of the royal army stationed in Catalonia placed 600 cavalry at his disposal. The church, too, was well disposed, seeing him as a saviour who would restore traditional Spanish virtues to public life after the corruption of recent decades.

At this point there was a chance of civil war, for Valenzuela, unlike Nithard, was not responsible to a Junta de Gobierno, and he could have decreed the use of force to defend his regime. But he lacked the nerve. He did his best to secure his wealth and fled to the Escorial for asylum. Now isolated among aristocratic advisers, Charles wrote to Don John inviting him to 'come without delay to assist me in this crisis'. Don John did not need inviting. He was inciting the country to violence, giving heated instructions to his par-tisans:

> Make known to people of every sort that what the grandees and other subjects have recently effected at court has been done with the knowledge, influence and approval of the Lord Don John; and that His Highness is now moving to take issue with any Spaniard, good or bad, who, failing God, king and country, tries to undo it. Incite all honourable and faithful men to oppose these people, and to employ themselves only in their de-struction.[31]

On 11 January 1677 Don John crossed from Aragon into Castile at the head of

[30] Ferran Soldevila, *Història de Catalunya* (3 vols., Barcelona, 1935), ii, 345–50.
[31] Maura, *op. cit.*, i, 254.

an army 15,000 strong, with most of the Aragonese aristocracy, and from Castile eighteen grandees and a flock of other nobility. The few ministers and nobles still around Charles II began to edge away; the Madrid garrison was disbanded; and Don John and the grandees entered the capital on 23 January virtually unopposed. They immediately secured the dismissal and banishment of Valenzuela, forced him out of his monastic asylum, and sent him as a prisoner to Consuegra. They were not satisfied until the king had stripped him of all his property and titles, including of course that of grandee, and exiled him to the Philippines. There he served a prison sentence of ten years. And he never saw Spain again. Waiting in Mexico for permission to return, he died from a horse-kick in January 1692. The rebels completed their work by insisting on the banishment of the queen mother to Toledo and the promotion to power of Don John.[32]

As an exercise in removing a prime minister this was one of the most vindictive in Spanish history. In its use of violence and terrorism the revolt of Don John and the nobility was a genuine *golpe de estado*. It was the first time a modern Spanish king had a government imposed upon him.[33] For this reason Don John is not to be classified as a *valido*, or even a prime minister. He did not advise the king, he coerced him. He was able to do this because he now had what he lacked in 1669 and 1675, the backing of almost all the aristocracy. On this occasion the grandees of Spain shed their political diffidence, if not their ineptitude, and acted together for the first time. The event which moved them was the formal promotion of Valenzuela to the premiership. Regarding Spain as an extension of their own estates, they were provoked in their honour, exclusivism and class consciousness when the king took his chief minister not from the natural ruling class but from the ranks of commoners or poor *hidalgos*. The savage sentence on Valenzuela was meant to be a warning against any further subversion of the social structure. The grandees did not revolt in order to re-establish personal monarchy, or to re-vitalise conciliar government, or to erect any institutional barrier against the absolute power of a prime minister. On the contrary, they sought to impose the personal rule of Don John, whom they regarded as their representative, a man who could be trusted to defend their group interest. This was not a political programme. As for Don John, he was seeking personal power, the power which had escaped him on two previous occasions.

The new leader was hailed as a political messiah.[34] In fact he was a *caudillo*,

[32] *Ibid.*, i, 246–62.

[33] Maravall, *Teoría española del estado en el siglo XVII*, pp. 305–6, with some exaggeration, describes Don John as a forerunner of the modern dictator.

[34] For a contemporary account of events in 1677–78 see 'Diario de Noticias de 1677 a 1678', *Colección de documentos inéditos para la historia de España*, lxvii, 69–133.

a strong man, a distributor of patronage, a ruler who improvised as he went along, living from day to day.[35] He rewarded the 'ins' and punished the 'outs'. Friends and creatures of Valenzuela were cruelly persecuted; and any leading noble who had not signed the grandees' manifesto was suspect. Other people were promoted, not on their merits, but on their record as rebels. The duke of Alba, for example, in spite of his notorious incompetence was appointed president of the Council of Italy. To satisfy his Aragonese supporters Don John insisted that the king visit Zaragoza. There the cortes voted a minimal grant—56,000 libras a year for eight years to support 1,500 troops—in return for cancellation of all previous debts to the crown and a promise not to request any further subsidy for the next twenty years. Indeed the price of Don John's success was aristocratic immunity. From the grandees of Castile he received little financial support. When in 1678 he requested a *donativo*, one after another of the higher aristocracy, their rents and estates now removed from service, declined to contribute. As usual, it was the bankers, merchants and *asentistas* who had to dip into their pockets, and the common taxpayers who had to increase their quota.

As fast as money was raised it was devoured in war. Louis XIV was perhaps Don John's worst enemy, for it was he who caused Spain's rising defence costs. After four years of precarious peace France had invaded the Low Countries again in 1672. In the subsequent war Spain and her allies—the United Provinces and the Empire—suffered one crippling defeat after another. Spanish armies were hard pressed in the Low Countries, Catalonia, and Sicily, where local insurrection gave France an opportunity to intervene. At the Peace of Nymegen (August–September 1678) Spain had no credit, and was forced to cede Franche-Comté (hardly worth fighting for) and further strategic territory in the Netherlands. Loss of distant provinces was less important than the strain on the Spanish economy. Now more than ever the government needed to economise. From 1677 Castile began to endure its most profound economic crisis of the seventeenth century, perhaps in its entire history.[36] In this area of government Don John could provide no leadership. As the economic crisis worsened and the government looked on helplessly, there was growing disillusionment. A satirical paper circulating in Madrid asked: 'Are there less taxes? Less *donativos*? Has the price of food come down? Have the fleets been repaired? Have we lost less in war? Are the prospects better that the people will be relieved, the kingdom saved and our condition improved?' Amidst mounting discontent Don John began to lose two specific bases of support, the army and the church. After a disastrous war and an ignominious peace, the military were now unoccupied and de-

[35] Maura, *op. cit.*, i, 271–315, regards Don John as a *cacique*, or political boss.
[36] See below, pp. 260–67.

moralised, and Don John had no panacea for their complaints. Meanwhile the hierarchy were having second thoughts about the messianic mission they had attributed to the new leader; their doubts were reinforced when they discovered that the clergy had less tax immunity than the aristocracy and were made to pay a higher *subsidio* as well as a *donativo*.

Don John reacted to criticism in two ways. He reshuffled his ministers, placing hard-core supporters, most of them second-rate, in presidencies, councils, and viceroyalties. And he silenced opposition by the classical methods of the *caudillo*, driving his enemies into prison or exile. The crown itself was his prisoner. He had the king's every movement watched, every public appearance and audience supervised, every letter opened. But this was no substitute for policy. With his rule disintegrating, his government empty of ideas, and resentment growing, Don John was only saved from political disaster by his death on 17 September 1679.

4. RETURN TO GOVERNMENT

While the fall of Valenzuela brought to an end the seventeenth-century series of *validos*, the death of Don John terminated Spain's brief experiment with *caudillismo*. Between 1680 and 1691 Spanish government was rebuilt on sounder foundations and, in spite of the last leaderless years of Habsburg rule, left a legacy of improved administration. Charles II himself contributed nothing to this development. He occasionally awoke to political affairs during interludes of better health, but in general his physical and mental abnormality forced him to abandon government to other men. These were prime ministers, not *validos*, for paradoxically to abdicate responsibility to a *valido* a king needed a modicum of determination in order to sustain his favourite against opposition. The new prime ministers reached power not as the personal choice of the king but through intense political intrigue. The successful candidates were a compromise between the needs of government and the demands of the aristocracy. They therefore combined some qualities of statesmanship, the minimum requirement of a country in prostration, and social qualifications, the test of their acceptability to the nobles. They were not slaves of their class, but they had to work within the existing social structure and they inevitably found this an obstacle to reform. Moreover a new dimension had been added to politics. In 1679 Charles II married Marie Louise of Orléans, niece of Louis XIV. The marriage had political implications. Having defeated Spain in war, the French now hoped to dominate her in peace and diplomacy; while Spanish opinion preferred a French to an Austrian marriage on the ground that one Austrian in the royal family—the queen mother—was enough. But this, and Charles's subsequent marriage

R

to Mariana of Neuburg, brought strong-willed queens and their diplomatic backers into Spanish politics and intensified the struggle for control of the crown.

After the death of Don John it took some time to reconcile the various interests and to find a prime minister acceptable to the aristocracy, the administration, and the two queens (Charles's mother and wife). Eventually, on 21 February 1680, the king appointed the duke of Medinaceli, explaining 'I now recognise that the form of government appropriate to my Monarchy and the exigencies of the moment both call for a prime minister'.[37] Medinaceli, one of the wealthiest of the grandees, was an unassuming and uninspiring man with administrative experience as president of the Council of the Indies.[38] He was not exclusively tied to class interests—he had not signed the manifesto of the grandees in 1676—and he did not claim to be a saviour of the nation. He saw his duty more simply—to relieve the king of all responsibility of government, to use the existing administration to provide law, order, and a sense of direction, and in particular to see the country through the great economic crisis of the years after 1677. He maintained the hard deflationary policy already devised by the financial administration.[39] But he also thought beyond economic restraint, necessary though it was. In an attempt to get the economy moving again he brought in a new president of the Council of Finance, Carlos de Herrera, former councillor of the Indies and of Castile, governor of Seville, and a man familiar with economic problems and merchant interests.[40] Medinaceli showed an interest in commercial–colonial reform untypical of the higher aristocracy and of his predecessors. He further strengthened his administration by recruiting José de Veitia Linaje, former treasurer of the Casa de Contratación, secretary of the Council of the Indies, and author of a celebrated treatise on American trade. Appointed *Secretario del Despacho Universal* in April 1682, Veitia Linaje worked as a kind of special consultant to the prime minister on plans to revive colonial trade and its yield. There was a vigorous attack on the more flagrant abuses of foreign commercial penetration at Seville–Cadiz, and greater attention was paid to imperial defence.[41] These efforts did not yield noticeable returns. According to the government's own statistics, of the 27,000 toneladas of merchandise exported to America in 1686 only 1,500 belonged to Spanish merchants.[42] Indeed there was no recovery of Spain's American trade before the eighteenth century. Nevertheless, for the first time in decades the government itself, as

---

[37] On the Medinaceli administration see Maura, *op. cit.*, i, 352–424.
[38] E. Schäfer, *El Consejo real y supremo de las Indias* (2 vols., Seville, 1935–47), i, 277.
[39] See below, pp. 263–64.
[40] Schäfer, *op. cit.*, i, 363.
[41] Girard, *Le commerce français à Séville et Cadix au temps des Habsbourgs*, pp. 159–70.
[42] Maura, *op. cit.*, i, 445.

distinct from the bureaucracy, showed an awareness of the problems and an anxiety to tackle them.

The fabric of Spanish life was too exhausted to be capable of sudden rejuvenation. The most that the Medinaceli administration could do was to provide political stability, recruit new talent, and improve the standard of government. It also had the courage to stand by its severe deflationary policy, and it refused to take the easy way out by manipulating the monetary system as previous administrations had done. This meant that life continued to be hard for the mass of the people, and even the aristocracy felt the pinch. On the basis of reports of acute distress in the peninsula, Louis XIV struck once again, invading the Low Countries and Catalonia. This was a small war, it is true, but it imposed painful defence costs and yet another punishing peace treaty (Ratisbon, August 1684), which deprived Spain of Luxemburg.

By 1684 Medinaceli was living on promise rather than performance and he had exhausted his credit with his sponsors. He agreed therefore to share the burden with someone else. In June 1684 the count of Oropesa, a member of the Council of State since 1680, was appointed president of the Council of Castile. Oropesa was of sufficient stature to turn his appointment into virtual co-government, and with the capricious support of the two queens and of disappointed aristocrats he gradually eased out Medinaceli. The latter resigned in April 1685. Charles II neither chose his prime ministers nor dismissed them: he had them imposed upon him; and he accepted the arranged succession of Oropesa without demur.

The author of a paper written some years later to discredit Oropesa described him as follows:

> He possesses considerable talent, sound judgement, and wide knowledge of affairs acquired from study. He applies himself to business, has good understanding, and a clear exposition. He is easy in his relationships and moderate in his conduct. All this may be enough for a good minister; but it is not enough for a good prime minister.[43]

Yet Oropesa was better qualified for the office than any other candidate. Between the needs of government and the demands of faction his appointment seemed to tip the balance towards the former. He was a man of ideas, capable and energetic, whose only apparent disadvantage was the possession of a notoriously pushing wife. Oropesa was also favoured with a first-rate colleague in the executive. Veitia Linaje had resigned along with Medinaceli and he was succeeded in the *Secretaría del Despacho* by Manuel Francisco de Lira, former diplomat, secretary for Italian affairs in the Council of State, an able if intolerant man.

[43] *Ibid.*, i, 419.

Oropesa stood for a policy of fiscal, administrative and ecclesiastical reform, and was ready to boost the economy by a moderate dose of reflation.[44] Impressed by the French style of government, and suspecting the efficiency of the Council of Finance, he assigned fiscal affairs to a new office, the *Superintendencia de Hacienda*. There were few outstanding candidates for the appointment, and imitation of French methods could not in itself revive Spain's finances and economy. But the experiment is chiefly interesting as an early attempt to construct a ministry outside the conciliar system; as such it anticipated the Bourbon reforms of the eighteenth century. The Spanish Colbert was the marquis of los Vélez, a benevolent and conscientious man though not greatly endowed with intelligence. According to current scurrility he was dissatisfied with his previous appointment as master of the queen's horse because excessive obesity prevented him from actually mounting a horse. As superintendent of finance he was energetic enough and soon produced an extensive memorandum as a working paper for the preparation of a new tax structure.[45] Oropesa and los Vélez thus gave a new stimulus to fiscal reform, and this was designed not only to reduce the chronic budget deficit but also to introduce an element of social justice into taxation. If their plans did not meet the success they deserved this was due to the opposition of vested interests, the aristocracy, the church, and office-holders. But a number of minor measures were implemented, and monetary readjustment brought some relief to the economy. Like many rulers who shelve issues, Oropesa was forced to divert his fiscal ideas into safer channels by the appointment of royal commissions. He created a *junta de medios* with membership drawn from the various councils and presided over by los Vélez to consider reform proposals; and to give greater weight to these proposals he appointed a *junta de estado*.

Frustrated on the financial front, Oropesa turned his attention to reform of the bureaucracy and the church.[46] Both institutions suffered from excessive recruitment. Oropesa campaigned against the number of false vocations in the church; he circulated the bishops requesting a temporary suspension of ordinations, and he sought to restrict the foundation of new religious houses. Under his initiative a special junta investigated the power of the Inquisition. The committee criticised the inflated jurisdiction, privilege and immunity of the tribunal; it recommended that there should be no excommunication for temporal reasons, that there should be right of appeal before secular courts against unjust sentences, that the tribunal's *fueros* should be

[44] For a fuller account of this policy see below, pp. 266–67. On the events of 1685–88 see the contemporary comments in 'Cartas del duque de Montalto a D. Pedro Ronquillo, embajador en Inglaterra (1685–1688)', *Colección de documentos inéditos para la historia de España*, lxxix, 299–475.
[45] Maura, *op. cit.*, i, 446–47.
[46] On administrative reform see below, pp. 267–73, 275–77.

more closely defined, and that its fiscal frauds should be investigated. It was easier to make these proposals than to implement them, but Oropesa kept up the pressure and achieved something, if only in ventilating the problem.

To threaten the aristocracy with taxation, the church with reform, and the bureaucracy with reduction, was to alienate the most powerful sectors of Spanish society. The Oropesa administration was not a failure; it made a contribution to Spain's slow recovery from prolonged depression, as will be seen. But many of its proposals were precocious and out of joint with the time and the place. They earned for Oropesa great unpopularity, which meant accusations of bad government by the interested parties opposed to his reforms. His opponents secured an ally in the new queen. After the death of Maria Luisa in February 1689 Charles II married Mariana of Neuburg, daughter of the Elector Palatine and sister of the Emperor Leopold. She was a calculating woman who easily dominated her husband and became the centre of much political intrigue. She also disliked prime ministers. But the Austrian marriage had further repercussions for Oropesa. It provoked Louis XIV to declare war on Spain yet again. As usual there were heavy defence costs with nothing to show for them, only predictable defeats in the Low Countries and Italy and the inevitable invasion of Catalonia. The prime minister was now vulnerable on domestic and foreign policy alike. Under pressure from the queen and a number of discontented grandees, Charles was persuaded, much against his will, to demand Oropesa's resignation; this he did on 25 June 1691.[47]

After the fall of Oropesa the government drifted without a prime minister. Queen Mariana, appropriating the sovereignty belonging to her husband, filled the Council of State with her own clients. Into the *Secretaría del Despacho* she put a particularly servile and uncultivated creature, Juan de Angulo, nicknamed *el Mulo*; and he was succeeded by another client of the queen, though a more presentable one, Alonso Carnero. In addition, a number of greedy German advisers were provided for in one way or another. But the Castilian aristocracy also had to be placated. There were so many aspirants to high office and the premiership that power was artificially divided among a number of competing candidates. On the advice of the duke of Montalto Charles was constrained to issue a decree in 1693, the so-called *planta de gobierno*, constituting a kind of senior junta of ministers and dividing the spoils among them. The successful candidates received the titles of lieutenant general and governor and were assigned different regions in which to deploy their talents. The Constable was appointed lieutenant general and governor of Old Castile; Andalucía and the Canaries went to

[47] Lira had already resigned from the Secretaría del Despacho; see Maura, *op. cit.*, i, 542–45.

the Admiral, the count of Melgar; Aragon and Catalonia to the count of Monterrey; and New Castile to Montalto himself.[48] This arrangement was followed by further manoeuvrings which reduced the four supremos to a triumvirate. Montalvo took the government of the Aragonese kingdoms and Navarre, with the presidency of the Council of the Indies; Galicia, Asturias and the two Castiles went to the Constable, a singularly stupid and overbearing man; and Andalucía and the Canaries to the Admiral. And the triumvirate was finally reduced to two, Montalto and the Admiral. These proceeded to squabble over the plunder, seconded by their respective factions, and the ridiculous territorial divisions gradually disappeared. In 1696 the queen demoted Montalto and dismissed Carnero. By now Spain was virtually without government, for the sole survivor from the *planta de gobierno*, the Admiral, dared not make a move without the queen's approval. And she was interested in other things than the internal government of Spain.

One of the great obstacles to Spain's recovery in the second half of the seventeenth century was French imperialism. Any neighbour of France could expect to suffer from aggression, but Spain was particularly vulnerable because of the various fronts she presented. Territorially she lost to Louis XIV little of real importance though he kept whittling away her possessions in the Rhineland and the Netherlands, and repeatedly struck her in northern Italy and Catalonia. The real cost to Spain was in men and money. Although she was still capable of sending subsidies to her overseas armies, these had to be paid in silver, which was in short supply in Spain where the currency was almost exclusively vellon. As for the peninsula itself Spain's only defences were the patriotism of her subjects and their notorious aversion to foreign invasion or domination. The aristocracy no longer fulfilled a military role and material defences were almost non-existent. When a decree for general conscription was issued in July 1691 it was stated that the country had 'insufficient ships and troops for its defence . . . and in most towns one can hardly find a musket, arquebus or pike'.[49] So Spain was in no position to resist Louis XIV's ultimate aggression, the War of the League of Augsburg, which brought further defeats in Milan, the Netherlands and Catalonia. Yet she emerged relatively unscathed: by the Peace of Ryswick (September 1697) Louis XIV returned all the gains he had made since the Peace of Nymegen. Spain's escape owed little to her own efforts. It was a consequence of two other factors. The combined pressure of the two great maritime powers, England and Holland, was at last turning the balance against France. And Louis XIV now had his eye on a greater prize, to be secured by diplomacy

---

[48] *Ibid.,* ii, 45–46; Cánovas, *op. cit.,* pp. 383–84.
[49] Quoted by Domínguez Ortiz, *La sociedad española en el siglo XVIII,* p. 368, n. 4.

rather than war, namely the whole of the Spanish Monarchy, or at very least a substantial part of it.[50]

By 1696–97 it was clear that Charles II had only a few years to live and would remain childless. An heir had to be found for Spain and her empire. The succession problem now obsessed the political life of the country and held government in complete suspense. For the real test of monarchy is the succession, and over this there was profound uncertainty. The two serious claimants were France and Austria, the former through Louis XIV's marriage to the Spanish Infanta, María Teresa, the latter through the emperor's marriage to Margarita Teresa. French and Austrian diplomatic pressure in Madrid, and the factions engendered in support of the rival causes, reduced the administration to impotence. Charles II suffered mental anguish in these years and in his desperate search for enlightenment had recourse even to exorcism. After intense lobbying, conflicting advice and constant vacillation, he finally made his will (2 October 1700) and left the Spanish dominions undivided to the French candidate, Philip, duke of Anjou, grandson of Louis XIV. This decision, the one moment of grandeur in his whole life, was influenced chiefly by the universal desire among Spaniards to keep their Monarchy and empire intact under a strong ruler who would reside in Spain.

Charles II, browbeaten for so long by the women of his family, was most influenced in his last days by Cardinal Portocarrero, archbishop of Toledo. On 29 October 1700 he signed a decree, doubtless prepared by his mentor, ordering that in the event of his utter incapacity, the cardinal should govern with complete power in his name.[51] But Portocarrero only enjoyed his power for three days. On 1 November Charles died, and on the following day, in expectation of the arrival of the new king, a Junta de Gobierno was established.

[50] See M. A. Thomson, 'Louis XIV and the Origins of the War of the Spanish Succession', *Transactions of the Royal Historical Society*, 5th ser., iv (1954), 111–34.

[51] Valiente, *op. cit.*, pp. 35, 191–92.

CHAPTER X
THE END OF HABSBURG SPAIN
1. Promise and Prejudice in Eastern Spain

In the last decades of Habsburg rule Spain resembled a corpse, picked at by noble parasites and foreign marauders. This, it would seem, was the horrifying nemesis of a society which turned its face against the world and the times in which it lived. Retribution was harsh and perhaps inevitable. Yet the conventional picture of Spain's final prostration has been overdrawn, or at least has lacked a sense of contrast and of movement. From the 1680's, amidst the ruins of government and economy, the country began to stir from its inertia and renew its life. Reform was in the air. Its authors were few in number, uncertain of themselves and frustrated by their fellows. But they cleared away some of the debris of the past and set up signposts for the future. This movement of recovery could be observed obscurely in Castile, more clearly perhaps in the periphery.

Eastern Spain moved independently of Castile. The second half of the seventeenth century was an Indian summer of provincial autonomy. After the costly failure to impose constitutional and fiscal uniformity, the central government left the regions severely alone. Don John appealed to Aragon and Catalonia—the first Spanish politician to do so—not to procure the vindication of their rights but to seek the support of rights already vindicated. To leave the regions alone was to leave them in the hands of their governing classes. In Aragon this perpetuated stagnation, and the province became an economic colony of France. In Catalonia it led to the first stage of economic advance. And in Valencia it led to peasant revolt.

In the last decades of the seventeenth century Catalonia began to emerge from its prolonged stupor.[1] It was assisted by two institutional conditions. Monetary autonomy saved it from the succession of state-imposed inflation and deflation experienced by Castile. In Catalonia monetary policy was determined by commercial not fiscal considerations. After 1659 the province enjoyed relative monetary stability; and it escaped the worst effects of the brutal deflation imposed on Castile in 1680. In the period 1688–99, however, Catalonia had enough inflation, without a corresponding wage rise, to

[1] J. Vicens Vives, *Manual de Historia económica de España*, con la colaboración de J. Nadal Oller (Barcelona, 1959), pp. 422–23.

ensure rapid accumulation of profits and conditions for further investment.[2] Another stimulus was provided by the freedom of commerce imposed in the Treaty of the Pyrenees (1659). While the neighbouring kingdom of Aragon was smothered by protection, which simply favoured low-quality goods and contraband, the Catalans enjoyed few tariff advantages and were forced to improve their own performance. Under the challenge of freer trade their textile industry underwent some renewal and expansion, shedding archaic privileges and equipping itself to compete more vigorously with French, English and Dutch goods.[3]

After a period of stagnation in 1664–74, maritime trade became more active from the late 1670's. On the evidence of *periatge* (guild merchant duty), it moved strongly ahead about 1680, and by the end of the century had expanded well beyond its level at the beginning.[4] In the late 1690's traffic in the port of Barcelona was almost double that in 1600. Barcelona now housed large-scale business firms, and these were turning from the narrow, pre-empted Mediterranean market towards the outer world, towards Cadiz and Lisbon, buying colonial goods—sugar, cacao and tobacco—and seeking to export Catalan products to the colonial markets.[5] The Catalan merchant marine was re-constructed and armed to deal with corsairs. While Barcelona was the centre of commercial activity, actual production developed elsewhere. Artisan conditions in the capital itself were still depressed in the second half of the seventeenth century, particularly in the silk and textile industries. The provinces on the other hand were forging ahead. Wine and brandy production experienced a minor boom, being exported to all parts of Spain, particularly Andalucía, where it was beginning to break into the Indies trade. Brandy was also sold to the English and the Dutch, and this further outlet was sufficient to cause expansion of vineyards, while some of the returns went into other local industries. Textile production in the provinces was doing much better than in Barcelona, and showing signs of assimilating technical improvement from France. And the minor ports of the principality were active in small-scale shipbuilding. This economic decentralisation was due not only to lower taxes in the provinces but also to rural population growth, which made the interior a good source of supply for labour. Whatever the reason, the inflation of agricultural prices was a sign of accumulation of rural profits.[6] In this period the bandits disappeared and the farmers got to work.

---

[2] Vilar, *La Catalogne dans l'Espagne Moderne*, i, 639–41, 646.

[3] José Fontana Lázaro, 'Sobre el comercio exterior de Barcelona en la segunda mitad del siglo XVII. Notas para una interpretación de la coyuntura catalana', *Estudios de Historia Moderna*, v (1955 [1957]), 197–219.

[4] This duty rose from 4,000 pounds a year in 1664–65, to 5,997 in 1680–81, to 9,785 in 1698–99; Smith, *The Spanish Guild Merchant*, p. 140.

[5] Vilar, *La Catalogne dans l'Espagne Moderne*, i, 648–49.   [6] *Ibid.*, i, 650–53.

The atmosphere was heady enough to produce a number of ambitious projects for promoting foreign trade. These were a common enough phenomenon in the seventeenth century, but the Catalan proposals, unlike those of earlier Castilian *arbitristas*, were a sign of optimism and incipient revival rather than a reaction to depression. The ideas came, about 1680, from individuals and consortiums who were candidates for the lease of the Barcelona municipal taxes and were capable of guaranteeing on their own security capital amounting to between 140,000 and 170,000 Catalan pounds. The type of organisation canvassed was the chartered company, as can be seen in the proposals of Narciso Feliu de la Peña, historian, economist and businessman.[7] In 1681 Feliu outlined a plan for a trading company on the model of those existing in Holland, France and England. It would be formed in Barcelona with capital subscribed by 50 shareholders; it would make loans to captains of ships, merchants and manufacturers, and would finance the construction of shipping; and it would send two ships a year to America, exporting fruits, clothing, and manufactures of iron, copper and glass.

The economic recovery of Catalonia in this period can be exaggerated. Projects like those of Feliu probably overestimated the prospects of the principality. Yet almost immediately after the change of regime in Madrid in 1700 the Catalans again tried to secure official admission to the Indies trade; and when they failed they soon began to force their way in regardless of the law. Their ability to engage in overseas trade did not develop overnight. It was the result of lengthy, if confused, preparation in the previous decades when Catalonia disengaged itself from the general depression lying over the peninsula. And as Catalonia began to emerge from its former myopia so it became less inhibited in its attitude towards the rest of Spain. Between 1653 and 1697 Barcelona contributed the considerable sum of 6,377,591 pounds to the crown, financial co-operation of a kind which Olivares had not managed to secure. In 1674 the Catalans formally objected to being classified as foreigners in Cadiz—and to their goods being taxed as such on landing. While not forgoing any of their regional prerogatives, they argued that Catalans were subjects of the crown and were 'Spaniards, Catalonia being indubitably of Spain'.[8] The crown acknowledged the justice of the complaint and by decree of 30 November 1674 removed the Catalans from the jurisdiction of the consul for foreigners.

Valencia, like Catalonia, enjoyed undisturbed possession of its *fueros* in the reign of Charles II. The crown exercised a limited power through its viceroy and its jurisdiction over a number of towns in the province. But the viceroy

---

[7] *Ibid.*, i, 653–67; Roland Dennis Hussey, *The Caracas Company 1728–1784. A Study in the History of Spanish Monopolistic Trade* (Cambridge, Mass., 1934), pp. 23–24.

[8] Carrera Pujal, *Historia política y económica de Cataluña*, i, 442–43, ii, 312.

had to operate within the framework of the *fueros*. The city of Valencia was administered by the Council of Hundred, its membership drawn from the various social groups, the majority representation, though not the greatest influence, being held by members of the guilds. And the *Diputación*, or standing committee of the cortes consisting of two nobles, two clerics and two commoners, supervised observance of the *fueros* and the administration of taxes. Even in towns under royal jurisdiction the king's power was confined virtually to taxation, the yield of which was consumed locally. Most towns, and their inhabitants, were in noble or ecclesiastical jurisdiction, and here the king's writ hardly ran. Some of these nobles held titles of Castile, such as the duke of Medinaceli and the duke of Infantado; others, like the duke of Gandia, were great territorial magnates, virtual sovereigns on their own estates.

The most significant event in Valencia's modern history was the expulsion of the moriscos. This massive amputation crippled the province for many decades after 1609.[9] The consequences were felt outside the rural economy. For the numerous *censos* (mortgage loans) on property farmed by moriscos were supplied from capital owned by urban groups and ecclesiastical institutions. These investments were now at great risk. The crown sought to compensate landowners for loss of their labour force by, among other things, reducing the interest rate on *censos*; but in any case the difficulties of repopulating morisco farmlands meant that payments on *censos* were often in arrears or in default. Thus the expulsion of the moriscos first damaged agricultural production, then hurt the feudal aristocracy, and finally penalised the latter's creditors; many of these were from urban middle groups, and were forced to consume their savings, which precipitated the failure of the municipal bank of Valencia in 1613.[10] While the landed aristocracy were compensated to some degree for loss of their morisco vassals, they were also in a powerful position to dictate the terms of re-settlement. Valencia lost about 25 per cent. of its 450,000 inhabitants, and most of those expelled were tenants or vassals of the aristocracy. There was no great rush of immigrants to fill the vacuum: by the middle of the eighteenth century Valencia's population still had not reached the level of 1609.[11] The bargaining power of the aristocracy, therefore, did not derive from surplus of labour but from sheer territorial sovereignty. A few colonists entered from outside the province, and there was

[9] Juan Reglá, 'La expulsión de los moriscos y sus consecuencias en la economía valenciana', *Hispania*, xxiii (1963), 200–18; Eduardo Asensio Salvadó, 'El arbitrista Jerónimo Ibáñez de Salt y su programa de recuperación de la economía valenciana en 1638', *Estudios de Historia Moderna*, iv (1954), 225–72.

[10] Reglá, 'La expulsión de los moriscos y sus consecuencias en la economía valenciana', *op. cit.*, pp. 206, 216–17.

[11] See above, pp. 48–49, 143–44.

some internal migration as artisans from the towns and peasants from more depressed areas moved into morisco farms in search of a living. What they found was hardly a colonist's dream.

In the southern part of the province the newcomers were settled on the great estates of the dukes of Gandia and Maqueda, the marquises of Guadalest, Denia and Albaida, and the counts of Cocentaina and Real. The terms of vassalage were harsh and extortionate. A typical example is provided by the settlement of Muro in the jurisdiction of the count of Cocentaina. The new tenants owed their lord tithes and first-fruits; they forfeited all common land to the lord, could not move without his permission, and were bound to stay for at least five years; they had no property rights except by grace and favour of the lord, who also reserved to himself all civil and criminal cases in first instance; the establishment of bakeries, shops and taverns was monopolised by the lord; tenants had to grind their corn only in the lord's mill, and they were forbidden to buy flour from outside; anyone manufacturing anything had to pay the lord 10 per cent. of production; on wines they had to pay a quarter of the product, and on sugar half of the canes collected.[12] These were only a number of major items of the pact; and similar terms were imposed by the duke of Gandia and the marquis of Albaida. There was no escape from an exclusively seigneurial relationship. The nobles—and the church—held all the cards: they dominated the apparatus of government; they owned the land; and they possessed jurisdiction. There was nothing to prevent them interpreting the pacts to their own advantage. The agrarian economy of Valencia, therefore, was rebuilt not by a free peasantry but on the backs of semi-servile vassals. This was one of the more glaring of the many opportunities missed by Habsburg government, an example of its crass neglect of responsibility and of its tendency to strengthen rather than loosen the existing social structure.

On top of the burdens of their vassalage the peasants of Valencia suffered a long series of calamities in the course of the seventeenth century—conscription, taxes, bandits, locusts, bubonic plague, earthquakes, the whole range of nation-wide afflictions in miniature. They became heavily indebted and incapable of keeping up with their numerous obligations—payments of interest, dues in kind and money to their lords, and taxes to the state. By the last decade of the century their situation was hopeless. The territorial magnates, lay and ecclesiastical, were a closely-knit group, with common interests and a united front. There was no rift in their defences, and they cursorily dismissed requests for the lowering of seigneurial dues or change of any kind. The peasants had no representation in regional institutions: the lay and

[12] Francisco de P. Momblanch y Gonzalbez, *La segunda Germanía del reino de Valencia* (Alicante, 1957), pp. 19–27.

ecclesiastical nobility controlled two of the three estates of the cortes of Valencia, and they also dominated the *Diputación*. As far as the peasants were concerned the *fueros* of Valencia were a savage mockery of constitutionalism, and they were forced to seek their own remedies. A clandestine movement began to take shape, centred round the Játiva region of southern Valencia and under the leadership of Francisco García Menor, a farmer from Ráfol de Almunia in the jurisdiction of the marquis of Almunia. By the early 1690's something like a peasant league existed, and its leaders initiated litigation before the viceroy, seeking a reduction of seigneurial dues and services on the ground that ancient privileges granted by the kings of Valencia exempted them from these exactions. But *fueros* were not for peasants. The marquis of Castel-Rodrigo issued a series of viceregal edicts denying their claims and declaring that in the post-morisco settlement the lords had acquired property and fiscal rights over tenants, that these had been confirmed by royal grant, and that the settlers had known the terms and accepted them. The peasants then took their case to Madrid and petitioned the king, with no better result. From the church they could expect no support. The archbishop of Valencia, Fray Juan Tomás de Rocabertí, a lord of numerous vassals, issued a pastoral letter (8 July 1693) admonishing the clergy under pain of major excommunication to explain in pulpit and confessional the grave sin committed by those who without just cause withheld the services and dues owed to their lords.[13]

The tension broke in the summer of 1693 when peasants refused to share harvest products with their lords in the customary proportions. On 9 July 1693 the duke of Gandia's bailiffs imprisoned four peasants of the village of Villalonga for not paying their dues. Peasants in the rest of the *senorío* came out in revolt and released the prisoners, and the movement swept through the estates of the marquis of Albaida, the count of Cocentaina and other lords. Soon the insurgents numbered about 1,000 and were recruiting more.[14] Francisco García was appointed *síndico* and assumed political direction, sending out emissaries throughout the province. And military command was conferred on José Navarro, a surgeon of Muro, who took the title *General del Eixercit dels Agermanats*, thus recalling the other *Germanía*, or brotherhood, of the 1520's.[15] The rebel forces were organised into companies, eight in all, and captains were appointed; and as their numbers grew, to about 2,000, villages came to their assistance with supplies. The plan was to assemble as large a force as possible and then march on the viceregal capital to place their cause before the crown and seek redress.

[13] *Ibid.*, pp. 43–49.
[14] *Ibid.*, pp. 51–63.
[15] See *Spain under the Habsburgs*, i, 41–42.

But the viceroy denounced the rebels as traitors and sent an army against them. On 15 July near the village of Cela de Núñez the peasant forces were scattered; a number of prisoners were taken and the rest fled in disorder to the mountains. The viceroy then offered an amnesty and a hearing to the rank and file; but to the leaders he offered nothing, and he placed a large price on the heads of the two principals, dead or alive. The villagers took the bait and again tried legal action, with no more success than before. So the movement was split, and three weeks after its beginning the rebellion was virtually over. García was never captured; but Navarro was taken and executed. Lesser rebels were sent to the galleys or heavily fined. In spite of the harsh repression the spirit of revolt was not extinguished. After 1700, during the War of Succession, the peasants of Valencia made another attempt to throw off their seigneurial yoke. But the Habsburg cause which they espoused was doomed, and the victory of Philip V was a victory for the landed aristocracy.

2. CASTILE'S TRAGIC DECADE

While Catalonia rebuilt its economy and Valencia erupted in social conflict, Castile passively endured its fate, trapped in a vicious circle of depression. A faulty agrarian structure and periodic pestilence precipitated demographic recession, which further diminished the consumer market for agricultural and industrial products. Falling output affected exports, which meant that Castile was unable to compete for European markets and even lost a major part of its American market. Shortage of foreign and colonial earnings perpetuated stagnation at home. This was almost a classical example of depression feeding upon itself. And in the background was a further factor, imperfectly understood by Spaniards who still believed that they possessed an El Dorado across the Atlantic if only it could be made to yield its wealth to them instead of to foreigners. They refused to accept that a fundamental shift of power had taken place within the Hispanic world, that the economic balance had now moved towards America, and that Americans now produced their wealth for themselves and not for Spain.

Castile was hardly in a position to endure more. Yet its worst crisis, incredibly, was still to come. Between 1677 and 1687 the country was struck by every conceivable adversity, reducing an already enfeebled frame to its last gasp. In this decade Castilians were visited by scourges of biblical proportions. The most relentless enemy was their own climate.[16] This was not a new experience. The countryside had suffered from the very beginning of the reign. There had been harvest failures in 1665–68, causing a sharp rise

[16] See the striking studies by Antonio Domínguez Ortiz, 'La crisis de Castilla en 1677–1687', *Revista Portuguesa de Historia*, x (1962), 436–51, and Henry Kamen, 'The Decline of Castile: the last crisis', *Economic History Review*, 2nd ser., xvii (1964–65), 63–76.

in the price of agricultural products, with wheat more than doubling its price between 1663 and 1668.[17] In 1670 crops in the province of Granada were destroyed by locusts. But these were only preliminary warnings.

In the spring of 1677 torrential rainfall caused heavy loss of crops in southern Spain and led to famine conditions in Andalucía. This was followed by two years of drought in the same region, and then an earthquake in October 1680. After a brief respite Andalucía had two more years of drought in 1682–83, followed in the winter of 1683–84 by a great deluge. Rain fell incessantly in the whole of Andalucía; rivers overflowed their banks, crops were inundated, and the few cattle that remained after recent droughts were swept away in floods. In the province of Granada the first four months of 1684 were like a monsoon; crops, roads, bridges and mills were destroyed or impaired, and in the city of Granada alone 6,000 houses were damaged. After this catastrophe Andalucía could expect no harvest in 1684, and three years later the region suffered yet another drought. Meanwhile northern and central Spain had not escaped. There was heavy flooding in 1679–81 and crops were further destroyed by hail. The great rainstorms of 1684 reached as far as La Mancha, and in 1685 there was severe drought in Galicia.

These meteorological conditions were bound to affect food supplies. Andalucía in particular became a major disaster area. Seville, normally one of the granaries of the south and a rich source of oil and livestock, reached the depths of depression. In 1684 the city authorities reported to the government on the plight of their people after eight years of drought or near-drought:

> The culmination of these afflictions came in the calamitous year of 1683, when drought left the fields barren and devoid of crops; food shortage became extremely critical, and people in their misery scratched the earth for grass and roots to keep alive.[18]

The chronicler Francisco Godoy recorded:

> During the whole of 1683, until the end of November, there was not a drop of rain. Almost the whole of Andalucía was in absolute drought. The crops were parched with heat, the trees burnt up, cereals destroyed. . . . Bread became so scarce and expensive that many people perished of hunger. No one in Andalucía escaped privation. There was a stock farmer whose 1,600 head of cattle was reduced to 200 because of drought and lack of fodder. . . . And I know another person who in addition to losing his cattle got only two bales of straw out of the 1,300 fanegas of grain he had sown.[19]

[17] Earl J. Hamilton, *War and Prices in Spain 1651–1800* (Cambridge, Mass., 1947), pp. 238–39.
[18] Quoted by Domínguez Ortiz, 'La crisis de Castilla en 1677–1687', *op. cit.*, p. 439.
[19] Quoted *ibid.*, p. 440, n. 14.

And when the rains came they brought no relief, only further disaster. All over Andalucía hungry peasants flocked to the towns in these years. The relief services provided by civil and ecclesiastical bodies broke down under the strain, powerless to prevent heavy mortality. Famine was a killer in itself. But its secondary effects were equally monstrous. Widespread malnutrition made the population easy prey to epidemic disease. And in a cruel coincidence pestilence now penetrated these debilitated regions.

The second half of the seventeenth century seems to have seen a reversal of the downward demographic trend, but there was a short-term recession in Castile in the 1680's, caused by the epidemics of 1676–85 which, while not as vicious as their predecessors, were more prolonged. The plague began in Cartagena in June 1676, imported perhaps from the eastern Mediterranean.[20] Quarantine measures were ineffective and the infection swept through Murcia, then eastwards along the coast to Andalucía. Málaga was badly hit. Antequera reported the loss of 12,000 inhabitants. Many villages lost half their inhabitants. The disease fed particularly on eastern Andalucía. From 1679 to 1681 Granada suffered grievously, and almost simultaneously Jaén, Córdoba and Seville were infected. In Seville a preacher promised immunity if the theatres were closed; the advice was sound enough on quarantine grounds and it was observed, but by then the infection had taken root. The poor harvests of 1682–83 enabled the epidemic to flare up again in a second wave which lasted from 1683 to 1686. While it revived in Andalucía, it now also penetrated parts of La Mancha and Extremadura. Terror struck the court when it reached Castile and approached Madrid itself; there were heavy losses in the provinces of Burgos, Toledo, Madrid and Valladolid. Total mortality between 1677 and 1686 amounted perhaps to 250,000.[21] So there was no real demographic recovery for Castile in the second half of the seventeenth century. In 1665 the kingdom had slightly over 5 million inhabitants; it had no more than this at the beginning of the following century. The setbacks occurred in 1677–86 when climate, crops and contagion all worked against the people of Castile and decimated their ranks once more. The economy also suffered. Trade was damaged by quarantine measures, which disrupted communications without preventing contagion; the revenue from taxes diminished; and labour shortage affected agriculture and other sectors of the economy.

On top of these natural calamities Castile experienced its worst monetary crisis of the century. Monetary disorder was more than a symptom of an ailing economy: it exacerbated as well as reflected depression. The basic object of monetary inflation was to bridge the gap between falling revenue

[20] Domínguez Ortiz, *La sociedad española en el siglo XVII*, pp. 75–81.
[21] *Ibid.*, pp. 81, 113.

and rising expenditure and to make good the failure of the economy to yield more wealth. Ironically the best industrial machinery in Spain was the mint at Segovia, installed by German technicians. Here and at other minting centres Philip IV had practised coinage debasement with reckless abandon. Inevitably gold and silver were driven out of circulation, and from the 1660's to the 1680's vellon may have constituted at least 95 per cent. of money spent in Castile. Government inertia in the first fifteen years of Charles II's reign allowed the problem to drift without solution. The premium on silver, the measure of public distrust of vellon, having fallen to 50 per cent. following Philip IV's violent deflation of 1664, rose to 115·5 per cent. in New Castile by mid-1665, to 175 per cent. by 1670, and to 275 per cent. by 1680.[22] Commodity prices in New Castile rose from an index of 69 in 1662 to 98 in 1670.[23] The following decade saw inflation at its peak, with the index moving from 96 in 1671 to 113 in 1679. In New Castile the price of wheat almost doubled between 1676 and 1678. This great price rise was conditioned to some degree by mutations in the coinage, the price curve almost coinciding with monetary inflation. In the case of agricultural prices, which reached their highest point in 1678, it was also aggravated by climatic conditions and crop failures from 1677, especially in Andalucía. According to the French ambassador, the marquis of Villars, on the basis of his experience in 1679–81, prices in Madrid were twice as high as the most expensive city in Europe.[24]

The cycle of inflation–deflation–inflation, the monetary and economic chaos, made life intolerable for Spaniards, destroying their savings and disrupting their trade. The ratio of wages to prices appears to have been favourable to wage-earners, and nominally they may have had sufficient for the necessities of life;[25] but the monetary disorder prevents serious estimate of the real value of wages; and in any case the continual depreciation of vellon, the only currency available to the poorer classes, eroded their earnings, while heavy taxation further reduced their actual income. Commerce was dislocated and Spanish merchants had real difficulty in conducting overseas transactions; and inflation was too rampant to be a stimulus to the economy.

Eventually the government of Charles II shed its lethargy. In response to public clamour for deflation, a decree of 10 February 1680 reduced the tariff of the 'rich vellon' struck under the ordinance of October 1660 by 50 per cent.; that of imitation vellon was reduced by three-fourths; and coins counterfeited abroad were cut by seven-eighths of their denominational value.[26] The law of 1641 limiting the premium to 50 per cent., which had

---

[22] Hamilton, *War and Prices in Spain 1651–1800*, pp. 9–35.

[23] Base 1671–80; see Hamilton, *War and Prices in Spain 1651–1800*, pp. 119, 121, 240.

[24] Marquis de Villars, *Mémoires de la cour d'Espagne, 1678–1682* (London, 1861), p. 3.

[25] Hamilton, *War and Prices in Spain 1651–1800*, p. 219.

[26] *Ibid.*, pp. 20–21.

S

been inoperative for 40 years, was reaffirmed. The premium now actually fell from 275 to 50 per cent. when the deflation took place and remained there for more than six years. By decree of 22 May 1680 the 'rich vellon' was demonetised, and the owners were paid its value in 'current money'. Pure copper vellon with extrinsic value slightly above its intrinsic worth was authorised. There were no further changes in the vellon coinage during the Habsburg period; the output of vellon was rigidly limited, if only through inability to secure copper; and no more sudden doses of inflation and deflation perturbed economic life.

The severe deflationary measures of 1680, necessary as they may have been in the long term, were excruciating in their immediate effects. The object was to entice gold and silver into circulation. It was also sought to bring down prices, which had become intolerably high for all those with fixed incomes. They were therefore accompanied by further decrees, notably that of 27 November 1680, fixing prices at an artificially low level. The combination of deflation and price-control produced a price collapse unparalleled in Spanish history: commodity prices fell by almost 50 per cent. in two years. Everyone suffered, from the beggar to the king. Shortage of money paralysed almost every sector of the economy. The government tried in vain to augment the amount of money in circulation by coining American silver when it arrived, by purchasing silver objects for minting, and by prohibiting the manufacture of articles from copper needed for vellon. But artisans, peasants and landowners continued to complain bitterly of the absolute lack of money and the minimal prices obtained for their products. Towns and villages could not pay their taxes, and the government was forced to condone arrears, especially in central Castile. In October 1681 the Council of Finance discussed the possibility of suspending all taxes created since 1656, lowering the municipal *sisa*, and making a new assessment of alcabala quotas, because communities simply could not pay the present level.[27]

The poor prices of agricultural products affected the whole Castilian economy, and the repercussions were felt in trade and industry. The calling in of old coin under the decrees of 1680 led in many parts of the country to a virtual stoppage of local trade, and some parts of Castile fell back on barter for lack of good currency. Merchants were unable to meet their liabilities or collect money owed to them. Administrators and lessees of public money, who had only old coinage in their possession, were left insolvent. The credit of financiers collapsed, and bankers lost half their capital through devaluation. Overseas trade was also affected. According to the French ambassador, 'The wool trade of Segovia, almost the only trade from which Spaniards still make a profit, slumped heavily as a result of devaluation, which caused the

[27] Domínguez Ortiz, 'La crisis de Castilla en 1677–1687', *op. cit.*, p. 449.

price of wool to double. Foreigners would no longer buy it unless the Spaniards would reduce its price proportionately'.[28] Altogether the years 1680–82 were tragic ones for Spain, among the most demoralising ever experienced by its people. And the agony continued.

Committees of inquiry sat in continuous session, but solutions were difficult to find. In November 1683 the government admitted that shortage of money was damaging trade and revenue as well as the income of the church and private landowners, and the Council of Castile was asked to propose a remedy. The Council could not agree on policy and gave an assortment of advice, none of it very convincing. The news reaching Madrid from the south of Spain in 1684 could hardly have been worse. In reply to a demand for greater tax efforts came a series of reports containing only lamentations. Córdoba, for example, insisted on its utter ruin:

> Great privation is suffered in this city and province. The flight of people from the countryside has filled the town with so many beggars that they have to be fed out of common stocks. But food is in short supply. The diminution of the harvests, the dearth of cattle, the destitution of labourers, the great bankruptcy of ecclesiastical and secular incomes, has left the greater part of the countryside uncultivated, and this is the only wealth of the province. So labourers are without work, owners without income; commerce is halted by lack of currency and by the export of money to buy grain from abroad. ... And to crown all the plague continues for its seventh year.[29]

Although Andalucía headed the list of distressed areas, New Castile was not far behind. In the course of 1684 the Council of Finance received numerous petitions from communities requesting a reduction of their tax quota on the grounds of depopulation, shortage of money, and poor prices. Many villages complained that their population had fallen steeply since 1680, one from 1,286 to 792, another from 500 to 158, others from 400 to 200, and from 200 to 80. And invariably the reason given was the low price of agricultural products since the savage deflation of 1680. A report of a minister of the Council of Castile in 1685 summed up the situation:

> The state of the whole kingdom of Castile is utterly wretched, especially Andalucía, where the aristocracy are without funds, the middle elements poverty-stricken, artisans reduced to vagrancy or beggary, and many dying of hunger, buried by the Brothers of Charity who used to give them relief but now have nothing to give. The women are also suffering.

[28] Villars, *op. cit.*, p. 276.
[29] Quoted by Domínguez Ortiz, 'La crisis de Castilla en 1677–1687', *op. cit.*, p. 449.

Necessity forces them to beg from door to door, for work does not yield a sustenance; others never leave the house, even to go to Mass, so destitute are they; and others—the worse pity—have prostituted themselves at all ages, simply to eat.[30]

One of the objects of the great deflation of 1680 was to bring gold and silver into circulation. In 1686 the government effected a partial revaluing of silver, a measure which had been demanded for some time as an economic stimulus and a means of preventing the flight of specie abroad.[31] By decree of 14 October the silver coinage was devalued by approximately 20 per cent. The premium on the new issue in terms of vellon was fixed at 50 per cent., and on the old at 87·5 per cent. And they remained fairly constant at this rate for the rest of the century. This devaluation of silver, the first in two centuries, was in effect an inflationary measure, but a sound and justified one. It put an end to a long period of monetary instability; silver came out of its hiding places and began to enter the market again; prices ceased to fall and underwent modest recovery; and the government helped things along by giving some tax relief. Even the weather improved, so that for a number of years harvests were more abundant. And the country was spared major epidemics for the rest of the century. The patient did not undergo a miraculous recovery. Periodic hunger and privation continued to visit the Castilian masses, and the Council of Finance was obliged to give further tax relief to numerous towns and villages unable to meet their quotas. But from 1687 the worst features of depression began to lift and Castile turned its back on the tragic decade.

Was the recovery of Castile merely an attenuation of the adversities of 1677–87, or was it an absolute revival, the basis of eighteenth-century development?[32] After 1686 the country enjoyed fourteen years of monetary stability, and Habsburg government bequeathed to its successor at least a sound currency. There was also a slow and modest rise in prices. The severe deflation of 1680 had brought commodity prices in New Castile down from an index of 113·4 in 1679 to 57·7 in 1686. In the subsequent period prices remained weak but showed a tendency to improve. In New Castile they rose from an index of 57·9 in 1687 to 67·1 in 1699; in Old Castile from 57·4 to 75·2; in Andalucía from 60 to 63·7.[33] This stabilisation of prices lasted from the mid-1680's to the 1730's, to be followed by a stronger rise, especially in the second half of the eighteenth century. In prices as in currency therefore

---

[30] Quoted by Maura, *Vida y reinado de Carlos II*, i, 396.

[31] Hamilton, *War and Prices in Spain 1651–1800*, pp. 22–23, 31.

[32] For varying interpretations see the two studies cited in n. 16 and Pierre Vilar, 'Histoire des prix, histoire générale', *Annales*, iv (1949), 29–45, especially p. 40.

[33] Hamilton, *War and Prices in Spain 1651–1800*, pp. 119, 136.

there was no abrupt break in 1700. The trough of Spain's great depression may be limited to the period 1640–85, and its greatest depth to the years 1677–85. The savage devaluation of 1680, the child and father of crisis, eventually restored confidence in Spanish currency, which in turn gave encouragement to financiers and manufacturers. And the slow and dependable price rise after 1686, if not a generator of growth, was at least a sign that the great depression had now spent itself; and the economy began to respond to moderate inflation. Perhaps the last decade of Habsburg rule was less disastrous for Spain than is often supposed.

3. BUREAUCRACY AND ITS REFORM

While the later government of Charles II was restoring confidence to Spain's monetary system, it was also taking the first steps in administrative reform, anticipating in some degree the more successful efforts of Bourbon reformers in the following century. The problem was clear enough. National revival was impeded by defective institutions. The bureaucracy, which had once been the strength of Spanish government, was now failing the country. In view of the vested interests involved, however, it was an achievement to get the matter on to a government agenda.

Spain had too many officials. Pursuit of office had become a mania, fed by the universities, current social values, the patronage system, and the government's own improvidence. The universities of Salamanca, Valladolid and Alcalá, among others, produced each year hordes of law graduates. Many of these had procured a virtually free education through entry in the Colegios Mayores, now a monopoly of the aristocracy; and many of them were sons and relatives of existing officials. With a university degree a man was almost guaranteed appointment in the law courts, the *audiencias* and the chancelleries, and from these he could expect promotion in due course to one of the councils. The close connection between university entrance and bureaucratic appointment tended to create a closed circle of administrators who monopolised public careers. For those who did not have a degree but possessed compensatory qualifications—aristocratic status or family relationship with officials—there was another means of entry into the bureaucracy, by way of offices known as *de capa y espada*. These appointments depended solely on royal favour and patronage; there was no limitation as to their number; no standards or formal qualifications were required; and the salaries of these additional officials were an excessive charge on government revenue. Appointments of this kind so greatly exceeded the needs of the councils that periodic attempts had been made to control them; in 1661, for example, Philip IV decreed that *capa y espada* councillors appointed to the *Junta de*

Guerra should wait for a vacancy before joining it, though they could receive salaries from the date of nomination.

Bureaucratic growth was both superfluous and harmful. In the Council of the Indies no less than 72 councillors were appointed in the 35 years of Charles II's reign. Of these 24 were appointments *de capa y espada*. A total of 48 were *consejeros togados* (legally qualified councillors); of these 23 died in office, 13 of them after serving only a short term, while 19 were quickly promoted to the Council of Castile. This lack of continuity in service was a serious obstacle to efficient administration: in the course of 35 years only 10 councillors served for more than 10 years on the Council of the Indies.[34] But there were further anomalies. One of these, of recent growth, was the habit of appointing supernumerary councillors, both *togados* and *de capa y espada*, who already held appointments elsewhere, frequently abroad. The sole object of this exercise was to augment salaries. Don Pedro Ronquillo, for example, while holding appointment in the Netherlands and then as ambassador in London, was appointed councillor of the Indies (and also of Castile), without ever setting foot inside the council chamber.[35] And former secretaries of the Council of State were sometimes appointed to the Council of the Indies simply as a form of pension on retirement.

Finally, there was a further entry to office, through purchase. This was regarded as patriotism, not corruption, and the office so bought became a piece of property, usually with right of renunciation, which meant that the owner could sell it, bequeath it, or give it away. Sale of office extended not only to notarial and municipal office, both very large groups, but to salaried offices in the central administration, including legal offices which were strictly speaking unsaleable. By the end of Philip IV's reign senior administrative posts of a judicial and financial kind, whose sale was generally regarded as inappropriate, were being put up to purchasers almost as a matter of routine.[36] The system embodied two abuses: it placed people in posts of responsibility for which they were morally or intellectually unfitted; and it encouraged peculation, as successful candidates had to pay off the interest on capital borrowed to purchase the office. In the reign of Charles II abuses multiplied. Now even conciliar appointments were sold. At least two *capa y espada* councillors of the Indies, both high-ranking aristocrats, the duke of Guastala and the marquis of Iscar, obtained their appointments through payment of a substantial *servicio*. And although all purchase of legal office was forbidden in law, Martín de Solis was appointed fiscal of the Council of the Indies on payment of 14,500 ducats. Towards the end of the

---

[34] Schäfer, *El Consejo real y supremo de las Indias,* i, 269.
[35] *Ibid.,* i, 269–70.
[36] Parry, *The Sale of Public Office in the Spanish Indies under the Habsburgs,* pp. 5, 48.

reign a child of nine years, the marquis of La Laguna, count of Paredes, inherited his father's office in the Council of the Indies along with other items of property.

Subordinate officials multiplied even more rapidly. In 1690 the Council of the Indies alone had 75 salaried officials. Its total strength of 100 included 50 supernumerary officials on salary in all grades from councillor to porter. This expansion occurred not in response to increase of business but to demands of patronage. Surplus staff were a great financial liability, and wages were usually in arrears, by August 1668 164,453 ducats in arrears. This may not have been serious for aristocratic supernumeraries, but it meant that lower officials lived constantly on credit or corruption. Apart from salaries—and pensions for widows—council officials also received a number of bonuses and fringe benefits, all of which were an additional burden for the council's financial allocation, at a time when its quota of remittances from Peru was becoming more and more irregular. So the financial position of the Council of the Indies was worse in the reign of Charles II than in any previous period. And this was one council alone. The others had similar problems of personnel and finance.

As the bureaucracy became a form of social security for its own members, so it deteriorated as an instrument of government. Its methods called for drastic overhaul. The *consulta*, originally a useful means of summarising subjects and opinions, degenerated into a long-winded and pointless exercise. The practice of recording the opinion and arguments of each individual councillor was rigidly followed even when these were unanimous or in substantial agreement. There was, moreover, a certain chicanery in the construction of *consultas*. By the mid-seventeenth century councillors had adopted the practice of leaving the council table after debate, recording their opinions in private, and then either incorporating them in a completed *consulta* or sending them direct to the king outside conciliar channels. Repeated prohibition of this practice in the 1650's and 1660's suggests that it was difficult to eradicate.[37] Further attempts to reform *consulta* procedure were made in the reign of Charles II, though without much success.[38]

At a certain level conciliar government could function with some efficiency; the receipt of reports by individual councils, and the transmission of outgoing replies and instructions, these tasks were performed well enough. But between these two stages, when the sovereign or his minister had to receive, consider and resolve material from a large number of councils, lay the weak link in the whole system and the point where it frequently broke down. Apart from the accumulation of business, the government did not

[37] Valiente, *Los validos en la monarquía española del siglo XVII*, pp. 201–2.
[38] See 'Orden de la Reina Gobernadora', 26 July 1672, *ibid.*, pp. 209–10.

possess an efficient registry; this meant that neither the councils nor the executive could lay their hands quickly on papers relevant to the file under discussion. The state archives at Simancas, outside Valladolid, were remote from the central organs of government; great delay could ensue if it were necessary to call for previous papers, especially as the filing system at Simancas was somewhat primitive.[39] Philip IV had attempted to remedy this situation. He ordered the creation within the royal palace of a current registry modelled on the permanent archives at Simancas. Here all conciliar papers would be filed for orderly consultation; material four years old would be removed and deposited in Simancas, but a classified inventory of their contents would be kept in the registry.

This large family of councils and their numerous offspring, the juntas, squabbled incessantly over jurisdiction. Overlapping areas of competence were a fertile source of dissension and kept the councils in permanent agitation, so that many of their *consultas* were concerned not with policy but with their own authority and alleged encroachment by other councils. Material which had come to a council, been processed into a *consulta* and remitted to the sovereign for decision, frequently had to be sent for execution to other interested councils, including the Council of State with its universal brief. These councils would then wish to see the original *consulta* from the first council, and if they disagreed with its contents they would start all over again, with new deliberations and new *consultas*. Philip IV on more than one occasion ordered this nonsense to stop. But relations among councils and cross-reference between their *consultas* continued to cripple conciliar government, causing endless paper work and retarding executive action.[40]

The only hope of success under this system lay in the quality of the executive. A strong minister could override or by-pass the councils in order to speed decisions and action. This was the crucial argument in favour of a prime minister, whether or not he was a *valido*. But the single executive which emerged in the seventeenth century, culminating in straightforward prime ministers under Charles II, depended on two further innovations to operate effectively. Prime ministers needed to consult frequently with other ministers without going through the cumbersome machinery of the councils; and the executive needed an efficient secretariat of its own independent of the conciliar secretaries. In the eighteenth century the Bourbons worked their way towards a kind of cabinet council, consisting of the king or first minister and a few ministerial colleagues. The idea at least had been anticipated. There were signs, obscure at the end of Philip IV's reign, more clear during the reign of Charles II, that government was moving towards this

[39] See the complaints of Philip IV, *ibid.*, pp. 199–200.
[40] *Ibid.*, pp. 162, 196–98, 205–6.

kind of extraconciliar consultation. Prime ministers and their colleagues, the presidents of councils, assembled together with some regularity and acquired a secretariat of their own. This was the *Secretaria del Despacho Universal*, which emerged from the secretariat of the Council of State but seems to have detached itself from it. The *Secretario del Despacho* was not confined to a specific area of foreign affairs, as were the two secretaries of the Council of State, but had a universal brief and combined the functions of consultant and secretary to the head of government, whether this was a Junta de Gobierno or later a prime minister. The holders of the office were men of some status and distinction, Blasco de Loyola, Pedro Fernández del Campo, Jerónimo de Eguía, José de Veitia Linaje, Manuel de Lira. The stature of the office made it an object of great competition, and accounts for the surprise evinced by the appointment of unworthy incumbents in the 1690's.

In the reign of Charles II these developments were limited by the mediocrity of the crown and the power of the grandees. Until the political power of the nobles had been broken by a powerful crown, absolute in practice as well as in theory and capable of choosing its prime minister irrespective of whether he were a grandee, then the executive could never completely bypass the aristocratic councils or fully control the administration. One attempt was made to provide an alternative to conciliar administration. In 1687 the count of Oropesa created a new office, the *Superintendencia de Hacienda*, designed as a single executive over financial affairs. This was inspired by French practice and was a curious precursor of eighteenth-century developments. But the functions of the office and its relation with the Council of Finance were never closely defined.[41]

The government of Charles II, therefore, had to accept the existence of councils and try to improve them. It made three attempts at reform. The first came in 1677 and its object, as defined by the royal decree of 6 July, was 'to obviate the great delay in the efficient dispatch of business caused by the increased number of ministers, as well as the rising cost of salaries'. The details are known only for the Council of the Indies, but similar provisions seem to have been made for the other councils. The personnel of the Council and of the Cámara de Indias was limited to a president, eight councillors, a fiscal, two secretaries, and eight minor officials; and it was insisted that the councillors should have had experience of service in the colonies.[42] Yet this admirable reform was virtually annulled by its final provision: it was conceded that no present incumbent would be retired, and that the Council would be reduced to its new size simply by not filling vacancies when they occurred. In view of the great numbers involved this would take a long time. As long

[41] See above, p. 250.
[42] Schäfer, *op. cit.*, i, 275–76.

as government was conceived in terms of grace, favour and patronage, there was little chance of basic reform. This decree had little effect, and the old abuses continued.

Under the inspiration of Oropesa the government returned to the problem in 1687. A decree of 31 January ordered the total suppression of purchased offices in the councils, leaving to the proprietors only the title and status and 5 per cent. interest on the sum paid for the office. The decree also suppressed supernumerary places acquired by grace and favour when they became vacant, and stated that on no account were there to be supernumerary offices in the future.[43] This was a limited measure, but it seems to have been more effective in practice than that of 1677.

The major reform was that of 1691. This too was prepared by Oropesa, though his dismissal prevented him from implementing it personally. By decree of 17 July membership of the councils was reduced in the interests of efficiency and economy. In the case of the Council of the Indies this meant a strength of one president, 8 councillors *togados*, 2 *de capa y espada*, 2 secretaries and a fiscal, and 9 minor officials. These were to continue to receive the customary salaries, but the numerous bonuses were reduced. All councillors over and above this number were to be retired, though they would remain on half salary with an option on vacancies when they occurred.[44] As a general measure the decree annulled all *mercedes* and grants made by the administration itself without royal cognisance. Similar decrees were issued for the other councils, and the whole can be regarded as an important announcement of administrative reform. But statements of good intentions were not enough, and the test came in the execution. These measures did not solve the financial problems of the councils or make good the arrears of salary. In 1694, it is true, the Council of Finance became the sole administrator of taxes in Castile, another anticipation of eighteenth-century rationalisation, but it was not given financial control over the bureaucracy. So each supreme council continued to have its own financial apparatus and its own income, and they were not controlled and paid by the treasury. Moreover, to accommodate clients, exceptions were immediately made—in two cases were written into the decree itself—allowing additional councillors *de capa y espada*. Finally, the execution of the decree was seriously handicapped by the collapse of government after the departure of Oropesa, though it might be added that early Bourbon government found it just as difficult to implement bureaucratic reform. For all these reasons the situation drifted back to normal. When in 1700 the Habsburg regime came to an end, the councillors of the Indies, whose number had been fixed at 10 by the decree of 1691, had

[43] *Ibid.*, i, 278.
[44] *Ibid.*, i, 279–85.

grown to 19, 7 of them *de capa y espada*; and substantial portions of salaries were five years in arrears.[45]

4. THE PRECURSORS

The years around 1680 were critical ones for Spain. It was then that the great depression of the seventeenth century, at its most acute from 1640, reached the most savage intensity. Yet the blackest period yielded the first glimmers of enlightenment. After the corruption and improvisation of the last *validos* and the first *caudillo*, the country was given political sanity and stability under the premierships of Medinaceli and Oropesa, an advance which was only halted by the intervention of the succession problem. Catalonia began to emerge from its provincialism, to renew its economy, and to raise its sights towards the outer world. On the basis of monetary soundness and moderate inflation, Castile laid the foundations for future economic recovery. And a programme of administrative reform was initiated, which promised more than it fulfilled, it is true, but which was subsequently imitated by the first Bourbon. The evidence, fragmentary though it is, justifies perhaps the projection of a new framework for modern Spanish history. For if this hypothesis is correct the chronology of depression must be revised. Spain did not pass suddenly from obscurantism to enlightenment in 1700 with the death of the last decrepit Habsburg and the advent of the first reforming Bourbon. If the performance of later Habsburg government was superior to its actual resources, that of the early Bourbons fell short of expectations. An alternative chronology, therefore, would postulate a period from 1680 to about 1760, in which successive governments arrested, if they did not reverse, the downward trend; this was followed, from 1760 to about 1790, by a programme of more vigorous reform which modernised Spain's government and strengthened its economy.[46]

In Castile ministers attempted to build upon the monetary reform of the early 1680's by putting the government's own finances in order. During the first half of the reign these continued in their pristine chaos. There were too many taxes, too many officials and tax farmers, and too little actual yield; income was further eroded by exemption and fraud, by the cost of collection, and by inflation.[47] The government survived by assigning taxes and other forms of revenue years in advance to bankers and creditors in return

---

[45] Nevertheless the Council of the Indies managed to produce in 1681, 78 years after the project was initiated, the *Recopilación de Leyes de las Indias*, a compilation of 6,400 laws in four folio volumes, 'a notable monument of colonial legislation'; see Haring, *The Spanish Empire in America*, p. 102.

[46] There are, of course, further refinements of chronology in the period 1700–1808.

[47] See above, pp. 234–250.

for immediate cash, and by borrowing from financiers and individuals on the security of *juros*. The latter became a dead weight of permanent obligation. Heavy liability had been inherited from the previous reign, for on 15 November 1663 Philip IV had declared his final bankruptcy and converted his debts into *juros*. A *juro* was a contract whereby a person or institution in return for an advance of capital to the crown, either voluntary or forced, was given an annual pension charged on a specific revenue.[48] This then became a piece of property which could be inherited or traded. The owners were hospitals, monasteries, widows, minors, *caballeros*, townspeople, all those people unable or unwilling to engage in work or business. But under Philip IV many merchants and businessmen were forced to buy *juros*, or received them in payment for sequestered capital.[49] Influential people such as bankers and *asentistas* speculated in these instruments, buying up depreciated *juros* and then persuading the treasury to pay the full income on them. Already by the reign of Philip III *juros* represented the massive sum of 4·5 million ducats, almost half the total revenue of the crown, and they were charged on the most lucrative and secure revenues. By 1667 they amounted to 9 million ducats and had become the treasury's biggest liability. The superintendent of finance, the marquis of los Vélez, reported on 10 May 1687:

> For all the great machine of this monarchy there remains to your Majesty no more than the revenue contributed by the provinces of Castile, whose value comes to 84,197,790 *vellon reales*: what is alienated and destined for *juros* comes to 122,971,550 reales, leaving a deficit of 41,578,230 reales.[50]

A substantial part of the revenue raised from *juros* was assigned to defence expenditure. This continued to be the biggest drain on government resources. In 1680 projected expenditure amounted to 19·5 million escudos, available revenue to 8·7 million; deficit for the year, 10·8 million.[51] As silver was the only Spanish currency acceptable abroad, the crown had to use its bullion on foreign payments while trying to live on vellon at home, the currency in which its taxes were also collected. The premium on silver rose to 190 per cent. in 1675, and to 275 per cent. in 1680. To send 1 million ducats to the Low Countries cost 2,750,000 ducats.[52] And by this time silver was a scarce commodity, for the treasure from America was much diminished. The entire sum remitted to the crown from Mexico in the period 1663–1700

---

[48] Domínguez Ortiz, *Política y hacienda de Felipe IV*, pp. 315–29.
[49] Although it is convenient to call *juros* government bonds, they were not bonds in the modern sense, for they were backed only by specific items of public revenue, not the whole.
[50] Quoted by Kamen, 'The Decline of Castile: the last crisis', *op. cit.*, p. 65.
[51] *Ibid.*, p. 66.
[52] Domínguez Ortiz, 'La crisis de Castilla en 1677–1687', *op. cit.*, p. 443.

amounted to no more than 13·5 million pesos; and between 1651 and 1739 only 36·9 million pesos came from Peru.[53]

From 1683 to 1685 the government initiated discussion of reform of the tax structure. In 1686 the *junta de medios* of the Council of Castile lent its support to the view that the incidence of taxation should be shifted from the lower to the upper income groups. It proposed that the *millones*, a tax on vital articles of food, should be reduced, while the *alcabala* and other taxes which fell more heavily on the affluent should be increased. The point was taken up in 1687 by the marquis of los Vélez, the newly appointed superintendent of finance, who produced an extensive memorandum on financial reform.[54] According to this, revenue was falling to 7–9 million ducats, while expenditure was rising to 10–11 million. The drop corresponded to the *millones*, which had originally been introduced as a tax on basic articles of consumption as an alternative to direct taxation of the privileged classes, the nobles and the clergy. The yield of the *millones* was gradually eroded by the excessive bureaucracy it attracted, by the charging of *juro* payments upon it, and by the frauds committed by nobles and clergy, who sold taxcharged articles from their own estates direct to the consumer and kept the tax for themselves. Vélez concluded that 'the *millones* is the most unjust and burdensome tax in the kingdom', as it fell primarily on the poor, benefited the rich not the treasury, and now yielded no more than 1·5 million ducats.

Although the majority of ministers agreed that the *millones* should be abolished and replaced perhaps by a direct tax, they feared the sudden loss of 1½ million ducats without a secure replacement. So the crown appointed another committee of the Council of Castile, headed by the superintendent of finance, to examine the financial situation in general and the proposal to reduce the *millones* in particular. And meanwhile an attempt was made to purge the tax of its administrative abuses and to charge it on the clergy. Strictly speaking the clergy were not exempt from the *millones*, but they resented it and took refuge in the periodic papal sanction which was required. On this occasion, with the excuse that papal permission had not yet arrived, the archbishop of Toledo, Cardinal Portocarrero, refused to allow the tax in his diocese and threatened the tax-collectors with excommunication. He remained adamant in spite of the pleas of Oropesa, the royal confessor, and Charles II himself. So the idea was dropped, and another reform was blocked by vested interest. Then, in February 1688, the Vélez committee reported; it concluded that while it was vital to alleviate the tax burden, the *millones* must

[53] Haring, *Trade and Navigation between Spain and the Indies in the Time of the Hapsburgs*, p. 167, n. 2; Rodríguez Vicente, 'Los caudales remitidos desde el Perú a España por cuenta de la Real Hacienda. Serie estadísticas (1651–1739)', *Anuario de Estudios Americanos*, xxi (1964), 1–24.

[54] Maura, *op. cit.*, i, 446–47.

be maintained, as it was needed for defence expenditure. It might have added that it was also a substitute for direct taxation of the privileged classes.

Frustrated in major reform by the rigid social structure of Castile, the Oropesa administration did what it could to adjust the fiscal system. It attempted to cut expenditure, and in fact reduced the budget for the royal household to 1·5 million ducats, a level little higher than that of seventy years previously. Offices were pruned, including those purchased, and those that survived were subject to a forced loan equal to a *media anata*.[55] There was a determined attack on pensions and *mercedes*: some were stopped, others were cut, and all were taxed, the only exceptions being those of service veterans and their widows, and the widows of ministers, though even these were taxed. While none of this added up to a complete programme, it was evidence of reform within the existing structure. And reform went beyond mere fiscal pressure. Not only did Oropesa and los Vélez try to tap the rich, they also sought to alleviate the poor. This can be seen in the removal of abuses attached to the *millones*, in the abolition or reduction of the *sisa* on a number of consumer goods, and in the lowering of the tax quota for communities who were particularly hard pressed. And they extended the hand of reform to the church, negotiating with Rome for increased revenue from the clergy, and initiating a campaign against the excessive number of clerics and false vocations.

Meanwhile, in response to mounting criticism from reformers and tax-payers, the government had launched a major campaign against *juros*. The crown had already added to the heavy *juro* liability inherited from its predecessor, particularly from 1672 when this device was used to finance defence expenditure against France. *Juros* of course had not been allowed to escape completely: in classical seventeenth-century manner, what weak governments had been unable to prevent they had taxed, by means of a *media anata*, equivalent to the first half-year's income from each *juro*. But from 1677 the government began a basic reform of *juro* finance, and attempted to divide its revenue fairly between past and present claimants.[56] In this year a distinction was made between (1) *juros antiguos* acquired before 1635, and (2) *juros modernos* acquired since then. The state annulled half the value of the first type, and charged a *media anata* and a tax of 5 per cent. on what remained. The second type, which had attracted greater speculation, were also annulled to half their value, and the remainder were charged a *media anata* and taxed at 15 per cent. Subsequent decrees of 1685 and 1687 reduced the exemptions

[55] *Ibid.*, i, 508.
[56] Alvaro Castillo Pintado, 'Los juros de Castilla. Apogeo y fin de un instrumento de crédito', *Hispania*, xxiii (1963), 43–70, especially pp., 64–66; Maura, *op. cit.*, i, 508; Domínguez Ortiz, *Política y hacienda de Felipe IV*, pp. 328–29.

allowed under the 1677 enactment, and further annulled *juros* by 50–75 per cent., restricting interest payments to 4 per cent. From the 1685 operation alone the state saved 4 million ducats. By a further decree of 1688 the government drew up a list of priorities on revenue, reserving an annual portion for state expenditure, and applying the balance in specific proportions to servicing debts, and paying *juros*, salaries and pensions. The attack on *juros* between 1677 and 1687 was part of the government's reaction to the great crisis which engulfed Castile in those years. Like the draconian monetary policy of 1680, the liquidation of *juros* caused great suffering in the short term, as individuals and institutions suddenly found their annuities annulled or devalued, and commercial houses involved in *juro* business lost some of their assets. But the new policy ended speculation in these instruments, penalised non-productive activities, and anticipated the final liquidation of the *juro* debt in 1727. As such it was a measure of long-term recovery.

The reforming aspirations of Charles II's ministers did not stop at public finance. They also tried to penetrate more deeply into Spain's industrial and commercial problems. In these sectors their efforts were piecemeal and confused, and they were overwhelmed by the magnitude of the task. They are evidence of promise rather than performance, of partiality to the idea that the state should play a more positive role in economic planning; and they foreshadowed more successful action by later governments. A law of 1679 sought to improve the status and conditions of factory owners by granting them, among other things, the right to import raw materials duty-free and reducing their liabilities for *alcabala*. Laws of 1682 and 1692 made it clear that industrial and entrepreneurial activities were legally compatible with nobility.[57] And by decree of 29 January the government set up a *Junta General de Comercio*. This consisted of ministers and experts, and was designed to deal with problems of depopulation and industrial depression; and it was instructed to found *montes de piedad*, or credit banks, to facilitate movement of capital. Great hopes were placed in the Junta, but they were not fulfilled. It received only intermittent support from the government, was starved of resources and periodically dissolved. The almost complete lack of evidence of its activities raises suspicion about their existence. But the Bourbons regarded it as a useful enough institution, for it was revived by Philip V in 1705. One of its purposes was to create factories, but little came of this. The few attempts at industrial revival in this period were made by foreigners, tempted into Spain by the country's underdevelopment and acting essentially on their own initiative, though with government backing. A law of 1679 encouraged the immigration of foreign craftsmen into Spain. In 1679 Flemish workers

[57] *Novísima Recopilación de las Leyes de España* (6 vols., Madrid, 1805–1807), V, xii, 2; VIII, xxiv, 1.

founded a paper mill at Arco in Segovia; a number of foreigners started new silk factories in Madrid and woollen factories in Cuenca; and in 1687 Frenchmen established a cloth factory in Sigüenza.[58] In the last decades of the century four stocking factories were established in Madrid and three in Valencia, with some export to England. Cloth was manufactured at Toledo and Segovia as well as at Cuenca and Sigüenza, but the product was coarse and had no market beyond the poorest classes. The silk factories of Valencia, Granada and Andalucía were still productive, though again the product was not of high quality.[59] Those at Valencia seem to have been profitable as well as productive, and before the War of Succession employed some 800 workers.[60] But none of this activity was sufficient to overcome the deep depression in the Spanish textile industry. Spain still remained unattractive to the best foreign experts. In 1677 the government tried to secure Dutch and English textile experts to revive the industry; but apparently they imposed conditions which the Spanish authorities found unacceptable.[61]

Commerce was almost as intractable as industry. In the eighteenth century, more particularly under Charles III, the government undertook a vast programme of commercial and colonial reform designed to appropriate the fruits of empire for its owner. In the late seventeenth century projects of this kind never left the council table, though at least they were extensively debated and the ideas canvassed are not without interest. Interested parties advanced a number of projects for chartered companies on the model of the English and Dutch East India Companies, some of them providing for the retention of the fleet system but with the administration of colonial trade and navigation focused in a single private corporation.[62] In 1683 the *Junta de Comercio* was reconstituted and initiated discussion of various reforms. One of the subjects under debate was a company for American trade, first proposed by Narciso Feliu, This envisaged a chartered 'armed company for the trade with the Indies', as a means of reviving Spanish manufactures and destroying foreign contraband in America; it would be modelled on English and Dutch companies, and foreigners might be admitted.[63] The Junta accepted the proposal and advised the government to give its sanction, which it apparently did, though the company was never actually created. For about

[58] Kamen, 'The Decline of Castile: the last crisis', *op. cit.*, pp. 68–69.

[59] N. Barozzi and G. Berchet, *Relazioni degli stati europei*. Ser. 1, *Spagna* (Venice, 1660), ii, 642–45; this is, however, an overrated source, containing inaccuracies and false impressions.

[60] Santiago Rodríguez García, *El arte de las sedas valencianas en el siglo XVIII* (Valencia, 1959), p. 26.

[61] Lonchay, Cuvelier and Lefèvre, *Correspondance de la Cour d'Espagne sur les affaires des Pays-Bas au XVIIe siècle*, v, 257, 282.

[62] Hussey, *The Caracas Company*, pp. 8–34; José Muñoz Pérez, 'El comercio de las Indias bajo los Austrias y los tratadistas españoles del siglo XVII', *Revista de Indias*, xvii (1957), 209–21.

[63] See above, p. 256.

a decade after 1687 the Council of the Indies considered a proposal for a company in the Netherlands, to be granted the sole right to trade to Hispaniola and Puerto Rico; it would be open to all Spanish subjects and even to capitalists of other friendly nations. Again, although the Council of the Indies seemed to favour the proposal, there was no outcome.

The most striking ideas came from the pen of Manuel de Lira, a cultivated and much travelled man who had spent some time in Holland. Lira was an official of independent views; as has been seen, he was Secretario del Despacho Universal from 1685 to 1691 when he left the administration in disgust at court intrigue and factionalism.[64] In 1690 the government appointed a junta to advise on the promotion of American trade, and subsequently asked Lira to comment on its report, which simply recommended rigid prohibition of trade with foreigners. Lira reacted sharply against the growing xenophobia, and he denounced prohibitive and unrealistic regulations and taxes. He argued that it was precisely the ban on trade with foreigners that induced the English, the Dutch and the French to establish settlements in the Indies. 'Excessive rigour has many disadvantages. I am convinced that it is better to govern with less absolutism.' It was one thing, he maintained, to prevent trade with enemies, another to prohibit trade with friendly foreigners. As an exponent of open trade and a critic of the Castilian monopoly, Lira advocated the formation of a commercial company at Seville or Cadiz; this would be open to all subjects of the crown and to the traders of England, the Low Countries, the Baltic ports, and other nations friendly or allied to Spain; to accommodate them they should be granted freedom of religion in Spanish ports. In addition to reviving and expanding American trade, which in turn would stimulate Spanish manufactures and merchant marine, Lira believed that his proposals would convert England and the United Provinces into firm allies, for they would have a stake in a vital sector of the Spanish economy and an interest in combating illicit trade.[65] Lira himself appreciated that his ideas had little chance of being accepted; and in fact they were not. Many of them would have simply legalised existing practice, and the government could not bring itself to do this. The proposal to admit foreigners to the American trade went far beyond the ideas of the time, including those of other nations. Even in 1765, when the government of Charles III began to reorganise colonial trade on the principles of *comercio libre*, it stopped short of admitting foreigners to the trade.

All of these schemes rose or fell in favour according to Spain's ability to

[64] See above, p. 251.
[65] Manuel Francisco de Lira y Castillo, 'Representación dirigida a Don Carlos II', in Juan Sempere y Guarinos, *Biblioteca Española Económico-Política* (4 vols., Madrid, 1801–1821), iv, 1–44; Antúñez y Acevedo, *Memorias históricas sobre la legislación y gobierno del comercio de los españoles con sus colonias en las Indias Occidentales*, p. 276.

T

defend her empire from foreign penetration. And they all failed. Shortage of capital, lack of confidence by foreign investors in Spanish officialdom, and the relentless opposition of the Seville *consulado* to any formal attack on its monopoly made failure inevitable. In any case the new promoters were attempting to copy the form of foreign trading systems without the substance; Spain did not possess the capital and industrial resources of her rivals. More than this, they missed the whole point of the crisis in colonial trade. They believed that it was sufficient to retrieve the trade from foreigners, whereas it was now the Americans themselves who absorbed most of the fruits of empire. Nevertheless it was only two decades later that the device of the chartered company was actually implemented and the Caracas Company was launched with Basque capital. The discussion had begun and the ground had been prepared in the reign of Charles II.

In the twilight of the Habsburg regime the balance sheet of progress was still unfavourable, in spite of the efforts of the precursors; and the mass of the Spanish people had little to show for the sacrifices demanded of them. After the fall of Oropesa in 1691 the reform movement begun in the 1670's lost its impetus; the political energies of the nation were now concentrated on the succession problem, and government virtually ceased to govern. The English ambassador reported in 1694, 'This country is in a most miserable condition; no head to govern, and every man in office does what he pleases, without fear of being called to account'.[66] For the common people the century ended as it had begun with living conditions hard and foodstuffs in short supply. In April 1699 there were bread riots in Madrid. A mob of 5,000 stormed through the town, frightened the grandees into hiding, and rampaged outside the royal palace. The prostrate king was forced to concede a change of corregidor, and to struggle from his sick-bed to appear in person before the mob with promise of redress. In May there were violent riots in Valladolid. Meanwhile peasants swarmed into the capital in search of food: 'We have an addition of above 20,000 beggars flocked from the country round, to share in that little there here is, who were starving at home, and look like ghosts'.[67] Scarcity of food reached famine proportions, and people fought like beasts over bread. It was a long haul out of the depression of the seventeenth century.

[66] Stanhope to Godolphin, 8 October 1694, in *Spain under Charles II; or Extracts from the Correspondence of the Hon. Alexander Stanhope, 1690–1699* (London, 1844), p. 53.
[67] Stanhope, 21 May 1699, *ibid.*, p. 138.

APPENDIX I

CURRENCY, WEIGHTS AND MEASURES

Maravedí. The basic unit of account.

Real. Standard silver coin; equalled 34 *maravedís*; the *real de a ocho* equalled 272 *maravedís*.

Ducado, or ducat. Formerly a gold coin, now a unit of account; equalled 375 *maravedís*.

Escudo. Standard gold coin; from 1609 equalled 440 *maravedís*.

Peso. American treasure was expressed in *pesos*; equalled 450 *maravedis'* worth of gold and silver; equivalent to 42·29 grams of pure silver. For purposes of conversion it is equal to 1·2 ducats.

Vellón. A fractional coin, originally a mixture of silver and copper; by seventeenth-century pure copper.

Lliura. A Catalan pound; equalled 10 *reales*, or just under a ducat.

Libra. A weight, roughly a pound.

Arroba. Equalled 25 *libras*.

Quintal. Equalled 100 *libras*.

Fanega. A measure of bulk; equalled about 1·6 bushels. A *fanega* of cacao, however, was a weight; equalled about 116 *libras*.

Tonelada. Had different meanings at different dates. Chaunu has devised a conversion factor for reducing original data into a standard draft tonnage of 2·83 cubic metres.

APPENDIX II

TABLE A

INDEX NUMBERS OF COMMODITY PRICES, 1651–1700
Base = 1671–1680[1]

---

[1] Reprinted from E. J. Hamilton, *War and Prices in Spain 1651-1800* (Harvard University Press, 1947), p. 120.

282

Table B

The Indies Trade, 1500–1650, as shown by the Tonnage of Shipping between Spain and the Principal Regions of America [1]

[1] From P. Chaunu, *Séville et l'Atlantique* (S.E.V.P.E.N., 1957), vii, 68.

283

BIBLIOGRAPHICAL INDEX

Guides to works used and to further reading are provided in the footnotes of each chapter. The following index contains the names of authors. The number after a name refers to the page where, in a footnote, the author's work is first mentioned and given full citation. Where the entry is followed by two or more numbers, these refer to other works by the same author. There are three indispensable bibliographies of Spanish and Spanish-American history: B. Sánchez Alonso, *Fuentes de la historia española e hispano americana* (3rd ed., 3 vols., Madrid, 1952); *Indice histórico español*, Universidad de Barcelona, Centro de Estudios Históricos Internacionales (Barcelona, 1953–); and *Handbook of Latin American Studies* (Harvard University Press, 1936–50, University of Florida Press, 1951–).

Actas de las Cortes de Castilla 3
Aguirre, Beltrán, G. 206
Aldea, Q. 230
Almeida, F. de 57
Antúñez y Acevedo, R. 173
Arcila Farías, E. 227
Arellano Moreno, A. 227
Artíñano y de Galdárano, G. de 150
Artola, M. 234
Arzáns de Orsúa y Vela, B. 218
Asensio Salvadó, E. 257

Báncora Cañero, C. 221
Bargalló, M. 204
Barozzi, N. and G. Berchet 278
Basadre, J. 220
Basas Fernández, M. 139
Belaunde Guinassi, M. 214
Beltrán y Rozpide, R. and A. de 222
Bermúdez Plata, C. 161
Borah, W. 112, 198, 201
Borah, W. and S. F. Cook 202
Boronat, P. 46
Bowden, P. J. 149
Boxer, C. R. 58, 59, 71
Braudel, F. 3
Brito Figueroa, F. 227
Brulez, W. 184
Brunel, A. 150

Cabrera de Córdoba, L. 16
Canabrava, A. P. 58
Cánovas del Castillo, A. 14, 17, 62
Carande, R. 80
Caro Baroja, J. 46, 140, 150
Carrera Pujal, J. 53, 149
Carter, C. H. 17, 31
Castillo Pintado, A. 276
Céspedes del Castillo, G. 163, 183, 214
Chaunu, P. 11, 41, 43, 111, 189
Chevalier, F. 185, 203, 209
Christelow, A. 159
Chudoba, B. 70
Cobb, G. B. 219
Colección de documentos inéditos 10, 36, 237, 241, 245, 250
Colmeiro, M. 88, 143
Cook, D. N. 213
Cook, S. F. and W. Borah 202
Crespo Rodas A. 219, 220

Danvila y Collado, M. 87, 88
Davidson, D. M. 206
Davis, R. 158
Deleito y Piñuela, J. 62
Descripción del virreinato del Perú 212
Desdevises du Dezert, G. 234
Díaz, J. S. 131
Diffie, B. W. 194

Domínguez Ortiz, A. 6, 19, 72, 75, 87, 91, 106, 122, 128, 134, 139, 140, 148, 155, 170, 230, 260
Dusenberry, W. H. 211

Elliott, J. H. 37
Espejo, C. 80
Essen, A. van der 79

Fernández Alvarez, M. 76
Fernández Duro, C. 174
Fernández Navarrete, P. 9
Firth, C. H. 123
Fontana Lázaro J. 255
Fraga Iribarne, M. 78

Gerhard, P. 180
Gibson, C. 194, 202
Giralt, E. 107
Girard, A. 139, 158
Goldwert, M. 214,
González Palencia A. 9
Guiard Larrauri, T. 150, 151
Guilarte, A. M. 135

Halperin Donghi, T. 43
Hamilton, E. J. 7, 9, 48, 152, 261
Hanke, L. 58, 218
Haring, C. H. 164, 184, 194
Harth-Terré, E. 217
Helleiner, K. F. 126
Helmer, M. 180, 219
Herr, R. 234
Hume, M. 62
Hussey, R. D. 176, 256

Incháustegui, J. M. 122

Janer, F. 47
Juderías, J. 62, 229

Kamen, H. 140, 231
Klein, J. 147
Koenigsberger, H. G. 184
Konetzke, R. 161, 214
Kubler, G. 213

Lafuente, M. 14
Lantery, R. 171
Lapeyre, H. 42
Larraz, J. 152
Laures, J. 33
Lefèvre, J. 41
Levene, R. 179
Lewy, G. 35

Lira y Castillo, M. F. de 279
Lohmann Villena, G. 213, 214, 220
Lonchay, H., J. Cuvelier and J. Lefèvre 75

McAlister, L. N. 201
McCulloch, J. R. 154
Macera, P. 216
McLachlan, J. O. 154, 158
Marañon, G. 64
Maravall, J. A. 16
Marrades, P. 69
Martínez Cardos, J. 92
Martorell, R. 139
Mateos, M. D. 234
Mattingly, G. 72
Maura, Duque de 145
Mauro, F. 59
Mellafe, R. 206
Mendes da Luz, F. P. 57
Mendoza L., G. 218, 219
Miranda, J. 202
Molina, R. A. 179
Momblanch y Gonzalbez, F. de P. 258
Moncada, S. de 4
Moore, J. P. 216
Morales Padrón, F. 175
Moreyra y Paz-Soldán, M. 224
Moxo, S. de 135, 148
Muñoz Pérez, J. 278

Nadal J. and E. Giralt 6
Neale, Sir J. E. 25
Novísima Recopilación de las Leyes de España 277
Novoa, M. de 22

Ots Capdequí, J. M. 216

Parry, J. H. 165, 194, 205
Peres, D. 55
Pérez Bustamente, C. 14
Pfandl, L. 229
Pirenne, H. 31
Pohl, H. 214
Prestage, E. 114

Quevedo Villegas, F. Gómez de 64

Rahola, F. 161
Ranke, L. von 15
Rau, V. 114
Recopilación de leyes de los reinos de las Indias 161
Reglà, J. 28, 49, 52, 124, 142
Riba García, C. 16
Roberts, M. 75
Ródenas Vilar, R. 75

Rodriguez, M. 179
Rodríguez Argua, J. 161
Rodríguez García, S. 149
Rodríguez Vicente, M. E. 112, 223
Rodríguez Villa, A. 77
Romero, E. 199
Rosenblat, A. 202, 213
Routledge, F. J. 123
Rowe, J. H. 213
Rowland, D. 176
Ruiz Almansa, J. 126

Saavedra Fajardo, D. 27
Salomon, N. 2
Salyer, J. C. 131
Sanabre, J. 105
Sánchez Granjel, L. 127
Sánchez de Sopranis, H. 141
Sandoval, F. B. 210
Sarrailh, J. 131
Scelle, G. 112
Schäfer, E. 18
Schurz, W. 225
Sempere y Guarinos, J. 279
Silva Santisteban, F. 217

Simpson, L. B. 202, 209, 210
Sluiter, E. 59
Smith, R. S. 139, 152, 184
Soldevila, F. 53
Stanhope, A. 280
Sureda Carrión, J. L. 33

Tejardo Fernández, M. 170
Thomson, M. A. 253

Usher, A. P. 152

Valiente, F. T. 24
Vargas Ugarte, R. 220
Veitia Linaje, J. de 151
Vicens Vives, J. 55, 128, 254
Vilar, P. 10, 51, 266
Villars, Marquis de 263
Viñas y Mey, C. 134, 139

West, R. C. 204
Whitaker, A. P. 221
Wright, I. A. 122

Zudaire Huarte, E. 96, 98

GENERAL INDEX

Acapulco, 181, 200, 225–26
Agreda, Sor María de, 117
Agriculture: in Castile: abandonment of, 2; and depopulation, 142, 144, 145, 262; and climate, 143, 260–62; common lands, 145; obstacles to, 146–48; crisis of, 264–66
— in Mexico, 194, 203–4, 207–12
— in Peru, 215–17
Alamos de Barrientos, Baltasar, 38
Alava, 31
Alba, duke of, 22, 243, 246
Albaida, marquis of, 258, 259
Albert, archduke of Austria, in Netherlands, 40, 41, 70
Alburquerque, duke of, viceroy of Catalonia, 53–54
Alcabala, 3–4, 35, 36, 38, 80, 91, 118, 124, 135, 141, 144, 234, 275, 277; in America, 164; in Mexico, 212; in Peru, 222–23
Alcalá, duke of, viceroy of Catalonia, 54
Alcalá, university of, 267
Alcalá de Henares, 235
Alcazar Arriaza, Jacinto de, *arbitrista*, 142
Algiers, 43, 128
Aliaga, Fray Luis de, confessor of Philip III, 29, 30, 44
Almadén, mercury mine, 139, 208, 220–21
Almazán, marquis of, viceroy of Catalonia, 53
Almojarifazgo, 163, 164, 193, 212, 222–23
Almunia, marquis of, 259
Ameixial, battle of, 115
America: trade and navigation, 11, 40, 41, 42, 43, 94, 151, 157, 159; monopoly, 160–63; taxation and fraud, 163–69; foreigners, 140–41, 157, 169–73, 180–84; fleet system, 173–74, 178; transatlantic defence, 175–78; Pacific defence, 178–84; depression, 184–93, 224, 227; reform projects, 248, 256, 278–80
— treasure, 11–12, 36, 37, 71–72, 74, 75, 76, 77, 85, 115, 122–23, 159, 164, 165, 168, 185, 186, 190, 274–75; sequestration of, 115, 120, 165–66, 224; causes of decrease, 168–69,

189, 195, 204–8, 219–23; relation with prices and trade, 186–87, 189
— economy, 13, 194–97, 228, 260; shipbuilding, 188, 189, 197–99; inter-colonial trade, 196, 218, 224–28; defence expenditure, 199–200; emigration to, 128–29
— Portuguese in, 58–59, 111–13; Dutch and, 58–61, 70–72, 120; England and, 122; English shipping, 151, 188, 191, 197
— See also Mexico; Peru
Amsterdam, 56
Andalucía, plague in, 6, 128, 262; prices, 7–8, 263; expulsion of moriscos, 47; foreigners in, 141, 158, 169–73; revolt of Medina Sidonia, 116; social unrest, 121, 142; population, 127, 145; agriculture, 143, 147; internal customs, 148–49; foreign trade, 155–56; American trade, 160–63, 193, 215; fleet system, 173–74; economic crisis, 261–66
Angola, 114
Angulo, Juan de, 251
Antequera, Mexico, 201
Antwerp, truce of (1609), 34, 42, 70
Aragon, *fueros*, 31; fiscal independence, 32, 38, 95; expulsion of moriscos, 44–50, 128, 135, 138; population, 45, 48, 126–27; plague, 128; policy of Olivares, 96–97; Union of Arms, 97–98, 103; internal customs, 148–49; and America, 160–61; Don John of Austria, 240, 244–45, 246, 254
Aragón, Pedro de, 243
Arbitristas, 83, 94, 142, 143, 256
Arcos, duke of, 234–35, 243
Arequipa, 219
Arica, 179, 180, 183, 218, 219
Aristocracy: in Castile: *señorío*, 2–3, 4, 135, 234; fiscal privilege, 5, 133–34, 138; and *validos*, 25; status and education, 130–31; hierarchy, 131–33, 232; as entrepreneurs, 134; office, 133, 135; land, 134, 146–47; finances, 136–37; *mercedes*, 136–37, 166–67; and government of Charles II, 229–30, 232–36, 240, 243–45, 247–48, 251–52, 271

— in Aragon, 50
— in Catalonia, 51–52
— in Portugal, 55–56, 109, 114
— in Valencia, 46, 49, 257–60
— in America, 194–95
— in Mexico, 201, 209
— in Peru, 165, 213–14
— in Venezuela, 195–96
Armada de Barlovento, 177, 197, 200
Armada de la guardia, 163, 174, 177
Armada de la mar del Sur, 180–84
Armada del Mar Océano, 177
Army, in Netherlands, 41–42, 69–70, 72, 74; in Germany, 78–79; in Castile, 77, 116, 125; in Catalonia, 103, 106, 107; in Portugal, 115, 123; battle of Rocroi, 119–20; casualties, 129; and Don John of Austria, 243–45, 246–47; disintegration, 252
Aróstegui, Antonio de, 23
Artois, 123
Asientos, 36, 37, 101, 102, 118, 119, 138, 139, 140, 143
Asturias, 127
Augsburg, war of league of, 252
Averia, 163–64, 165–66, 171, 190; termination of, 192–93
Avila, 87, 234, 235
Azores, 174, 191

Badajoz, 114
Bahama channel, 174, 175, 191
Bahia, 71, 72, 110
Baltic, Olivares's policy in, 75; naval stores from, 150, 151, 197
Barbados, 183
Barbastro, 97
Barcelona, 51, 54, 73, 98–101, 104–07, 150, 152, 255–56
Basque. *See* Vizcaya, Guipúzcoa, Alava
Bavaria, Maximilian, duke of, 70, 75, 78
Béjar, dukes of, 136, 233
Benavente, count of, 243
Benavides, Juan de, admiral, 75, 174
Bermúdez de Pedraza, Francisco, 24
Bilbao, 150, 151, 154
Blake, Robert, admiral, 122–23, 174
Bleda, Jaime, 44
Bois-le-duc, 77
Bourbons, Spanish, 250, 270, 272, 273, 277
Braganza, duke of (John IV of Portugal), 109, 113–14
Brazil, development of, 58–59, 110; Dutch and, 60, 70–72, 74, 77, 102, 110–11, 179, 190; Dutch expelled from, 114
Breda, capture of, 3; loss of, 101, 111

Breisach, 101
Brouwer, Hendrick, 182
Buccaneers, in Caribbean, 177, 178; in Pacific, 182–83
Buenos Aires, and Brazil 111, 112 n. 49; closure of, 178–79, 226
Bureaucracy, sale of office, 81; reforms of Philip IV and Olivares, 82; condition and reforms under Charles II, 267–73
Burgos, depopulation 7, 139, 262; in cortes, 87; economic collapse, 154

Cacao, 195–96, 198, 227–28
Cadiz, English attack on (1625), 73; English naval blockade (1655–56), 122–23; foreigners in, 141, 151, 169–73, 248; American trade, 162–63, 188, 189, 190, 191–92; fleet system 173–74; Catalans in, 255–56
Calais, 122
Calderón, María, 238
Calderón, Rodrigo, 26, 28
Callao, taxes at, 164; fiscal fraud, 168; transatlantic trade, 179, 223; Pacific defence, 180–84; Pacific trade, 218, 226
Callejón de Huaylas, Peru, 215
Canaries, the, 162, 173
Cañete, García Hurtado de Mendoza, marquis of, victory of Peru, 215–16
Cano, Tomás, 151
Caracas, 195, 227
Caracas Company, 162, 280
Caracena, marquis of, viceroy of Valencia, 46
Cardinal Infante, Ferdinand of Austria, in Germany, 79, 86; in Catalonia, 100; in Netherlands, 101
Cardona, duke of, 51
Caribbean, Dutch in, 59, 72, 74; English in, 122, 175–76, 178; trade and navigation, 185, 189
Carnera, Alonso, 251, 252
Cartagena, Spain, 262
Cartagena de Indias, 176; Portuguese in, 170; fleet system, 174; taxes, 193; shipbuilding, 198
Casa de Contratación, 160, 167, 169, 171, 172, 248
Castel-Rodrigo, marquis of, viceroy of Valencia, 259, 260
Castile, agriculture in, 1–6, 143–48; population, 2, 6–7, 127, 142, 144–46, 262; aristocracy, 3–4, 5, 91–92, 116, 132–37, 232–36; 243–45; prices, 7–9, 263–67; revenue, 30–39; 80–86, 117; expulsion of moriscos, 42–50, 128; and Netherlands, 42; and Catalonia, 51–55; and Portugal, 55–61,

Castile (*cont.*)
108–115; and crown of Aragon, 94–108; cortes, 86–93; foreigners in, 140–41; industry, 148–53; American monopoly, 160–63; economic crisis, 246, 249, 260–66; recovery, 266–67, 273, 277
Castrillo, García de Haro y Avellaneda, 2nd count of, 116
Castrillo, García de Haro Sotomayor, 3rd count of, 239
Catalonia, *fueros*, 31; fiscal independence, 32–33, 38, 95; population, 99, 126; policy of Philip III, 51–55; views of Olivares, 96–97; Union of Arms, 98–101; and war with France, 101–103; revolt, 104–105, 116, 123, 129; under France, 106–108; and America, 55, 107, 160–62, 190–91, 255–56; ship-building, 150; industry, 152; Don John of Austria, 107, 244; invasion of in reign of Charles II, 246, 249, 251, 252; economic recovery, 254–56, 273
Caylloma, Upper Peru, 222
Cela de Núñez, Valencia, 260
Censos, 89–90, 92, 132, 135, 143, 147, 257
Chancay, Peru, 215
Charles I, king of England, 73
Charles II, king of Spain (1665–1700), birth, character and upbringing, 124, 229; aristocratic control of government, 230–36; minority, 236–42; and Valenzuela, 242–45; and Don John, 245–47; marriages, 247, 251; ministry of Medinaceli, 248–49; ministry of Oropesa, 249–51; the succession, 252–53; prime ministers, 270–71
Charles III, king of Spain (1759–88), 279
Cherasco, peace of, 76
Chile, Dutch and, 120, 181, 182; transatlantic trade, 178; Pacific trade, 199, 215, 218, 219
Chiloe, 182
Chimbo, 199
Chinchón, count of, 22–23
Chocaya, Upper Peru, 222
Church, tithe, 4, 81; revenue from, 35–36, 231–32, 275; and government of Charles II, 229, 231, 232; condition of, 230–31; and Don John, 244, 246–47; attempted reform by Oropesa, 250–51; in Valencia, 258, 259
Ciriza, Juan de, 23
Ciudad Real, 152, 234, 235
Claris, Pau, 105
Cocentaina, count of, 258–59
Cochabamba, 219
Cochineal, 153, 156, 158, 164, 203
Colima, Pedro de, shipbuilder, 151
Commerce. *See* Trade

Commoners, careers, 137; entrepreneurs, 137–38; taxation, 138; foreigners, 139–41
Conflent, 107
Conselho da Fazenda, Portugal, 56–57
Conselho da India, Portugal, 57
Consuegra, 239, 245
Consulado, of Burgos, 139; of Bilbao, 151, 154; of Seville, 155–56, 160, 163–64, 172, 173, 187, 190, 192, 193, 226, 280; of Lima, 161, 165, 214; of Mexico, 200, 201
Corbie, 101
Córdoba, Spain, 87, 152, 235, 262, 265
Córdoba, Río de la Plata, 179
Córdoba, Fray Gaspar de, 22
Corregidores, 133, 135
Cortes: of Aragon: 97
— of Castile: Olivares and, 66; revenue, 85–86, 88–90, 101, 121; constitution, 86–88; aristocratic composition, 91–92, 135; comments on fiscal structure, 2–3; on depopulation, 7; on church, 230–31
— of Catalonia, 52, 98–99, 100–101
— of Valencia, 97–98, 257, 259
Costa Rica, 182
Council: government by, 17–21, 267–71; reform of, 271–73
— of Aragon, 17–18, 28, 43, 100
— of Castile; *consulta* of 1 Feb. 1619, 9, 37, 39, 48; under Philip III, 17, 18; under Philip IV, 74, 96, 136, 155, 156; under Charles II, 239–40, 242, 249, 265, 268, 275
— of Finance: under Philip III, 18–19, 28, 67; under Philip IV, 79–80, 82, 83, 84, 86–87, 91, 94, 135; under Charles II, 233, 248, 250, 264, 266, 271–72
— of Flanders, 17–18
— of the Indies, 17–19, 20–21, 28, 66, 166, 248, 252, 268, 269, 271, 272–73, 279
— of the Inquisition, 17, 19
— of Italy, 17–18, 241, 246
— of Portugal, 18, 56–57, 72, 110
— of State: under Philip III, 17–18, 20, 22–23, 24–25, 28, 29, 44–45, 133; under Philip IV, 66–67, 68, 76–77, 100, 118; under Charles II, 237, 242, 249, 251, 268, 270–71
— of War, 17, 21, 23, 77, 100
Cromwell, Oliver, 114, 122, 123, 156
Cruzada, 35–36, 139, 231; in America, 164
Cuba, battle of Matanzas, 74, 174; fleet system, 174–75; defences, 177; shipbuilding, 197
Cuenca, 87, 149, 152, 278
Cuernavaca, 203, 211
Cumaná, 195, 199
Curaçao, 178

Currency: vellon, under Philip III, 34–35; under Philip IV, 83–85, 88–89, 115–16, 120–21; under Charles II, 252, 262–67, 274; and American trade, 186, 189, 191
Cuzco, 220

Darien, 183
Dávila Ponce de León, Rodrigo, 234
Denia, marquis of, 258
Díaz Pimenta, Francisco, 176
Diputació, 53, 54, 99, 100–101, 103, 104, 105
Disease. See Plague
Donativos, 165, 232–33, 246, 247
Downs, battle of the, 102, 113, 129
Duero, river, 144
Dunes, battle of the, 123
Dunkirk, 72, 119, 120, 122–23
Durango, 204–205
Dutch. See Netherlands, United Provinces of

Eguía, Jerónimo de, 271
Elvas, battle of, 115, 123
Emperor (Austrian), Spanish subsidies for, 69–70, 75, 78, 86; and Charles II, 246, 251; and Spanish Succession, 253
Encomiendas: in Spain (military orders), 132 — in America, 166–67, 168, 233; Mexico, 201, 209; Peru, 213–14
Enghien, duke of, 119
England, peace of 1604, 34, 40; war of 1625–30, 72–73, 77, 155; war of 1655–59, 121–23; in Andalucía, 141, 160, 171; trade with Spain, 149, 153, 154, 155, 156–57, 158–59; attack on Spanish-American trade, 174, 191; in Caribbean, 175–78, 182, 195; in Pacific, 183; vessels in American trade, 189–90; returns from American trade, 192, 279; and Triple Alliance (1668), 239; and War of League of Augsburg, 252
Enríquez, family of, admirals of Castile, 136, 233
Escorial, 14, 29, 244
Esquilache, marquis of, viceroy of Peru, 181–82, 222
Evora, 109
Excusado, 36, 231
Extremadura, population, 127, 130, 145, 262; agriculture, 143; señorío, 234

Feliu de la Peña, Narciso, 256, 278
Feria, duke of, governor of Milan, 69, 73
Fernández, Duarte, 140
Fernández de Córdoba, Gonzalo, governor of Milan, 76
Fernández del Campo, Pedro, 271

Fernández Navarrete, Pedro, arbitrista, 9, 38, 94, 142
Finance: administration of: under Philip IV, 79–82; under Charles II, 272; reforms of Oropesa, 250, 273–77. See also Council of Finance
— Revenue: under Philip III, 30–39; from Castile, 35–39; under Philip IV, 79–93, 118–19, 124; from Union of Arms, 98–101; from Catalonia, 52, 102–3. See also America; Juros
— Expenditure: in Netherlands, 33, 36, 37, 83–84, 86, 101, 118–19, 123, 274; under Philip IV, 101, 118–19, 121, 124; under Charles II, 276
Fleets, Indies: New Spain, 74–75, 76, 85, 115, 177; Tierra Firme, 85, 115; losses to England (1656–57), 122–23; fleet system, 173–74; Callao, 183
Florida, 197, 199
France, peace of 1598, 34, 40; and expulsion of moriscos, 47; hostilities with Spain 1625–59, 73, 76–77, 78–79, 101–102, 119–20, 121, 123; and Catalonia, 105–108; and Portugal, 113–15, 120; Peace of Pyrenees, 123–24; in Andalucía, 141, 160, 170–71; trade with Spain 155–56 157–58; in Peru, 170; trade with America, 173, 185, 192; in Pacific, 183; Louis XIV's wars with Spain, 238–239, 249, 251, 252; and Spanish succession, 252–53
Franche-Comté, 239, 246
Franqueza, Pedro de, count of Villalonga, 26
Fuenterrabía, 103
Fuggers, Augsburg bankers, 84, 139

Galápagos islands, 183
Galicia, in cortes, 87; population, 127; Portuguese war, 129; agriculture, 143, 261
Gandia, duke of, 243, 257, 258, 259
García Menor, Francisco, 259–60
Genoa, Genoese, bankers, 84, 119, 139; in Andalucía, 141, 160; American trade, 192
Germany, Spanish intervention in (from 1618), 29, 37, 69–70; Olivares's policy, 75, 77–79
Gerona, 104, 152
Godoy, Francisco, chronicler, 261
Gondomar, Diego Sarmiento de Acuña, count of, report on Castile, 10, 144, 148
González de Cellorigo, Martín, arbitrista, 4, 5, 6–7, 138
Granada, 47; in cortes, 87, 144; silk industry, 149, 278; depression, 261, 262
Guadalajara, 2, 87, 145
Guadalest, marquis of, 258

Guadalquivir, river, 162
Guanajuato, 205
Guanbacho, Peru, 215
Guano, 215
Guatemala, 166, 226
Guayaquil, shipbuilding, 180, 198–99; defence, 181, 183; trade, 218, 226, 227–28
Guevara, Fray Antonio de, 26
Guipúzcoa, fiscal autonomy, 31, 95; French invasion, 103; grain imports, 148; metallurgy, 149–50; shipbuilding, 150–52
Gustavus Adolphus, king of Sweden, 76, 78
Guzmán, Enrique Felípez de, illegitimate son of Olivares, 116
Guzmán, Pedro de, 21

Habsburg, cause in Germany, 29, 70–71, 77–79; collapse of alliance, 119, 125
Hacienda, in Mexico, 201, 209–212; in Peru, 216–17
Hanse merchants, 75, 155, 156; vessels in American trade, 190
Haro, Luis de, valido, 117–18; policy, 118–19; foreign policy, 123; and aristocracy, 133, 136
Haro, Simón de, 201
Havana, and fleet system, 177, 191; shipbuilding, 189, 197
Herrera, Carlos de, 248
Heyn, Piet, 72, 74
Hidalgos. See Aristocracy
Híjar, duke of, 116
Hispaniola, English attack on (1655), 122; fleet system, 174, 175, 279; sugar, 203
Horn, Cape, 180, 183
Huancavelica, 208, 220–21, 223

Ibarra, Esteban de, 23
Ica, Peru, 215
Idiáquez, Juan de, comendador of León, 22, 27, 44
Indians: in Mexico: demographic recession, 12, 168, 189, 202–203, 205; Chichimecs, 204; and mining, 205–6; and agriculture, 202, 209–211
— in Peru: population, 213; and agriculture, 215, 217; mita, 215–216; in mining, 218–21, 223
Industry, obstacles to, 148; performance of, 149–53; crisis under Charles II, 264–65, 277–78
Infantado, 6th duke of, 22, 44
Infantado, 7th duke of, 136
Infantado, duchess of, 243
Infante, Sebastian, royal judge, 234

Inquisition, Spanish, 35, 250; Peruvian, 113; Portuguese, 140
Isabella, Infanta, wife of archduke Albert, 70
Isabella of Bourbon, first wife of Philip IV, 63
Italy, revenue from, 31–32, 95; war of Mantua, 76–77; expenditure in, 86; Louis XIV's wars in, 251, 252

Jaén, 87, 262
Jalapa, 211
Jamaica, Spanish neglect of, 175, 176; English capture of, 122, 177, 178, 182
James I, king of England, 72
Játiva, Valencia, 259
Jerez, 87, 234–35
Jesus, Society of, in Spain, 131; in Portugal, 114; in Peru, 216–17, 218
Jews, in Spain, 80, 84, 85, 119, 138; in Portugal (Marranos), 56, 57–58; in Spanish America, 113, 170
John IV, king of Portugal (1640–56). See Braganza, duke of
John of Austria, Don (Juan José de Austria), illegitimate son of Philip IV, military career, 107, 115, 123; political ambition, 237–43; revolt and government of, 243–47
Junta, government by, 21, 67
— de armadas, 67
— de estado: under Philip IV, 67–68, 118; under Charles II, 250
— de gobierno, under Charles II, 235–42
— de guerra de Indias, 21
— de hacienda, 21
— de medios, 86, 250, 275
— de población, 130
— general de comercio, 277, 278
Juros, 36–37, 80, 83, 84, 86, 89, 90, 92, 101, 118, 119, 124, 132, 135, 143, 165; state of, 274; liquidation of, 276–77

La Barranca, Peru, 215
La Coruña, 192
La Laguna, marquis of, 269
La Mancha, 261, 262
Larrea, Juan Bautista, 135
La Selva, 104
Lasma, Peru, 215
Laynez, Joseph, 16
Leeward Islands, 173
L'Heremite, Admiral Jacob, 181
Lhermit, Denis and Jacob, 197
Le Maire, Jacob, 181
León, 87
Lérida, 106, 116, 119

Lerma, Francisco Sandoval y Rojas, duke of, character and career, 15–16; and councils, 20–21, 22; as *valido*, 23–29; fall of, 29–30, 81; grants to, 3, 33; and expulsion of moriscos, 43–49; and Catalonia, 52; and Portugal, 57

Lima, Portuguese in, 113, 170; merchants, 214, 219, 224, 225; treasury, 222–23

Lira, Manuel Francisco de, *Secretario del Despacho*, 249, 271; and reform of American trade, 279

Lisbon, 56–57, 60, 109, 111, 113, 162

Lison y Biedma, Mateo de, 144, 230–31

Loaysa, García de, archbishop of Toledo, 16, 21, 22

Loeches, 117

London, treaty of (1604), 40

López Bravo, Padre, 142

Louis XIII, king of France, 107

Louis XIV, king of France, 238–39, 246–47, 249, 251, 252, 253

Loyola, Blasco, 271

Luanda, 114

Luisa de Guzmán, doña, wife of John IV of Portugal, 114

Madrid, migration to, 2; in cortes, 87; population, 138–39, 262; aristocracy, 235; prices, 263; industry, 278; bread riots, 280

Madrid, treaty of (1670), 178

Magellan, Straits of, 180–81, 183, 223

Málaga, plague in, 128, 262; silk industry, 149; wine, 215

Manila, galleons, 179, 181–83; trade with Mexico and Peru, 189, 200, 225–26

Mantua, war of, 76–77, 85

Maqueda, dukes of, 258

Maracaibo, 175, 177, 195; shipbuilding, 197–98

Margaret of Austria, wife of Philip III, 14

Margaret of Savoy, princess, 109

Margarita, island, 195

Margarita Teresa, daughter of Philip IV, 253

María Teresa, daughter of Philip IV, 123, 253

Mariana of Austria, second wife of Philip IV, 63, 115; queen regent in reign of Charles II, 229, 236; and Nithard, 237–38, 239–40; and Valenzuela, 241–43; and government of Charles II, 248–49

Mariana of Neuburg, second wife of Charles II, 248, 251

Mariana, Juan de, 33, 35

Marie Louise of Orléans, first wife of Charles II, 247, 248, 251

Marquesado del Valle, 203, 211

Marranos, in Spain under Olivares, 140. *See also* Jews

Matanzas, capture of New Spain fleet in bay of, 74, 174, 190

Mazarin, cardinal, 120, 123

Media anata, 121

Medinaceli, duke of, 243, 257; prime minister, 248–49

Medina de las Torres, duke of, 100

Medina del Campo, 7

Medina Sidonia, 9th duke of, 116, 136

Medina Sidonia, 10th duke of, 243

Mediterranean, Islam in, 43

Melo, Francisco de, 119

Mendoza, doña Antonia de, countess of Benavente, 166

Mendoza, Rodrigo de, 181

Mercedes, royal extravagance in, 81; in Catalonia, 98; and aristocracy, 136–37, 166–67, 233, 234, 241; control of, 272, 276

Mercury, 207–8, 220–21, 223, 224

Mérida, Extremadura, 130

Mesa da Consciencia e Ordens, Portugal, 56–57

Mesta, 147

Metallurgy, 149–50, 154

Metedores, 169, 171

Mexico, economy, 1, 12–13, 200–201; population, 12, 201–203, 205; silver production, 11–12; mining, 168, 194, 201, 204–8; remittances to Spain, 99, 164, 181, 185–93, 274–75; fleet system, 173–74; Pacific defence, 181–84; *situados*, 199–200; trade and navigation with Spain, 164, 185–93; agriculture, 194, 203–4, 207–8; *hacienda*, 209–12; treasury, 212; trade with Peru, 215, 218, 224–26; trade with Venezuela, 227–28; Portuguese in, 112

Mexico City, 201, 203, 208

Michoacán, 211

Milan, 32, 37, 69, 73, 101–2, 124

Millones, 4, 35–36, 38, 86, 90, 91–92, 94, 133, 141, 144, 232, 275–76

Mining, American, 186–87; Mexico, 11, 189, 194; Peru, 11, 194, 218–23

Miranda, count of, 22, 23

Mita, in Peru, 213, 215, 217, 219, 220, 221

Mixteca, 201, 203

Moluccas, 180

Moncada, Sancho de, *arbitrista*, 4, 9–10, 150, 153, 230

Montalto, duke of, 251–52

Monterrey, count of, 243, 252

Montesclaros, marquis of, 100

Monteleón, duke of, viceroy of Catalonia, 52

Montferrat, 76

Monzón, 97, 106

Monzón, treaty of, 73

Morgan, Henry, 177, 182
Moriscos, expulsion of, 6, 42–48; its conse-
quences, 48–50, 128, 138, 143–44, 257
Moscoso, doña Leonor, 166
Mosquito Shore, 182
Moura, Cristóbal de, 22, 27
Municipal government, 80; aristocracy in,
132, 133, 146–47, 235; and taxation, 80,
141
Münster, treaty of (1648), 120, 178
Murcia, in cortes, 87; population, 127, 262
Muro, Valencia, 258, 259

Naples, revolution in, 119, 121
Navarra, Melchor de, 241
Navarre, 95, 127, 148, 149
Navarro, José, 259–60
Navy, 75, 102; in South Atlantic, 72, 111; in
Atlantic, 113; war with England, 114;
casualties, 129; transatlantic defence, 173–78.
See also Armada
Negroes, slave trade, 175–76, 195–96; in
Mexico, 206, 211; in Peru, 213, 214, 215,
216–17
Netherlands, Spanish, under Philip III, 29;
revenue from, 31, 95; expenditure in, 33,
36, 37, 83, 84, 86, 101, 118–19, 123, 274;
truce of 1609, 34, 40–42; renewal of war,
69; and Germany, 77–79; war with France,
101, 119–20; Peace of Pyrenees, 123–24,
125; under Charles II, 238–39, 246, 249,
251, 252
Netherlands, United Provinces of, truce, of
1609, 34, 40–42; and Portuguese empire,
58–60; and Brazil, 60–61, 70–72, 74, 77,
102, 110–11, 190; Olivares and renewal of
war with, 68, 70, 76–77, 101–2; and Spanish-
American trade, 74, 120, 174, 192, 195, 279;
vessels in American trade, 189–90; and
revolt of Portugal, 113–14; war with
Spain, 119, 151; Treaty of Münster, 120;
in Andalucía, 141, 160; trade with Spain,
155, 156, 157–58; in Caribbean 175–78; in
Pacific, 180–82; Triple Alliance, 239;
alliance with Charles II, 246; War of
League of Augsburg, 252
Nevers, duke of, 76
Nevis, 176
New Galicia, 204
New Granada, 193, 215
New Viscaya, 204
Nicaragua, 182–83, 198, 199, 226
Nithard, John Everard, *valido*, 237–40
Nördlingen, battle of, 79, 86
Nozca, Peru, 215

Núñez Saravia, Juan, 140
Nymegen, peace of, 246, 252

Oaxaca, 203. *See also* Marquesado del Valle
Obrajes, in Mexico, 202, 225; in Peru, 217
Ocana, 152
Office, sale of, 81, 268–89, 272; in America,
165; aristocracy and, 133, 146–47; commoners and, 137; municipal, 235
Olinda, 110
Olivares, Enrique de Guzmán, 2nd count of, 64
Olivares, Gaspar de Guzmán, count duke of,
rise to power, 62, 63–64; *valido*, 65–66; and
institutions of government, 66–68; and
Thirty Years War, 68–79, 156; financial
policy, 81–86; and cortes of Castile, 86–93;
theory of empire, 95–97; Union of Arms,
97–101; and Catalonia, 102–6; and Portugal,
108–9, 111, 112–14; fall of, 115–17; and
aristocracy, 133, 136, 233; and marranos, 140
Oñate, count of, 78, 79, 100
Oquendo, Antonio de, 102
Oropesa, Manuel Joaquín Alvarez de Toledo,
count of, and revolt of grandees, 243;
prime minister, 249–51, 271, 272, 275–76, 280
Oruro, 220, 222
Osorno, 151
Ostend, 41, 72
Osuna, dukes of, 81, 243
Ottoman empire, 43

Pachuca, Mexico, 205, 206
Paita, Peru, 226
Palafox, Juan de, bishop of Osuna, 232
Palafox y Cardona, Juan de, 166
Palatinate, 69–70, 72, 73, 78
Palencia, 87
Panama, 112; fleet system, 178, 179, 180;
defence, 182–83, 184, 199, 223; shipbuilding,
198; Pacific trade, 215, 218
Paria, 199
Paris, 101
Parral, 204, 205, 206, 208
Pastrana, family of, 136, 233
Paz, Manuel de, 140
Peasantry, in Castile, feudal burdens, 2–4;
tithe, 4, 81; rent, 405; taxes, 80, 92, 141,
146; social condition, 5, 142–43, 148; during
great depression, 264–66; in Valencia,
revolt of, 257–60
Pechelingues, 180. *See also* Netherlands, United
Provinces of
Peñalosa y Mondragón, Benito de, 142
Peñaranda, Gaspar de Bracamonte, count of,
241, 243

Pernambuco, Dutch conquest of, 77, 110, 111
Perpignan, 116
Peru, economy, 1, 12, 212; Portuguese in, 59
112–13; transatlantic trade, 164, 178, 185–93,
223, 224; remittances to Spain, 100, 164–65,
185–93, 199, 221–24, 275; fiscal fraud,
167–68; foreigners in, 169–70, 218; Pacific
defence, 180–84, 199, 222, 223; mining and
output, 11–12, 194, 208, 213, 214, 218–23;
capital resources, 187–88, 196, 199, 224;
population, 213; agriculture, 215–16, 217;
hacienda, 216–17; merchant marine, 218;
trade with Mexico, 215, 218, 224–26
Peru, Upper, Portuguese in, 112, 179; transatlantic trade, 178; as market, 217; mining,
218–23
Peruleiros (Brazil merchants in Peruvian trade),
112
Peruleros (Peruvian capitalists or their agents
in Spain), 187–88, 196
Philip II, king of Spain (1556–98), 3, 14, 15, 17,
22, 24, 30, 50, 56, 57, 58, 71, 73, 81, 132, 147,
203, 218, 236
Philip III, king of Spain (1598–1621), character
and upbringing, 14–15; critical years of
reign, 9–10; aversion to work, 20; government personnel, 21–22; and Lerma, 3, 23–29;
and Uceda, 29–30; finances of, 10, 30–39,
81, 83, 165; and Netherlands, 40–42; and
expulsion of moriscos, 42–51; and Catalonia, 51–55; and Portugal, 55–61; and
aristocracy, 132–33; death of, 30, 62
Philip IV, king of Spain (1621–65), upbringing
and character, 62; habits of government, 63,
267–68, 270; and Olivares, 64–68; and
Thirty Years War, 73, 74, 75, 78, 119–20;
finances of, 3, 10, 79–86, 118–19, 120–21,
135, 165, 168, 274; and cortes of Castile,
86–93; and Union of Arms, 96, 97; and
Catalonia, 98–108; and Portugal, 108–9,
110–11, 112–14, 115, 124; and fall of
Olivares, 116–17; and Haro, 117–18; and
England, 73, 121–23; and aristocracy, 132–
33, 136, 232, 233; balance sheet of reign,
124; political testament, 236–37, 238, 239,
240
Philip V, duke of Anjou, king of Spain
(1700–46), 253, 260, 277
Philippine Islands, 199, 216, 225–26, 245
Pisco, Peru, 215, 218
Piura, Peru, 199
Plasencia, 235
Plague, in Castile (1596–1602), 6–7; in Spain,
127; (1647–52), 128; (1676–85), 128
Population: Castile, 2, 6–7, 126–30, 144–46,

149; and expulsion of moriscos, 44–49;
and great depression, 262
— Aragon, 45, 48, 126–27
— Catalonia, 99, 126
— Valencia, 45, 48, 126
— Mexico, 201–3, 205
— Peru, 213
Portobello, taxes, 164; bullion fraud, 167;
fleet system, 174, 178, 224; defence, 182–83
Portocarrero, Pedro, inquisitor general, 16, 21
Portocarrero, Pedro, cardinal archbishop of
Toledo, 232, 241, 253, 275
Porto Viejo, Peru, 199
Portugal, fiscal independence, 32, 38, 95;
under Philip III, 55–61; marranos, 56, 57–58,
80, 84, 85, 113, 140, 170; and Brazil, 58,
70–72, 110–11; in Spanish America, 58–59,
112–13, 170, 178–79, 195, 218; and Olivares,
102, 108–9; revolt of, 113–15, 120, 123, 129;
independence of, 124; revolt of and Ameri-
can trade, 190–91
Potosí, 11; Portuguese in, 59, 112, 179;
foreign penetration, 178–79; supply of,
217, 218, 226; mining and output, 218–23
Prada, Andrés de, 23
Prices, in Castile, 7–8, 263–67; grain, 146; and
American trade, 185–87
Priego, marquis of, 136
Puebla, 201, 203
Puerto Rico, 72, 176, 279
Puna, island of, 198
Punta de Araya, 59
Pyrenees, peace of, 107, 115, 118, 123–24, 158,
255

Querétaro, 211
Quevado y Villegas, Francisco de, 62, 64
Quinto, 164, 167, 181, 207, 221–22

Ráfol de Almunia, Valencia, 259
Ramírez de Guzmán, Juan, procurador of
Seville, 89
Ratisbon, peace of, 249
Real, count of, 258
Realejo, Nicaragua, 198, 226
Recife, 110, 114
Recopilación de leyes de los reinos de las Indias,
161
Repartimiento (labour), in Mexico, 205, 206,
210; in Peru, *see* Mita
Richelieu, cardinal, 78, 102, 105, 113
Rímac, Peru, 217
Rio de Janeiro, 111
Río de la Hacha, 195

Río de la Plata, Portuguese in, 59, 112; foreign penetration, 169, 178–79; trade to Potosí, 219

Rivera, Juan de, archbishop of Valencia, 44, 46

Rocroi, battle of, 119–20

Rojas, Antonio, 196

Ronquillo, Pedro, 268

Rosellón, 106, 107, 123, 126

Ruidiaz de Pineda, Francisco, procurator of Seville, 89

Ryswick, peace of, 252

Sá, Salvador de, 112

Saavedra Fajardo, Diego, on *valido*, 27; in Germany, 78

St. Kitts, 176

St. Martin, 176

Salamanca, in cortes, 87; depopulation, 144; *senorío*, 234; university, 267

Salces, 103

Salinas, count of, 57

Sandoval, Bernardo de, 16

San Juan, river, 182

San Lucar de Barrameda, 162, 173, 174, 175

San Luis Potosí, 204, 205

San Sebastian, 147

Santa, Peru, 217

Santa Bárbara, 204

Santa Catalina (Old Providence), 176

Santa Coloma, count of, viceroy of Catalonia, 103, 104

Santa Cruz, marquis of, 73

Santa Cruz de la Sierra, 219

Santa Cruz de Tenerife, 123

Santander, 6, 192

Santo Domingo, 175, 176

Santos de San Pedro, Miguel, 96

Sarmiento de Valladares, Diego, 242

Scheldt, 111, 120

Schapenham, Hugo, 181

Schomberg, count, 115

Secretary of state, office of, 24–25

Secretario del Despacho Universal, 248, 249, 251, 271, 279

Segadors, 104

Segovia, in cortes, 87; industry, 149, 152, 263, 264, 278

Senorío, secular, 2–3, 4, 132, 135, 146, 234, 257–58; ecclesiastical, 230, 234

Servicios, 4; *servicio ordinario y extraordinario*, 35, 36, 91, 134

Sessa, duke of, 116

Seville, plague (1599), 6, (1649), 128, (1679), 262; depopulation, 7, 162; Portuguese in, 58–59, 140; Dutch in, 60, 141; in cortes, 87,

89–90; unrest, 121; businessmen, 138, 160, 167; industry, 149, 152; shipping, 151; *almirantazgo*, 155; American trade, 162–63, 166, 189, 190, 191–92, 200, 224, 227; foreigners in, 169–73, 248; *Peruleros* in, 187–88, 196; aristocracy, 234, 235; great depression, 261

Sharp, Bartholomew, 183

Shipbuilding, in Spain, 150–52, 172; in America, 188, 189, 197–99

Sicily, 32, 121, 246

Sigüenza, 278

Silver. *See* America, treasure

Simancas, archive of, 270

Sisa, 80, 134, 264, 276

Slavery, Indian, 206; Negro, *see* Negroes

Solis, Martín de, 268

Solórzano, Juan de, 161

Soria, 87

Speilbergen, admiral Joris von, 180–81

Spínola, Ambrosio, marquis of los Balbases, councillor of state, 23; in Netherlands, 41–42; occupies Palatinate, 69–70; advocates peace in Netherlands, 70, 76–77; captures Breda, 72; death in Italy, 76

Strong, captain John, 183

Suárez, Simón, 140

Subsidio, 35, 36, 247

Succession, war of, 278

Sugar, Mexico, 203, 208, 210–11; Peru, 215, 216–17

Superintendencia de Hacienda, 250, 271

Sweden, 76, 78–79, 119, 239

Tamarit, Francesco de, 105

Tapia, Pedro de, archbishop of Seville, 232

Taracena, 2

Tarija, 220

Taxation, social inequality of, 3–5, 80–81, 90–92, 141–42, 144, 146; regional inequality of, 30–33, 38–39, 94–95. *See also* Finance, revenue

Textiles, in Spain, 149, 278; in America, 12, 200–1, 202, 215, 217, 222–23, 225

Tierra del Fuego, 181

Tierra Firme, Dutch and, 59, trade and navigation to, 173, 175, 185–93, 198, 224; plantation economy, 195–96

Tithe, 4, 81, 146

Tobacco, 195, 198, 227

Toledo, depopulation, 7, 145; in cortes, 87; textiles, 149, 278; arms industry, 150; university, 153; aristocracy, 234, 235; plague, 262

Toledo, Antonia María de, countess of Priego, 167
Toledo, don Fadrique de, 72, 111, 176
Toro, 87, 117
Torre, conde da, 111
Tortosa, 105, 106
Tortuga, 175, 176
Trade, foreigners in Spanish, 140–41; internal customs, 148–49; Spain's foreign, 153–59; great depression, 264–65, 278–80. See also America, trade and navigation
Triana, Seville, 152
Trinidad, 175, 195
Tromp, admiral, 102
Trujillo, Spain, 235
Trujillo, Peru, 215, 218
Tucumán, 59, 112, 219
Tulancingo, Mexico, 112

Ubursil, 151
Uceda, Cristóbal de Sandoval y Rojas, duke of, 29–30, 81
Union of Arms, 97; Aragon-Valencia, 97–98; Catalonia, 98–104; Portugal, 108–9; America, 99–100, 164
United Provinces. See Netherlands
Universities, 131, 267

Valdivia, 182, 184, 223
Valencia, prices, 8; fueros, 31, 256–57; fiscal independence, 32, 38; expulsion of moriscos, 44–50, 128, 135, 138, 143–44, 257; Union of Arms, 97–98, 103; population, 126; plague, 128; social unrest, 142, 235; agriculture, 143–44, 147; industry, 152, 278; and America, 160–61; senorío, 234, 257–58; second germanía revolt, 258–60
Valenzuela, Fernando, valido, 241–45
Valido, government by, 16–17, 236–37, 245, 247, 270; Lerma, 23–29; Uceda, 29–30; Olivares, 63–68; Haro, 117–19; Nithard, 237–40; Valenzuela, 241–45
Valladolid, depopulation, 7, 144, 262; in cortes, 87; church, 231; offices, 235; depression, 267; food riots, 280
Valparaiso, 218
Valtelline, 69, 73
Vázquez de Arce, Rodrigo, president of Council of Castile, 21–22
Veitia Linaje, José de, author 151 n., 173 n.; administrator, 248, 249, 271
Velasco, family, constables of Castile, 22, 136, 233, 251
Velasco, Luis de, viceroy of New Spain, 203; viceroy of Peru, 221
Velázquez, Diego Rodríguez de Silva, 74
Vélez, Pedro Fajardo Zúñiga y Requesens, marquis of los, 106
Vellon. See Currency
Venezuela, Spanish trade with, 162; foreign penetration, 175–76; plantation economy, 195–96; trade with Mexico, 224, 227–28
Vera Cruz, 174, 177, 191
Villalonga, Valencia, 259
Villanueva, Jerónimo de, 100
Villars, marquis of, 263
Villaviciosa, battle of, 115
Vizcaya, fiscal autonomy, 31, 32, 95; population, 127; internal customs, 148–49; metallurgy, 149; shipbuilding, 150–52, 188, 189; and America, 162

Wages, 8–9, 148 n., 187, 263
Weimar, Bernard of, 101
Westphalia, peace of, 106, 120
Wine (Peru), 215, 216–17, 218, 224, 226
Wool, production, 147, 157; trade, 153–54, 158

Yucatán, 174, 210

Zacatecas, 204, 205, 206, 208, 211
Zamora, 86–87
Zaragoza, 116, 246
Zúñiga, Baltasar de, as ambassador, 22, in Council of State, 29, 30; and Olivares, 65